ROCK *deluxe*

Research, writing, photography, design and typesetting by Kate Sinclair and Ivan Vostinar.

© 2004 Kate Sinclair and Ivan Vostinar

Distribution enquiries:
NZAC Publications
PO Box 786
Christchurch

ph: (03) 3777-595

fax: (03) 3777-594

email: publications@alpineclub.org.nz

web: www.alpineclub.org.nz

Printed by:
Saxon Print, Christchurch

Cover photo:
Scott Kerr on *High Ideals and Crazy Dreams* (22), The Chasm. KATE SINCLAIR

This photo:
Chris Burtenshaw on *Hotline to Jim* (18), Mt Somers. MARK WATSON

Rear circle–top:
Charleston

Rear circle–middle:
Spittle Hill. DEREK THATCHER

Rear circle–bottom:
Mt Somers

Rock in the South Island is about as diverse as it could be. Sea cliffs, 'old-school' trad crags, an international bouldering destination, relaxed sport climbing areas and volumes of alpine rock are all within a few hours drive. This variation is what makes rock climbing here so good. We don't have a Yosemite, an Arapiles, a Lake District or a Squamish, but we do have an extreme range of climbing styles packed on to one funky island.

The South Island is also ideally set up for road trips. Wagons are cheap and camping is hassle free. Many climbing destinations are near population centres like Christchurch, Wanaka, Queenstown and Dunedin but there are also some secluded crags in rural areas and National Parks. Whether you are local or a traveller, there is bound to be enough here to keep you sidetracked for countless days.

Craig Buckland on *No. 79*,
Map 2 Quantum Field.
KIRILEE RAMSEY/INSPIRED PHOTOGRAPHY

This is a book for rock climbers. Before embarking on any of these climbs make sure that you have the skills and experience to climb safely. We have indicated when we feel that climbs are inherently dangerous and can not take responsibility for mishaps.

Contents

This Guide

A rock guide can be many things; a travelling companion, a microcosm of experiences or just a reliable source of information. What it can't be is all things to all people. We wanted to create something with a personality that evolved from the landscape of the South Island, the people and the rock. It is a slice of time and a story about the developments and trends that have created the vibrant scene and sub-culture of rock climbing in this part of the world.

This book is borne out of a year of research and climbing immersion. We climbed more than 95% of the routes to get accurate information and consistency. Previous guides provided route names and ascentionist details, but all of the route descriptions, protection information and safety details were collected by us in 2003-2004 on a road tripping marathon.

We produced a selected guide to focus on quality and easy route finding. So, while you will not find everything here, you will get accurate information for the best climbing without having to spend a lot of time ferreting around for the gems or getting lost moaning about guidebooks.

We hope that this guide will give you a good background to the best crags in the South Island and some inspiration to get to some new places. If you get hooked on an area, the best place to get more information is usually a local guide. These are listed on page 401. If you have feedback or new route information, drop us a line at rockdeluxe@alpineclub.org.nz

Enjoy!

Kate and Ivan

Andrew Smith on *Nasal Slip* **(V4) Spittle Hill.** MARK WATSON

Alpine Rock

Alpine rock climbing in New Zealand often requires long approaches, mountaineering skills and equipment. While this may make the climbs more committing, there is some outstanding rock to be found in the backcountry.

The Darran Mountains in Fiordland have undoubtedly the best alpine rock in New Zealand. The granite peaks and valleys have steep glacial-carved walls and the rock has amazing friction. The climbs are generally long, multi-pitch outings and there is vast potential for new routes. Many climbs can be done in one day from Homer Hut, but there are definitely some awesome multi-day trips to do in the area. The only downside is the annual rainfall. Yvon Chouinard was right in saying that Fiordland would be one of the best big wall/multi-pitch areas in the world if it wasn't for the weather.

Craig Jefferies is currently producing a new NZAC guide to this area (due spring 2005) and *The Darrans Guide* by Murray Judge and Hugh Widdowson (1990) is still available.

Sarah Garlick traversing Barrier Knob in the Darrans with Lake Adelaide below. DANIEL JENKINS

Twin Streams. KATE SINCLAIR

Greywacke in the Southern Alps is arguably best to climb when it's covered in snow or ice. Sitting at the boundary of two active tectonic plates, the mountainous spine of the South Island has grown very quickly, but is also eroding just about as fast. The main process of erosion is freeze-thaw, which is why the rock in the Alps is referred to as 'weetbix.' There are, however, several areas that have surprisingly compact sections of weathered rock.

The most well known alpine rock destination in the central South Island is Twin Stream in the Ben Ohau Range near Aoraki/Mt Cook. This broad buttress of rock has been developed as a multi-pitch crag. It is 3–4 hours walk from the road and a lot faster by helicopter. The best place to get route information for this area is the NZAC *Barron Saddle – Mt Brewster* guide (2002) by Ross Cullen.

All of the rock/mountaineering routes in the Mt Aspiring National Park are documented in Allan Uren and Mark Watson's NZAC guide to the Aspiring region. The rock routes in The Remarkables, near Queenstown, are covered in *Rock the Wakitipu Way* (2003) by Kerri Dann and Andy Mills.

In the spirit of postmodernism, rock climbing has evolved to include a huge range of ethics and attitudes. For most boulderers and sport climbers, it is not about ascending great heights, but producing enough power to link sequences of difficult moves. Alpine rock and traditional climbing enthusiasts often focus on the line or the journey and many of us like to engage in all aspects of this diverse sport.

This retrospective traverses the seminal moments in the development of rock climbing in the South Island and looks at the progression from the early days of mountaineering through to the bouldering craze and most things in between.

The First Steps. In late nineteenth century New Zealand, early rock ascents were tackled with mountaineering equipment—hawser-laid ropes and leather boots. One of the obvious areas for mountaineers to tune up their rock climbing skills was at Sebastapol Bluffs near Mt Cook Village. It is thought that Tom Fyfe made the first ascent (solo) of the classic *Red Arête* (13) in 1894 before his successful attempt on Aoraki/Mt Cook.

While New Zealand remained mountaineering-focused in the early twentieth century, developments in Europe began to have a major influence on rock climbing styles and standards. Karabiners and pitons were invented around 1910 and during the pre-war period, rock climbing benefited from this new equipment and the drive to push technical mountaineering standards. Climbers in Central Europe had been rock climbing since the mid-1800s and by 1921, they were making ascents of grade 19/20 routes.

Simultaneously, but separately, a strong free-climbing school developed in the Lake and Peak Districts in England on gritstone outcrops. Pitons were used sparingly, not so much for environmental reasons, but out of a belief that they diminished the challenge and made a climb less glorious (post World War II, Joe Brown imposed a limit of one piton per pitch on his first ascents). This encouraged a bold approach that still prevails in England.

In pre-war New Zealand, climbers had little exposure to developments in Europe. Technology and methods remained isolated because climbers did not have the resources to travel. In population centres like Christchurch and Dunedin, most of the activity was restricted to the wide chimneys and easy gullies. One of the earliest recorded ascents was *Hellfire Gully* (10) at Castle Rock by Edgar Williams in 1913.

As in the rest of the world, there was not much recorded activity on the rock during the First and Second World Wars. The only known ascents in the South Island were Neil Hamilton's efforts at Castle Rock with *Hawk* (12) and *Eagle Cleft* (10), both in the 1940s.

After the main peaks were knocked off in New Zealand, climbers who wanted to ascend technical alpine routes started to hone their skills at local crags. This was still seen as training for the real thing. Peter Crew, for example, in his *Dictionary of Mountaineering* (late 1950s) suggested that the term 'outcrop climber' was used by mountaineers in a derogatory sense to describe a 'climber who frequents outcrops, or a particular outcrop, either because he prefers to climb on small cliffs rather than mountains or because of the difficulties involved in travelling to a mountain area.'

In the 1950s Johnny Cunningham, a charismatic Scot, emigrated to Christchurch with the entire Clogwyn du'r Arddu Climbing Club due to appalling weather in the British Isles. Johnny claimed to have 'climbed every crack on the front of Castle Rock.' This would have meant climbing up to grade 20 as early as 1952 in New Zealand!

Of developments in the 1960s, Bob Cunninghame's *Kindling Crack* (19, 1966) at Long Beach was a milestone. This is still regarded as a solid lead, even with modern protection. Cunninghame's other contribution was to introduce machine nuts and wood chocks to the Dunedin scene as an alternative to piton protection. Also of note at this time was Murray Jones and partners' landmark ascents of the *North Buttress of Sabre* (17) and the *Cleddau Buttress of Moir* (17) in the Darran Mountains in 1967.

Further north, enough routes had been done in the Port Hills by 1968 to inspire Don Hutton to write New Zealand's first European-style guide, describing routes with the

British grading system (*Hangman* 17 was graded 'Very Severe'). The *Guide to the Port Hills* contained some early Castle Rock lines, such as *Excalibur* (19) and *Guinivere* (18) by Don Hutton (1967), and at Rapaki Rock, *Body and Soul* (19) by Gavin Wills (1967). In his review of the book, Graham Ellis thought that the name was 'a little grandiose—it is really a guide to a few rock outcrops' (we wonder what he would think of *Rock Deluxe?*) and he disapproved of the deletion of traditional names; '…perhaps this is a reflection of the youth of today's disregard for tradition…' However, he may have reflected the general attitude of the time by saying 'I must admit that I like many others regarded its arrival with trepidation but, if this booklet is to set the pattern, most of my fears are allayed' (NZ Alpine Journal 1969 p. 294).

Long after the guide's publication New Zealand adopted the Ewbank grading system. Starting in Auckland then implemented in Christchurch around 1975-76.

The Development of Free Climbing.
As rock climbing began to grow as a pursuit in its own right new ethics were developed. This was ultimately to lead to a new paradigm: 'free climbing.' This now means climbing a route without resting, falling or aiding (initially called 'artificial climbing'). The progression to free climbing in New Zealand is hard to pinpoint because climbers always tried to climb ground-up, without resting or aiding if they could and many of the early, easy-grade climbs were done this way. However, around this time developments in Yosemite Valley fuelled a small aid craze, a few saw aiding as an entity in its own right and questioned if some of these routes could ever be done free. Cutting-edge free climbing required problem solving and multiple attempts, ethics which would take time to embed themselves in the psyche of New Zealand climbers.

In the early phases of free climbing, if a climber couldn't complete a route clean first go, they would fall off or rest, then continue. They would repeat this as many times as necessary to get to the top and claim the ascent. A key factor in this style was that they **still did all of the**

Laurie Kennedy on the 1st ascent of *End Rib* (12) Long Beach. ALAN DONAGHUE

moves and protected the climb ground-up. Many climbers recall team sieging missions, where one climber would lead as high as they could and then get lowered. The next climber would then top-rope to the nasty spot and try to push on, still placing gear on lead. Finally, someone would climb the route from the bottom in one push. This was a common occurrence until the late 1970s and it was not until the early 1980s that pulling the rope down after each attempt became good form.

Alongside the development of free climbing in New Zealand, was the influence of an international trend called 'clean climbing.' This originated in the early 1960s when passive protection in the form of nuts (variously known as wires, chocks or stoppers), became a viable alternative to piton protection. Climbers realised that repeated ascents of routes using pitons were causing obvious and permanent damage to the rock. Following the example of the British, Americans Royal Robbins, Yvon Chouinard and Doug Robinson began to promote natural protection and what they called 'clean climbing.' Nuts were adopted with great enthusiasm by the climbing world and hexes followed hot on their heels. Climbers found that this gear was easier to place and remove than pitons and that the process of protecting a climb became more creative.

With the development of this new natural protection, climbers were inspired to free old aid routes. Much of Lyttelton Rock was initially considered too steep and sparsely protected for free climbing. *Scratching Julius* (21) is a good example of the change in perception. Originally aided by John Visser and Stu Allan in 1971, John returned and freed it in 1982.

The free climbing revolution was initially frenetic because it opened up so many new challenges, but just when it started to become self-limiting, a new clean climbing gadget appeared—the spring-loaded camming device. Cams enabled climbers to protect perfectly parallel cracks, which opened some routes in the south, but it was at Whanganui Bay (North Island) where they had the biggest impact.

There were some outstanding climbers contributing to the development of clean/free climbing in New Zealand in the 1970s. The grades established in the

Lindsay Main on *Judgement* (20) Castle Rock
IAN WHITEHOUSE

North Island were cutting edge and leagues ahead of activities in the south. The Quarry, in Auckland, was the scene of the country's first 23 (1974) and 24 (1975). The strongest climbers at the time were Rick McGregor and Robbie McBirney, who climbed the country's first 26— *Supergroove* at Mt Eden Quarry in 1976. It was the hardest route in Australasia and remained that way until Kim Carrigan freed *Procol Harem* (26) at Mt Arapiles two years later. While Robbie remained local, Rick traveled extensively, leaving many challenging and classic lines in the South Island.

In terms of hard routes, rock climbing was comparatively comatose in the south through the 1970s. However, the climbers who were active produced a valuable body of mid-grade classics. Ross Gooder was one of the most promising of his generation, but died in the Dolomites soon after establishing *Gargantua* (16), *Smaug* (originally 19, now 17) and the super-classic *Hotlegs* (17) at the Tors. In 1972, Colin Dodge climbed *Court Jester* (20) at Castle Rock, which was one of the steepest and most cruxy routes in New Zealand at the time.

It was also in the 1970s that a new breed emerged. They committed themselves to alpine rock, but also transferred their route development skills to local crags. The most prolific of this group was the formidable trio of Murray Judge, Phil Herron and Bill Denz (both Herron and Denz died young in the mountains). Of the three, Murray went on to contribute a huge amount to development in the South Island. Predominantly focused on the Darrans, he was one of the best all-round climbers at this time. Calum Hudson also actively added to the clean climbing ethic in the 1970s particularly at Mihiwaka where he produced the classic *Aqualung* (17) in 1973.

The Apex of Trad and the Emergence of Bolts

Bolts were used extensively in the United States and Europe for aiding from the 1950s onwards and began to be used as free climbing protection in the late 1970s–early 1980s. In New Zealand, bolts were placed with a staunch trad ethic in mind and were only used if no other protection could prevent injury or death in the event of a fall. Great trepidation accompanied any new bolt. Climbing boldly and within their abilities, climbers made new ascents with minimal numbers of small bolts. It was a quirky kind of compromise whereby the placement of permanent protection became ethical, so long as the fear factor was preserved. The effort required to place a bolt was also a limiting factor. Only hand drills were available and even placing a short, small diameter bolt took hours.

At about this time, there was a separation in the climbing world. The traditionalists believed that ultimate style and difficulty lay in climbing with no fixed protection, while a new group of climbers saw that the ultimate gymnastic achievement could only be reached if the danger was decreased or eliminated. While both approaches are now widely accepted in the climbing world, this is still the main division between climbing styles.

Alongside the bolting revolution came some major shifts in the way climbers approached difficult climbs. Somewhat unexpectedly, new methods of ascent were trialled on trad climbs and not bolted routes. The first 28 in the world was *The Phoenix*—a difficult 'finger tips' crack by Ray Jardine (Yosemite 1977). This new level of difficulty required 'working,' a technique that was labelled 'hangdogging' in the States.

The gear was pre-placed and the moves were tried repeatedly until the whole climb could be done in one push. This allowed climbers to concentrate on the moves and not the danger or the extra effort needed to place gear. Hangdogging proved to be beneficial in the development of difficult lines and enabled climbers to improve at an incredible rate.

At this time John Allen, John Howard and a little later, Dave Fearnley were undoubtedly at the forefront of development in the South Island. Dragged to New Zealand by his parents in 1977, John Allen was responsible for kicking the South Island scene back to life. Although he was initially disillusioned with Christchurch rock, he did achieve some impressive results. With no one to equal his ability, he picked off the best and boldest trad lines in the Port Hills, most of which still remain testing leads. In an ironic twist, John was responsible for introducing bolts to the South Island with *Nether Edge*

Ton Snelder leading the 1st ascent of *Cave Route* (26) Castle Rock. TON SNELDER COLLECTION

(21, Castle Hill 1979) and *Wall of Shame* (23, Castle Rock 1980). But the first true sport climb, *Jim Takes a Tumble* (24), was put up at Whanganui Bay by Brian Fish during the 1980 'two car raid' to the North Island.

British climbing magazines smugly claimed that John Allen would push standards in New Zealand by 10 grades, however when he tried our national test piece *Supergroove* (26) on the same trip, he promptly dislocated his shoulder.

One of the few locals who could repeat John's routes very quickly and add others of similar difficulty or seriousness was John Howard. Some of his highlights are *White Wizard* (22) and *Yo-Yo* (21), both at Mt Bradley (1979), *A Bridge Too Far* (22, Rapaki 1980) and the rather serious *Falter* (22, Otepatotu 1980).

One of the strongest North Island climbers in the early 1980s was Charlie Creese. He made numerous trips to the South Island and established some of the first routes at Paynes Ford. He tested the limits, putting up the country's first grade 27, *Blam, Blam, Blam* (Mt Eden Quarry 1981).

'In retrospect, I think John Allen used to only operate at the level of the climb he was on to make life more interesting. I mean at the age of 16 he was one of the best climbers in Britain, doing unprotected 26s and 27s above mutilatory landings, a bona fide rock star and then his family moved to Christchurch. That would be about 1977, when the hardest routes here were 19s.

I don't think he hardly climbed at all for a year or so, but he did a few routes like *Nudity*, that people had looked at but were too scared to lead... He got back into climbing in 1979 to get fit for a trip to Australia... Anyway, he sometimes used to scratch around on climbs and make out that he was desperate, but the fact is I never saw him on a climb he couldn't do when he wanted to.' **Dave Fearnley**. Climber 24 p.31

> **John Allen's Classics**
> ★★ Nudity (20)–The Tors 1977
> ★★ Future Legend (19)–The Tors 1977
> ★★ Rambandit (21)–Castle Hill 1979
> ★★ Nether Edge (21)–Castle Hill 1979
> ★★ Go (23)–Mt Pleasant 1979
> ★★ Thin White Duke (23)–Mt Bradley 1979
> ★★ Career Girl (22)–Mt Pleasant 1979
> ★★ In the Night (22)–Mt Pleasant 1979

Dave Fearnley has had more impact and made a more significant contribution to South Island rock climbing, than any other climber to date. He has established numerous very staunch routes and was at the heart of the 1980s punk rock climbing culture. He left his mark both in terms of the quality of his routes and the difficulty or seriousness of the climbing.

In a way, Dave's timing was perfect. When his climbing came to fruition, few hard trad lines had been established in New Zealand and bolts were only just appearing on the scene. He had the ability and boldness to pick the cream of the crop and consequently many classics are attributed to him. Difficulty and aesthetic qualities always go hand in hand on Dave's routes and when it wasn't difficult it was usually bloody dangerous. At most South Island crags, you will find a Fearnley test piece. They were character-

Dave Fearnley on *Barking Up the Wrong Tree* (25) Mt Pleasant. TON SNELDER

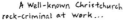

A Well-known Christchurch rock-criminal at work...

A Funkencartoon

istically undergraded due to Dave's fondness for sandbagging, or just out of his '19 or 23' grading rule. In a 1988 NZAC Bulletin he commented that there 'seem to be a lot of 23s around this season,' after he had climbed (and graded 23) *Rage Sur la Plage*, *Drop the Bomb* and *Dominion*. These are now respectively graded 25, 26 and 27!

Dave's Classics
- ✳✳ Hyperformance (22)–Mt Horrible 1982
- ✳✳✳ Up the Schrunds (23)–Charleston 1986
- ✳✳✳ Rage Sur La Plage (25)–Lyttelton Rock 1987
- ✳✳✳ Make My Day (25)–Paynes Ford 1988
- ✳✳✳ Dave's Arête (24)–Paynes Ford 1988
- ✳✳ Subculture (24)–Castle Hill 1988
- ✳✳ Instrument of Torture (26)–Long Beach 1988
- ✳✳ Dominion (27)–Mt Pleasant 1988
- ✳✳ L'Air du Temps (24)–Castle Hill 1989
- ✳✳✳ Adios Gringos (25)–Castle Hill 1989
- ✳✳ Fauvism (28)–Paynes Ford 1991

Power and Performance Becomes the Goal

Until the mid 1980s, the majority of routes in the South Island had cruxes that most skilled climbers could master. If the route was rehearsed, it was usually due to the lack of protection rather than a physical barrier imposed by the difficulty of the moves. Bolting provided an opportunity for climbers to focus purely on the physical moves and aim for the seemingly impossible. This either required more power, which in turn required training (shock horror!), or the patience and persistence to work a route until it could be climbed.

Cave Route (26, Castle Rock 1984), a joint achievement by Ton Snelder and Dave Fearnley is perhaps where this new tangent began in the South Island. A year later, visiting North Island climbing legend, Roland Foster, established *Suicide by Hallucination* (26, Castle Hill). At this time he had already put up many wonderful routes on the ignimbrite at Whanganui Bay. The first three 28's in the country are to his credit, including the classic *El Topo* and the dauntingly-bolted *Repulsion,* both in 1984/85. At this time, Roland was on par with the strongest Australian climbers and had made a name for himself in England for bold trad climbs.

The next route which took face climbing to a new and monumentally difficult level was 17 year-old, Colin Pohl's *Moment of Greed* (29, Castle Hill 1989). From this point on the South Island seized the North Island's yellow jersey and wears it to this day. All of the major advances in difficulty and the sheer volume of hard climbs were to be concentrated south of the Strait. But to be fair, many of the climbers doing these routes are rock-refugees from the north.

Roland Foster on *Labours of Love* **(24) Long Beach**
PHIL DE JOUX

Over the next few years more face-climbing test pieces appeared, including *Dreamweaver* (28, Hanging Rock 1989) by Tony Rooney and visiting Swiss Eric Talmadge's *Dance of Silence* (29, Castle Hill 1990). Talmadge also established the still unsurpassed pinnacle of fingery climbing, *Angel of Pain* (32, Dark Castle 1991). Diabolical monos on a steep bulge and then the mantle of all mantles—this makes *The Unrepeatable* (V6, Quantum Field) seem like a walk in the park. Although tried by many Australasian hotshots, *Angel of Pain* has still not seen a second ascent.

At this time, there was one young climber who managed to repeat almost all of the test pieces; Nick Sutter. He excelled at fingery climbing and added a good collection of classic hard climbs, including *Protoplasm* (29, Hanging Rock 1991), *Electrocution* (27, Paynes Ford 1991) and *Stoned Monkey* (28, Paynes Ford 1992). However, what propelled him into the hall of fame was the fact that he climbed *Punks in the Gym* (31) at Mt Arapiles before an Australian!

Until the early 1990s there were very few female rock climbers in New Zealand. Carol Nash was perhaps the most notable, climbing grade 28/29 routes in France after beginning her career in New Zealand. Lydia Bradey, although her goals were more mountaineering orientated, was also an active and strong rock climber at this time.

While the technical face climbers were pushing standards, a new breed of climbers started to enjoy the horizontal. These people sweated in the darkness,

Eric Talmadge on *Angel of Pain* (32) Castle Hill
SIMON MIDDLEMASS

Mayan Smith-Gobat on _Fuel_ (29) Babylon. PAUL ROGERS

slowly moving from one grotto to another leaving behind new routes with a gradient never before experienced. Ton Snelder's _Gone Bimbo_ (27, Lyttelton Rock 1989) was the beginning of a new trend towards roof climbing.

The Cave was discovered in 1993 and was mainly developed by Matt Evrard and Peter Taw, who both contributed popular classics and a few impressive projects. Taw did _Let There be Bolts_ (28, 1993) and _Bogus Machismo_ (29, 1994) and Matt climbed _Gorilla Grip_ (27, 1993). Stamina was the main requirement of the Cave routes thus far, but Matt upped the pace with _Space Boy_ (31, 1994). This cruxy new route required power endurance and gave all who tried a good spanking—apart from Kaz Pucia. In 1995, Kaz applied the brute strength he had gained from intensive campusing to _Space Boy_, extending it by another third which added another crux as well as a grade.

Two women who have excelled at roof climbing are Pat Deavoll and Rachel Musgrave. Pat has been the most active female developer establishing dozens of routes up to grade 28. Both Rachel and Pat have redpointed many 27's and a few 28's.

In the mid-to-late 1990s not much happened in terms of cutting-edge climbs. A young generation of climbers, more keen on bouldering, pushed the levels of difficulty but rarely applied their strength to route climbing. When some of these climbers turned their attention back to route development, the volume of difficult climbs increased markedly. Four new 32's were completed in a productive 2003 Cave season by

Murray Judge is probably the most significant developer in the South Island. He has discovered numerous new areas, tackled everything from crags to big wall missions and put up hundreds of new routes from beginner level through to the very serious and difficult.

It has been said that the best thing that ever happened to New Zealand rock climbing was Murray getting a petrol drill in the 1990s (although some may debate this, after encountering his uniquely angled bolts!). With Andy Macfarlane, he wielded this with great success at alpine crags like Twin Stream, Mt Somers and Chinaman's Bluff. The terrain that he opened up in the Darrans has been nothing short of phenomenal, with some of the most committing and stunning lines in the country set in a remarkable environment.

More recently Murray's development has offered people challenges that are closer to home and of a less committing nature. Mt Somers is a great addition to the South Island rock library; a collection desperately lacking long naturally protected routes. Chinaman's Bluff has become a popular pilgrimage and first multi-pitch experience for many climbers.

Murray Judge new-routing in Charleston
MURRAY JUDGE COLLECTION

Murray's Classics
- ✳✳ Judgement (20)–Castle Rock 1973
- ✳ Guillotine (16)–Mt Bradley 1975
- ✳ Jumping Jellyfish (19)–Long Beach 1976
- ✳✳ Labyrinth (21)–Barrier Knob 1988
  –with Paul Rogers
- ✳✳ Skate (22)–Mt Somers 1994
- ✳ Pain and Pleasure (24)–Mt Somers 1994
- ✳ Wailing Wall (22)–Mt Somers 1994
  –with Andrew Macfarlane
- ✳ Ravages of Time–Chinaman's Bluff 1999
  –with Andrew Macfarlane and Steve Carr
- ✳ Blue Lagoon (21)–Chinaman's Bluff 2000
  –with Matt Squires
- ✳ Third World Assassin (20)–Chinaman's Bluff
  –with Wayo Carson, Kate Wolfe & Jamie Foxley

Kaz–*Dracula* (32), Ivan Vostinar–*Ride of the Valkyries* (32) and *Centrifuge* (32) and Derek Thatcher–*The Enigma of Kasper Hauser* (32).

In mid-2003, the focused Mayan Smith-Gobat climbed *Fuel* (29, Babylon). Seven months later, she followed with *You're Either Dread or You're Not* (29, Paynes Ford) on her second attempt, plus a slew of 28s over that summer. This has been the result of a long period of intensive climbing, which has included many other hard routes and staunch boulder repeats. Mayan has consistently climbed harder than most male contemporaries, not to mention pushing the standard of female climbing in New Zealand to a new high.

Recently, the most exciting discovery has been the beautiful blank wall of Babylon near Milford Sound. In the summer of 2003/2004, Derek Thatcher put up a bunch of difficult lines, including the testing and thin *Katalepsis* (32, 2004). Derek is the only current climber to have systematically 'dispatched' almost all of the hardest test pieces New Zealand has to offer, both in bouldering and route climbing. He has also added great numbers of seldom-repeated boulder problems.

Indoor Vogue.

By the late 1980s the first rock climbing gyms started to appear, spurred by the efforts of Doug Carson, the organiser of New Zealand's first sport competition at Island Valley in 1989—complete with international hotshots. The gyms have had an indirect and significant impact on outdoor rock climbing. They are a safe environment to learn basic skills and are often more inclusive than the outdoor scene. They also provide an incubation venue for young climbers who eventually make the leap to outdoor rock.

Indoor competition climbing started alongside the development of gyms. The New Zealand Sport Climbing Federation was established and for the first time in rock climbing, there was a governing body that set standards and protocol for one aspect of the sport. Initially, most keen climbers were attracted to the competition scene. The National Series in the mid 1990s drew crowds that included most of the strong outdoor climbers at the time. This is no longer the case with the growing popularity of hard rock routes and bouldering, but the Federation has been active in promoting climbing competitions to young people and schools and has developed a strong following in the North Island.

The widening of the climbing scene has occured alongside the development of real 'sport' crags in Wanaka, Queenstown, Paynes Ford and Christchurch. The development ethic of these crags has made the transition from gyms to the rock a lot easier. It has also resulted in many more women participating in rock climbing. With the development of these crags, climbing crossed the line from being a fringe activity to becoming reasonably mainstream.

Steve Carr on *Via Magma* (23) Lovers Leap
DAVE BRASH

Developers. Starting in the early 1970s and continuing to the present, Lindsay Main is the South Island's most prolific route developer. From early trad climbs on the Port Hills and Banks Peninsula to modern sport areas such as Britten Crag, Lindsay has continually developed new areas, as well as adding a considerable number of routes at established crags. He also produced *Port Hills Climbing* (1998), the first comprehensive Port Hills guide.

Joe Arts, also a Cantabrian climber, has made a significant contribution to the pool of Canterbury climbs. *Feeding Time at the Zoo* (21, Lyttelton Rock 1982), *Citizen Kane* (22, Lyttelton Rock 1984), *Colonel Malone* (22, Lyttelton Rock 1989) and *The Monkey Wrench Gang* (22, Three Sisters 1990) are some of his best.

In Dunedin, Graham Love can be credited with being the most active developer at Long Beach. Some of his stellar lines are *Acid Queen* (23, 1984), *Crime & Punishment* (22, 1984), *Surreptitious* (20, 1984) and *Drury Lane* (20, 1985). Al Mark also made a big contribution to Long Beach and the torch has since been carried forward by current developers, such as Mike Simpson. Recently, Lovers Leap has come to fruition as an outstanding new addition, not only to the Dunedin area, but as one of the best walls in the South Island. It's emergence is mainly due to the efforts of Steve Carr and Dave Brash, who have established the majority of the new routes.

The seacliffs of Charleston have been climbed on since the mid 1970s, but the real renaissance occurred in the mid-late 1980s. The new routes were primarily developed by local climbers, Rick Harding, Ronan Grew and Paul Wopereis in a traditional style that is well-suited to the character of the crag.

The development of Wanaka rock climbing started in the 1970s with climbers picking off the obvious cracks, but it wasn't until Guy Cotter started bolting the longer faces at Phoebe Creek in 1988 that things began to gather pace. The style of development has been to establish accessible recreational climbing for the masses. This has been

Lindsay's Classics

- ✳ Judge and Jury (17)–Three Sisters 1977
- ✳ Prometheus Busted–Three Sisters 1977
- ✳ Son of Hangman (17)–Mt Bradley 1978
- ✳ Andromeda (19)–The Monument 1979
- ★ Rubicon (21)–Lyttelton Rock 1983
- ✳ The Promised Land (17)–Lyttelton Rock 1983
- ✳✳ Surgical Strike (22)–Cattlestop 1996
- ✳ Collateral Damage (21)–The Tors 1996

helped along by the Wanaka Rock Club and many keen locals, including Nick Cradock, Glen Einam and more recently Ed Nepia and David Hiddleston. Nick picked off a lot of the quality lines, Glenn has added vast volumes of routes in the valley while Dave and Ed both concentrated their efforts on difficult grades.

Ian Binnie is a passionate developer who has focused on quality rock and making routes accessible. He was one of the pioneers of Hanging Rock and later the driving force in Wye Creek action. While Wye Creek was explored and climbed in the early days, it was bolting that really opened the area. Ian established the majority of the routes and credit should go to him for having the fore-sight to use the best bolting technology available. As a result, Wye Creek is one of the best set up crags in terms of hardware.

The days of Kiwi spots, no mats and *Babyfood* (V5) at Cave Stream. IAN WHITEHOUSE

This is matched by Dave MacLeod's development at the central Queenstown crags.

Paul Rogers is enthusiastic and prolific in his climbing and development. He is a South London geezer with an eye for the aesthetic and a self-confessed granite devo-tee. His routes are likely to be positive, safe experiences always on good rock and often on wild terrain. Some of his best routes are *African Head Charge* (26, Paynes Ford 1992) and at the Chasm with Steve Walker, *Day Tripper* (24, 1993), *High Ideals and Crazy Dreams* (22, 1993) and *One Way Ticket* (24, 1993).

Tony Burnell is also a British climbing export and a focused developer. He has systematically worked his way through all known Christchurch climbing areas, adding dozens of routes and climbing virtually everything in the Port Hills. Of particular interest is *Mt Pleasant Butcher* (24, Britten Crag 1999), *Face Race* (21, Britten 2000) and *Peer Pressure* (24, Three Sisters 1998).

Numerous other climbers have contributed to the recent sport route boom in Christchurch. Of these, Richard Kimberley stands out both for his work on the Port Hills and for his exploration, with Alan Hill, of new trad routes on Banks Peninsula.

See page 135 for Roland Foster's take on development styles.

Pete Smale on an early Matt Warwick problem (V5) Flock Hill. JOHN McCALLUM

Bouldering has been practised over the decades for warming up or just clambering about. It was always seen as secondary to route climbing, as route climbing was once secondary to mountaineering. As a result boulder problems were never graded or named and apart from the odd exception, it was seen as a side show.

Derek Thatcher on *Joker* (V9) **Spittle Hill.** DANIEL JENKINS

It was at Castle Hill that the first serious bouldering occurred in the late 1970s. There was quite a marked distinction between this and what had occurred before, which was mainly just mucking around at the base of Castle Rock. At the time, there were only a few devotees, such as Bill Atkinson (known for his one-arm pull-ups), John McCallum and Matt Warwick, who saw that you didn't have to climb routes to find quality moves and vast climbing potential. In the 1980s, the group visiting 'The Hill' grew to include most of the passionate developers and climbers. John Allen probably did the first V6 by climbing the thin crack of *The Day the World Stood Still* (1980).

From the early days, one boulder problem stands out in New Zealand as a breakthrough in terms of difficulty. At Baring Head, Wellington, the young Charlie Creese established *Show of Strength* (V8, 1981). An impressive problem for the time internationally, it was the beacon to aim for and was not to be surpassed until over a decade later.

Boulder Comp at Spittle Hill MARK WATSON

North Islanders, John Palmer, Sebastian Loewensteijn and Derek Thatcher flexing at 'The Hill.' SEBASTIAN LOEWENSTEIJN COLLECTION

Meanwhile, Castle Hill received the usual interest, which climaxed in a rather large rock meet in 1988 at Flock Hill and Dry Valley. Climbers at the time enjoyed having high-volume days running around with friends and brushing up new boulders. While the problems were technically devious, none were extremely difficult (mostly up to V5 and a few V6's). There was so much to do at every grade, that climbers tended not to work on particular problems, but came to sample the delights of the whole boulder field. The advent of the Boreal 'Ninjas' also made all-day climbing a lot more comfy.

Elephant Rocks and Hulk Hogan were also developed for bouldering in the late 1980s. This was predominantly the work of Murray Judge and Doug Carson, who were scouting around for a venue for the first National Sport Climbing competition. Many Dunedin visitors have since made good contributions to this area.

In the early 1990s, Steve Grkovic pushed the standards with two mega classics *Bio Hazard* (V7) and *Quantum Mechanics* (V7) at Castle Hill. The next grade in bouldering difficulty appeared in the North Island when Colin Pohl established a painful and awesomely fingery test piece in Wharepapa, Froggat; *The de Flow Humpty Funk* (V9).

By the late 1990s, bouldering was on the verge of exploding. This was inevitable, given overseas trends and the quality of Castle Hill. Ivan Vostinar actively developed problems in Quantum Field for a new bouldering guide. It wasn't that climbers needed to be shown the boulders, but problems graded for the first time, which appealed to a lot of people (what else would they talk about at parties?).

Along with the promotion of bouldering competitions (which peaked at four per year), swarms of people started to visit 'The Hill.' Mainstream bouldering became the eventual distillation of the move to fuss-free, social and safe climbing. While trad climbing may have been seen as risky and fringe, bouldering was totally the opposite (and the moves were rad). It has been the most inclusive climbing movement to date, with all ages, abilities and genders being well represented.

Tim Clifford on
***Cold Fusion* (V12)**
RANDY PURO

The next jump in difficulty in South Island bouldering was only to be realised years after Kaz Pucia climbed *The Joker* (V9, 1998). He originally graded the problem V6, partly innocently, partly out of annoyance at North Island down-graders. At this stage thousands of problems had been established along with multitudes of highballs, even up to V8. All of these were done without bouldering mats, which only made it across the Tasman when young Australian climbers turned up in 1998 to film *EOS1*. Mats not only encouraged more people to get into bouldering, but also upped the height of problems that climbers tackled. Many of these would have previously been considered solos.

Over the past twenty years, Baring Head (the sole Wellington training ground) has spawned numerous strong-fingered climbers and unleashed them on the South Island. Of the most prolific are Derek Thatcher, Sebastian Loewensteijn and John Palmer. The new crew added volumes of V8's and V9's, but it was Boone Speed (US) who pushed the grades up with *House of Pain* (V10, 2000 Spittle Hill). Not to be outdone, the locals got progressively stronger and in 2003, Derek Thatcher established *Ristretto* (V11, Quantum Field). Upping the standards again, visiting Tim Clifford (UK) added two V12's, *Cold Fusion* and *Headbanger* (both at Quantum Field 2004).

The Anchor. Rock climbing's notable diversity has come about through the fast-paced development of equipment, ethics and styles. It is common for a boulder-er to enjoy racking up at a trad crag and city rock climbers are often partial to the odd alpine rock excursion. Routes are established bottom up, top down or somewhere in between.

Who knows what's next? In our travels we have seen some potential for new routes at existing crags as well as a lot of climbed out areas. More importantly, there are many worthy lines that never get climbed, cleaned or maintained. As climbing grows, we are bound to see a focus on quality over quantity and a developing aware-ness of the need to look after what we have already created.

Whatever happens the future is bound to be colourful and full of unique characters. While much of climbing is now mainsteam, hopeful-ly a fringe element will remain.

Ode to Jane Fonda (2004) DEAN MACKENZIE

Climbing Equipment

The development of climbing technology has had a direct and major impact on rock climbing standards, ethics and styles. When climbers look back on the grades that the elite were doing in the past, they may seem quite moderate, but we have to consider their achievements within the context of the equipment that was available to them at the time.

Ropes. The early hawser-laid ropes were sufficiently strong for aiding, top-roping and abseiling but not for holding a decent lead fall. The development of nylon ropes was a major advance for climbers. This new material added some dynamic properties, but more importantly it did not break! It wasn't until 1953 that Edelweiss produced the first kern-mantel rope (with a separate core and sheath). This was an incredible leap for climbing because it allowed for greater stretch, strength and abrasion resistance.

Protection. Perhaps the most ancient protection was supreme or foolhardy self-confidence. Along with hawser-laid ropes, this worked most of the time on easy ascents of peaks or bluffs. At best, rope slings were threaded or placed around flakes and spikes. The first real protection arrived when climbers started to place chockstones in cracks. In England, climbers started to select well-rounded pebbles lying at the bottom of the crags and carry them up the climb in their trouser pockets. Once the stone was wedged in the crack, the climber would untie the rope, thread it around the chock, retie and continue (if they did not have karabiners). The first recorded use of deliberately placing stones in cracks to act as chocks was credited to Morley Wood during the ascent of *Piggot's Climb* (Clogwyn du'r Arddu, North Wales 1926). In the mid 1950s, the chockstone technique was pushed into another level by the introduction of metal machine nuts.

Pitons. The development of karabiners and pitons opened up a vast untapped potential for rock climbers and paved the way for modern protection. The first person to design a series of pitons was Hans Fiechtl from München in about 1910. Wood or metal had previously been hammered into cracks for rudimentary protection or aiding. Hans refined these improvisations and shaped the metal into something that had the first resemblance to modern pitons. The major step was to use molybdenum alloy steel which allowed the piton not to deform when inserted and could therefore be removed. This was a revolution in aid climbing.

Hardened steel piton

Mild steel piton

Karabiners had been used in sailing for some time but it wasn't until Otto Herzog (one of Fiechtl's contemporaries) saw München firemen use a ring with an opening bar that he realised they could be used for climbing. The early karabiners were mild steel, then heat treated high tensile steel became standard. Light-weight, aluminum karabiners were developed during WWII. For mountaineering and big walls, in particular, the weight difference helped considerably. Since then only cosmetic changes have occurred to karabiner design.

Steel karabinar

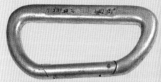

Aluminium karabiner

Wires. In 1961, a blacksmith from Sheffield, John Brailsford, created the first ever purpose-designed nut, the Acorn. Three sizes (1 inch, 3/4 inch and 5/8 inch) were turned on a lathe from extruded aluminium alloy and were threaded with rope. Charles Curtis was probably the first to make wired nuts in 1961 in the Geology Department at Sheffield University.

Since the mid 1970s, Australian Roland Pauligk, made the ultimate tools for hair line cracks, RPs. Small wires were already on the market, but Pauligk's silver soldering process allowed RPs to be far narrower, whilst maintaining maximum wire strength. He initially sold his micro brass wedges in campsites during climbing trips around the world, and the invention filled a huge hole in the size range of available protection.

No.8 Stopper

No.8 Wedge

No.1 and No.2 RPs

Hexes. While wedges and pitons covered small to medium placements, larger cracks were often unprotectable until the asymmetrical hex was developed in 1971. These gadgets are lightweight and still unparalleled in bottleneck placements. They were used extensively from the 1970s through to the 1990s and have since been superseded by cams to a certain extent.

No.11 Hex

No.2 Friend

Cams. The idea of a spring loaded camming device (SLCD) first came from Greg Lowe, who invented a device based on a constant cam angle. These early models were highly unreliable and didn't have a trigger.

Ray Jardine, a former aerospace engineer, bought some of these early designs and refined the idea. In the spring of 1974, Jardine, Kris Walker and Lou Dawson covertly used a collection of size 2.5 and 3.5 'Friends' (the name for their little helpers) to cut the three day speed record for climbing the Nose in half, getting to the top after only twenty hours of climbing. Eventually Jardine sold the rights to his invention to Mark Vallance, who founded Wild Country. Friends were released to the public in 1978.

Since then the biggest developments have been flexi-stems, which added versatility and enabled the production of sub #1 sized cams and twin-axle Black Diamond Camelots, which have increased the camming range of each unit.

Shoes. The first foorwear used in rock climbing were stiff mountaineering boots, leather or canvas shoes and bare feet. All these were okay for some things but still utterly useless overall. In the late 1950s the first rock climbing boots, PAs were designed by Pierre Allain and soon after EBs arrived on the scene named after Eduard Bourdineux. Much like modern shoes, they had a smooth rubber sole and a canvas upper. However, they were considerably stiffer than modern shoes, and the rubber was nowhere near 'sticky.'

In New Zealand it was difficult to get rock climbing shoes until well into the 1980s. There were few outdoor stores and the ones that did sell climbing gear would only stock a few pairs of shoes at a time. As a result in the early 1980s some climbers used 'spoon

EBs

boots.' These were made by Para Rubber and were not bad for bouldering.

The sticky rubber revolution began with the arrival of Firés in 1984/5 and suddenly some of the most technical and smeary problems became quite straightforward. Since then shoes have made great progress in the shape to become better fitting with increased performance.

Bolts were used overseas since the 1950s on big walls and in the mountains. They were small in diameter and short because of the effort required when hand drilling. They were mostly terrier or compression bolts, if climbers could get their hands on such technology. If not, then the sophisticated 'carrot bolt' was used. This involved grinding the end of a 10 or 12mm engineering bolt (anything found around the house or garden would do) down to a point and then pounding it into a slightly smaller hole. Getting the ratio correct between the bolt and hole diameter was critical—too tight and the bolt would stick out or bend, too little and it may come out again. Carrot bolting was used on local hard rock to some extent, but it was in limestone where this became the method of choice.

The omnipresent chain-link anchor

The first expansion bolts were 6mm in diameter which made them more practical to place but did not offer any factor of safety and only lasted a few years before corrosion made them frightening even to look at.

After petrol and battery drills became available bigger bolts could finally be used. Now expansion masonry bolts became the easiest to place but climbers still opted for cost effectiveness and so used zinc plated or galvanised material. By the late 1990s most climbers accepted stainless as the only suitable material and 10mm as the smallest diameter.

Old extracted 6mm compression bolt

During the 1980s proper hangers became available, but due to the cost they were mostly avoided. A climber either placed a wire over the end of a bolt or used a special removeable hanger, which was placed over the head of the bolt and then clipped. When hangers were opted for it was mostly chain link or even some home made ones. It wasn't until the late 1990s that stainless hangers become standard.

By the early 1990s glue-ins started to be used sporadically, mainly for steeper rock. This method is acknowledged to be excellent, but due to extra cleaning needed, glue drying time and the greater cost, glue-ins remain a rarity.

10mm expansion bolt

8mm terrier bolt

12mm carrot bolt

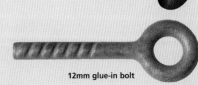

12mm glue-in bolt

Geology

Subhorizontal layers in gneiss at Charleston were formed as the New Zealand crust was stretched before finally breaking away from Australia and Antarctica.

New Zealand is a young country. In fact, if geological time were compared to a human lifespan, most present day landscapes would have been formed in the last few hours.

For most of its geological history, New Zealand has been a fringe dweller, attached to the eastern edge of the Gondwana supercontinent. About 80 million years ago, New Zealand finally broke away from Gondwana. Since approximately 25 million years ago, New Zealand has been at the boundary of two continental plates, the Indo-Australian Plate to the west and the Pacific Plate to the east. The islands move like a cork, riding the tectonic forces between the two plates. The South Island is being pushed up, while some of the North Island is being submerged at the plate boundary. The land is also moving sideways about 3–5cm per year (about as fast as hair and fingernails grow) along the Alpine Fault. All of this movement explains why, although we come from ancient origins, most of the South Island is less than one million years old.

The Makings of the West Coast

The oldest rock in New Zealand is found in the Cobb Valley in Nelson and dates back about 540 million years. At this time, volcanoes were spewing magma and ash onto the sea floor along the coast of Gondwana. After they died down, the volcanic rock was covered with sediment that settled and was compressed over a very long period.

It was not until the first main period of uplift, the Tuhua Orogeny (approximately 370 million years ago) that this seafloor sediment was brought to the surface. The uplift crumpled the skin of the earth into giant folds, which were lifted out of the ocean to form a new mountain range. By the end of this upheaval, many of the basement rocks of Fiordland and northwest Nelson were formed, but the new land was still part of the Gondwanan coastline.

The East Coast Takes Shape

About 250 million years ago, a fledgling chain of volcanic islands formed a 'volcanic arc' along Gondwana's eastern coastline. It was very active, erupting huge volumes of ash into the ocean. This material settled on the sea floor and mixed with sand to create layered sedimentary rocks, known as the Arc rocks. These Arc rocks are found mainly in eastern parts of New Zealand, including a large part of Southland and east Nelson.

While the Arc rocks were forming, a new rock type, known as the Torlesse Group, was being deposited on another part of the seafloor. This is mainly greywacke, built from layers of sandstone and mudstone that were later intensely folded and now makes up more than half of New Zealand's landmass.

Geologists think that most of the Torlesse Group rock originated from huge underwater landslides. These were triggered when material from Gondwana was swept into the sea and built up on the edge of the continental shelf. When this became unstable, it tumbled into offshore canyons and gathered speed, ripping up the seafloor as it went. At the mouth of the canyons, these giant landslides fanned out and settled on the seafloor, depositing thick layers of sand and mud **(diagram 1)**.

Jaap Overtume on *Hanging Around* (18) Charleston. DANIEL JENKINS

Seafloor spreading caused the Torlesse Rock to move towards the chain of islands where the Arc rocks were forming. Seafloor spreading occurs when convection currents in the mantle of the earth bring molten material to the surface at the boundary between two continental plates.

Over millions of years, this process moved the Torlesse Group rock along the Gondwana coast. When this rock met the plate boundary, the heavy oceanic crust was pulled down towards the centre of the earth (**diagram 2**). The seafloor sediments were too buoyant to follow and were scraped up and pushed against the volcanic sediments (Arc rocks).

As more Torlesse material arrived it started to jam the subduction trench. Shearing and buckling movements pushed huge slices of the sea floor into a contorted and crumpled skin, tens of kilometres thick. This long period of collision is known as the Rangitata Orogeny and it lasted for about 50 million years.

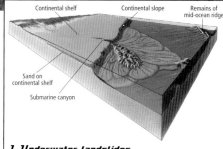

1. Underwater landslides.

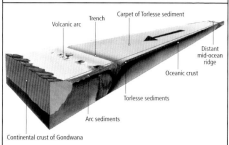

2. The Rangitata Orogeny

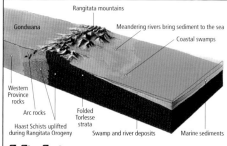

3. The Cretaceous

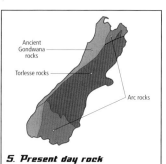

5. Present day rock

4. New Zealand leaves Gondwana

Diagrams by Geoffrey Cox from *The Rise and Fall of the Southern Alps*. Canterbury University Press (2002).

Geologists do not know how high the mountains were on this new landscape because most of the evidence has been destroyed. However, they do know that by approximately 150 million years ago, the pile up of sediment was left to cool. Its weight pushed down against the rock at the bottom of the stack, subjecting it to intense pressure and heat. This pressure caused a huge area of sedimentary rock to be altered from its original form. The result was the Haast Schists, found mainly in Central Otago (Wanaka and Queenstown). The Rangitata Orogeny was also associated with the melting of the earth's mantle and crust to produce igneous rocks such as the diorite of the Darrans and much of the granite of Rakiura, the Paparoa Range and Charleston.

A New Land in the Pacific
At the end of the Rangitata Orogeny, all of New Zealand's foundations had been laid down. A large mountainous land reached thousands of kilometres along the coast of Gondwana (diagram 3).

New Zealand then entered a major erosional phase in the Cretaceous period. The weather ate away the young mountains and rivers meandered across fertile plains, carrying the sediment back to the sea. Some of the first plants to appear on earth flourished in the swamps, dinosaurs roamed the plains and pterosaurs circled over early forests.

While New Zealand was developing a distinct ecosystem, big changes were happening beneath the earth's crust. Magma started to well up again beneath the coast of Gondwana and giant cracks appeared in the earth's surface. The new phase of sea floor spreading started a rift that, between 85 and 60 million years ago, pulled New Zealand away from Gondwana. The Tasman Sea flowed between the two lands and finally New Zealand found its own foothold in the Pacific Ocean (diagram 4).

The early Tertiary period (65 million years ago) was a geologically tranquil time in New Zealand. There were no major mountain building episodes, and the earth's crust cooled and solidified. With the end of seafloor spreading in the Tasman Sea, New Zealand became part of the Indo-Australian Plate and, as that plate pulled away from the Antarctic Plate and drifted north, so did New Zealand.

At this time most of New Zealand was submerged and new sediments were gently deposited over the basement rocks. These included layers of sandstone, mudstone and limestone that have mostly been eroded away in the South Island. Only small patches have been protected from erosion by tectonic uplift. Castle Hill Basin, because it is bounded by faults on all sides, is one of these remnant pockets of Tertiary rock.

Modern New Zealand Arrives
About 25 million years ago, New Zealand entered a period of gentle mountain building, which has become dramatic in the last 5 million years. The Pacific Plate, which stretches all the way to Los Angeles, started to collide with the Indo-Australian Plate along the Alpine Fault. This complex junction of forces has created a geological jigsaw that has shifted rock thousands of kilometres from its origins.

The two plates meet in the North Island at the Hikurangi Trough, where the Pacific Plate is subducting under the more buoyant Indo-Australian Plate. As this happens, the downward moving oceanic crust dehydrates and rising fluids cause the mantle and lower crust to melt. The molten rock rises to the surface again as magma. This is the origin of the Taupo Volcanic Zone in the Central North Island.

The Hikurangi Trough peters out just north of Kaikoura. From this point, south, the two plates are colliding in a constant battle to sink one another. This mammoth wrestling match has produced enough force to build the Southern Alps in a very short time. 'The hills' are growing about 7mm per year and if no erosion had occurred, the mountain chain would extend 20km into the sky. Were it not for this convergent boundary, New Zealand would still be under water.

As well as colliding head on, the two plates are also sliding past one another along the Alpine Fault. This has caused about 480km of sideways movement in the last 100 million years. The crust on the West Coast is moving north relative to the eastern side, which explains why some of the same rock is found in Nelson and Fiordland (**diagram 5**).

Rock Types in New Zealand

Sedimentary rock is material that settled in a lake or sea as grains or fragments and was then packed down and hardened. Greywacke is the most common sedimentary rock in New Zealand and tends to be quite brittle. Freeze-thaw cracks shards of this rock off the Southern Alps and the weather helps transport it back to the ocean.

Limestone is a sedimentary rock made from lime (calcium carbonate). This substance comes mainly from the shells and the bodies of marine creatures. In shallow oceans this material accumulates and either stays intact (large shells are often found in limestone areas) or dissolves and recrystallises. The chemical reaction of water with limestone forms caves and sinkholes and, of course, amazing holds and pockets.

Metamorphic comes from Greek words meaning 'change of shape.' It refers to rocks that have been changed by heat and pressure without actually melting. This results in rock with a new texture and chemical composition. In Fiordland, where some of the best friction climbing in the country is found, some of the igneous diorites and gabbros have been recrystallised during metamorphism to form gneiss (e.g. Milford Sound). The Haast Schists in Wanaka and Queenstown were also formed by metamorphic activity. The minerals that separated into layers during metamorphism have given the rock its striped look.

Igneous rock is formed by melting of the mantle or older crust. These magmas may reach the surface and form volcanos (where it cools quickly), or may freeze deeper in the earth as coarser grained rock, like granite or diorite.

Volcanic magma may erupt explosively or quietly ooze from the earth's surface. Erupted rock is usually aerated and brittle, whereas rock that has oozed from the surface is more compact. More than 90% of the world's volcanoes are basalt, and all of the volcanic crags in the South Island are made of this rock type.

The geology section was prepared with help from Andy Tullock, GNS.

Andrew Smith on *Burn Hollywood Burn* (21). STEVE EASTWOOD

How to use this guide

The Crag

At the beginning of each section you will see the following symbols in the top bar to give you quick reference information.

 Approximate walking time to the closest wall of the crag.

 Important to wear a helmet due to loose rock on or above the climb.

 There is drinking water near the crag. This should be safe but, if in doubt, boil it for at least 3 minutes.

 There is either camping or hut accommodation reasonably close to the crag.

 The crag is on farmland and subject to lambing restrictions. You may need to call the farmer to ask permission to climb. Read the information section for more details and specific dates.

Access and Information

Everything that you should know before going to a crag is described in the following sections.

 Driving access instuctions.

 Foot access instructions.

 This gives crag-specific information about the climate, the gear required, handy climbing tips and anything else we thought may help you plan your first trip to an area.

The Tab

Each climb has a grey tab alongside the route description. This gives information on the protection and safety of the route. It should be used in conjunction with the symbols on the photo topo to give a good idea of what to expect from the climb.

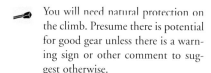 You will need natural protection on the climb. Presume there is potential for good gear unless there is a warning sign or other comment to suggest otherwise.

8🛠 The number of bolts on the climb. It does not include belay bolts.

👍 The route will have evenly spaced, secure placements with plenty of options for protection.

⚠ The danger sign refers to lack of gear, groundfall potential, loose rock or a combination of these.

Photo Topos

The photo topos indicate route direction and show anchor details. Make sure that you read the crag intro to find out more about the anchors in each area.

All routes within the guide are described from left to right.

❹ The reference number of the climb always relates to the number on the photo. If a climb is not on a photo topo, it will not have a reference number in the text.

⚫ The natural gear anchors are a grey circle to indicate the area where you will find suitable gear or blocks.

- A bolted anchor. Will be double bolts, unless otherwise stated.

- A tree anchor.

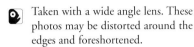 Taken with a wide angle lens. These photos may be distorted around the edges and foreshortened.

Indicates where the photo was taken from.

Quality

This guide uses a three star system. The stars may be different to the historical ratings. We definitely found unsung gems and three star imposters out there, but experiences on a route obviously vary for every climber. The stars have nothing to do with the safety of the route.

✷✷✷ The climb has all or most of the following qualities: it looks great, climbs well, has excellent quality rock, some individuality and a great setting.

✷✷ Expect a sterling climb with good virtues. Bound to be a satisfying experience.

✷ Still a top-notch climb that is well worth your time. Should have a couple of 'three star' qualities.

Grades

New Zealand uses the open-ended Ewbank (Australian) grading system for routes. This starts at about 10 and currently goes to 32.

A V-grading system is used for bouldering. This starts at VE (easy)/VM (medium) and then goes from V0 to V12.

Both systems are based on endurance, power and technical difficulty all summed up in one number. They don't take danger into account.

Gear Requirements

This is a run-down on what most New Zealand climbers use at the crag. Any other equipment that is necessary or useful, is listed in the crag information section.

Climbing Equipment:

- A single rope is sufficient for most crags.
- A rope tarp is always useful.
- Most crags require about 12 quickdraws.
- A standard rack will consist of a full set of wires (and sometimes double-ups and offsets), and a range of cams up to #4.
- A nut key/tool is essential at trad crags for cleaning and gear removal.
- Short slings are useful for protection, but you may often need long slings to set up anchors.
- Prusik cord is essential for safety/rescue.

Other Paraphenalia:

- Sunscreen/glasses: The sun conditions are harsh in New Zealand, apparently due to the proximity of a large ozone hole.
- 2 litre water bottle.
- Climbing tape.
- Plastic brushes for cleaning.
- A carpet for bouldering to keep your shoes clean and dry, and the rock clean.
- Boulder mat.

Clothing

The weather in New Zealand is changeable and most climbers take a down jacket or some sort of wind stopper to the crag, even in summer.

NZAC Code of Conduct for Rock Climbers

Permission
Before entering private land permission is usually obtained. Any agreements made must be strictly followed. Accept that sometimes you may be refused permission to enter the land because of current circumstances, e.g. family gathering, lambing/calving.

Impact
Any rock climbing must have the lowest possible impact on the crag and environs. Points to note are:

- No climbing on special areas such as burial grounds, artefact sites, stalagmites and stalactites, areas of rare wildlife or other such identified areas.
- Rock climbers should limit their activities at a crag to the cliff, its top and its base, preserving areas such as native bush and reserves for all.
- Keep tracks to a minimum.
- All rubbish should be taken from the crag, including biodegradables.

Route Preparation
This should be done with minimum impact while ensuring the route is safe to climb. Talk to the landowners/managers before cutting or removing vegetation. It is important that the route be prepared properly so the job does not have to be done twice. All ropes, slings etc. used in cleaning must be taken when leaving the crag, as these are often unsightly.

Fixed Gear and Anchors
In some areas climbs may have to be equipped with bolts or pegs. It is stressed that this gear is placed only for safety reasons. Where possible use the same belay point for several routes. At bolt station belays, the double bolt and chain set-up is the minimum standard. Bolts, where necessary, should be placed using the following as a guide:

- Make every bolt safe to use.
- Use the best and most appropriate type for the rock.
- Use care when considering bolt placements—note the distance between bolts, and ease of clipping.

Naming Routes
The prerogative of the first ascentionist. Care should be taken not to offend others with the selected name. It is not worth incurring the wrath of the local iwi, ranger, farmer or landowner for the sake of a crude or derogatory route name. This can cause a crag to be closed.

Behaviour
Remember that your voice carries some distance from the cliff, sometimes far enough to be heard by landowners and other land users who may be upset by obscenities and offensive phrases uttered in the heat of the moment on a climb. Before stripping off for a swim, consider if nudity might be offensive to landowners. It sometimes is!

On a Farm
- Leave gates as you find them (open or shut).
- Cross fences at stiles or posts and cross locked gates at the hinged end.
- Leave your dog and gun at home.
- Do not distress the stock.
- Before driving across farmland you must check with the farmer.

Cultural Considerations

Where crags have special cultural significance, any issues such as burial grounds or tapu sites, must be resolved before climbing commences. Relevant specialists may need to survey the crag.

Communication

Maintain good communication. A few minutes of polite discussion can mean an uninterrupted days climbing, whereas a few hurled insults can result in no further access. Be courteous and respectful.

Camping

Camp only in designated areas and keep a tidy camp. Completely extinguish any campfire after use.

Safety

Inherent in climbing is an element of risk. Some flaunt it, others respect it, some choose to ignore it. In the final analysis you are responsible for your own safety. Nobody has to do a particular route. If a route is too necky for you, back off.

Climb as safely as possible. Beware of loose rocks; they cause considerable damage to people and equipment when dislodged.

Some crags are notorious for having loose rocks on the routes and on access/descent tracks. Wearing a helmet could save you from serious injury.

All things being equal, softer rock is more likely to have protection fail; keep this in mind when placing wires at some of the softer rock crags. Treat all fixed gear with suspicion—you do not know its history.

Access to crags is a privilege not a right!

Acknowledgements

We wish to extend our appreciation to the NZAC who have supported this publication from the word 'go.' Thank you especially to the Publications Committee, Mark Watson and Richard Wesley—for their ongoing support and advice.

Thank you Daniel Jenkins for not only working on this guide for the first few months, but also for ideas and awesome images.

Our gratitude goes out to the reviewers and local experts who have all added a huge amount: Peter Allison, Joe Arts, Hana Black, Dave Bolger, Dave Brash, Tony Burnell, Chris Burtenshaw, Steve Carr, Rob Dunn, Rick Harding, Tom Hoyle, Phil de Joux, Murray Judge, Jo Kippax, Tim Lewis, Sebastian Loewensteijn, Dave MacLeod, Lindsay Main, Simon Middlemass, Andy Milne, Tom Riley, Paul Rogers, Mike Simpson, Derek Thatcher, Andy Tulloch, Carl Waddick, Wanaka Rock Club, Mark Watson and Bruce White.

The climbing retrospective was constructed with the help of many famous people. They graciously allowed us a personal audience, reviewed the drafts, provided photos and the anecdotes. Thank you to Stu Allan, Joe Arts, Dave Brash, Phil de Joux, Dave Fearnley, Roland Foster, Murray Judge, John McCallum, Lindsay Main, Simon Middlemass, Paul Rogers and Ton Snelder.

Thank you also to all of the people who also contributed to the project and gave us ideas, shelter and moral support: Brigid Allan, Andre Dahlman, Jonathon Clearwater, Kim Cousins, Kate Finnerty, Nick Flyvbjerg, Milo Gilmour, Murray and Bronwyn Judge, Dean MacKenzie, Jess McVeigh, Kaz Pucia, Tim Robertson, Mark Scaife, Fiona and Mike Simpson, Dave Woodman, Ben Yates and Simon van der Sluijs.

Paynes Ford

The swimming hole
opposite Hangdog is
the best place to
frolic at the Ford.
STEVE EASTWOOD

Paynes Ford personifies all that is good. It is a scenic reserve with some of the best limestone walls and swimming holes in the country, all set in native bush. Takaka, the chill-out hippy epicentre of New Zealand, is just down the road and offers a mouthwatering array of wholesome cafés. It is also a summer party venue, with some of the best multi-day dance parties held around New Years Eve.

The climbing's great. There are two main outcrops of hard, weathered limestone and these are littered with horizontal ripples and range from slabs to roofs. The characteristic style will see you pulling down on subtle edges, trying to find that one good hold among the multitude of pretenders, but there are foot holds aplenty.

Paynes Ford itself contains over 200 routes and there are about 90 in nearby Pohara. This guide covers more than 100 of the best routes at Paynes. For a comprehensive look at the area we recommend *Golden Bay Climbs* by Simon Middlemass and Mark Watson. Hangdog Camp also produces a well-priced local guide. This has route descriptions for all climbs up to grade 23 and listings for the other routes.

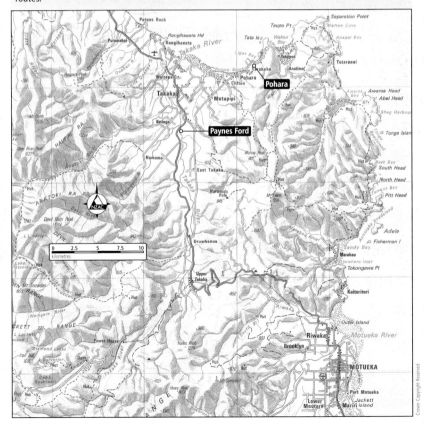

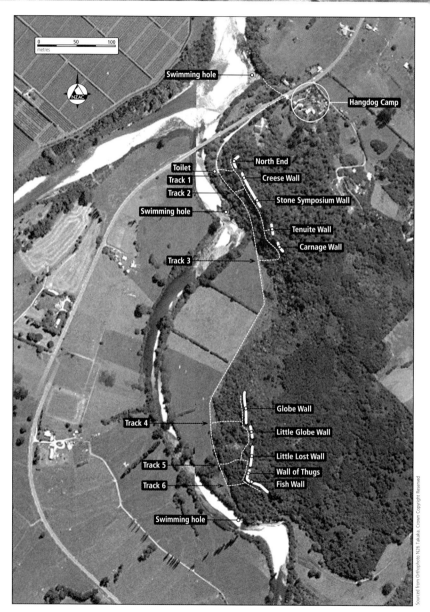

Swimming hole

Hangdog Camp

North End

Toilet
Track 1

Creese Wall

Track 2

Stone Symposium Wall

Swimming hole

Tenuite Wall

Carnage Wall

Track 3

Globe Wall

Track 4

Little Globe Wall

Little Lost Wall

Track 5

Wall of Thugs

Track 6

Fish Wall

Swimming hole

0   50   100
metres

NZAC

The first step is to get to Motueka. From here, drive another 60km over the Takaka Hill to the Paynes Ford Bridge (over the Takaka River). 100m past the bridge on the right-hand side is Hangdog Camp. This is 5km before the Takaka township.

From Hangdog camp-ground, turn left onto the main road towards the bridge and veer left into the carpark and reserve. A farm track starts here and runs all the way to the farthest cliffs. From the farm track there are six access tracks which lead to the main walls.

i The majority of climbs are bolted with only a few mixed routes (these usually only require a placement or two). Most of the bolts are stainless and in excellent condition thanks to the local bolting fund. Contributions to this can be made at Hangdog and are always welcome and put to good use.

The crag is on a DOC reserve and they have had a good relationship with climbers. It is important to respect this environmentally significant area, stay on the tracks and look after the crag. The vegetation should not be removed from the walls or boulders or anywhere (apart from if it is growing on your body). There are toilets at the start of the farm road.

The place to stay is Hangdog Camp. It has a long and charismatic history and is a mere 5 minute stroll from the crag. Since Willy Butler instigated the institution, any one who's anyone has been seen hanging at Hangdog. Camping is only $4 (showers an extra $1) and the bunkhouse is $10 per night (that's where Aucklanders stay).

The camp is sardine packed with climbers in the Christmas/New Year period and Easter is also popular, otherwise it's pretty quiet.

Paynes Ford is climbable for most of the year. Rain is the main problem in winter and spring, but some of the steep routes stay dry.

Takaka has a small supermarket, good cafés, a petrol station and cinema. For drinks, food and good local bands, The Muscle Inn (20km towards Collingwood) is the place. They brew several tasty beers of great quality as well as cooking amazing local seafood.

What to Wear:

This is always a dilemma when packing for the Ford. It has definitely got to be hip and if you can climb in it, it helps. Here's Chris Burtenshaw's take on what was hot in the nineties: 'To cut it with this crew, and therefore be socially 'with it' at the Ford, you'll need some serious army surplus pants, tough enough for camp living and hip enough for the 'Big G.' (the Gathering dance party). Weird hair for everyone, 'tribal' is definitely still in. Jewellery for the boys; tatoos for the girls…both boys and girls are in sarongs. Boys' hems have staggeringly, come up to just below the knee this season…(Climber vol. 26 p.5).' Not much has changed really apart from boys' hems, which are becoming indecently high.

The next most important thing after your 'look' at Paynes has always been your transport. Chris reckons 'if you haven't got a van turn your car or your tent into one.'

North End

Officially the closest wall to Hangdog, this is a good quality wall with short, quite testing routes. Head up Track 1 (unmarked) just before the toilet block. Before you reach the Creese Wall, hang a left. The first route is at the left end of the wall behind a tree.

① ★**22 Big Sharks at Night 13m**
2 Short, technical and bears teeth if you mess up the crux sequence. *Brian Alder 1990*

② **25 Gangrene 14m**
2 An easy ramp to the 1st bolt, then two crimpy cruxes through the bulges. *Ivan Vostinar 2000*

③ ★**18 Terror, Illness and Rebellion 15m**
2 A steep arête with a layback crack and tricky rock-over past the 2nd bolt. The long run-out to the tree can be protected with a sling. *Pete Garlick 1990*

④ **19 Herbal Infusion 12m**
2 An attractive wee face that is let down by some flaky rock. Avoid gripping too hard. *Callum McLellan 1998*

③ ★**21 Checkmate 12m**
3 Big jugs to the 1st bolt, but these totally disappear over the bulge. *Karen Ashbury/Ivan Vostinar 2000*

③ ★**23 The Darling Buds of May 14m**
3 A steep arête that gets devilishly pumpy up high. *Phil Castle 1992*

Creese Wall

The first wall to be developed at Paynes, this is an open, pleasant hangout that gets heaps of traffic. From the farm track head up Track 1, past the turn off to the North End to meet the following climbs:

⑦ ★**16 Blobbet 14m**
4 Fun climbing on good holds until some tricky slopey moves leap out to surprise you near the end. *Floppy the Dog 1996*

⑧ ✹**17 Good Bye Cream-Poofters 15m**
4 One of the first climbs developed in Paynes and an obligatory classic. A tricky bulge, then up to an exhilarating top-out. *Charlie Creese 1980s*

⑨ ★**16 Re-election Blues 16m**
2 The obvious groove that is overcome with crafty bridging. Step left to the bolt and take on the juggy finish.

✷✷**14 Mid-Wife Crisis 18m**

7 Excellent for your first grade 14. It's long, well protected with some groovy moves at the 3rd bolt. *Kath Meek 2001*

12 Calling All Hobbits 8m

1 A juggy arête. *Tony Clearwater 1995*

★**18 Elvis Lives in Takaka 18m**

⑫ 3 Many claim to have seen him but few can guarantee that they weren't on hallucinogens at the time. This one has a bit of a reputation for injuring climbers who fall before the 3rd bolt. Be aware of the ledge, otherwise, it's quite delightful. *Rob McLeod 1980s*

⑬ ★**19 Blockbuster 18m**

4 Moderate climbing accumulates to become quite a pump fest. Start from *Bite My Chunk* and drift left to share the anchor with *Elvis Lives in Takaka.* *Rob McLeod 1980s*

⑭ ★**19 Bite My Chunck 18m**

5 Looks a bit dodgy due to the bulge out right, and also a bit contrived (as the bulge is not meant to be used). However, the climbing above is well worth it.

On the right wall of the gully:

⑮ ★**20 The Fearless Vampire Killers 18m**

3 Climb past the killer stake, clip then place a thread. Commit to a couple of moves over the bulge and good holds will come your way. Take a sling and don't forget your garlic. *Spence Pomeroy*

The next two mixed routes are grade 15 and share the same start. Both have three bolts and threads for protection and they climb to the top of the wall.

The following four climbs are on the wall left of the Rawhide Roof and finish at anchors on the ledge.

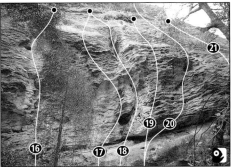

⑯ 19 Hula Yula 14m

4 A steep start past the hole then move over the bulge and onto the slab.

⑰ ★23 Spotty Brit 14m

4 A bit tricky to clip the 1st bolt, then cranky moves over the bulge to a positive pocket. Continue up the slab. *John Row 1996*

⑱ ★20 Tongue in Groove 14m

4 Really neat with excellent potential for getting yourself wedged. Casual slab up to the chain. *John Row 1996*

⑲ ★21 Sweet Dreams 16m

3 A radical, juggy and steep start to a fingery crux past the 2nd bolt. Most enjoyable. *Colin Daniel 1993*

⑳ ★18 Hunting Tartan 24m

8 A long, exhilarating number. Start just right of the *Tongue in Groove* hole and traverse right past *Sweet Dreams*. Climb past the hole, over the bulge and to the top of the wall. *Willie Butler 2002*

Rawhide Roof

This is an impressive roof with crazy, rounded jugs. The next three routes all start from the left-hand side of the roof but soon diverge and converge again at the anchor.

㉑ ★21 Something Precious 18m

3 The left side of the roof past a ledge with a small cam to the steep face above. Eventually the terrain becomes nice and slabby. *Dave Skilton 1985*

㉒ ★★22 Rawhide 18m

5 The holds are large, but the climbing is steep and pumpy. Boulder out to the rest just after the 1st bolt and charge up the roof. Don't loose it on the slab, it's still pretty tricky. *Mike Rockell 1987*

㉓ ★23 Rumplestiltskin 18m

6 From the 1st bolt of *Rawhide,* go right through the big roof. Follow the slab and arête past the lip. *Kristen Foley 1993*

㉔ ★V4 Easiest Out

Start on the block at the back of the roof (1m left of the big boulder) and exit to the lip the easiest way possible.

㉕ ★V8 Straight Out

Unique but burly bouldering. Start on the block at the back of the roof and head directly out on good but spaced holds.

㉖ ★24 The Golden Bay Connection 16m

7 Gain the traverse break above the Rawhide Roof and head left past 3 bolts before kicking upwards to the anchor. *Paul Rogers 1995*

This next climb is along the cliff track, past the next big vegetated corner:

㉒ ★22 Woop, Woop Pull Up 12m

2 Double plus good! Short with pleasurable, hefty moves on excellent rock. *Rob McLeod*

Rat Trap Wall

Walk past the next undercut roof with a narrow squeeze between the cliff and a tree at the right end. At this point you will be below the Rat Trap Wall. The following three routes start by climbing the featured short slab behind the tree (use threads for pro) to the ledge.

㉘ ★21 Tales By Firelight 25m

8 Once on the ledge, traverse left then climb the face to a crux at the bulge at half-height. *Tony Clearwater 1995*

㉙ ★20 Rat up a Drainpipe 25m

6 From the ledge, scuttle into the faint groove. Things get run-out at the top, but the holds are all good. *Andrew Taylor 1991*

㉚ ★21 Bilbo's Great Adventure 24m

8 A straight line through the scoop to the break. Tackle the cruxy bulge with Hobbit bravery but you may need to be a bit taller than Bilbo to pull this one off. *Tony Clearwater 1995*

The next two routes start right of a small boulder and share the first 2 bolts.

㉛ ★21 No Rest for the Wicked 22m

7 Motor up the face to the break. Things get cruxy over the bulge (no surprises there), then there's an awesome finish. *Zippy 1992*

㉜ ★22 The Immaculate Deception 21m

6 Just left of the flowstone-vine arrangement. This route has some technical climbing with a few exciting run-outs. *Ben Yates 1996*

Stone Symposium Wall

Past the vegetated gully is a very high looming wall with a gorgeous arête in the middle (*R for Ranger, D for Danger*).

㉛ ★18 Temples of Stone 27m

8 Wonderful climbing with enough good holds to hang back and savour the view. Start at the ring bolts, head to the arête and find a nice climax on the bulging finish. *Tony Clearwater 1995*

47

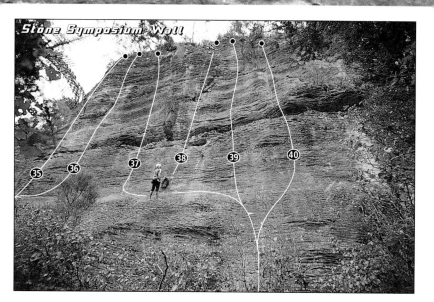

Stone Symposium Wall

3 ⭐**20 Jimmy the Torn Piece of Paper gets a Hand From Frederick the Friendly Roll of Sellotape 11m.** Hardest at the start and easing to a slab. Can be used as a direct start for *Temples of Stone* or *R for Ranger, D for Danger*. *Chris and Jeremy Butler 1997*

35 ⭐⭐**21 R for Ranger, D for Danger 27m**
4 Climbs in a stunning position on, or just right of, the obvious and proud arête. Start direct from ground level and tackle the first cruxy steep section before the ledge. Take a #3 cam and wires. *Rob Gray 1989*

36 ⭐⭐**21 Stone Symposium 18m**
6 The face just right of the arête. Start as for *R for Ranger, D for Danger* but branch right at the ledge. Thin face climbing eventually leads to jugs on the upper section. *Rob Gray 1989*

8m right is a single start point to access all the routes on the wall.

37 ⭐**18 Stroking the Tiger 18m**
7 From the belay ledge, climb past two breaks/ledges to enjoy the cruxy lay-back crack and ever-increasing dream holds. *Tony Clearwater 1995*

38 ⭐**18 Wazzo Jugs 18m**
7 Cruxy through the bulge to huge tracts of jugs. *The Toad 1995*

39 ⭐**18 Autumn Leaf 18m**
6 Can be lead directly to the ground. Hardest at the start then kick-back and smoke up to the top. *The Toad 2001*

40 **19 Sacred Forest 18m**
8 The right-most route on the wall. Predictably it has a crux low down and a few more interesting bulges. *Tony Clearwater 1995*

Follow the cliff track right for 40m to reach the Tenuite Wall access track. Turn left and scramble up the steep path just before the yellow rock with an orange arrow. Be careful if it is wet.

Tenuite Wall

Perfect rock and a superb setting makes this a wicked wall, sporting a few steep and pumpy routes. It's often protected from the rain. If you are coming from the farm road take Track 3 to the Carnage Wall and turn left to find the access track.

41 ✸**20 Hi I'm Doctor Terrific**

4 **14m.** Starts innocently enough but quickly gets you sweating. Long cranking with some lovely jugs near the top. *Simon Middlemass 1992*

42 ✸**21 Headplant 14m**

4 Pleasurable with big holds. Climbing fast may help you avoid the fading. *Martin Wilson. 1992*

43 ✸**20 Loose Unit 15m**

3 Same, same but different. In fact, a little longer than the previous two routes. Choice top-out. *Kiersten Price 1992*

44 ✸**22 Go with the Flow 14m**

4 Devious moves around the flowstone keep you on your toes. Once through the cruxiness, continue on good edges to the anchor. *John the Possum Swallower 1992*

45 ★**19 Fat Cats 15m**

4 Up the right side of the wall. Face climbing via crimps eventually joins the arête. *Simon Middlemass 1993*

Back at the cliff track, continue along for 10m to a nice short slab:

2 ★**16 Romancing the Stone 11m**
A vague ramp of holds leads left and up a groove to finish. Falling in some places would be unadvisable. *Tony Clearwater 1996*

2 ★**14 Grey Warbler 8m**
A tricky slab start leads to big holds on the arête. For more pleasure, continue up the arête to the *Romancing the Stone* anchor. *Chris and Jeremy Butler 1995*

Go up the hill past some crusty routes and right 30m to the next main wall.

Carnage Wall

A popular area which contains some classic steep lines. The quickest access from the farm road is via Track 3.

Carnage Wall

48 **★18 Carnage at the Crossroads 18m**

4 May not look the flashest but it climbs well. Up the ramp to the pillar then step right onto the face. *Tony Stempa 1988*

49 **★27 There is No Spoon 18m**

6 Start straight up the face, heading for the groove. Veer left to join *Carnage at the Crossroads* after the 4th bolt. *Ivan Vostinar 1999*

50 **★★25 Skiing Off a Convex Slope 13m**

5 Fantastic cranking up this proud line left of the arête. With strong shoulders you should be able to muscle through the crux. *Colin Pohl 1990*

51 **★★25 Responsible Lunges 13m**

5 Impressive climbing on the right side of the arête. Rest in the hole and brace yourself for the crux, with plenty more opportunity to blow it before the anchor. *Murray Hamilton*

Around the corner on the right arête:

52 **★22 No Fly Zone 8m**

3 Jugs lead to 'the hole' then a very strange crux solution. A couple more tricky sloper moves are thrown in to finish. *Karen Ashbury 2001*

The next short wall has five routes at grades 22, 20, 18, 20 and 17.

This is the end of this half of the crag. To get back to the farm road, walk right and down Track 3 for 2mins.

Globe Wall

From Track 3, continue along the farm track for 5mins past an area of regenerating bush until you stumble upon Track 4. The first wall you come to at the top of the track is the *Superconductor* arête. Walk left for 2mins along the bottom of the wall past many inspiring lines and through a tight gap to reach the next two routes.

2 **★20 Super Blonde 14m**

2 Don't be put off by the run-out to the 1st bolt. A couple of moves put you on an easy slab and a way cool finish. *Simon Middlemass 1992*

1 **★18 Feisty Red 14m**

The first two moves are cruxy, from then enjoy positive holds and interesting climbing. Sling the thing and ride the groove which is the crux. *Simon Middlemass 1992*

Back through the gap are the next three routes:

3 **★★22 Burly But Sensitive 13m**

3 Stem up the corner and charge into a delicate crux. Follow this up with a dyno left to the arête. A technical test piece with perfectly placed bolts. *Suzy Ruddenklau 1990*

❹ ✴**23 Red-lining to the Max 13m**

3 🔩 Beautiful rock and quite sneaky really. Smeary foot holds, fingery, even a mono move past the 3rd bolt. Wow! *Andrew Taylor 1992*

❺ ★**20 Voice of the Beehive 13m**

3 🔩 Negotiate your way around the arête, gradually ascending with the dulcet tones of a parliamentary session ringing in your ears. *Brian Alder 1990*

Just right is the next wall.

❻ ★**25 Sweetest William 14m**

4 🔩 After the start and crux of *High Voltage,* drift left and up the white streak. A grade 27 variation can be done by moving hard left after the 1st bolt. *Marc Elliot 1993*

❼ ✴**23 High Voltage 18m**

5 🔩 Crux past the 1st bolt, then drift right to unrelenting climbing on the arête. *John Skilton 1990*

Go right to the next very prominant arête.

❹ ✴✴**24 Dave's Arête 16m**

4 🔩 A great route for big air. Start through some big cranks and head right onto the faint arête. Gets extremely pumpy and quite run-out. *Dave Fearnley 1988*

❾ ✴**28 Dancing on a Skewer 25m**

9 🔩 Traverse from the right to the 1st bolt, do the power crux thing and veer right to a big rest. Now embark on the slopey and pumpy section. This leads to another rest before the thin face finish. There is a grade 29 variation which eliminates the rest by charging left and up after the 2nd bolt. *Matt Evrard 1993 (Variation Derek Thatcher 2003)*

Paynes Ford

**Globe Wall
Left Side**

⑩ ✶✶24 Amino Pro 25m

8 Climb the vague arête, hoof it up the slab, step left and continue to the top face which definitely won't bore. *Bill McLeod 1991*

⑪ ✶✶21 Make my Grumpy Cat Dance 16m

5 The left leaning ramp of reddish rock. The start may look run-out but the clipping stances are positive. Cool balancy climbing to the anchor. *Simon Middlemass 2001*

⑫ The Killing Time 2 Pitches

5 **P1. 25 16m.** Same start as *Make my Grumpy Cat Dance*, then head right at the 2nd bolt. Ascend the arête to finish. *Brian Alder 1990*

4 **P2. 28 12m.** Climb slightly right through the beast crux, then up on bigger edges. *Nick Sutter 1993*

⑬ ✶31 The Unforgiven 16m

5 Up the lovely face just left of the crack. Interesting climbing leads to smaller and smaller edges, culminating in a two move crux. *Sebastian Loewensteijn 2002*

The following piece of rock is one of the finest walls not only at Paynes but in the South Island. The routes are sportingly bolted and climb brilliantly.

⑭ ✶✶25 Feeling Lucky Punk 15m

3 An awesome route up the white face. Fingery climbing on tiny holds, winds up to an intricate top crux. *Nick Sutter 1991*

⑮ ✶✶25 Make My Day 15m

3 The red face with medium holds but burly moves. Steep and sustained with the crux near the top. The 3rd bolt sees heaps of air time. *Dave Fearnley 1988*

⑯ **⚡24 Gravity 16m**

4⚡ Hard start to big pockets; rest then charge into the challenging finish. The run-out is a real sting in the tail. *Dave Fearnley 1988*

⑰ **⚡23 Power Failure**

4⚡ **15m.** A bouldery start to a super comfy rest. Put your foot down for the final bulge. *Neil Parker 1988*

⑱ **★25 Body Nazis 15m**

5⚡ The most powerful route on this wall. Slopey holds and some underclings lead to a rest on the slab. Finish up the face. *Simon Middlemass 1991*

4⚡ **★24 Celluloid Heroes**

15m. Again the start is the hardest. Battle the usual array of Paynes edges and waltz casually to the top. *Simon Middlemass 1991*

5⚡ **★24 Weetbix Heroes**

12m. Funky moves around the arête and various ways solve the crux. *Pete Smale 1991*

Beast Wall

The next wall has a beautiful blank-looking band of perfect rock between the 1st and 2nd bolts. Here you will find the greatest concentration of hard routes at Paynes. Up higher most of the routes get easier but also more run-out.

Globe Wall Right Side

4⚡ **28 Monkey Master 18m**

Boulder to the roof, where a small cam protects to the bulge. Hard moves over this, and then it's still a long way to go, but things do ease off. *Sebastian Loewensteijn 2004*

㉒ **★28 Stoned Monkey 18m**

4⚡ Just left of the alien head, this has a fingery and powerful crux. *Nick Sutter 1992*

Paynes Ford

The next two climbs start just right of the alien head.

㉓ ✹26 The Beast Within 5 🔩 **18m.** Good edges, sustained and very run-out. After the break, head boldly left. Get psyched for the top and unleash your alter ego. *Nick Sutter 1991*

㉔ ★27 Papageno 15m 4 🔩 Up the reddish streak. The crux culminates in a couple of exceptionally small crimps. Once over the lip, it's easy. *Helmut Neswadba 1993*

㉕ ★27 Cloud Walker 18m 5 🔩 Hoon up the start (carefully) to jugs, do a massive move right, then use trickery to gain good holds. *Nick Sutter 1991*

The next wall is 10m to the right. It has a DOC enclosure and platform to protect a rare native plant. Please be careful where you stand and put your gear.

5 🔩 **✹✹22 Electricorp Production 18m** Up the left side of the wall. Weave your way up the steep face to a defined crux and more pumpiness to the top. *Damian Carrol 1991*

㉗ ✹✹23 Send a Gorilla 18m 4 🔩 This route is mega sustained with fantastic holds. Take an optional #1.5 cam to use after the 1st bolt. *Al Mark 1989*

Max Farr on *Creative Confusion* (27)
MARK SEDON/OFF PISTE PHOTOGRAPHY

The next route is on the arête, right of the platform. This is where Track 4 emerges.

❷❽ 🔨23 Superconductor 25m

7 This arête is visible from the farm road and is one of the most amazing routes around. From the flat boulder, veer diagonally left to the 3rd bolt (don't head straight up the arête). The steepness kicks back to interesting slab climbing. *Neil Parker 1988*

❷❾ 🔨27 Creative Confusion 15m

7 Up the middle of the overhanging face, just right of the arête. Beautiful holds to a dyno, then it gets easier to the anchor. *Eric Talmadge 1991*

Tomorrow Gully

A narrow, parallel-sided gully to the right of the *Superconductor* arête.

❸⓿ ★28 Futurism 14m

5 Go up the short corner on red rock just left of the flowstone. Once on top, take a breather before tackling the very reachy crux. *Ivan Vostinar 2001*

❸❶ 21 Wreck Tangle 13m

2 Bridge up the groove just right of the flowstone to the easy right-leaning ramp with ample gear possibilities. *Kirsten Rabe 1990*

❸❷ ★22 Clutch Cargo 12m

3 The 2nd pitch of *Wreck Tangle* and a most worthwhile one at that. Faint stemming to negotiate the bulge then up the high face. *Brian Alder 1990*

❸❸ 🔨28 Fauvism 13m

2 A technical test piece with unusual and devious climbing on textured, multicoloured rock. Preclip the 1st bolt. *Dave Fearnley 1991*

Little Globe Wall

This wall is just to the right of Tomorrow Gully. The best access is up Track 4, or by traversing around from the Little Lost Wall. You'll find three great 22's here as well as one of the finest face climbs at Paynes.

❸❹ 🔨22 You're Either Dead or You're Not 14m

3 A snaking crack line that is utterly delicious to climb. Head right after the last bolt. *Brian Alder 1990*

❸❺ ★22 Short Circuit 12m

2 A short and bouldery route that starts left of the slimy tufa. Climb left at the start and then trend right to the anchor. *Pete Hunt 1990*

❸❻ ★22 Lights Out 13m

3 A very tricky crux past the 1st bolt and then it's just a little pumpy at the top. *Bill McLeod 1990*

❸❼ 🔨27 Electrocution 13m

4 Awesome in its blankness. Technical and fingery down low but it eases off to phat slopers near the top. Finish as for *Lights Out. Nick Sutter 1991*

Little Lost Wall

A neat little area with short but interesting climbs. Track 5 will lead you to the base of *Doo-Little*. The first route is 20m left of this.

❸❽ 16 Winkle 9m

3 On the far left side of the wall next to the totara tree. Face climb to the break and ooze over the bulge. *Peter Fountain 1998*

❸❾ 18 Candy Man 9m

4 Face climbing that gets bouldery in places. Avoid the big flake at the start. *The Toad 1998*

3 **16 Jerry Garcia 9m**
Layback the flake then grope your way up the blobulous flowstone. The crux is at the 2nd bolt (watch you don't land on the flake). *The Toad 1995*

3 ✴**21 Lost Soul 9m**
A stimulating face. Slopey holds eventually give way to bigger specimens. *Simon Middlemass 1993*

On the next section of wall:

5 ★**14 Ecological Itch 9m**
3 A steep, juggy start relents to massive holds in the middle. *Penny Excell 1992*

6 ✴**16 Doo-Little 9m**
3 Thoroughly good. Use cunning to outwit the slopers. *Polly Stupples 1992*

7 ★**14 The Wrong Trousers 9m**. The arête just right of *Doo-Little* with a sneaky side pull move past the 1st bolt. Lovely to the top. *Kirstie MacLeod 2002*

The next section of wall is a good beginners spot. It is quite laid-back with a profusion of sculpted holds and incuts.

8 **12 Wobbly Bits 9m**
2 A steep ramp to a wee bulge. *The Toad 1995*

9 **13 Lucy in the Sky with Prismatic Raindrops 9m**. Above a practice anchor on an endearing strip of rock. *Willie Butler 2002*

10 ★**11 The Bell Ringer 9m**
2 Super holds until it thins out before the anchor. *The Toad 1995*

11 ★**12 Mind the Hebes 9m**
2 A strip of ladder-like holds, culminating in a thin finish. *The Toad 1995*

12 **14 Damsel in Distress 10m**
3 Just left of the flowstone, this is a glam little number that is a bit steeper than other climbs here, but it has some pert jugs. *Willie Butler 1997*

4 ✴**18 Nicknack Paddywack 15m**
Left of the arête is this adventurous climb on featured holds. Take care clipping the 1st bolt, then enjoy the odd tricky move above. *The Toad 1996*

Wall of Thugs

Little Lost Wall

Fish Wall

- ㉕ ★ **26 Smells Like Fish**
- ㉖ ★★ **26 African Head Charge**
- ㉗ ★ **24 Jive Bombing**
- ㉘ ★★ **25 Fish on Heat**
- ㉙ ★ **26 Fish and Chips**
- ㉚ ★ **23 The Good, the Bad and the Dread**
- ㉛ ★ **24 Subliminal Seducer**

Rhinoceros Wall

Track 6

5 **✹27 Mea Culpa 16m**
On the face right of the arête. Don't be put off by the scuzzy start as it leads to awesome holds and moves on the rest of the climb. A cam or wire is often placed close to the anchor. *Brian Alder 1992*

Wall of Thugs

This very high roof provides some exciting routes on big jugs. The exposure is wonderful if you are into that sort of thing. The wall can be reached via the Little Lost Wall or the Fish Wall. At *Mea Culpa*, head uphill via a steep gully to reach *1080 and the Letter G*. To access the other routes lead across the ledge. Downclimbing is the quickest method of stripping the routes.

⑮ **✹23 1080 and the Letter G 13m**
6 An exposed line with only a short crux to get you flustered. Mind the gap as you step across to the 1st bolt and after the cruxy moments, jug haul your way to glory. Desperate individuals can crawl into the rest hole near the top. *Colin Pohl and Lionel Clay 1991*

⑯ **✹22 Typhoon Tongue 13m**
6 A worthy neighbour of *1080 and the Letter G*. Climb the flow features to flat jugs and crank, crank, crank. *Chris Burtenshaw 1998*

⑰ **★22 Java Jive 12m**
6 A straight line on generous jugs that heads slightly left of the top crack. *Simon Middlemass 1998*

⑱ **★21 Burn Hollywood, Burn 13m**
6 Pull through steep ground and traverse left at the break just before the top horizontal roof. Join *Java Jive* to finish. A good name, if only it would happen. *Simon Middlemass 1998*

⑲ **21 Wilt 10m**
4 Climb just right of the flowstone and head right to the exposed, jutting prow. *Al Mark 1992*

⑳ **24 Intensive Scare 12m**
5 From the anchor, veer right across the void to a couple of reachy moves before the jug fiesta. *Martin Wilson 1992*

Fish Wall

On the right of the Wall of Thugs, is this impressive wall with some fantastic pumpy climbs. It is accessed via Track 6 or by traversing across from the Little Lost Wall. The next few routes start below and to the left of the Fish Wall.

㉑ **28 Dreadful 17m**
8 Start up the block and traverse left across the lip–not the nicest rock, but unusual for the roof climbing start. This is followed by two beefy cranks one of which is off a non-existent sloper. Join *Dread Carefully* on the arête. *Chris Plant 1993*

㉒ **Dread Carefully–2 pitches**
Martin Wilson/Richard Kirk 1992
5 **P1. ✹23 15m.** Climb onto the block just above the track, then traverse left past 2 bolts to the arête. Charge up this, eventually veering right for some more excitement.

6 **P2. ✹24 12m.** From the ledge, head right up the steep arête. Very exposed and great fun.

㉓ **✹27 Big Mama Jama 12m**
7 Climb the 1st pitch of *Dread Carefully* to the belay ledge. From here, start climbing up the arête but head left at the 3rd bolt. *Jeremy Strang 1992*

㉔ ✸**29 You're Either Dread or You're Not**
11 **26m.** A long and varied route with the same start as *Dread Carefully,* but head straight up the face to the roof. Rest here and then embark on the bouldery crux with great whipper potential. Once over the roof, relax on good holds and join *African Head Charge* for its crux. *Alfonso Garcia 2000*

Go slightly uphill to the belay ledge for the Fish Wall. Almost all the climbs start from here and diverge.

㉕ ✭**26 Smells Like Fish 21m**
7 Start on the far left of the belay ledge, go over the cruxy bulge and onto easy slab climbing. Slowly drift right across *Fish on Heat* towards a thin, edgy finish and a hell sloper (straight from Mephistopheles own garage wall). Go directly up to share the anchor with *Fish on Heat. Lionel Clay 1989*

㉖ ✸**26 African Head Charge 25m**
10 Wild and exposed are the adjectives that spring to mind. Start at *Fish on Heat*, but traverse left just above the lip. Go almost as far as the African head, but don't be a wuss and sit on it. Head up small edges to finish. *Paul Rogers 1992*

㉗ ✸**24 Jive Bombing 23m**
10 An awesome route through steep terrain that provides a few good rests. No single move is too hard but there's just a lot of it. Start as for *Fish on Heat* but traverse left. Once over the first bulge it's funky climbing to the anchor. *Paul Rogers 1992*

㉘ ✸**25 Fish on Heat 21m**
8 The second start on the wall. After a small traverse, move up through juggy/streaky stuff and head for the middle of the grey bulge. Once you are on the bulge, well and truly pumped, head right to the anchor. *Lionel Clay 1989*

㉙ ✸**26 Fish and Chips 21m**
7 Start as for *Fish on Heat*, but go straight up at the 2nd bolt. Once half way, go slightly left to join *Smells Like Fish* for its crux. *Tony Ward-Holmes 1992*

㉚ ✸**23 The Good, the Bad and the Dread**
4 **13m.** The superb red-streaked face. It climbs really well and is pleasantly pumpy and run-out to the anchor. *Paul Rogers 1996*

㉛ ✸**24 Subliminal Seducer 21m**
6 The obvious red corner makes a stunning line. Interesting moves up the corner give way to a typical pumpy Paynes finish. *Paul Rogers 1991*

2 **22 American Spoon 13m**
A chickenhead start onto slopey edges to finish at 2/3 height (strange when most things American go over the top). *Mike Rockell 1991*

6 **24 Slaprobatics 18m**
A seasonal climb that gets moist in winter. Two sections of cruxy climbing are split by the break. *Neil Parker 1991*

5 ✭**24 System of the Down 16m**
Starts under the bulge right of *Slaprobatics*. Traverse left and up to the thread. A straight up and pumpy finish. *Sebastian Loewensteijn 2002*

Rhinoceros Wall

10m right from the last route in the Fish Wall is this sheltered and shady wall. The grove of totara trees makes the atmosphere ambient and it's perfect for mid-summer.

35 ✸**19 Gobble, Gobble, Yum, Yum 13m**
4 A beautiful route with interesting and sustained moves. *Claire Healing/Robin Hood*

36 **22 The Great New Zealand Clobbering**
4 **Machine 13m.** The direct start to *Gobble, Gobble, Yum, Yum,* just left of the chimney. A short, fingery crux just past the 2nd bolt, then lean out left to clip the 3rd bolt before joining the previous route. *Martin Clark 1992*

37 **21 Feeding the Rat 15m**
4 Stay on the left side of the arête until past the 3rd bolt. Enjoy the mono crux then veer slightly right for a left-trending finish. *Simon Middlemass 1991*

38 ★**19 Rhinoceros 14m**
4 Just left of the totara, this has quite a technical start, then it's enjoyably run-out on wonderful holds. *Jeremy Butler 1996*

39 **22 Black-Eyed Beauty 12m**
4 A worthwhile route with good moves that is let down by the hollow sounding triangular thing by the 3rd bolt. Be careful. *Tony Burnell 2002*

40 **26 Berlin Wall 12m**
4 The good-looking face on the right hand side of the wall. An easy start followed by death crimps to the lip. *Ingo Machelheidt 1996*

41 ★**22 The Ground's the Limit 12m**
3 Up the interesting flowstone-like arête. Weave your way around this feature on unusual holds. *Kevin Nicholas 1991*

Huntley and Palmers Wafer, Pohara.
GRAHAM CHARLES/IMAGE MATTERS

Charleston

Tim Robertson watching the swell roll in on
Shark's Breakfast (18). DEREK GRZELEWSKI

To put it simply, Charleston is gneiss. The sea crag is on the beautiful West Coast with handy camping and the shortest pub–crag distance in the South Island. There are is array of routes and grades all on rock with extremely good friction. Most climbers come to sample the delights of the classic Wonder Wall, but there are lots of other worthwhile nooks and crannies to explore.

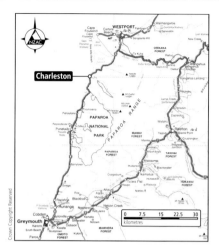

Crown Copyright Reserved

Charleston is 28km south of Westport and 77km north of Greymouth.

At the township, turn off to the Constant Bay Reserve to reach the camping area and the Southern Cliffs.

From Constant Bay, take the Lookout Track past two small bays. Turn off at a 'warning' sign onto a small track through the flax. You will emerge at Ushers Rock.

i The climbing is divided into two main areas, the Northern and Southern Cliffs. We have not covered the Northern Cliffs in this guide because the climbing is dispersed and harder to access. It does, however, have much potential.

The cliffs drop directly into the tidal zone. In good conditions it can be safe to wander around the base of the climbs, but when there is a good swell it can be an extremely dangerous place to be. Freak waves have killed several people and many climbers have been drenched on their belay or even sucked towards the blowhole in Ushers Cove! Please err on the side of caution and if in doubt, clip in at the base of climbs.

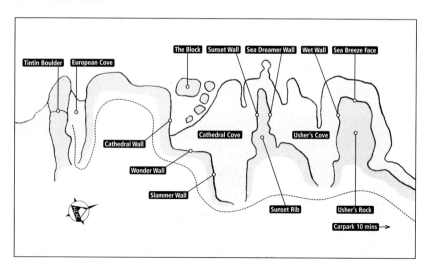

The rock is generally good, but there is the odd fragile hold. Placing more gear than you normally would is good practice because some of the cracks have a grainy/sandy surface (gear could rip through).

A standard rack augmented with lots of large cams is the way forward. There is a mixture of natural and bolted anchors.

Camping at the reserve seems to be fine. The drinking water is in a tank by the toilet block.

There is also a motor camp in town and just up the road at Little Totora River (5km north) is an interesting restaurant and guesthouse called Jack's Gasthof.

Usher's Rock

This is the first (most northern) outcrop of rock. The northern and western faces are sunny and well-featured.

Sea Breeze Face

One of the best quality walls in Charleston, this faces west, has perfect rock and interesting holds. We have listed most of the main lines but there are plenty of variations.

13 Heatwave 17m

The chimney on the far left, just around the arête. This is hardest at the start before wide bridging makes the finish quite comfy. *Ronan Grew 1985*

❷ ★14 Badjelly 17m

Awesome climbing up the round well-featured arête. Drift slightly left at the end. *Paul Woperis (solo) 1986*

❸ ★10 Flight of Stairs 16m

The main corner and crack with millions of pro possibilities. *Ronan Grew 1985*

❹ ★16 Calypso 16m

Up the centre of the main face. Wonderful fat slopers but spaced protection. *Andrew Taylor 1986*

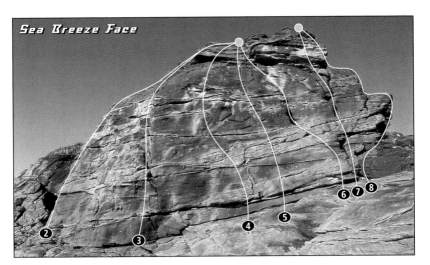

Sea Breeze Face

Sea Breeze Face

Usher's Cove

⑨ ⑩ ⑪ ⑫ ⑬

---

❺ ★16 Nashira 16m

Up the face with tricky pro to the blind crack near the top. *Paul Woperis 1986*

❻ ★13 Adams Apple 16m

Lovely climbing up the big, left slanting ramp. *Dave Adam 1985*

❼ ★15 Making Plans for Dave 16m

The fat crack. Cruise on big slopers, jugs and good jams. *Dave Adam 1985*

❽ 20 White Punks on Chalk 17m

A steep overhang, short crack just right of the arête. Thuggish moves to some jamming. *Ronan Grew 1986*

'The best training was to go to the pub, drink 5 pints of beer, and talk about climbing.' **Ron Fawcett**

Wet Wall

This is the south face of Ushers Rock. It has some nice lines but tends to get damp. Access is via the cave at the head of the cove.

❾ 24 33 Brut 17m

The next weakness through the steepness. Power through the hand jams up the short crack. *Dave Fearnley 1991*

❿ ★16 Reach for the Sky 17m

The leftmost prominent crack. Juggy climbing through the bulbous section gives way to a perplexing overhang. This may require some grovelling.

⓫ 13 Far Out and Solid 17m

Climb the crack and rock up to a cruisy upper section. *Dennis Kelly 1985*

Sea Dreamer Wall

Usher's Cove

12 **14 Blah, Blah, Blah 17m**
Climb the thin crack up the face and continue on blobby terrain to the top blocks. *Ronan Grew 1985*

13 **12 A Day in the Life of a 20c Piece 17m**
The right-leaning crack on the right side of the wall. It turns into a chimney at half-height. *Rick Harding (solo) 1978*

Sunset Rib

This is the next outcrop south of Ushers Rock. The Sea Dreamer Wall faces north and the Sunset Wall faces south.

Sea Dreamer Wall

On the left side of this wall is a black slab with three glue-in anchor bolts at the top. It is a good place to invent top rope variations. There are some short and fiesty climbs to the right.

14 **16 Stop Procrastinating 21m**
Climb the crack through an overhang and step merrily leftwards up the long slab to the bolted anchor at the top of the rib. *Dave MacLeod*

On the next triangular rib:

15 **10 4th Form Alley 17m**
The solo/access route. Start in the groove and keep following the dominant crack.

16 **★21 Short, Sharp and Shithot 14m**
Strenuous climbing up steep grooves just left of the arête. Jams lead to the rest ledge, where cams fit the break. The first ascentionist took a head first dive into the rocky slot below while soloing this. *Ronan Grew 1987*

Charleston

Sunset Wall

Cathedral Cove

㉓ ㉔ ㉕ ㉖ ㉗ ㉙ ㉚ ㉛ ㉜ ㉝ ㉞

---

❶⓱ ★**15 Hoop's Mistake 14m**
Fabulous rounded holds up the left corner.

⓲ 16 Sparrow Fart 14m
The 2nd corner (leans left at the top). Lots of big cams make this a safe lead. *Dennis Kelly 1986*

⓳ ★17 Thinking 14m
The crack 2m right of the keyhole. A pumpy and overhanging finish. *John Skilton*

⓴ ★15 Sweating Up 14m
Head up the juggy face directly to the small notch and move right up the crack through the bulge. *Richard Pearson*

㉑ ★15 All Stars 14m
Just left of the arête, climb to the ramp and follow the jagged crack. *Andrew Taylor 1986*

The next route is on the front face of the rib. It is a very daunting place if the sea is big.

㉒ 17 Sunset Arête 12m
A nice line up the steep crack to the overhang. *Paul Woperis 1987*

Sunset Wall
The south-facing side of the rib is littered with good holds and great protection, but may be damp. The rock is fun to climb and it is a good place to practice placing gear.

㉓ 19 Cream Puff 12m
A sustained, jagged crack up the left side of the face. *Mike Dunn 1986*

㉔ ★17 Combination 14m
Take the most prominent of the cracks on the left side of the face through to a horizontal break. *Paul Woperis*

25 17 Still Steaming 14m

Crack features 3m left of the keyhole. Drift right at the top. *Mike Dunn 1986*

26 ★16 Keyhole 14m

The wide crack with a distinct 'keyhole' feature. Climb over the bulge with great gear. *Andrew Taylor*

27 10 Aid in Line 14m

This corner faces the sea and has massive holds. Take big cams.

17 Red Shark 14m

From the scoop under the prow climb the steep crack. It eases back on the slab at the top. *Ronan Grew 1986*

29 ★17 Atomic Chevrolet

Climb the right-leaning diagonal slash up the prow and move around the bulge to the slab. *Ronan Grew 1986*

30 16 Black Cadillac 14m

The next right-leaning crack. Vertical climbing leads to a blocky slab. *Ronan Grew 1986*

31 10 Gully, Gully, Gully 14m

A prominent gully with cruisy bridging and ample holds. It makes a good solo.

32 13 Summer Holiday 12m

Up the left side of the blocky arête with jugs.

33 ★17 Out of Your Mind 12m

Easy moves through a blocky start. Pull through the centre crack, bisecting the small roof, to luscious holds over the lip. *Dennis Kelly*

34 11 Green Corner 12m

Up the corner, stepping right to a mini arête. Easy to the top.

Cathedral Rock

This area contains the longest and best routes at Charleston. The Slammer Wall and Cathedral Wall face north, and the Wonder Wall faces out to sea.

Slammer Wall

This is a beautiful north-facing wall with excellent rock. The climbs on the left side make good warm-ups before venturing to the Wonder Wall, but watch the run-out over the grass to the anchors.

35 16 Sweat and Sin 18m

Up the bouldery face (crux) to a ledge with a big loose block. Head up the left crack and go left onto the face to top-out. *Dave MacLeod*

36 ★16 Grunt, Grip and Grasp 18m

A wide chimney with twin cracks. Climb over the block, rock onto the ledge then stem and place gear mostly in the right crack. Exiting right feels more exposed but at least you are climbing on rock rather than dirt. *Dave MacLeod*

37 ★★17 Lonely on the Lead 20m

A sustained Charleston classic. Start up the deep crack and trend right up the diagonal seam to reach upper cracks. Head back 10m to anchor. *Paul Woperis 1986*

38 ★24 Louise's Climb 22m

Start up the middle of the face on steep rock. Crank into the short crack and go right one metre along the ramp of holds. Climb the short crack and exit up the easy slab. Overall the pro is sparse. *Louise Shepherd 1986*

Wonder Wall
Slammer Wall
P2
㉟ ㊱ ㊲ ㊳ ㊴ ㊵ ㊶ ㊷ ㊸ ㊹ ㊺ ㊻ ㊼ ㊽ ㊾ ㊿ (51)

㉟		16 Sweat and Sin
㊱	★	16 Grunt, Grip and Grasp
㊲	★★	17 Lonely on the Lead
㊳	★	24 Louise's Climb
㊴	★★★	23 Up the Schrunds
㊵	★★★	18 Humpty Dumpty
㊶	★★	16 Rolling Dice–2 Pitches

㊷		18 Think About It
㊸	★★	18 Rattle Your Dags
㊹	★★	20 Dead Trousers
㊺	★★★	18 Wild Horses in the Sun
㊻	★★★	17 Stinger
㊼	★	18 Over the Top
㊽	★★★	18 Hanging Around

Cathedral Wall

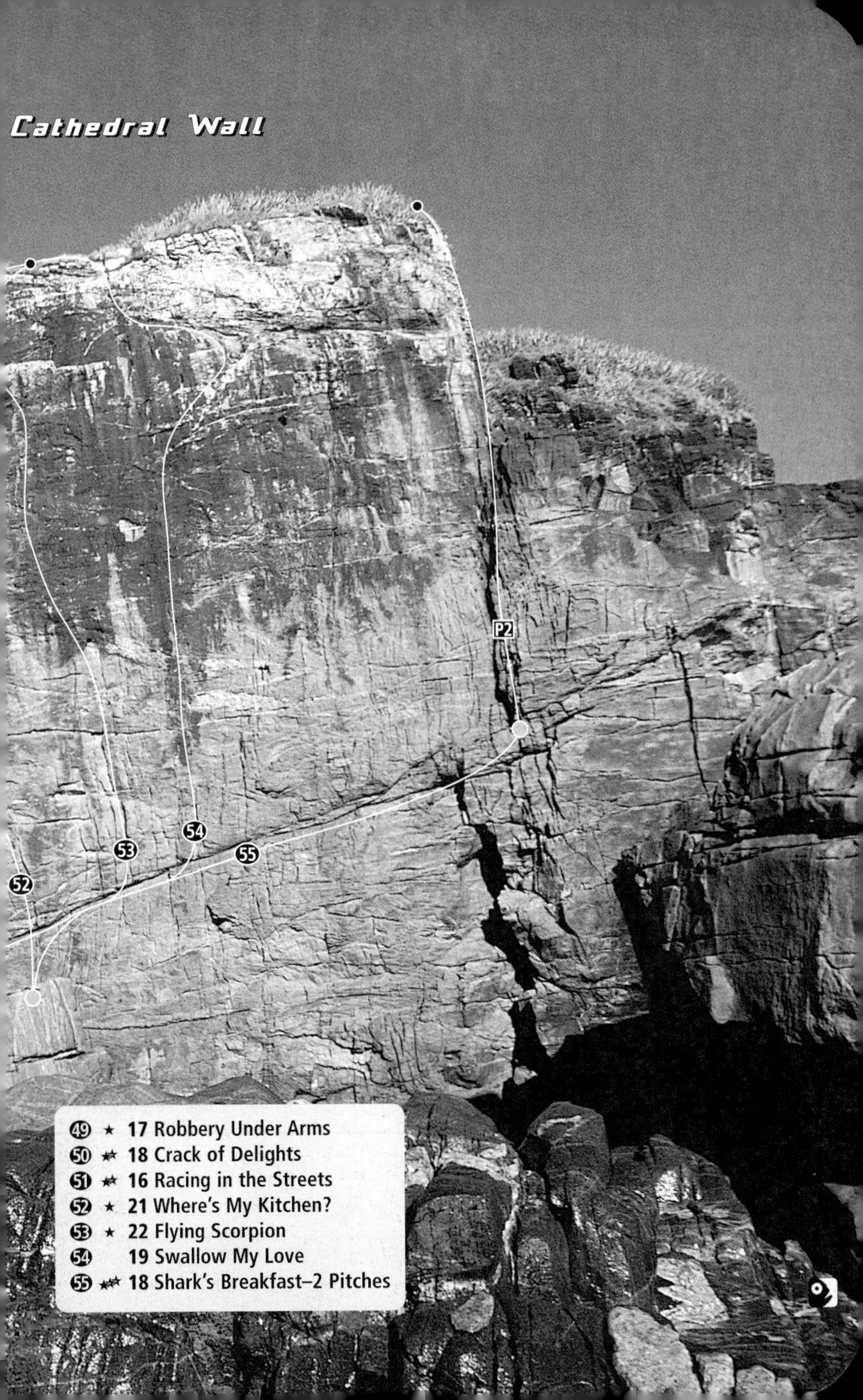

P2

52
53
54
55

Wonder Wall

39 ★★**23 Up the Schrunds 22m**
A superb route up the arête between the Slammer and Wonder Walls. The gear is suspect on the lower half (the scene of one serious accident), but is great after the crux. Start up the wide short crack left of the arête. This leads to a strenuous crux before the angle changes to a pleasant and protectable slab. Big cams are essential at the start. *Dave Fearnley 1986*

Wonder Wall

This wall has long and varied routes on fantastic rock. It is undoubtedly the best climbing on the West Coast.

40 ★★**18 Humpty Dumpty 30m**
Climb the short crack to the ledge then go straight up and over the mini roof where the holds are at their biggest. Veer right to find pro and more slabby climbing to the top. *Rick Harding 1987*

41 **Rolling Dice–2 Pitches**
A snaking route which must be pitched due to rope drag. Belay at the far right of the sloping ledge.

P1. 13 14m Start up an easy crack and head right along the sloping ledge.

P2. ★16 20m From the belay head up, place good gear and embark on the obvious leftward traverse (no gear for a while). This leads to a large flake near the arête. Climb the shallow corner to the top. *Paul Woperis*

42 **18 Think About It 10m**
A short route to reach the ledge and a good alternative start to the longer lines. One cranky move before lovely jugs. *Andrew Taylor*

43 ★**18 Rattle Your Dags 30m**
Gain the ledge, head slightly right via flakes, then left following whatever gear you may find. Stay several metres left of the bolt two thirds up. Eventually head past some birds' nests and good holds. Great climbing but sketchy on the pro side. *Rick Harding 1990*

44 ★**20 Dead Trousers 30m**
Once you make the ledge, charge directly up to the bolt at two thirds height, firstly on massive holds then to smaller edges. Head slightly right past the bolt and finish up a small corner at the top. *Richard Thomson 1986*

45 ★★**18 Wild Horses in the Sun 30m**
Up the face on the left side of the big slab then move onto the arête. Head over the small roof using the finger crack, veering right to meet the shelf on *Stinger*. Now the route climbs about 3m left of the *Stinger* corner. *Rick Harding 1987*

46 ★★**17 Stinger 30m**
Up the low-angled slab to a ledge, then embark up the left corner to the main roof. Step left from below the roof to a small ledge and climb the left-leaning corner to the top. *Paul Woperis*

47 ★**18 Over the Top 30m**
Start as for *Stinger* but go up the overhang, through the face and past a bolt to finish. *Rick Harding 1990*

48 ★★**18 Hanging Around 30m**
Start 4m left of the main corner. Climb up the slab then breathe deep and head through the overlaps. Finishes left of *Robbery Under Arms*. *Rick Harding 1987*

49 ★**17 Robbery Under Arms** 30m

From the belay halfway up the main corner, climb 2m before veering left to the most defined crack on the upper wall. There is some loose rock in the upper crack. *Rick Harding 1987*

50 ★**18 Crack of Delights** 30m

From the belay station halfway up the corner, climb 4m before veering left into the thin crack 2m left of the corner. The finish can be unpleasant if wet. *Rick Harding 1987*

51 ★**16 Racing in the Streets** 30m

This is a very popular corner between the Wonder Wall and Cathedral Wall. There are bolts at the belay ledge at half-height and making it into a 2 pitch outing gives you time to enjoy the atmosphere up this wild line. *Dennis Kelly/Ronan Grew*

Cathedral Wall

It looks impressive but has a nasty streak. The lower half is great rock but the upper half, while slabby, is on the loose side with sparse protection. The wonderful *Shark's Breakfast* avoids this issue by traversing the good stuff.

52 ★**21 Where's My Kitchen?** 30m

Not up here luv! Follow the crack that curves slightly left on great rock, then embark on the hairy journey before you. Finish on the dark rock. Serious. *Louise Shepherd 1986*

53 ★**22 Flying Scorpion** 30m

An extremely serious route with virtually no gear and poor rock on the upper half. Climb up the crack directly to the traverse, move right and take another wide crack up the impressive face. Veer left on a crimpy and run-out, crusty section. *Dave Fearnley 1991*

Jaap Overtoom on *Robbery Under Arms* (17). DANIEL JENKINS

54 **19 Swallow My Love 30m**

Climb to the traverse line and once above the flake, charge up the faint crack. The gear is poor and spaced. *Dave Fearnley 1986*

55 **Shark's Breakfast–2 Pitches**

P1. ✹✹18 25m This wild traverse line heads out towards the Tasman over the 'pit of doom.' Technically it's not grade 18, but you do get tired placing enough gear to make it safe for the second. A total classic. *Paul Woperis 1986*

P2. ★17 17m After the long traverse, most people put in a belay before heading up the crack. Finish up the arête on suspect rock. *Keith Dekkers 1986*

The Block

This large block shelters Cathedral Cove from the smashing waves. If it were in a grassy meadow it would be a boulderer's dream.

56 **A1 Blockhead 10m**

A route which defies description. Needless to say this can only be attempted in calm conditions! *Keith Dekkers 1986*

Brian Anderson on *Thinking* (17). BRUCE WHITE

European Cove

This little nook is well-hidden from the main cliffs. It has some intimidating but interesting climbing. Most of the long climbs are on the north wall and there are some short sporty numbers on a large flat boulder on the opposite side of the cove.

The descent into the cove is an awkward scramble and some people prefer to abseil off the Tintin boulder or from the belay above *Warrior* (the easiest).

① ★**19 Great White Shark Hunt**

32m. Follow the main corner through a small roof and continue climbing past a bolt to the top corner. This route can be divided into 2 pitches at the single bolt which can be backed up with pro. *Ronan Grew (first pitch). Rick Harding*

② ⚡**18 Way of the Lion 32m**

Start on georgeous grey rock over the cracked blocks. Veer left below the roof and then cut back right to join the arête. The pro is sparse on the top section. *Rick Harding 1988*

③ ⚡**19 Flowers on your Grave 32m**

Charge straight up the arête on big, rounded holds that lead slightly right to a rest under the roof. Hard moves over the bulge are followed by slabby crack lines. *Rick Harding 1990*

④ **Open Project 26m**

A superb crack at the start, which includes awkward hand jamming and another typically problematic bulge. An easy slab after the bouldery crux.

⑤ ★**17 Warrior 26m**

Climb the prominent crack on easy ground then move through the bulgy crux, grappling with a flared layback crack. It is easy but sparsely protected to the anchor. *Rick Harding 1989*

On the east wall (facing the sea):

⑥ **18 Fool's Gold 23m**

A little nerve wracking due to the spaced pro and the occasional suspect hold. Start up the middle and head right to find pro, or left for a fat cam and more exposed smearing. Finish straight up the middle. *Dave MacLeod 1986*

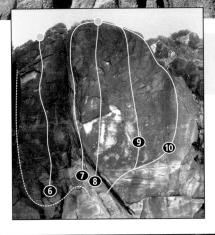

Tintin Boulder

This is a bolted slab facing the sea. The routes are very enjoyable and thought provoking with plenty of good smears.

❼ 20 Rastapopulos 12m

3 Up the left arête on flakey holds. Steep and pumpy climbing. *Wayo Carson 1997*

❽ ★18 Marlinspike 12m

2 Up the interesting slab with some reachy moves and underclings. The start needs natural protection.
Andrew Macfarlane 1997

❾ ★19 Red Rackham's Treasure 12m

2 A well-featured start leads to small holds and full tilt smearing
Andrew Macfarlane 1997

❿ ★19 Thompson and Thompson 12m

2 Climb right across the slab to the arête. Use this to gain height and easier ground.
Wayo Carson 1997

'When you ride your bike, you're working your legs, but your mind is on a treadmill. When you play chess, your mind is clicking along, but your body is stagnating. Climbing brings it together in a beautiful, magical way.' **Pat Ament**

Rick Harding on *Wild Horses in the Sun* (18)
BRUCE WHITE

Sebastian Loewensteijn on *Crash and Burn* (V10), Quantum Field.

Castle Hill

The Castle Hill Basin is a unique quasi-alpine area nestled between two mountain ranges. There are two main areas of large boulder fields which contain thousands upon thousands of sculpted limestone boulders. Much of the rock surface of the boulders is blank, with the odd pocket, edge or feature to layback, smear or grovel up. But there is no avoiding the omni-present mantles, which conclude many of the boulder problems.

The rocks best lend themselves to bouldering, but some stunning routes are to be found. While there are over 200 routes in the basin, they are not often climbed and thus dirty, it is the bouldering which is world class and receives all the attention nowadays.

Castle Hill is known for it's technical and often powerful climbing style. People either love it or find it challenging, until they work out what smears hold and build up those mantle muscles.

View of the Basin from Castle Hill Peak
MARK WATSON

The fields vary in their style and level of development. Spittle and Quantum are the most developed and also the most polished. The Flock Hill and Dry Valley boulders are more featured and tend to require less mantling and slapping. There are also some boulders by Cave Stream and doing the 30min walk through the cave is great for a rest day.

Camping and clean streamwater is available at the Craigieburn Shelter (10km down the road towards Arthurs Pass). This is free to use but is not suitable for leaving your tent or gear there while you are away. There is a backpackers at Castle Hill Village or for more fancy accommodation try the Flock Hill Lodge (4kms past the Craigieburn Shelter). The nearest mini metropolis is the village of Springfield which has a pub, dairy, café and backpackers.

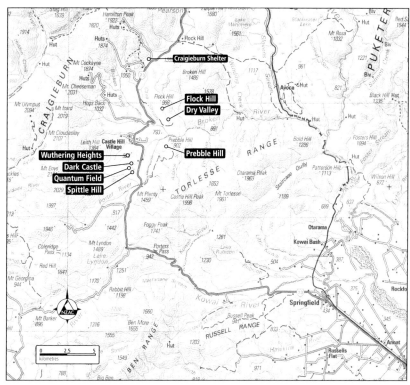

From Christchurch: Head out on SH73 towards the West Coast, but after Yaldhurst take the Old West Coast Rd which eventually joins SH73 again. From Porters Pass it's another 5kms. The first rock areas you will see are Spittle Hill and Quantum Field on the left side of the road.

From the West Coast: From Kumara Junction drive inland following SH73. From Arthurs Pass its 45km to Flock Hill, which is the first boulder field on the left (a couple of kms before Castle Hill Village).

A small carpet, tooth brush and whacking cloth are handy for clean bouldering. To clean the rock perfectly and to help preserve the friction, wash the holds with water and a soft brush.

Most of the landings are good but a boulder mat helps. If you are route climbing bring your usual sport rack, plus wires to slip over the naked coach bolts (removable RP hangers won't fit).

The ascentionist details for routes and boulders (V6 and above) are on page 407.

Bring plenty of water and sun protection.

Rambandit Boulder

Dark Castle is opposite the north edge of Quantum Field and contains about 60 routes. Many of these are long and excellent but are almost never climbed. As a result they are dirty and now almost impossible to climb. If you are a keen route climber, having fossick and doing some cleaning would be rewarding. A few of the great routes have been included as they are too important to leave out.

❶ ⚹V9 Fidel Castro
Sit-start on slopey holds and do two very long moves. Finish at the big jug.

Rambandit Boulder
This large boulder contains four classic, historically important and testing routes. No casual clip-ups here.

❷ ★25 Smile as You Sin 14m
On the left side of the Rambandit wall. Good edgy climbing but a scary run-out to the one and only bolt.

❸ ★25 Jesus Chrysler 14m
An even more serious face climb to the high bolt. A bold test piece.

❹ ⚹⚹21 Rambandit 14m
The striking, splitter crack. A hard start leads to some delightful jamming. Often lead with pro then soloed afterwards.

❺ ⚹24 Mental Block 14m
A hard bouldery start to climbing through large pockets.

Go up the gully above Rambandit and through the small notch, once on top, turn right to see the following route.

❻ ★32 Angel of Pain 12m
A short but an intense climb on painful monos to a mantle crux. This climb sees little attention and when people try they usually strugle on either the monos or the mantle.

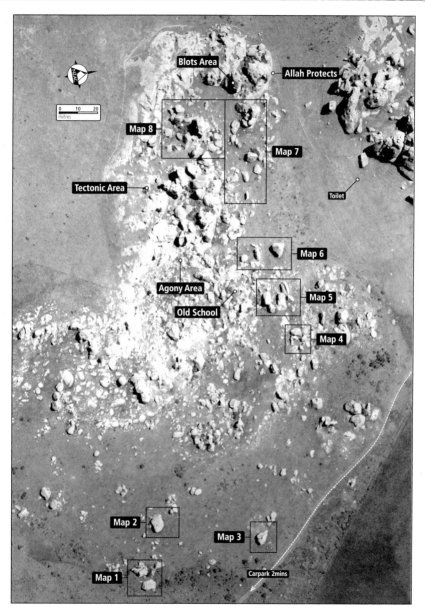

Blots Area

Allah Protects

Map 8

Map 7

Tectonic Area

Toilet

Map 6

Agony Area

Map 5

Old School

Map 4

Map 2

Map 3

Map 1

Carpark 2mins

0 10 20
metres

❶ **V0** Massive jugs.
❷ ✷ **V2** Offwidth.
❸ ★ **V3 Fission.** Sidepulls to the short slab.
❹ **V0** The short snaking handcrack.
❺ ✷✷ **V1** Fantastic exposed arête.
❻ ✷ **V1 Indiana.** Head for the upper layback jugs.

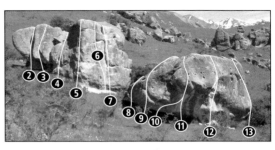

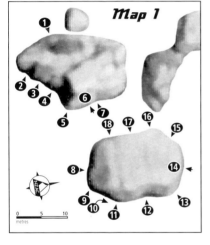

Map 1

❼ ✷✷ **V1 Jericho.** A long lovely layback.
❽ **V0** Palm up the scoop.
❾ ★ **V2 Dharma.** Up the round arête.
❿ **V8 Fierce Crimpy.** Sit-start and traverse right. Exit up *Tricky*.
⓫ **V6 Tricky.** Yellow holds to undercling.
⓬ ★ **V4 Quake.** Reach high into the crack.
⓭ ✷✷ **V6 Halloween.** Hop-start and veer left.
⓮ ✷✷ **V4 Pain and Pleasure.** Delightful and devious up the face.
⓯ ★ **V3** Up the scoop.
⓰ **VM** Low mantle
⓱ ★ **V3 Bingo.** Mantle using small dimples.
⓲ **V2 Cocoa.** Mantle the low lip.

Mushroom Boulder

⓳ **V4 Moister than Most.** Small pockets.
⓴ ★ **V10 House of Pain.** Tiny pockets.
㉑ **P** Long moves and a blank top.
㉒ **P** Tiny holds to a two finger pocket.
㉓ ★ **V9 Desiderata.** Undercling the pocket and reach high to a gaston.
㉔ ★ **V6 VRB.** Up the middle of the wall.
㉕ ★ **V7 Generation X.** Two wide cranks.
㉖ ✷✷ **V2 Pillar of Faith.** Up the narrow face.
㉗ **V2** Grovel up the crack.
㉘ ★ **V5** A delicate, high rock-over.
㉙ **V7 Vice Grip.** Jump, slap and clamp.

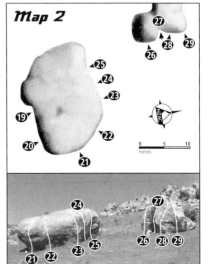

Map 2

Map 3

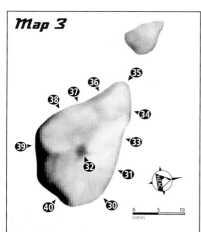

Map 4

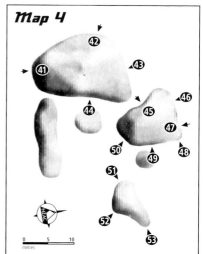

Submarine Boulder

30 ✹ **V4 Torpedo.** Dynos between jugs.

31 ✹ **V1** Big pockets.

32 ★ **V1 Terror Scope.** The second pitch involves a committing rock-over.

33 ✹ **V2** Big pockets but harder.

34 ✹ **V6 Undertow.** Crack to a mantle.

35 ★ **V4** Up the rounded arête.

36 **V0** The slab to the bush.

37 **VM** The middle slab.

38 **V1** Lots of wee pockets.

39 ★ **V2 Sonar.** Over the steep arête.

40 ✹ **V6 Red October.** Through the scoop.

Blue Area

41 **V0** Easy start and go right.

42 ★ **V6 Mantle Mania.** Slopey rock-over.

43 ★ **V8 Tiger Eyes.** Two small pockets.

44 ★ **V4 Red.** Crank to a sidepull.

45 ★ **V4 Blue.** Up the slabby scoop.

46 ★ **V6 Vaseline.** A hideous smeary slab.

47 **V3** Jugs to pull over.

48 ★ **V7 The Prophet.** Pocket to round top.

49 ★ **V6 The Revelation.** Start between the two boulders to a blank top.

50 **V0** Face to a smeary atête.

51 ★ **V7 Gluttony.** Sit-start to mantle.

52 ★ **V1** Sharp arête to pocket.

53 ✹ **V2** Long laid-back arête.

Tales From the Riverbank (16)
DANIEL JENKINS

Spittle Hill

Map 5

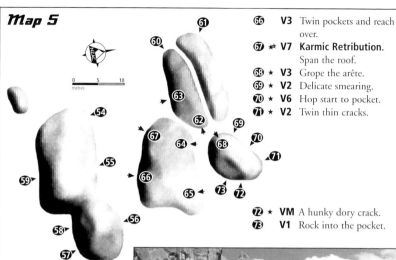

66		V3	Twin pockets and reach over.
67	✹	V7	**Karmic Retribution.** Span the roof.
68	★	V3	Grope the arête.
69	★	V2	Delicate smearing.
70	★	V6	Hop start to pocket.
71	★	V2	Twin thin cracks.

| 72 | ★ | VM | A hunky dory crack. |
| 73 | | V1 | Rock into the pocket. |

Usurper Area

54	✹✹	V3	Long arête.
55	✹✹	21	**Usurper.** Follow the thin crack.
56	✹✹	V5	**Let There be Malt.** Long Slab.
57	★	V3	**Big Cheese.** Start low to mega jugs.
58	★	V1	Jugs deluxe.
59		15	Short with large pockets.
60		V3	Layback the short arête.
61		V6	**Animal Attraction.** Slopey bulge.
62		V3	A couple of hard moves.
63	★	V5	Undercling up to nothing.
64		V4	Dyno.
65		V4	**Shisle My Nisle.** Round rock-over.

Old School (V2). DANIEL USSHER

90

Map 6

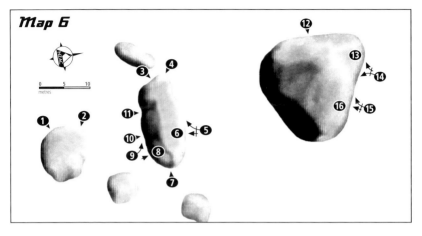

①   **V0**   Two crimps and smear.

② ★ **V3**   Very polished sit-start.

Nasal Slip Boulder

③   **V10** **When Animals Attack.** Sit-start from fearsome small edges.

④ ★ **V5**   Grunt onto the arête.

⑤ ✷ **V2**   Traverse right accross the slab.

⑥ ✷✷**V4** **Nasal Slip.** The high slab test piece.

⑦ ★ **V0**   Layback and hoon up the arête.

⑧   **V1**   Slippery foot holds.

⑨   **V6**   **Ride the Snake.** Traverse left, exiting up the V3.

⑩ ★ **V5**   **The Element.** A hard crimp move.

⑪ ★ **V3**   Get into the groove.

Cyclops Boulder

⑫ ✷ **16** **Cyclops Slab.** Hard rock-over and easy up the middle of the slab.

⑬ ✷✷**V5** **Koolstie.** Very high arête.

⑭ ✷ **V5** **Where Love Crawls on All Fours.** Up the groove then head left.

⑮ ✷✷**V5** **Cyclops Boulder.** Through the central eye/scoop to a high top-out.

⑯ ✷ **V8** **Diablo.** A dastardly rock-over, tiny sharp pocket and high top-out.

⑰ ✷✷**V2** **Old School.** A popular offwidth crack, which is easier than it looks.

⑱ ★ **V8** **Sloper Madness.** Arête rock-over.

91

Spittle Hill

Agony Area

⑲ 18 The left slabby arête.

⑳ ★ 29 **Agony.** A blank looking wall with the mother of all rock-overs.

㉑ ✶ 27 **Honey I Shrunk the Holds.** Traverse right accross the ramp.

㉒ ★ 17 **Jumped Up Country Boy Who Never Knew His Place.** A two pitch excursion with two starts.

㉓ 21 **Noxious Fish Plot.** Traverse the pockets to the arête via pitons.

㉔ 22 Steep and yellow with drilled holds.

㉕ ★ 20 Very smeary slab to the arête.

㉜ ★ 24 **Lily of the Valley.** Face climbing to slopey sidepulling.

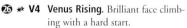

㉖ ✶ V4 **Venus Rising.** Brilliant face climbing with a hard start.

㉗ ★ V0 Step-ups through big pockets.

㉘ VM **Ocelot.** A hard start to easy groove.

㉙ VM Up the arête.

㉚ ✶✶17 **Tales From the Riverbank.** A very pleasing climb on pockets. Head left at the top.

㉛ 16 **Dark Side of the Moon.** Up the slab to anchor at at the ledge.

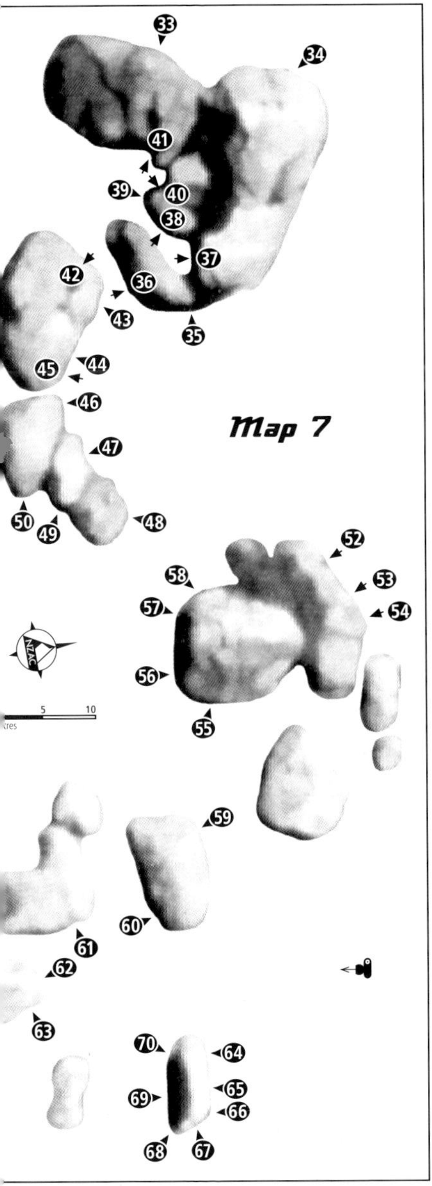

㉝ ★★ **V4** **Piccalilli.** Mantle the ledge.
㉞ ★ **V8** **Episto.** From edges go right.
㉟ **V3** Mantle to the upper ledge.
㊱ **V4** **Gumbo.** Very high step-up.
㊲ **V4** **Horrible Edges.** From the right end of the ledge.
㊳ ★ **V2** Mantle the low lip.
㊴ **V6** **Jackie Chan.** Slap-fu your way across the blank bulge.
㊵ ★ **V7** **Terra Forma.** Climb into the groove and do a high top-out.
㊶ ★★ **V6** **The Air Below.** Climb the steep arête and swing left to the lip.
㊷ ★ **V5** **Supernatural.** Pocket pulling.
㊸ ★★ **V7** **Philtrum.** Mantle the bulge.
㊹ ★ **V3** Into the runnel.
㊺ ★ **V4** Over the runnels.
㊻ ★ **V6** **Duel.** Campus then grovel.
㊼ ★ **V1** Nice edges lead into the scoop.
㊽ **V2** Sit-start in the pocket.
㊾ **V1** Good holds, smeary feet.
㊿ ★ **V4** **Showdown.** Pockets, but no feet.
(51) **V3** Slab with pockets.
(52) ★★ **V2** Beautiful rock-over up the face.
(53) ★ **V1** Edges up the face.
(54) ★ **V3** Use the arête and the face.
(55) ★★ **V8** **Chasing the Dragon.** Traverse right on pockets, easy finish.
(56) ★★ **V4** **Sinsemilla.** Through the scoop then the exciting top crux.
(57) ★★★ **V7** **Opium.** Pockets, dyno, sloper.
(58) ★ **V4** **The Tonic.** Go left via pockets.
(59) ★ **V4** Rock out left up the slab.
(60) **V1** **Caramel.** Big pockets.
(61) ★ **V4** Small holds and lunge up.
(62) **V4** Arête and small pocket.
(63) ★ **V2** Great sidepulling up the crack.
(64) **V1** Slab.
(65) ★ **V4** Veer right up the slab.
(66) ★★★ **V6** **On the Edge.** Delicate up the edge with a few tiny foot holds.
(67) ★★ **V7** **Tuppi Master.** Sit-start and slap the arêtes. Awesome moves.
(68) ★★★ **V3** The angular steep arête.
(69) ★ **V3** The face with small pocket.
(70) **V3** Short with tiny mono pocket.

Spittle Hill

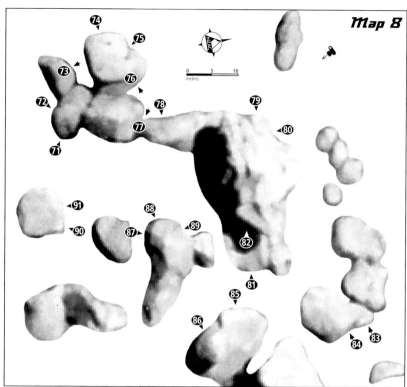

Map 8

0   5   10
metres

71 ★ **V2** Grab pockets, rock-over the arête.

72 ★ **V6 The Flex Capacitor.** Cool name for a tricky problem into the runnels.

73 ★ **V4 Monster Munch.** All good until the top, which tends to catch people out.

74 ★★★ **V9 The Joker.** A mega classic which sports all kinds of moves.

75 ✳ **V2 Botanica.** A long adventure up the groove. Easiest to get off by jumping the gap on the back of the boulder.

76 ★ **V7** Lots of pockets up the high slab.

77 **V0 Tunnel.** Grovel up the slot.

78 ★ **V3** Mantle on the right end of wall.

79 ★ **24** Short edgy face.

80 ★ **18 That Obscure Object of Desire.** Head straight up, then go left.

81 **V2** Short slab with pocket.

82 ✳ **24 L'Air du Temps.** A winding route to the top of the Perfume Bottle.

83 ★ **V2 Inner Space.** Jump start to pocket.

84 ✳ **V7 Mecca.** Pockets to mantle.

85 ★ **21 Baby Boom.** Smeary antics up arête.

86 ★ **V3** Up the groove and exit right.

87 **V1** Slab with edges.

88 ★ **V9 The Gift.** Start off a cheat stone and crank on edges to a lunge.

89 ✳✳ **V4 Beautiful Edges.** Angled edges on the face. Keep left.

90 ★ **V1** Up the right side of the face.

91 **V4 Fetish.** Small edge and crank left.

92 **V3** Pockets up slab.

93 ✳ **V7 Fat of the Land.** Radical slopey top.

94 ✳ **V4 Time Bandit Arête.** Sidepull and pocket start to a mantle.

95 ★ **18 Yet Another.** Follow the ramp right and then tackle the pockets.

96 ★ **V5 The Final Cut.** A line of pockets veering slightly right. SSV8

97 **V3** Move right to a fat sloper.

98 **V5 Post Haste.** Layback the slot.

99 ★ **21 Tectonic Awareness.** Lovely arête.

Sickly Rebel Yellow 23
What's This? 18
Blots 24

★ **23 Sickly Rebel Yellow.** Bridge the groove.

✳ **24 Blots.** Bouldery face climbing, heads right to finish.

★ **18 What's This?** Big pockets.

Allah Protects 23

✳✳ **23 Allah Protects.** A devious groove and then move right up the face.

Quantum Field

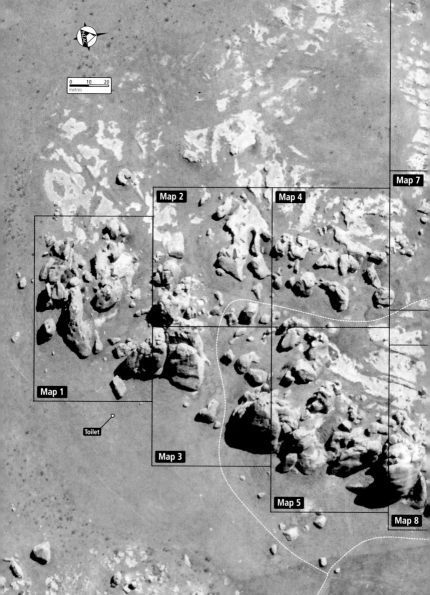

Map 7

Map 2

Map 4

Map 1

Toilet

Map 3

Map 5

Map 8

Carpark 5mins

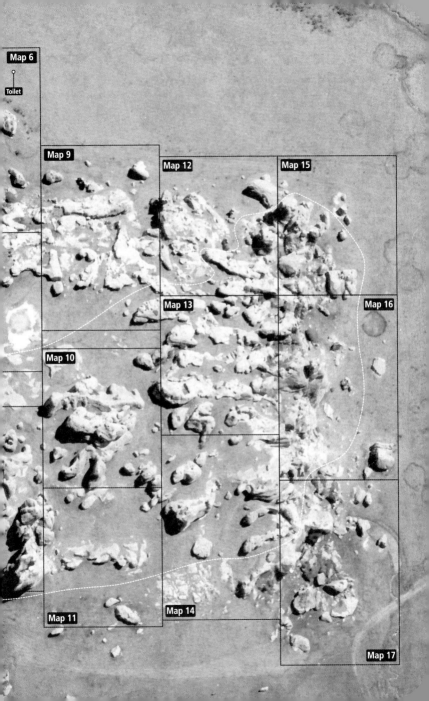

Map 6

Toilet

Map 9

Map 12

Map 15

Map 13

Map 16

Map 10

Map 11

Map 14

Map 17

Quantum Field Map 1

① ★ **V1** Finger jam it.
② ★ **V7** Miss Swish. Slopey and balancy.
③ ★ **V6** Mr Sumo. Over the bulge.
④ **V3** Hump. Mantle the protrusion.

Sunny Side Wall

⑤ **V6** High rock-over.
⑥ **V9** Traverse far left and up slab.
⑦ ★ **V6** Dog Eat Dog. A hard rock-over.
⑧ ★ **V5** Eagle Eye. High-step onto face.
⑨ ★ **V7** Warp Eight. Up blunt arête. SSV9.
⑩ ★ **V6** Satan's Sleeves. Mantle.
⑪ **V2** Smear.
⑫ ★ **V5** Sit-start and up to slopers.
⑬ ★ **V10** Everything's Gone Green. Two hard moves over the bulge.

Toilet Wall

⑭ **V4** San Fran' Punks. Hard start.
⑮ ★ **V1** Small sidepull.
⑯ ✹ **V1** Slopey pockets.
⑰ ✹ **V1** Slopey pockets.
⑱ ★ **V1** Slopey pockets.
⑲ ★ **V0** Reach high to slopers.
⑳ **V1** Omerta. Jump to jug. SSV9.
㉑ ★ **V0** Up the lovely arête.
㉒ ★ **V6** Limpet. Sit-start with choice holds.
㉓ **V3** Jump to pocket.
㉔ ★ **V8** UFO. Sit-start and traverse right.
㉕ ★ **V5** Dyno left to jug.
㉖ ✹ **V0** Smeary arête.
㉗ ★ **V0** Smeary arête.
㉘ ✹ **V3** Layback and smear left up the slab.
㉙ ★ **V0** Slab.
㉚ ★ **V2** Slab.
㉛ ★ **V1** Slab, drift right.
㉜ **P** The horizontal crack. Go right.
㉝ **V0** The chimney between boulders.
㉞ **P** Up the face, just to the grass.
㉟ ★ **23** Sea Egg. Steep cranking with a dyno that leads to a run-out finish.
㊱ **V4** Slopers to pockets.
㊲ ★ **V3** Pockets.
㊳ ★ **V2** Pockets.
㊴ ✹ **V9** Dolomite. Technical and it tops out.
㊵ **V4** Up corner.
㊶ **V1** Line of pockets.

㊷ ★ **V5** Remorse. Finish up or right.
㊸ **P** High and steep wall.
㊹ **V2** Up the high groove.
㊺ ★ **V5** Climb up and exit left to the ledge.
㊻ **P** Steep and high.
㊼ ✹ **26** Suicide by Hallucination. The yellow wall, edges and pocket crux.
㊽ ✹ **29** Moment of Greed. An amazing blank face. Very fingery.
㊾ **25** Toxic Avenger. Traverse right.
㊿ **P** Arête with bad landing.
51 **V9** Sloper Groper. Sit-start and traverse left on hideous holds.
52 ★ **V4** Sit-start on the left and mantle.
53 ★ **V6** Willy Nilly. Up the face with edges.
54 **V2** Short face with crack thing.
55 ★ **V5** Meat Wipes. Start from the ground.
56 **V3** Pizza. Step from rock to face.
57 **P** The staunch-looking face.
58 **VM** Step up the broken jugs.
59 ★ **V0** Hard start.
60 ★ **V4** No hopping, just smear!
61 ✹ **V4** Mantle/smear.
62 ✹ **V4** Mantle (can be done with style).
63 **VM** Grovel up between the boulders.
64 ★ **V9** Cuba. The slopey arête.
65 **V7** Nefarious. Jump to crimp.
66 **V5** The Opera House. Hard rock-over.
67 ✹ **V5** Open Book. Up the corner.
68 ★ **V5** Eye Spy. Slopers.
69 ★ **V4** Pockets.
70 ★ **VM** Line of pockets.
71 **V2** Bridging/smearing.
72 **V3** Traverse right along the ledge.
73 ★ **V3** Rust. Start on crimps.
74 ✹ **V3** Arête with shallow pockets.
75 ★ **V7** Sloper System. Slopey arête.
76 **V10** Infinite Jest. Sit-start in the middle.
77 **P** Slopers to pockets on arête.
78 ★ **V2** Jungle Line. Jugs going right.
79 ★ **18** Brooke Pantyshields. The offwidth.
80 ★ **22** Superlicker Man. The yellow face.
81 **V2** Mantle
82 ★ **V5** High Five. Jump to the sloper.
83 ★ **V3** Hobie. Jugs and slopers.
84 **V10** Ignition. Dyno left to slopers.

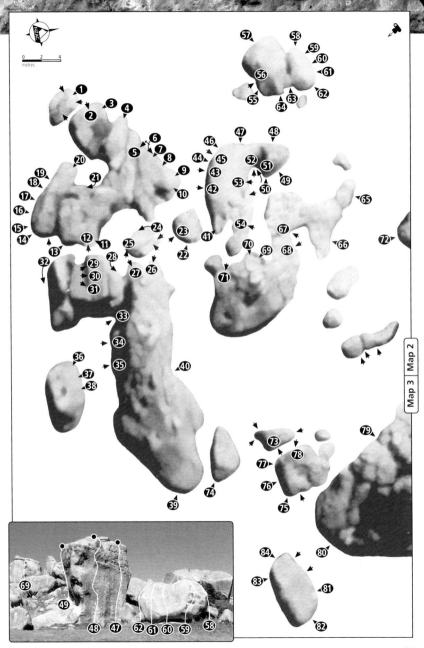

Map 3 | Map 2

Quantum Field Map 2

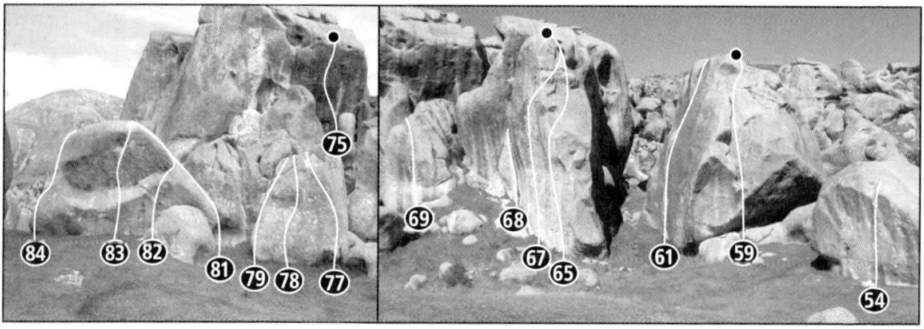

① ★ **V2** Layback crack.
② ★ **V5** **Snax.** Up small face to a good edge.
③ **V2** Very grippy rock.
④ ★★ **V2** Crack.
⑤ **V8** **Diplomacy.** Crimp left, slap arête.
⑥ ★ **V6** **The Echo.** Dyno left to sloper.
⑦ **V1** The short groove.
⑧ ★ **V5** **Snow White.** Slopey holds.
⑨ ★★ **V5** **The Classic.** Layback the ear.

Horseshoe Boulder

⑩ **V6** Slopers up a scoop.
⑪ ★ **V5** Big crank on good pocket.
⑫ **V8** **Predator.** Quite a cranky sit-start.
⑬ ★ **V3** Traverse left to top-out.
⑭ **V1** Mantle.
⑮ **V1** Mantle.
⑯ ★ **V2** Slopers.
⑰ ★ **V2** **Egypt.** Slopers.
⑱ ★ **V4** **Retrograde Motion.** Undercling.
⑲ ★ **V6** **Something Appropriate.** Scoop.
⑳ ★★ **V0** Smear up the corner, exit right.
㉑ ★ **V7** **Something Blank.** The bulge.
㉒ **V8** **Leverage.** Pull on and go to sloper.
㉓ ★★ **V2** Fat undercling.
㉔ **P** Straight into the groove.
㉕ ★ **V4** **Ameros Peros.** Nasty slab. Go left.
㉖ ★ **V5** **You Will Bleed Profusely.** Straight.
㉗ ★★★ **V1** Jump from boulder onto face.
㉘ ★ **V4** Underclings for start.
㉙ ★★ **V0** Pockets.
㉚ ★★★ **VM** Up the arête. Try no hands.
㉛ ★★ **V0** Pockets.
㉜ ★ **V1** Long reach.
㉝ ★ **V1** Mantle.
㉞ ★★ **V3** Tricky start then mantle.
㉟ ★ **V4** Smear straight up.
㊱ **V3** Mantle onto lip, smear up.
㊲ ★ **V8** **Archvile.** Sit-start and exit out left.
㊳ **V9** **Continuity.** Crank off tiny holds.
㊴ ★ **V3** Mantle.
㊵ ★ **V4** Slopey holds to jug.
㊶ ★ **V9** **Reflections.** Small holds and dyno.
㊷ ★ **V6** **One Move Boulder.** A long move.
㊸ ★ **V5** Terrible feet, sketch up somehow.
㊹ **V8** **Simple Things.** Lots of small crimps.
㊺ ★ **V4** **Sidewalk.** Scoop with small lip.
㊻ ★ **V6** **Brine.** Crank to pocket.
㊼ **V3** Sidepull.
㊽ ★ **V3** Sidepull.
㊾ ★ **VM** Pockets.
㊿ ★ **V1** Jump to pocket.
(51) ★ **V3** Pockets then mantle.
(52) ★ **V9** **Karmageddon.** Small holds mantle.
(53) ★ **V1** Rock-over using the mono. SSV5
(54) ★★ **V7** **Quantum Mechanics.** Two cranks.
(55) **V1** **Venus.** Run and jump up.
(56) ★ **V4** Smear and static reach.
(57) **V2** Smear and snatch.
(58) ★ **20** **Chit Chat.** Go left. Right is a 22.
(59) ★ **20** **Heretic.** Hard start up the crack.
(60) **V3** **Chipped Dyno.** Dyno to pocket.
(61) ★★★ **V2** **Wide Offwidth.** All the way.
(62) ★ **21** **Mantle Block.** Big slopey arête.
(63) **P** Jump to pocket and up.
(64) **V2** Edges up the face, exit right.
(65) ★★ **21** **Nether Edge.** Beautiful arête.
(66) ★ **V7** **Beta Master.** Traverse left and exit.
(67) ★★ **24** **Hunters Bar.** A superb face climb. Exit right to the arête.
(68) ★★ **V3** **Orifice Fish.** Tricky start, into hole.

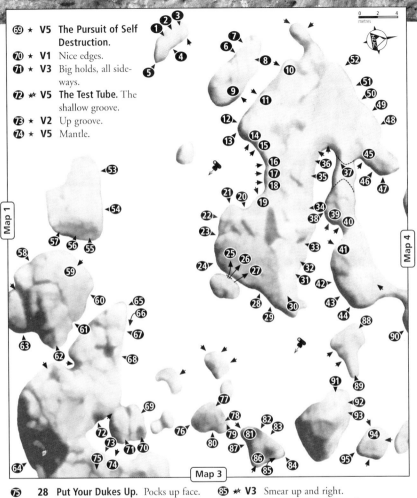

69 ★ **V5** **The Pursuit of Self Destruction.**
70 ★ **V1** Nice edges.
71 ★ **V3** Big holds, all sideways.
72 ✹✹ **V5** **The Test Tube.** The shallow groove.
73 ★ **V2** Up groove.
74 ★ **V5** Mantle.

75 **28** **Put Your Dukes Up.** Pocks up face.
76 **V3** Up the arête with some hugging.
77 ★ **V7** **Blade Runner.** Right side of face.
78 ★ **V6** **It's Love.** Face with tiny edges.
79 ★ **V3** Arête.
80 **V2** **Miso.** Run and jump to the jug.

Lung Boulder
81 **V9** **Rastapopoulos.** High-step.
82 ★ **V3** Escape right to the arête.
83 ✹✹ **V4** **Lung Dyno.** Dyno from jug.
84 ✹✹ **V3** **Lung Arête.** A smooth cruise.

85 ✹✹ **V3** Smear up and right.
86 ✹✹ **V1** High step then big pockets.
87 ✹✹ **V5** **Cyclops.** The single pocket
88 ★ **V6** **Crucifixion.** The round bulge.
89 **V2** Devious, small arête.
90 ★ **V7** **Lobotomy.** Run/jump to pocket.
91 **V2** Crack.
92 ★ **21** **Max Blank.** An attractive slab.
93 ★ **V1** Offwidth.
94 ✹✹ **V6** **Old Timer.** Arête with crimpy top.
95 ★ **V7** **Wasabi.** Clamp up the arête.

Map 1

Map 4

Map 3

Quantum Field Map 3

❶ ✲ **V1** **The Soft Machine.** Handcrack.

❷ ★ **?** **Unknown.** Up wall in the gully.

❸ ★ **23** **Roid Rage.** Up face to corner.

❹ ✲ **24** **Heisenberg.** The pocketed arête.

❺ ✲ **26** **Schrodinger.** The blank, exposed face left of the arête.

❻ ★ **24** **Bonza Pipeline.** The cute groove.

❼ ★ **20** **Kiss in the Dreamhouse.** Nifty face.

❽ ✲ **V6** **Dreamhouse.** Go right on pockets.

❾ **V4** **Bad Memory.** Arête.

❿ ★ **V6** **Technophobia.** Weird down-palm.

⓫ **V6** **Sushi.** High-step.

⓬ **P** Jump to pocket, then to top!

⓭ ✲ **V2** Traverse right, same way down.

⓮ ★ **V3** Into the right scoop.

⓯ ✲✲**V5** **The Flat Lands.** Straight up.

⓰ **V2** Into the left scoop.

⓱ ★ **V1** Straight up or go left.

⓲ **P** Crimps on the face.

⓳ ★ **V5** **Cobra.** Big crank to edges. SSV7.

Meat Market Boulder

⓴ **V5** **Liver.** Jump to fat sloper.

㉑ **V6** **Belly.** Onto rounded arête.

㉒ **V1** The short bulge.

㉓ ★ **V3** **Mince.** Step onto the boulder.

㉔ ✲ **V2** **Corned Beef.** Pockets.

㉕ ★ **V5** **Paté.** Crank over and up slab.

㉖ ✲ **V5** **Spam.** Lunge to the sloper.

㉗ **V7** **Propulsion.** Traverse and dyno right.

㉘ **V0** Mantle.

㉙ ★ **V2** Weird undercling in big pocket.

㉚ ★ **V1** Hop to pocket.

Dan Armachump on *Fatwa* **(V7) Map 9.**
DEREK THATCHER

Map 2

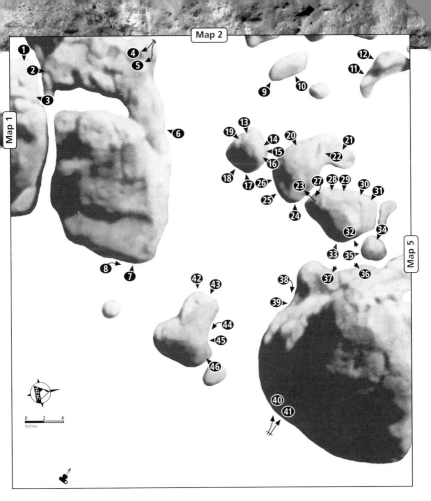

Map 1
Map 5

③ ★ **V1** Hop to pocket.

㉜ **V7** **Mono Logic.** Use the mono.

㉝ ★ **V6** **Leningrad Cowpats.** A hard start.

㉞ **V5** **The Pill.** The round arête.

㉟ **V4** **Decay.** Try to use solid holds.

㊱ ⁂ **V2** **Fallopian Tube.** Groove.

㊲ ⁂ **V1** **Xanadu.** Smear up to the high arête.

㊳ **V7** **The Froggatt Simulator.** Sit-start.

㊴ **V0** Grovel up.

㊵ **21** **Like Cockatoos.** Go left up the face.

㊶ **22** **Sleazy Skankin'.** Get into the groove.

𝒯𝒽𝑒𝑜𝓇𝓎 𝐵𝑜𝓊𝓁𝒹𝑒𝓇

This is the large boulder at the bottom of the Heisenburg Gully.

㊷ **P** Faint arête.

㊸ **P** Futuristic face.

㊹ **V6** Jump to pocket and go left.

㊺ ⁂ **V9** **The Outcast.** Big cranks on pockets to a tricky mantle.

㊻ ★ **V4** **Guinea Pig.** Step into pocket from boulder, then up the slab.

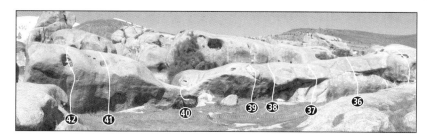

① ★ **V7 Gripper.** Fat sidepull, traverse left.
② **V6 Yuk.** Short and awkward.
③ **V3 Play Dough.** The smeary arête.
④ **V5 Give Birth.** Up the groove.
⑤ ✷ **V1 Latte.** Sidepull to good holds.
⑥ ★ **V3** Smeary arête.
⑦ ★ **V0** Reach high to jug.
⑧ **V2** Mantle.
⑨ **V6 Growler.** Very slopey mantle. SSV8.
⑩ ★ **V1** Layback the arête.
⑪ **V6 Cold Turkey.** Start on a stone.
⑫ ✷ **V2** Small edges then big pocket.
⑬ ★ **V3** Arête.
⑭ **V2** Face with pockets and rounded top.
⑮ **V2** Grovel up.

⑯ ★ **V6 Kung Fu Mojo.** Crank to the slopey lip and wrestle with this.
⑰ **V0** High step or mantle.
⑱ ★ **V4 Yoga Master.** Bridge up.
⑲ ✷✷ **V6 The Day the World Stood Still.** The long, thin finger crack.
⑳ ✷ **V5 Slop Slop Splat.** Straight up.
㉑ ★ **V5 Martin Goes Mountain Biking.** Up then go left to the arête.
㉒ ✷ **V9 Cuidado las Llamas.** Use start stone.
㉓ **V3** Into scoop.
㉔ ★ **V2** Layback.
㉕ ★ **V5** Tricky arête.
㉖ **V4** Face.
㉗ ★ **V2** Smear.
㉘ ★ **V6 Sapid Sloper.** Sit-start.

Joerg Zeidelhack on *No. 11* (V2) Map 3. MARK WATSON

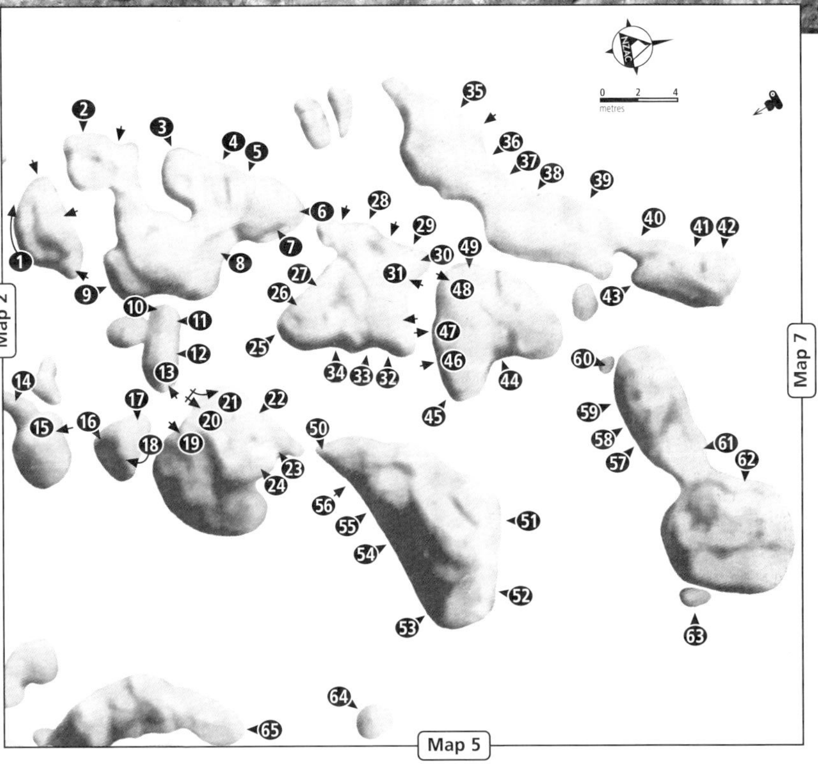
NZAC
0 2 4
metres
Map 2
Map 7
Map 5

㉙ V5 **The Apprentice.** Cranky mantle.
㉚ ★ V1 Smeary arête.
㉛ ★ V3 Use mono and go right.
㉜ V0 Big pocket.
㉝ V0 Twin grooves.
㉞ V1 Reach high for holds.
㉟ ★ V4 Pockets then mantle.
㊱ V1 Work feet up high.
㊲ ★★ V3 A devious, technical problem.
㊳ V3 The two-finger and heel hook.
㊴ V0 Jug.
㊵ V8 **Loop.** Loop the loop.
㊶ ★ V5 **Sputnik.** Jump to the sloper.
㊷ ★★ V3 Dyno to pocket then mantle.
㊸ V5 **Luna.** Jump up to the jug.
㊹ ★★ V1 **Pink Carpet.** Smear up ramp.
㊺ ★ V6 **Skin Graft.** Up the slopey bulge.
㊻ V1 Pockets.
㊼ V1 Pockets.
㊽ ★★ V7 **Thin Lizzy.** Small crimps/feet.
㊾ ★★ V5 Big move to pocket then smear.
㊿ ★ V2 **The Fin.** Layback up either side.
(51) ★★ V6 **Murad.** Crimp up face.
(52) ★★ 22 **Dr Squat.** Great face climbing.
(53) ★★ V6 **Better Than Jesus.** Slopey edges lead to a nice top-out.
(54) ★ V8 **Bastille.** Slopey edges.
(55) ★ V6 **Bypass.** The scoop with edges.
(56) V2 Crack-like thing.
(57) ★ V3 Line of pockets.
(58) ★ V1 Pockets.
(59) V5 **Trust Thyself.** A big run and jump.
(60) V1 **Spinal Tap.** Step across from rock.
(61) V2 Leg up and hoon up the slab.
(62) ★ V1 **Magic Beans.** Wind up to the top.
(63) ★★ V2 **Bird's Head.** Interesting climbing.
(64) V2 **Nipple Mantle.** Mantle the pert…
(65) ★ V4 **Road To Nowhere.** Smear up slab.

Quantum Field Map 5

❶ ★★V3 Beautiful layback.
❷ ★★ V6 **The Beast Within.** Arête/face.
❸ ★ V8 **Agent Provocateur.** Tricky start leads to a hard, crimpy crux.
❹ V2 Pockets up arête.
❺ ★ V5 Devious crank and smear.
❻ V4 **Jack in the Pock.** Jump up.
❼ ★ V5 **Focus Pocus.** Smear then dyno.
❽ 18 **The Graze.** Slab. Does not top-out.

Ode to Joy Boulder

❾ ★ V8 **Anthrax.** Up face, arête then slab.
❿ ★★ V8 **Nuns and Poodles.** Traverse left.
⓫ ★★V2 Great jug pulling.
⓬ ★★ V6 **Mantle Block.** Start from the left or go direct. Tricky top-out.
⓭ ★ V7 **Beached Male.** Campus up.
⓮ ★ V0 Slab.
⓯ ★ V0 Slab.
⓰ P Up the steep arête to *Bio Hazard*.
⓱ ★★V7 **Bio Hazard.** Traverse right on pockets to the smeary arête. SSV10.
⓲ ★★V1 **Ode to Joy.** Good holds.
⓳ ★ V10 **Apocalypse.** Big moves on edges to a very high mantle. Slab finish.
⓴ ★★V9 **Juggernaut.** Up underside of arête.
㉑ ★★ V5 **Out to Lunge.** Middle of the face.
㉒ ★★V6 **Pie Stop.** The attractive arête.
㉓ ★ V6 **Constant Force.** The single pocket.
㉔ ★ V7 **Slapper.** Very rounded arête.
㉕ ★ 13 **El Vista.** Up arête to great view.
㉖ ★ V7 Groove with some holds.
㉗ V2 Mantle the slopey blob.
㉘ ★ V3 The lip then easy slab.
㉙ V2 Rock-over onto the slab.
㉚ ★ V0 Great pocket.
㉛ ★★ V3 Arête.
㉜ ★★ V6 **Pickpocket.** Face with small pockets.
㉝ ★ V4 Traverse left to the arête.
㉞ ★★ 25 **Vicious Games.** Climb right.
㉟ ★ 23 **Boozin'.** Start up *Squashed Gecko,* but head right when you can.
㊱ ★★ 17 **Squashed Gecko.** The offwidth.
㊲ ★★ V1 **Crippler.** Go right on positive holds.
㊳ ★★ V4 **My Left Thigh.** Up pockets, then head left and do a leg press.
㊴ ★ 25 **Pig Dog.** Traverse left on pockets. Start from a high cheat stone.
㊵ P Straight up.
㊶ ★ V4 **Acid Roof.** Nice steep moves.
㊷ V0 Wee arête.
㊸ V2 Tricky.
㊹ P Up the arête.
㊺ V1 Short sit-start.
㊻ ★★V0 **Ladder.** The cute line of edges.
㊼ ★ V2 **Traveller.** Traverse right along lip.
㊽ V1 Good jug on arête.
㊾ V0 Step-up.
㊿ ★ V3 Step-up.
(51) P Face.
(52) P Face.

High Rise Boulder

(53) ★★V5 **High Rise.** Face exit right. SSV6.
(54) V1 Crack between the boulders.
(55) ★★V2 **Head Spin.** Lovely pockets. Exciting.
(56) VM Jump onto the boulder.
(57) ★ V2 Long reach to pocket.
(58) VM Pockets.
(59) V5 **Philderbeast.** Jump to pocket.
(60) V6 **Hustler.** Big move to bad sloper.
(61) ★ V2 The interesting groove.
(62) ★ V0 Pockets, drift right.
(63) V0 Climb over the block and up.
(64) ★ V7 **Granada.** Dyno to jug.
(65) 25 **Scrotum.** Jam the steep crack.
(66) ★★ 23 **Arseyboo.** The edgy, rounded arête.
(67) ★ 19 **What's on the Slab.** A slippery slab.
(68) V0 Slopers and smears up slab.
(69) ★★ V9 **Atlantis.** From the gap, traverse left.
(70) ★ 24 **Sid Lives.** Hard start up the arête.
(71) ★★ 28 **The Treadmill.** Crack through bulge.
(72) ★ 22 **Digging for Fire.** The wide groove.
(73) ★★ 26 **Gone with the Wind.** Pretty arête.
(74) ★ V2 Waves of slopers.
(75) 20 **One Arm Pull-up.** Slab with slopers. Finish at the 3rd bolt.
(76) P Impossible-looking face project.

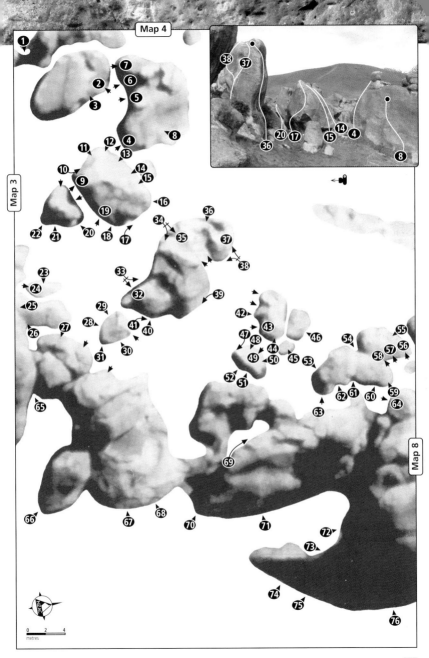

Map 4

Map 3

Map 8

0   2   4
metres

❶ **V0** Slopers.
❷ **V6** One Flew Over the Cuckoos Nest.
❸ ★ **V5** Mid Summer Scrape. Jump to jug then crawl over.
❹ ★ **VM** Left onto the slab and cruise up.
❺ **V5** Strange Traverse. Go left on pockets.
❻ ★ **V7** Aliens are Real. Navigate slopers.
❼ **VE** Big jugs.
❽ **P** Very blank, very steep.
❾ **P** Dyno from slopers.
❿ **V0** Drift left through pockets.
⓫ **VM** Large pockets. Head left.
⓬ ★★ **V1** West Side Story. Classic layback.
⓭ ★ **V3** Smeary arête.
⓱ ★ **26** I'm the Boss. Crimpy wall.
⓲ ★ **24** King of the Road. Bouldery arête.
⓳ ★★ **V8** Pythagoras. Right-leaning feature.
⓴ ★ **V8** Super Suprise. Dyno up steep wall.
㉑ **24** Deceptive Bends. Up the arête.
㉒ **V6** Mr Fervent. The rounded arête.
㉓ **V4** Reach to slopey pocket.
㉔ ★ **V2** Rock-over/palm-down.
㉕ ★★ **V0** Slab with rock-over start.
㉖ ★ **V5** Insertion. Pockets to arête.
㉗ **V1** Pockets.
㉘ **V1** Pockets.

Stage Boulder

㉙ ★★ **V6** Smear Right. Hop start, hard slab.
㉚ ★★ **V5** Smear Left. Hop start, easy slab.
㉛ ★★ **V4** Exit Stage Right. The right start, go to middle and finish right.
㉜ ★ **V4** Exit Stage Left. The left start, same middle (crux) but finish left.
㉝ ★★ **V3** Pilgrimage. Pockered face.
㉞ ★ **V3** Jump to jug then pockets.
㉟ ★ **V1** Jump to pocket.
㊱ ★ **VM** Arête.
㊲ ★ **V5** Day of the Triffids. Start from the stone and onto the slab and arête.
㊳ ★ **V8** The Power of Equality. High face.

Tunnel Wall

㊴ **V0** High-step.
㊵ ★ **V1** Strenuous pulls.
㊶ ★ **V5** Jump to holds and up.
㊷ ★ **V12** Headbanger. Static start on small pockets to a difficult, slopey top.
㊸ ★ **V0** Hole. The hole.
㊹ ★★ **V5** Eight Legged Groove Machine. A long reach to a lovely groove.
㊺ **V8** The Leonard. Pockets.
㊻ **P** Up through scoop.

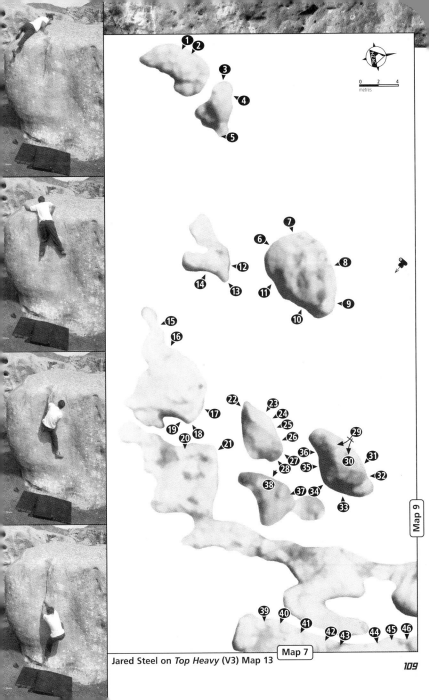

Jared Steel on *Top Heavy* (V3) Map 13

Map 9

Map 7

Kate Finnerty on *Round About* (V2), Map 8
MARK WATSON

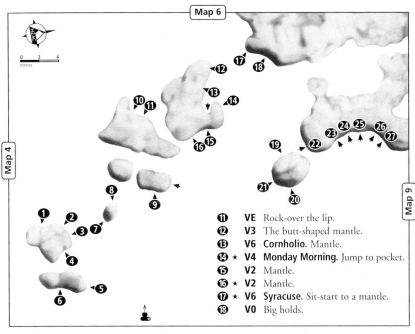

Map 6

Map 4

Map 9

⑪	**VE**	Rock-over the lip.
⑫	**V3**	The butt-shaped mantle.
⑬	**V6**	**Cornholio.** Mantle.
⑭ ★	**V4**	**Monday Morning.** Jump to pocket.
⑮	**V2**	Mantle.
⑯ ★	**V2**	Mantle.
⑰ ★	**V6**	**Syracuse.** Sit-start to a mantle.
⑱	**V0**	Big holds.

❶	**V5**	**Abomination.** Start under lip.
❷	**VM**	Good holds.
❸ ★	**V0**	Up the front through big holds.
❹ ★	**V1**	Into the scoop and up.
❺ ✸	**V3**	Up the rounded arête.
❻	**V0**	Slopers.
❼	**V6**	**Chunky Farmer.** A sensitive problem.
❽	**V2**	Slopers.
❾	**V2**	Scoop.
❿ ★	**V0**	Crack.

⑲ ✸	**V0**	A lovely crank off the pocket.
⑳	**V3**	Jump to jug and up.
㉑ ★	**V2**	Traverse to the right.
㉒	**VE**	Crawl under/around the lip.
㉓	**V3**	Somehow get over the lip.
㉔	**V0**	Reach high to slopers.
㉕ ★	**VM**	Lay off the crack.
㉖ ★	**V3**	Slopers and undercling.
㉗	**V1**	Crank off the pocket.

Map 8

(1) V0 Jump to jug.
(2) P Small crimps.
(3) ★ V4 **Skin Deep.** Run and jump.
(4) V6 **Weird Arête.** Crusty rock.
(5) V2 Mantle
(6) ★ V7 **Rapt.** Slopey mantle.
(7) ★ V6 **Mongolian Cluster.** Mantle.
(8) ★★ V6 **Deadline.** Face and arête.
(9) ★★ V5 **Roger.** Jump from the phallus.
(10) ★ V2 **Jalapeno.** Tricky rock-over.
(11) V8 **Dumbo.** Powerful rock-over.
(12) ★ V0 A nice rock-over.
(13) ★ V1 Arête.
(14) V6 **Lavender.** Crank far to slopers.
(15) ★★ V4 Classic friction problem. Smears.
(16) V4 **Beach Ball.** Pop from sidepull.
(17) V3 **Bounce.** Smeary arête.
(18) ★★ V6 **Phallic Aesthetics.** Face to mantle.
(19) ★ V2 **Round About.** Single pocket.
(20) ★★ V6 **Übermensch.** Traverse left and up.
(21) ★ V5 **Nipple Scrape.** Jump to pocket.
(22) V8 **Super Saiyan.** Up the scoop.
(23) V1 Mantle.
(24) V4 Very slippery.
(25) ★ V2 **Mixed Plonk.** Smear up the groove.
(26) ★★ 21 **Mac's Plank.** Slab traverse left.
(27) P Direct start to *Mac's Plank.*
(28) ★ V6 **Quantum Leap.** Big jump to jug, then smeary top-out.
(29) ★ V7 **Alleoupe.** Traverse right into scoop.
(30) V6 Crimps up the bulge.
(31) ★ V6 **Syzygy.** Run and jump to sloper.
(32) V4 Up slab then right.
(33) ★★ V3 Up slab with pockets.
(34) ★★ V3 **Magic Line.** High slab.
(35) ★★ V4 **Video Camera.** Traverse left.
(36) ★★ V5 High jamming in crack.
(37) ★ V2 Reach high to pocket.
(38) V2 Wedge up the gap.
(39) V0 Rock into the pocket.
(40) ★★ V1 Nice holds but very high.
(41) ★ V3 **Trollop.** Slab–don't fall to the right!
(42) ★ V6 **Power Slab.** Pocket cranking.
(43) ★ V4 **Wide On.** The big groove.
(44) 21 **Hurt so Good.** Pockets on arête.
(45) ★ V3 Jump to pocket then top-out.
(46) ★ V5 **Get Bent.** To mono and out right.
(47) ★ V6 **Get High.** Contains slopers.
(48) ★★ V8 **Graphenburg.** Use a start stone.
(49) P Up face and right arête.
(50) P Overhanging crack.
(51) ★ V3 Up left side of face.
(52) ★ V7 **Mr Grevious.** Up the groove.
(53) ★★ V2 **The Unbearable Lightness of Being.** Pocketed face with 2 bolts.
(54) ★ 28 **Houdini.** High-step on pockets.
(55) ★ 21 **A Taste of Things to Come.** Go left.
(56) 22 **Afternoon Delight.** Straight up.
(57) ★ 19 **Snug as a Thug on a Jug.** Arête.
(58) P Up the arête.
(59) P The arête.
(60) V3 Arête.
(61) P Pockets then the left arête.
(62) ★★★ V6 **Ocean.** Interesting bridging.
(63) ★ V3 A tricky jump onto the slab.
(64) ★ V6 **Mr Tangent.** Run and jump slab.
(65) P Wrestle with the bulging rib.
(66) ★★ V3 Arête.
(67) ★ V7 **Amitabha.** Shallow groove.
(68) ★ V6 **Amnesia.** The right arête.
(69) ★ V3 **Night of the Long Knives.** SSV7.
(70) ★ V6 Into the groove.
(71) ★ V5 Grope the round arête.
(72) ★★ V8 **Retro Vertigo.** Interesting.
(73) ★ V2 The faint corner. SSV4.
(74) V3 Mantle.
(75) 14 **Critical Mass.** Big pockets
(76) ★ 23 **Spoonerama.** Traverse left.
(77) V6 Pockets.
(78) V4 Pockets.

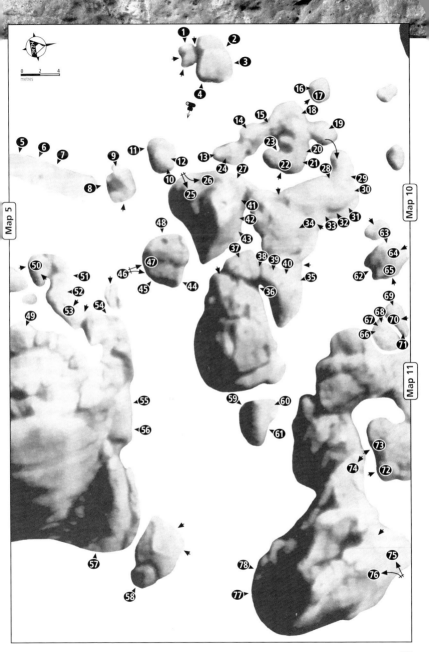

Map 5

Map 10

Map 11

Quantum Field Map 9

❶ V4 **Nana.** Static to the sloper.
❷ ★★ V2 **Clean Living Girl.** Crank to pocket.
❸ ★★★ V0 Straight up.
❹ ★ V6 **Rubic Arête.** Delicate slab climbing.
❺ ★ V8 **Concentrate.** Small crimps.
❻ ★ V5 **Turn.** Palm-down in the pocket.
❼ V3 Long reach to pockets.
❽ V4 **The Cube.** Sidepull and straight up.
❾ ★ V5 **Rubic.** Go left on nifty slopers.
❿ V0 Smear up the long slab.
⓫ V4 **Hammer Time.** Steep arête. SSV6.
⓬ V3 Bridge in the scoop.
⓭ V1 Arête.

Goldilocks Wall

⓮ ★ V10 **Rumplestiltskin.** Very blank.
⓯ ★★ V2 **Father Bear.** Rock into pocket.
⓰ ★★ V6 **Mother Bear.** Into pocket then slab.
⓱ ★ V2 **Sister Bear.** Pocket then smear.
⓲ V8 **Hansel.** Start from the left.
⓳ ★ V8 **Gretel.** Straight up into the scoop.
⓴ V2 **Blood On The Rocks.** High slab.
㉑ ★★ V5 **Pock Face.** Up the small pockets.
㉒ ★ V3 **Grooving.** The water groove.

Run and Jump Slab

Once you have done all the lines, try backwards, sideways, one hand one foot, eyes closed and the popular classic—using no hands.

㉓ ★★ V8 **Shaman.** Awesome line veering left.
㉔ ★ V7 **Knee Banger.** Tricky static start.
㉕ ★★★ V0 **Run and Jump Slab.** There are many variations. Left is easiest.
㉖ ★ V4 **Side Attraction.** Undercling at start.
㉗ ★ V7 **Jump'n'Slap.** Jump to hideous holds.
㉘ ★★ V5 **Jump For Joy.** Jump to the pocket.
㉙ ★ V10 **Restoration.** Small holds, high step.
㉚ ★★★ V6 **Spent.** Face moves, slopey top-out.
㉛ ★ V0 Grass-filled crack.
㉜ ★ V2 **Flapper.** Pockets then slopers.
㉝ ★ V5 **Pigs on the Wing.** Slopey. SSV6.
㉞ ★ V4 **Misty Frequency.** Undercling. SSV9.
㉟ ★ V4 A weird pull on.
㊱ ★★ V10 **Fade Away.** Sit-start to slopey top.
㊲ ★ V6 **Peer Pressure.** Mantle.
㊳ V2 A nice short crack.
㊴ V6 **The Remedy.** Pocket/long move.
㊵ V0 Long reach.
㊶ ★ V7 **Mental Mantle.** Up blank bulge.
㊷ ★ V9 **Nullification.** Tiny holds to scoop.
㊸ V6 **Break Beats.** Weasely arête.
㊹ V8 **Inositol.** Small holds up arête.
㊺ ★★ V3 Slopers.
㊻ V0 Mantle.
㊼ ★ V6 **Misfit.** A nice crank to edge.
㊽ ★★ V2 Up the arête.
㊾ ★★ V5 **Learning Curve.** Slopey arête.
㊿ ★ V3 **Smiley Face.** Edges to gain scoop.
(51) ★★ V2 **Vlad the Impaler.** Big crank. SSV6.
(52) V6 **Höger Vänster.** Dyno/crank right.
(53) ★ V8 **Placebo.** Very long dyno out right.
(54) V6 **Biopsy.** Jump and mantle.
(55) ★ V2 **Lock and Load.** Jump to lip.
(56) ★ V7 **Raw Terror.** Overhanging arête.
(57) ★★ V7 **Fatwa.** Mantle the bulging thing.
(58) V3 **Colt.** Tricky slopey thing.
(59) ★ V8 **Trojan.** Sit-start mantle.
(60) V1 Sidepull.
(61) V0 Long reach to good holds.
(62) V5 **Sunday School.** Mantle.
(63) V4 Mantle.
(64) V1 Slopey holds.
(65) ★ V4 Smear left up the slab.
(66) V4 Hop up into the pocket.
(67) V6 **Big Bubba the Buddha.** Mantle.
(68) V4 A pleasant mantle.
(69) V0 Pocket.
(70) P Will be the mother of all rock-overs.
(71) ★★ V6 **Small Balls.** The overhanging lip.
(72) ★ V1 Juggy rock-over.
(73) ★ V2 Good holds then rock-over.
(74) ★ V5 **Big Balls.** Slopers to get a leg over.
(75) ★ V6 **Push Me Pull Me.** Hard mantle.
(76) V2 Mantle.
(77) V3 Mantle. Start from left or right.
(78) ★★★ V7 **Fingers of Fury.** To the toilet bowl.
(79) ★ V6 **Simultanous Equation.** Traverse right and up *Fire Fingers* exit.
(80) ★★ V7 **Fire Fingers.** The powerful undercling problem.
(81) ★★★ V7 **Odyssey.** From scoop to slopers.
(82) ★ V5 **Jandal.** Big moves, good holds.
(83) ★ V3 **Thong.** Bridge up.

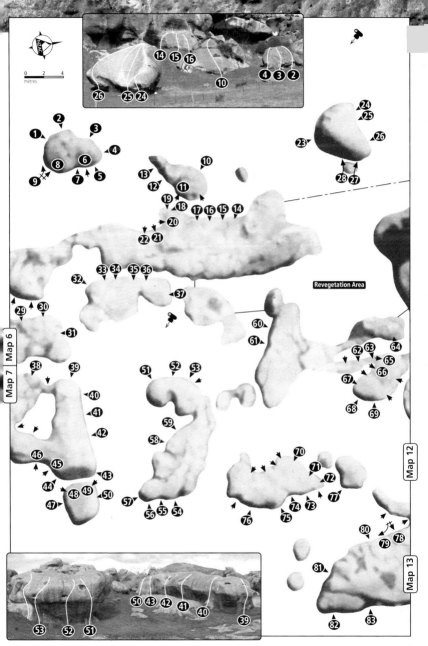

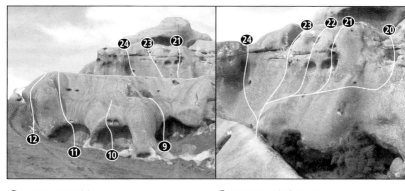

❶ ★ **V4 Hepatitis.** Jump to hold.
❷ **P** Long reaches.
❸ ★ **V6 The Package.** Awesome sloper.
❹ ★ **V5 Mirage.** Very slippery slopers.
❺ ✻ **V5 Prettier than a Snow Flake.** Slab
❻ **V4** Crack and smearing.
❼ **V4** Slab.
❽ ★ **V3** The groove to the top.
❾ ★ **V11 African Man Horse.** Over the lip.

❿ ✻ **V10 Leviathan.** Up the scoop.
⓫ ✻ **V8 Monkey and the Magic Peach.**
 Large scoop and groove.
⓬ ★ **V7 Coda.** Two big pockets on bulge.

The Eastern Front

The problems along this wall (apart from the *Highball Wall),* are all short and good for warm ups or fun easy climbing.

⓭ ★ **V5 Indecision.** Very slopey, smeary arête.
⓮ **V0** The single pocket.
⓯ ★ **V1** Smeary arête.
⓰ **V5 Bastard.** Crawl into the groove.
⓱ ★ **V3** Tenuous arête.
⓲ ✻ **V2 Crash Test.** Pockets and scary top.
⓳ ★ **21 Limestone Cowboy.** Crack to face.

Highball Wall

⓴ ★ **V4 Moonlight Drive.** Traverse right.
㉑ ✻ **V1 Leisure King.** Pockets to right.
㉒ ★ **V4 Lounge Lizard.** Freaky finish.
㉓ ✻ **V0 Lizard King.** Up the high slab.
㉔ ✻ **V2 Mojo Rising.** Up groove on left.
㉕ ✻ **V5 Joe 90.** Up the middle of face.
㉖ **V4 Get Some Lard In Ya.** Offwidth.
㉗ **V6 Superstition.** Tricky start.
㉘ ✻ **V2 Rimmer.** Big moves, good holds.
㉙ ★ **V5 Candy.** The pocketed groove.
㉚ ✻ **V1 Oxygen.** Line of pockets.
㉛ **P** Run and jump.
㉜ ★ **V4 Comet.** Jump up to jug.
㉝ ★ **V5 Black Hole.** Big crank up.

Jonathon Clearwater on the *Phoenix* (V7), Map 13
ANDRE DAHLMAN

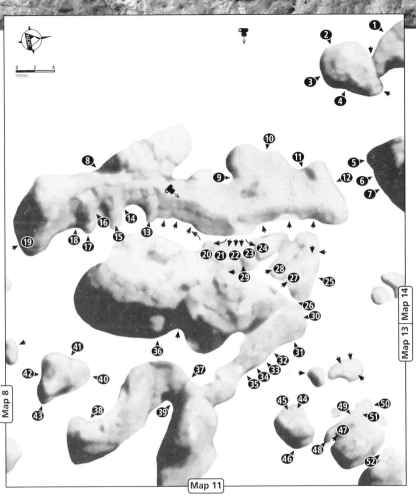

㉞	**V6**	**War Machine.** Mantle.	㊹	**V4**	**Curse of the Apocalypse Chicken.**
㉟	**V1**	Smear.	㊺ ★	**V0**	Jump to jug.
㊱	**V4**	**Short Circuit.** Small, slabby face.	㊻ ★	**V3**	**Boca Grande.** Travese right.
㊲	**V1**	Crack.	㊼	**V2**	Bridge.
㊳ ⚹	**V6**	**Hunchback.** Go right and up arête.	㊽ ★	**V4**	Arête.
㊴	**V3**	The right line of pockets.	㊾	**V3**	**Cavalier.** Mantle.
㊵	**V2**	Pocket.	㊿	**V5**	**Grindstone.** Jump to fat slopers.
㊶ ★	**V5**	**Mongrel Mob.** Into the scoop.	51 ⚹	**V0**	A boulder of three parts to the top.
㊷ ★	**V7**	**Phalanx.** Gain the pocket, mantle.	52 ⚹	**V4**	**The Great Chimney.** Long and
㊸ ★	**V6**	**Global Underground.** Tricky arête.			wide. Same down climb.

Quantum Field Map 11

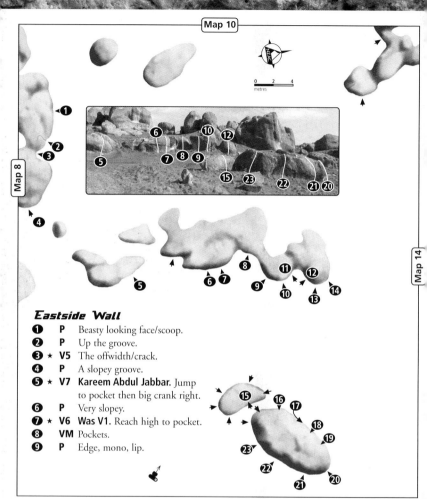

Eastside Wall

1   **P**   Beasty looking face/scoop.
2   **P**   Up the groove.
3   ★ **V5**   The offwidth/crack.
4   **P**   A slopey groove.
5   ★ **V7**   **Kareem Abdul Jabbar.** Jump to pocket then big crank right.
6   **P**   Very slopey.
7   ★ **V6**   **Was V1.** Reach high to pocket.
8   **VM**   Pockets.
9   **P**   Edge, mono, lip.

10   ★ **V7**   **Point Break.** Cranky moves on the bulging rock with pockets.
11   **V0**   Pockets.
12   **V0**   Pockets.
13   ★ **V2**   Pockets.
14   ★ **V1**   Pockets.

Eastside Boulder

15   **V2**   Edges up the face.

16   **V8**   **Top Gun.** A crimpy pull-on.
17   ✸ **V5**   Sit-start the crack. Traverse left.
18   **V1**   Rock-overs in pockets.
19   ✸ **V3**   Up the face with some pockets.
20   ★ **V4**   The arête.
21   ★ **V3**   Rock into the pocket. Nice ending.
22   ✸ **V4**   The layback thing. Interesting moves.
23   ★ **V3**   Faint groove on the face.

118

Lionel Clay *on Nether Edge* (21), Map 2
JOHN McCALLUM

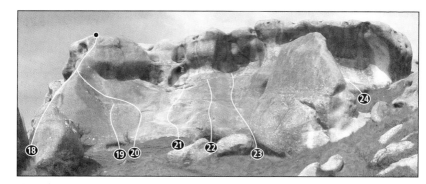

❶ **V3** Mantle.
❷ **V3** Layback and high-step.
❸ ★ **V3** **Zig Zag.** Wind up the beautiful wall.
❹ **V5** Slopey mantle.

The Great Weekender

By Chunky Farmer

Picton ferry. 1am. Steak & cheese pie was a bad idea. If the swell doesn't bring it up, the salty stench on the car deck will. Head lights on, gunning for Blenheim. Right to Paynes or left to Castle Hill? Left. Dead rabbits and service station coffee. Only 45 minutes 'til dawn.

Bright sun, nor'west arch and dust, dust, dust. How does the tussock survive this heat? Springfield for breakfast—not literally. Skid marks on Porter's Pass—another anxious climber? Or was it the pie?

Boulders, boulders, boulders, boulders. Elbows tense, the mind relaxes. 24 hours of heaven (and hell). Push me, pull me, small balls, big balls, one move wonder. Ticks or tests? Both. Did you bring the rope? Silly question.

Stiff and sore. Back hurts. Chest hurts. What chest? Refuelled and resigned to another day of second and third attempts. The cost/benefit analysis looks bleak—and then the sequence appears. As if by magic. More than I can handle now, yet it's never enough. Home! James.

Picton ferry. 1am. Work tomorrow. I'll sleep in the library and dream of nothing but…

---

❺ **V6** **Gibbosity.** The bulging arête thing.
❻ **V2** Long reach and mantle.
❼ **V5** Smear and bridge.
❽ ★ **V4** **Little Kid's Play Thing.** Corner.
❾ ★ **V2** Smear.
❿ ★ **V4** **Blancmange.** Smear up the wave.
⓫ ★ **V1** Smear up.
⓬ ✷ **V5** **Interjection.** Climb through scoop.
⓭ ★ **V2** Crank to hold.
⓮ ★ **22** **The Downtrodden.** Smeary arête.
⓯ **23** Up the groove.
⓰ **V4** Up to the scoop.
⓱ ★ **V1** High climbing up the slab.
⓲ ✷★ **17** **Shout to the Top.** Lovely arête.
⓳ ★ **V5** Delicate smearing.
⓴ ★ **20** **Slip up.** Up then join the arête.
㉑ ✷ **VM** **Broadwalk.** Easy long slab.
㉒ ★ **V3** **Palm d'Or.** Crux is a palm down.
㉓ ✷★ **V3** **Phil's Palm Down.** Smear and twist.
㉔ ★ **16** **General Ledger.** Left and into hole.
㉕ ★ **V3** Layback/smear.
㉖ ★ **V2** Reach the shallow pockets.
㉗ **V1** **Toilet Brush.** Sit start offwidth.
㉘ **V0** Mantle.
㉙ **V1** Mantle.
㉚ **V2** Mantle.
㉛ **V1** Pocket.
㉜ ★ **V3** **Popeye.** Up the small groove.
㉝ ★ **19** **James' Slab.** Long and run-out.
㉞ ★ **25** **The Black Vegetable.** Cruxy groove.
㉟ ★ **V5** **Wuspus.** Through the scoop.

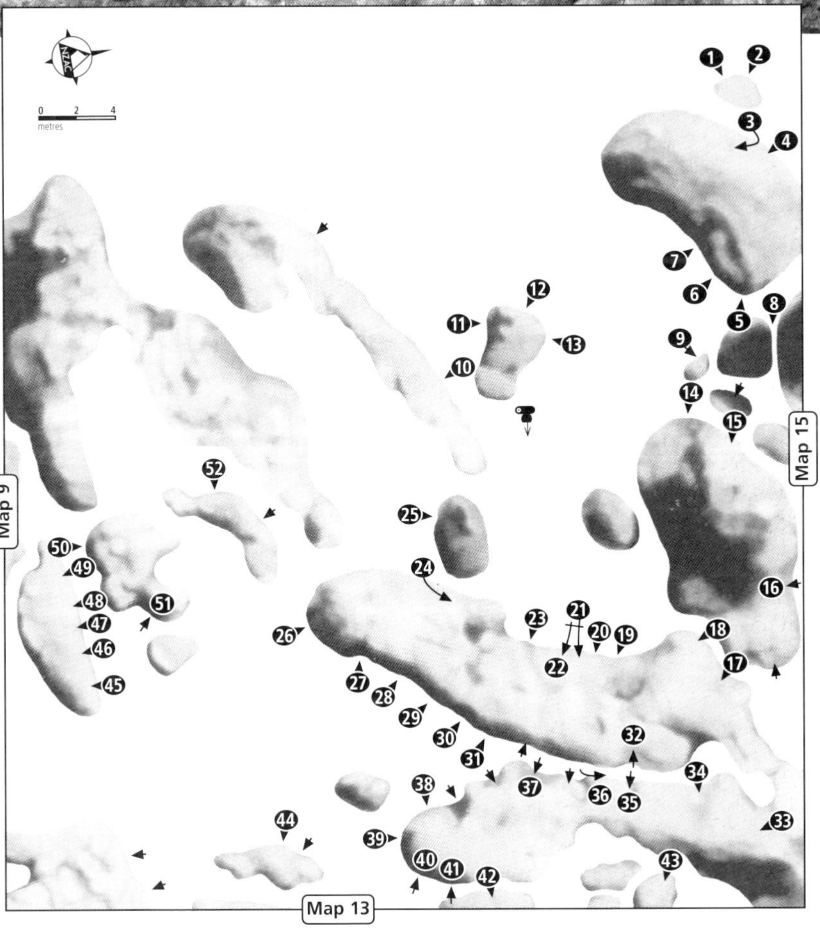

㊱ ★ **V7** **Glampus.** Traverse left, over bulge.

㊲ **V5** **Karate.** Slopers and bad feet.

㊳ ★ **V1** Up the slab.

㊴ ★★★ **V4** **Curvature.** Pockets straight up.

㊵ **V6** **The Force.** Edges up to slopes.

㊶ **V0** Pockets.

㊷ **V4** Crack.

㊸ ★★ **V3** **Body Bag.** Go bravely left up slab.

㊹ ★★★ **V6** **The Unrepeatable.** This is the one; the mantle test piece of Quantum.

㊺ ★ **V0** A smeary step-up.

㊻ ★★ **V5** **Sidetrack.** The groove.

㊼ ★ **V4** Start low and crank to the lip.

㊽ **V1** Start low on good holds.

㊾ ★ **V3** Rock-over into the single pocket.

㊿ **V7** Sit-start and grovel over the lip.

(51) **V1** Reach high and crank up.

(52) ★ **V3** **Slug.** Short and slopey.

'We may easily become physically strong, but as long as the spirit is weak the person is weak' Tadashi Nakamura.

Quantum Field Map 13

❶ ✳ **V4 Snail.** Static, smear/palm-down.
❷ **V11 Prototype.** Small two-finger pocket.
❸ ★ **V3** Sit-start the roof crack.
❹ ✳✳**V7 The Phoenix.** Very cool arête.
❺ **V7 Stoner.** Mantle into the groove.
❻ ★ **24 Second Floor.** Two cruxes.
❼ ✳ **V3 High Flyer.** The curving face.
❽ ★ **V3** Smear up the vague bulgy arête.
❾ **23 Mung Bean.** Through the scoop.
❿ ✳ **V4 Hot Spots.** Dyno right to big holds.
⓫ **V1** Bridge/smear.
⓬ **V1** Pockets.
⓭ ★ **V8 Dismantle.** Sloper to sloper.
⓮ **V5 Van Damme.** Short but blank.
⓯ ★ **V3** Mantle.
⓰ ✳✳**V1 Henry Moore.** Line of pockets.
⓱ ★ **V1** Pockets.
⓲ **V3 Doph Doph Music.** Hop onto it.
⓳ ★ **V12 Cold Fusion.** Very slopey pockets.
⓴ ★ **V6 Rocket Pants.** Dyno to sloper.
㉑ ★ **V6 Seppuku.** Very high leg kick up.
㉒ ★ **V1** Jump to jug.

Project Wall

㉓ ✳✳**V9 Energy Follows Thought.** Pockets.
㉔ ✳ **V7 Oil.** Slopey finish out right.
㉕ ★ **V7 Finger Monster.** Top-out left.
㉖ ✳ **V6 Ape.** Directly to the bad pockets.
㉗ ✳ **V9 Snake Eyes.** Drift right and up.
㉘ **V9 The Secret of Slow Twitch Motion.**
㉙ **V4 New Electra.** Short arête.
㉚ ★ **V6** Bridge and smear up the groove.
㉛ ★ **V4** Mantle.
㉜ ✳ **V3 The Curse.** Short slab with lip.
㉝ **V2** Committing step-up.
㉞ ★ **V1 Traffic Arête.** The arête.
㉟ **V1** Jump, then jug haul.

㊱ ★ **V5 Deliverance.** Strenuous top-out.
㊲ **V4** Sidepull dyno right to pocket.
㊳ ✳ **VM Biggles.** Nice smearing.
㊴ ✳ **V3 Top Heavy.** The arête with groove.
㊵ ★ **V6 Future Proof.** Crank to slopey lip.
㊶ **V6 Snakeoid.** Tricky start off the stone.
㊷ ★ **V2 Bad Ass Lawyer.** Up pockets.
㊸ ★ **V5 Land of Plenty.** Dyno or static.
㊹ **V11 Legion.** Sit-start to tiny holds.
㊺ ✳ **V5 Oracle.** Go left then crank up.
㊻ ★ **V5** Bridge then slopey top-out.
㊼ **V7 Aki.** Use a pinky in the small pocket.
㊽ ★ **V4 Hepatitis.** Jump to jug, up slab.
㊾ ★ **V5** Delicate slab.

Bonsai Boulder

㊿ ✳ **V4 Right Wing.** Face with pockets.
51 ✳ **V3 Left Wing.** Face, drift left.
52 **V6 Jihad.** Undercling/layback.
53 ✳✳**VE Bonsai.** Nice big pockets.
54 **V6 Trash.** Hard with bad foot holds.
55 **V6 Something Short.** High-step.
56 ★ **V5** Sloper start to good pocket.

The Cauldron

57 ✳ **V4 The Cauldron.** Bridge the scoop.
58 ✳ **V6 The Sorcerers Apprentice.** Go left.
59 ★ **V5 Frictionless.** Slither left.
60 **V5 The Savage.** Hug the vague arête.
61 **V5** Awkward mantle.
62 ★ **V0** Head right to high jugs.
63 ✳ **V4 Milk.** Traverse crack from the right.
64 ✳✳**V5 Cream.** The scoop and wild lip.
65 **V6 Hello Jug.** Steep and bulgy.
66 ✳ **V3** Traverse left then up slab.
67 ★ **V1 Right Buttock.** Up scoop.
68 ✳ **V3 Left Buttock.** Up scoop.
69 **V3** Grope the slopers.

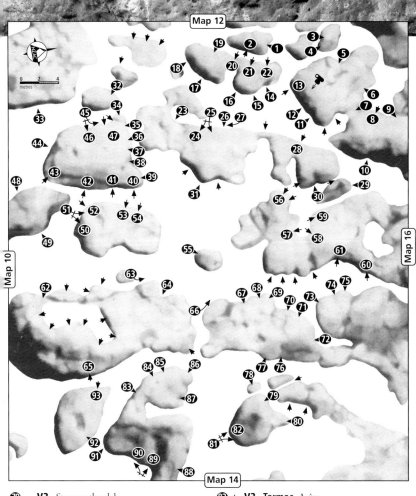

Map 12

Map 10

Map 16

Map 14

70	**V3**	Step on the slab.	
71	★ **V4**	**The Kelvinator.** Run and jump.	
72	✹✹ **V3**	**Bliss.** A delightful Slab.	
73	★ **V7**	**Funky Charmer.** The vague arête.	
74	★ **V1**	Mantle.	
75	**V1**	Edges to slab.	
76	★ **V2**	Jump to pocket.	
77	**V3**	**Sneaky.** Couple of nice smears.	
78	✹ **V0**	**The Red Carpet.** A nice slab.	
79	★ **V5**	**Saucy.** Smeary slab.	
80	★ **V2**	Slab.	
81	★ **V2**	**Sussex Sidestep.** Right to crux end.	

82	★ **V3**	**Tarmac.** Arête.
83	★ **V4**	The overhanging crack.
84	**V6**	**Walrus.** Mantle over slopey lip.
85	✹ **V4**	**Whale.** Start low in scoop.
86	★ **V6**	**Spanner.** Up the yellow rock.
87	✹✹ **V4**	**Old Chimney.** The groove.
88	★ **V7**	**Wax on Wax off.** Jump into scoop.
89	✹ **V3**	Up face then safe, high top-out.
90	★ **V6**	**Ice.** Very difficult smearing left.
91	★ **V6**	**The Big, the Bad and the Ugly.**
92	**V6**	**Cat Food.** Scrape over the bulge.
93	**V1**	**Alaskan Man Whore.** Jugs.

1   P   Mount the bulge.

2 ★ V3   Mantle the big edge.

3 ★ V1   Bridge/mantle.

4   V1   Jump to jug.

5 ★ V7   **Travelling Around the World at the Speed of Sound.** Dyno to sloper.

6   V0   Mantle.

7   V1   Reach high to sloper.

8   V6   **The Village Bicycle.** Slopey edges.

9   V2   Into scoop.

10 ✹ V1   Slab.

11 ✹ V2   Slab.

12 ★ V5   **Village Idiot.** Scoop to high slab.

13   P   Silly overhanging lip.

14 ★ V9   **Maya.** Jump and then campus.

15   V8   **Aztec.** Long reach to hold.

16 ★ V8   **Inca.** Dyno far to hold.

17   P   Over bulge on slopers.

18   P   Traverse and dyno right.

19   V0   Pockets.

20 ★ 24   **Pathetic Gropes.** To the arête.

21 ✹ 26   **My Feet are my Friends.** Groove.

Caffeine Wall

22 ★ V5   **Decaf Soy Latte.** Nice slab.

23   V9   **Piccalo.** Lots of tiny dimples.

24   V8   **Robusta.** Undercling to dimples.

25 ★ V4   **Hop into palming the scoop.

26   V0   Through the scoop.

27   V7   **Arabica.** Crank up and high-step.

28 ★ V5   **Turkish.** Jump to jug.

29 ✹ V6   **Short Black.** Crank to lip, mantle.

30 ✹ V7   **Double Espresso.** Rock up pockets and dyno up high to mega jug.

31 ★ V11 **Ristretto.** Tiny pockets. Big moves.

32   V5   Sit-start the arête.

Ring Finger Wall

33   V2   Slopey edges.

34   V0   Reach back the good holds.

35   V1   Long reach.

36 ★ V3   Arête.

37   P   Pocket then shallow groove.

38 ✹ V3   Through scoop.

39 ★ V2   Layback.

40   V6   **Rhythm and Stealth.** Edgy face.

41 ★ V2   Small pockets.

42   V5   Small pockets.

43   V4   **Zoom.** Small holds and then jug.

44 ★ V2   Long reach to pocket.

45 ★ V1   Into scoop.

46   V1   Pockets.

47   V1   Pockets.

48   V0   Mantle.

Index Finger Wall

49 ★ V2   Pockets.

50 ✹ V2   Small then large pockets.

51 ★ V5   Another line of pockets.

52 ★ V5   Edges and pockets.

53 ✹ V3   Jump to pocket.

54 ✹ V2   Line of pockets.

55 ✹ V5   Go right to pockets.

56 ★ V1   Reach high to big pockets.

57 ★ V1   Pockets.

58 ★ V2   Pockets.

59   V5   **South Side.** A bit slopey.

60 ★ 20   **Floppy Banana.** The pocketed face.

61   VM   Slab with pockets.

62   VM   Slab with pockets.

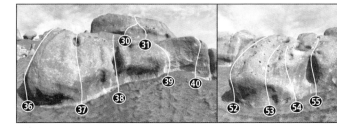

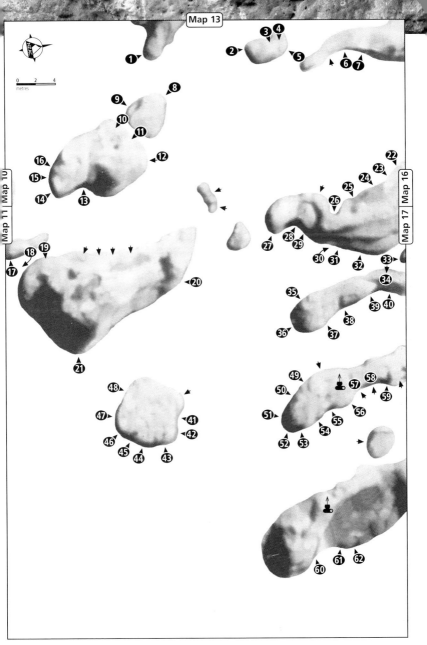

Map 13

Map 11 | Map 10

Map 17 | Map 16

1	**V2**	High reach.
2	**V4**	Tricky top.
3	✹**V6**	**Midnight Milk.** Pull over lip. SSV9.
4	✹ **V7**	**Monkey See Monkey Do.** Ooze up the arête and exit out right.
5	★ **V3**	Crank or hop to hold.
6	★ **V4**	Jump to hold.
7	★ **29**	**Pumpkin.** Right side of the face.
8	**25**	**Strangers on Journeys.** Face.
9	✹ **24**	**Subculture.** Excellent face climbing.
10	**21**	**Voodoo Child.** Right of the arch.
11	★ **21**	**The Arch Route.** Through the arch and exit out right.
12	**22**	**Two Eyed Sloth.** Top-rope the arête.
13	**19**	**Weasel.** Next to the cave/corner.
14	**V1**	Up the slot/crack.
15	★ **20**	**Viola.** The curving small slab.
16	✹ **V3**	The crack and chimney.
17	★ **15**	**Cold Ethyl.** Left up the slab.
18	**13**	Up the right side of the slab.
19	★ **VM**	The right arête.
20	✹ **V0**	Up the middle of the slab.
21	**V1**	Smear leftwards up the slab.
22	★ **V2**	**Elvis Died for Our Sins.** Arête/face.
23	✹ **V1**	**Scully's New House.** Groove.
24	★ **12**	**Love Buckets.** Slab with pockets.
25	★ **V0**	Long slab with big pockets.
26	**21**	**Slap and Tickle.** Slabby arête.
27	**V1**	Tricky start.
28	**P**	Blank slab.
29	✹**V1**	Beautiful layback.
30	✹ **V2**	The wide groove.
31	✹ **VM**	Into scoop then up.
32	✹ **V3**	High step-up.
33	★ **VM**	Big holds, up then left.
34	★ **V4**	High step-up.
35	★ **V1**	Up the middle of the face.
36	✹ **VM**	**Stairway.** Smear out left.
37	**V7**	**Quandary.** The lip and slab.
38	**V7**	**Alloy.** A fingery step-up.
39	★ **V2**	Work your feet into pocket.
40	**V2**	Across the scoop.
41	★ **V3**	Smear and palm down.
42	★ **V3**	Mantle.
43	**V5**	**Leper.** Small disappearing holds.
44	**V2**	Reach left then up.
45	**V3**	Fingery slab.
46	✹ **VM**	**Arm Chair.** The fun mantle.

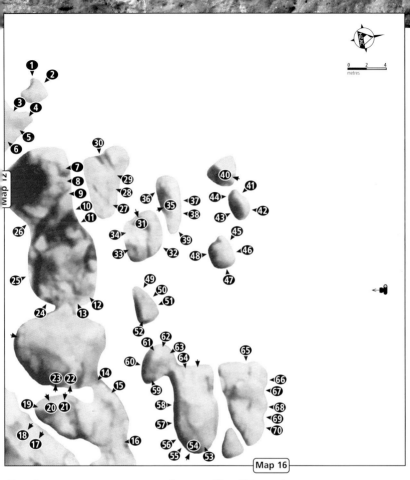

Map 16

47	**P**	From scoop to mono to mantle.
48 ★	**V6**	**Breasty Dumpling.** Pinch the…
49 ★	**V0**	Go rightwards up the slab.
50 ✹	**V2**	The slab with small holds.
51	**V6**	**Lorax.** Hop start and put foot up.
52 ★	**V0**	Arête.
53 ★	**V3**	Step high then pull over.
54	**V6**	**Super Shifter.** Sidepulls and mantle.
55 ★	**V3**	Start from small boulder.
56	**V6**	**Swing.** Undercling and sloper.
57 ★	**V2**	Slopey foot holds.
58 ★	**V2**	High reach.

59	**V5**	Mantle.
60	**V3**	Arête.
61	**V4**	**Dancing With the Devil.** Devious.
62 ★	**V1**	**Geng Kian Waan.** Up the face.
63	**V1**	Start from left or right.
64	**V4**	Up the right side of the face.
65 ✹★	**V4**	**Think Tank.** The scoop classic.
66 ★	**V1**	Arête.
67 ✹	**VM**	**Think.** Easy slab up wide groove.
68 ★	**V3**	Tricky start then high-step.
69 ✹	**VM**	Smeary groove.
70	**V3**	**Compost.** Slab with small holds.

127

Quantum Field Map 16

❶   21   **Lonesome Cowboy.** Traverse left.

❷   V5   **Jonho.** Round arête.

❸ ★ V6   **Honjo.** Up the face in the gully.

❹   V3   Angular holds, head right.

❺ ★ 18   **Phil McKrakin.** Rap to the crack.

❻ ★ V5   **Jesus I was Evil.** Underclings.

❼ ★ 18   **The Yellow Peril.** The blocky wall.

❽   V2   High step-up.

❾   V2   Pockets and palm-down.

❿   V2   Reach back to good holds.

⓫   V2   Arête.

⓬   V2   Good holds, strange position.

⓭ ✸✸ V5   **Dominatrix.** Awesome cranks. SSV7.

⓮ ★ V4   Mantle or go right.

⓯ ✸✸ V4   Up slab. Use start stone.

⓰   V8   **Ming the Repugnant.** Use elbows.

⓱ ★ V5   **Buster.** Mantle.

⓲ ★ V4   Mantle.

⓳   VM   Mantle.

⓴ ✸✸ V3   **The Regurgitator.** The offwidth.

㉑   P   The line of small pockets.

㉒ ★ 26   **The Haptic Channels.** The continuation to *Marmaduke*.

㉓ ★ 23   **Marmaduke Goes Chipping.** Face with flake. Finish at the 4th bolt.

㉔ ★ 27   **Chocolate Coated Razor Blades.** Eventually joins *Adios Gringos*.

㉕ ✸✸ 25   **Adios Gringos.** Classic face climb up the obvious streak.

㉖ ✸✸ 29   **Dance of Silence.** Blank wall/slab on the left side of the wall.

㉗   21   **Pete's Eats.** Up the groove.

㉘ ★ 18   **Epics Incorporated**. Low angle slab.

㉙ ★ V1   **Extrinsic.** Mantle over lip. Scary!

㉚ ✸✸ V5   **Cheese Grater.** Long slab.

㉛   V7   **Uncle Sams Safe Smacker.** The low traverse going right.

Headlights Boulder

㉜ ★ V4   **Jenny Craig.** Trend left.

㉝ ★ V4   **Takaka Death Trip.** Narrow face.

㉞ ✸✸ V7   **Crimp Operator.** Right side of face.

㉟ ✸✸ V5   **Right Taillight.** Steep slab.

㊱ ✸✸ V4   **Left Taillight.** Classic. Head left.

㊲ ★ V1   Grovel up the chimney.

㊳ ✸✸ V10   **Crash and Burn.** Right up arête.

㊴ ✸✸ V4   **Right Headlight.** Fun climbing.

㊵ ✸✸ V7   **Fender Bender.** Dyno to pocket.

㊶ ✸✸ V4   **Left Headlight.** Straight up.

㊷ ✸✸ V7   **Spirulina.** Traverse from the left.

㊸   V3   Slopey holds and onto arête.

㊹   25   **Ramases Nibblick.** Slabby face.

㊺ ★ 14   **Good Girls Spit.** A pleasant slab.

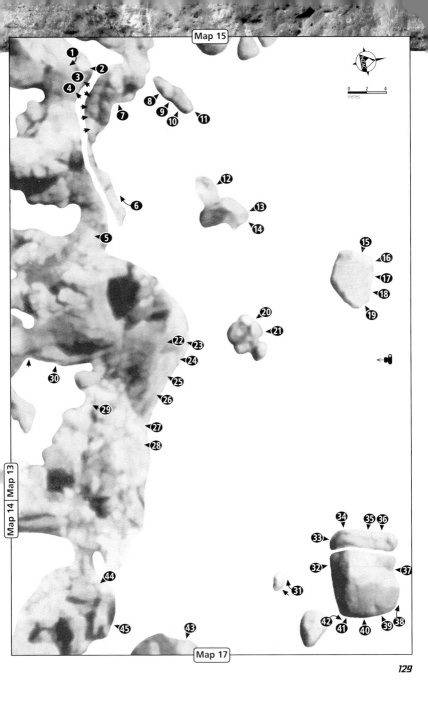

Map 15

Map 17

Map 13

Map 14

Quantum Field Map 17

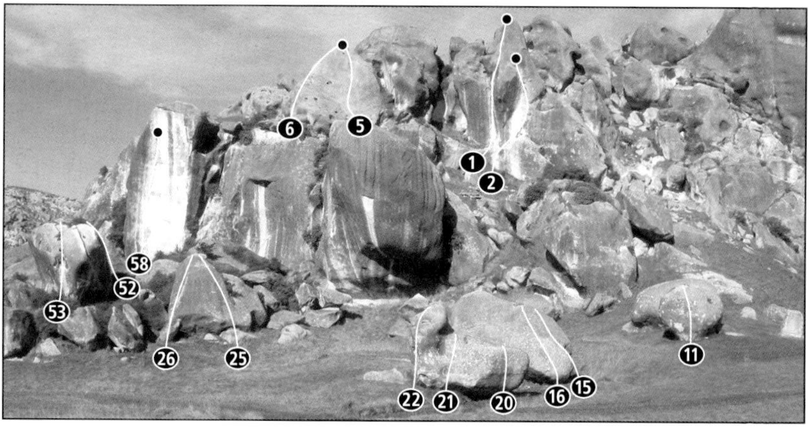

❶ ★★ **26** **Gascrankinstation.** Beasty edgy face.
❷ ★★ **22** **Bad Boys Always Swallow.** Face.
❸ ★ **V3** Pockets up the lower wall.
❹ **P** Crimpy face.
❺ ★★★ **17** **On Some Faraway Beach.** Slab.
❻ ★ **14** **Girls Just Wanna Have Fun.** Arête.
❼ ★ **V0** The tasty crack.
❽ ★ **V3** **Heave Ho!** One hard move.
❾ **V2** Don't bridge.
❿ **V2** Jump to holds.
⓫ **V5** Rounded face.
⓬ **V6** **Steve's.** One very big crank.

Waterworks Boulder

The following four boulders are accessed from the steam via stepping stones.

⓭ **P** Climb left and around.
⓮ ★★ **V5** **Gas Man.** Groove to sidepull.
⓯ **P** Up the undercling.
⓰ ★★★ **V3** **Hydroslide.** Slab.
⓱ **V5** Smeary arête.
⓲ **V5** **Vertex.** Pockets.
⓳ **V2** **Slippery When Wet.** Nice rock-over.
⓴ **P** Start from the stream.
㉑ ★ **V1** Bridge, smear or mantle.
㉒ **V1** Nice moves up arête.
㉓ **VM** Pocket and smear up.
㉔ **V0** Slab.
㉕ ★ **V4** **Side Show Slab.** Right side of slab.
㉖ ★★ **V7** **Ebb and Flow.** Span the wide arête.
㉗ **V1** A weird start with some holds.
㉘ **V1** The short crack thing.
㉙ ★ **V5** **Cannibalism.** Balancy climbing.
㉚ ★ **V2** Mantle.
㉛ **P** Jump to horrible slopers.
㉜ **P** Slap as you have never slapped before.
㉝ **V0** Mantle.
㉞ **V1** Smeary arête.
㉟ **V2** Face.
㊱ **V1** Mantle.
㊲ **P** Monster crank to small pocket.
㊳ ★ **V4** Line of pockets.
㊴ **V2** Big pockets on lip.
㊵ ★ **V6** **Boone's Dyno.** Dyno up face.
㊶ **V1** **Sand Bag.** Monos to lip. SSV8.
㊷ **V1** Jump to jug.
㊸ **V0** Edges and rock-over.
㊹ **VM** Face.
㊺ ★ **V2** Corner.
㊻ ★ **V4** **Liver and Bacon.** Face to arête.
㊼ ★★ **V2** **Tofu and Sprouts.** The arête.
㊽ ★ **V1** **Dirt Bag.** Grovel up the chimney.
㊾ ★★ **V5** **Petrol.** Jump to slopers.
㊿ ★ **V6** **Diesel.** Undercling the big hole.

Death Boulder

(51) ★★ **V0** **Lesbian Seagull.** Hard arête.
(52) ★★ **V4** **You Make Me Wear Dresses.** Slab.

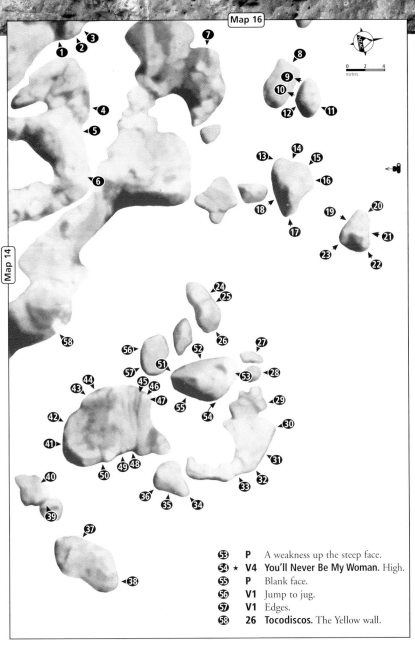

Map 16

Map 14

53	**P**	A weakness up the steep face.
54 ★	**V4**	**You'll Never Be My Woman.** High.
55	**P**	Blank face.
56	**V1**	Jump to jug.
57	**V1**	Edges.
58	**26**	**Tocodiscos.** The Yellow wall.

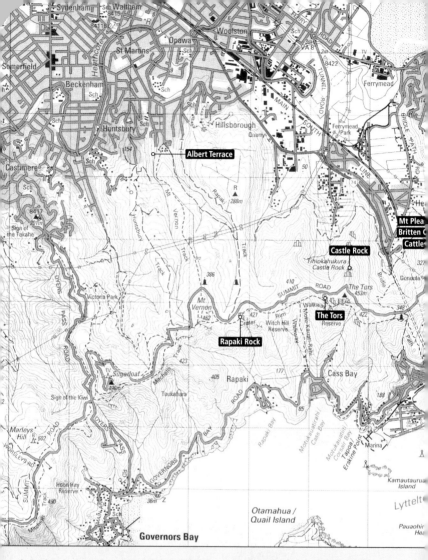

Christchurch city is framed by the Port Hills, the northern edge of an old volcanic crater. The rock offers a broad range of climbing, from older style trad and sport routes (Castle Rock, Lyttelton Rock, The Tors) through to modern sport crags (Britten Crag, The Cave). There are a few great beginner areas, which cater for both trad and sport climbers (Rapaki Rock, Albert Terrace). As well as there being a good spread of grades between the crags, you'll find that they have very different characters and are suitable for various weather conditions. The sheer number of routes makes climbing in Christchurch diverse, handy and never boring.

Port Hills

Christchurch is home to the largest rockclimbing population in the South Island. While it is never over crowded, on most sunny days you'll find at least a few parties at the major crags. While not all the routes on the Port Hills are classic or on excellent rock, you will find special gems at each crag. This makes it important to keep exploring and check out different areas.

There are many minor crags not included in this guide. For more information on these see *Port Hills Climbing* by Lindsay Main.

2 mins

The only suburban crag in Christchurch, Albert Terrace is a recent addition to the Port Hills collection. The positive holds and thought-provoking moves make this little basalt wall an excellent transition from the gym to the rock. With good double bolt anchors on all climbs, this is an excellent top-rope arena and the bolts are well spaced for first leads.

Most climbs were established in 1997 by Ross Cullen and Rob Blackburne as trad routes. They have since been retro-bolted which has vastly increased their usability. This guide covers the bolted lines on the best wall of this crag. The other trad lines are poorly protected, often on friable rock.

At the main roundabout on Centaurus Rd in St Martins, turn into Albert Terrace. Follow this to the end and park before the gate. The crag is visible from here.

From the car park, follow the valley track to the bushy gully.

i This is a user-friendly sport crag, and is not too gear intensive. You will need about 7 quickdraws, gear for top-roping and a rope-tarp.

If you are setting up top-ropes, run the rope through your own carabiners rather than through the anchor rings to help reduce wear.

❶ ★19 Peggy Peggy Phew 11m
2 Climb onto the big ledge and clip carefully. Move through the crux on thin holds with delicate footwork. From the 2nd bolt continue up the flake to the anchor. *Paul Roberts 1997*

❷ 14 Quacker 11m
4 A blocky start takes you to a juggy slab. *Ross Cullen 1997*

❸ 13 Defenced 11m
3 Up a ledge system to the 1st bolt and through the central gully line. *Ross Cullen 1997*

❹ 14 Kinny 11m
5 Through two bulges with tenacious moves between the 3rd and 4th bolts. *Ross Cullen 1997*

❺ ★15 Itbeckonstan 11m
4 Follow the juggy holds left of the cave. Resist the temptation to duck for cover, instead rock across the roof and run up the slab. *Ross Cullen 1997*

❻ 14 Ramahana Road 11m
5 Climb past the right side of the cave on a slab with positive holds. A little feisty at the top. *Ross Cullen 1997*

❼ 14 50 Cents Worth 10m
5 An ex-trad line, now well-bolted. Move into the left-leaning crack and luxuriate in undercling and layback moves. *Ross Cullen 1997*

❽ 13 Kopus Edge 10m
4 A pleasant arête, but watch some of the blocks. *Rob Blackburne 1997*

❾ 13 Chinese Ladder 10m
5 A nice line up incuts in the centre of the face. A bouldery start to the 1st bolt. *Ross Cullen 1997*

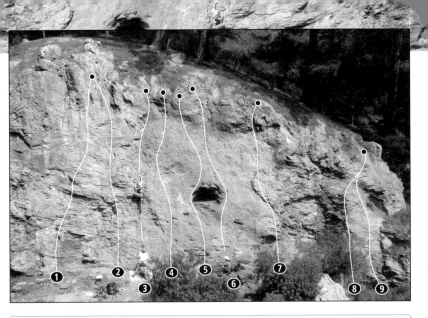

For one university paper I researched the practices of new route developers and the arguments they make to justify these practices. Three predominant styles of new route developer based on their preferred practices were distinguished.

The Explorer cleans quickly and spasmodically and is most reluctant to chip climbs, but will usually remove large loose blocks. Bolts are useful but expensive and are usually tailored to the first ascentionists needs. Indeed, if you can get away without them, it saves time and allows more routes to be developed. However, it is sometimes difficult to think up names for all those esoteric gems, and time is precious because there are lots of other adventurous places and pursuits to explore.

The Fanatic began to emerge in the early eighties and is easily distinguished by a more persistent focus on one sport at a time. Initially this was rockclimbing but further specialisms of style, angle, rock and hold type (e.g. slopey boulder problems or thuggy sport routes) may become the focus for the same person at different times. The eagerness to uncover perfect rock can result in deforestation on a massive scale and hard climbs require very clean holds. Most 'fanatics' are against chipping, especially the short-sighted improvement of single holds on cruxy routes. However, a line of completely manufactured holds on a blank roof may be more acceptable, particularly if it's pushing standards. Lack of bolts and under-grading may help to create mystique, which is reinforced by obscure and intimidating naming and, for this reason, they seldom favour retro-bolting.

The Best Selling Author gained prominence when the electric drill appeared. The emphasis shifted to seeing how many people you could get to do your route, rather than how many you could scare off. Cleaning and bolting routes became a fine art and these artworks required thoughtful naming and lots of word-of-mouth publicity. Although chipping is mostly deplored by this group, sharp holds may be comfortised and a classic 22 with short grade 28 crux might be improved to make the climb more continuously classic. 'The best selling authors' are more likely to equate safety with quality arguing that only the best bolting technology be used for new retro-bolting of classic lines.

These new routing styles reflect an emphasis on quantity, difficulty and quality respectively and routes can often co-exist at a particular crag. It is, therefore, important to know the predominant style of the developer who designed the experience that you are about to undertake. It's probably wise not to try busting your first grade 24 lead on a Fearnley route, but if you have a sense of history and a cool head, it may be just the ticket.

Roland Foster

Rapaki Rock

1 ★ 13 Left Arête
2 16 Left Face
3 ★ 12 Crow's Nest
4 ★ 16 Face
5 ★ 14 Barricoe
6 ★ 16 Bosun's Chair
7 ★ 12 Ratlines
8 14 Fo'c'sle
9 ★★ 13 Scurvy
10 ★ 13 Monkey Poop
11 ★ 23 Penile Decay
12 ★ 16 Galley Gully

Rapaki Rock is a crescent-shaped dome on the Summit Road, and is probably New Zealand's most climbed crag. Although top-roped by all 'n' sundry from the Scouts to the Army, most climbs make very good leads. The rock is quite unique and some of the best climbs have weird and wonderful geological features to negotiate.

⑬ ★ **22 The Bridge Too Far**
⑭ ⚹⚹ **18 Spinnaker**
⑮ ★ **16 Forecourse**
⑯ ⚹⚹ **16 Main Royale**
⑰ ⚹⚹ **17 Yardarm**
⑱ **17 Mizzen**
⑲ **22 Freakey's Wall**
⑳ ★ **19 Body and Soul**
㉑ **19 Dr Rock and the
Carbo Kid**
㉒ **15 Bilge**
㉓ ⚹⚹ **14 Flying Jib**

Rapaki Rock

From the Sign of the Kiwi, turn left onto the Summit Rd. You will see the crag after about 6km at the top of Rapaki Track. There is a car park on the right side of the road.

All climbs use natural protection and the anchors consist of big blocks at the top of the crag. Apart from a standard rack, long slings for the anchors are useful and these may need to be extended a few metres for top-roping.

The descent off the crag is straightforward at both ends, but it may be more efficient to set up a separate abseil rope to service several climbs at once.

❶ ★13 Left Arête 17m
At the left extremity of the crag, this three tiered arête is nice climbing. There are plenty of solid options for gear, so best refrain from using the hollow blocks.

❷ 16 Left Face 16m
A great looking face with intriguing climbing and pro that needs some thought.

❸ ★12 Crow's Nest 16m
Climb over the blocks and past the cave into a hideaway scoop. Have a breather, place some cams and launch into the mantle finish.

❹ ★16 Face 16m
Easy ground gives way to nifty slab moves. The well protected top-out is definitely exciting.

❺ ★14 Barricoe 15m
Scramble up to the roof. The enticing crack is short 'n' sweet.

❻ ★16 Bosun's Chair 16m
A crack of two halves—easy up to a great wire and funky moves through the crux to a vegetated rest. A #5 camalot can protect the crux, otherwise enjoy a little exhilaration. Follow the right leading crack to victory.

❼ ★12 Ratlines 14m
After the flared crack at the base, this climb follows two parallel cracks separated by a block. It is varied climbing that can be well-protected with big gear (up to a #4 cam). Finish right, or take the harder direct finish (13) from the flake.

❽ 14 Fo'c'sle 18m
Tip toe up old graffiti on the slab to a rock protrusion. This square block is loose and should be avoided for pro. From the cave, take the right-leaning crack. Good fun.

The next 2 climbs are on either side of the big horizontal block:

❾ ✶13 Scurvy 18m
A charming, arced crack with sustained juggy climbing. It is a nice length and a recommended lead if you are just starting to place gear.

❿ ★13 Monkey Poop 17m
A tricky slab to start, but then move onto easy ground with better pro right of the nose. Trundle up the wide crack to finish.

⓫ ★23 Penile Decay 17m
Get your brain into gear for bizarre moves on slopers. From the 2nd bolt, drift right to the jug and rock delicately onto the arousing slab. *Steve Elder 1989*

⑫ ★16 Galley Gully 15m
Left-facing corner with nice bridging and finger jams. Once past the crack, step left and finish on easier ground.

⑬ ★22 The Bridge Too Far 16m
Tricky bridging and a couple of questionable pieces of gear lead to a crux with good pro. Pull over the bulge on slopey holds to a rest stance and ramble to the top. *John Howard 1980*

⑭ ✦18 Spinnaker 16m
Dance around the thin cracks using the slippery arête to get to the ledge. Climb the blotchy face into the groove and finish straight up. *Lindsay Main 1979*

⑮ ★16 Forecourse 18m
Start up the corner on the left side of the fractured face and go left to gain the holds. Move back into the central crack aiming for the intimidating overhang. Use the sneaky undercling to pull over the roof and breathe a sigh of relief.

⑯ ✦✦16 Main Royale 18m
Totally lounge—this classic is smack bang in the middle of the fractured face. Pretty fly through the roof too. Rest in the scoop and climb the roof through the middle crack.

⑰ ✦✦17 Yardarm 18m
A very impressive route through an Arapilesque arch. Head up the corner on the right side of the face to the thread. Once at the top of the arch step right onto the pillar and relish the solid rock and sensational holds. Otherwise keep following the arch to the easy crack.

⑱ 17 Mizzen 18m
A thin crack with a cave at the top. Begin up the rib where a thread through the small pillar helps to keep the pro in if you fumble the face. Follow the crack to the cave and finish out left on big holds and good pro.

⑲ 22 Freakey's Wall 18m
Start at the juggy dog-leg crack to an egg pod. Up the thin face to exit through the notch. Difficult climbing and marginal gear. *John Allen 1980*

⑳ ★19 Body and Soul 18m
A steep broken crack line which leads to a bulging top crux. Exciting! Crank on the horn, rock-over to juggy ground and ooh ooh ooooh. Do take cams. *Gavin Wills 1967*

㉑ 19 Dr Rock and the Carbo Kid 16m
Start up a broken crack on the slab and move through the bulge. Watch what you pull on and follow the right-leaning crack. *Dave MacLeod 1988*

㉒ 15 Bilge 15m
The bowels of this ship. Climb the boomerang-like chimney with some awkwardness. Move up to the roof and step left.

㉓ ✦✦14 Flying Jib 17m
Very elegant sailing up a curvaceous red slab with a crack. Exit right at the block.

> 'I think a lot about climbing still, but not during the daytime. I think about it mostly at night, and on special occasions. I think about climbing when I am fed up with life in general. When I wish I could go over to the rocks or the trees. I enjoy my dreams about climbing.' **Fritz Wiessner** after a stroke at 87.

The Tors

The Tors is an impressive plug of basalt that overlooks Cass Bay. It sports some very good routes and a day here can be happily spent warming up on some easy climbs at the left end and working your way around the pick of the lines. It has some long lines that are not as exposed as some of the classics at Castle Rock, but they are very good quality and seldom crowded.

 Follow the Summit Rd from Dyers Pass, past the Sugarloaf TV tower, Rapaki Rock and around a sweeping bend. The crag is on the right side of the Summit Rd and is very prominent on the sky line. Park just before the crag on the left.

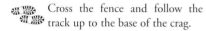 Cross the fence and follow the track up to the base of the crag.

i The blocks at the top are good for setting up anchors and it's easy to descend from both ends. Just take the usual rack and some long slings.

The crag faces south-west and is very cold in winter but is out of the sun for some of the day in summer when it is scorching on the Christchurch side of the Summit Rd. The wind tends to buffet the outcrop so be careful wandering around on the top.

❶ ★13 Pantagruel 12m

Climb the slabby corner to a little garden then bridge up steepening ground. *Ross Gooder 1970*

❷ 17 No Nirvanas 12m

Doddle up the vegetated corner to the arête at half-height, where the fun kicks in. Nice climbing left of the block. *Lindsay Main 1977*

❸ 17 Smaug 12m

RPs are essential to protect this thin crack (if they hold). Easy climbing up the slab culminates in two edgy moves to gain the block. From here the gear is good. *Ross Gooder 1970*

❹ ★10 Mr Baggins 14m

Generous holds for hobbit hands. The crack up the middle of the face has enough gear for all the Shire.

❺ ★10 Gollum 14m

No fishies on this one, but you might find a pideon preciousss. Slither up the left-facing corner. Suprisingly good holds and gear. *Ross Gooder 1970*

❻ 16 Gumbo 16m

Follow the curvy crack over the bulge to the jumble of dodgy-looking blocks. These seem to be fairly stuck, but negotiate them with caution. *Lindsay Main 1977*

❼ ✷19 Future Legend 16m

Done back in the day when few people were climbing 19, this route was a precursor of things to come. Doddle to the bulge and haul into the V-corner. A gripping traverse on underclings and tenuous smears takes you to success around the corner. Small cams are useful (sub #1). *John Allen 1977*

❽ ★26 Someone Else's Girl 16m

A short climb with staunch crimpy moves. Rock up the slab to the overbearing face. Put pedal to the metal and climb the left side of the face. *Tony Ward-Homes 1993*

❾ ★15 Crapbreech 16m

A wide crack (way more elegant than its name) that climbs on juggy and positive face holds. A couple of big cams are useful and hexes would work a treat. *James Jenkins 1973*

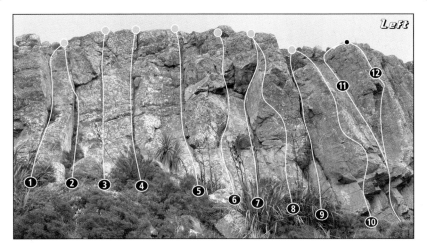

Left

⑩ ★18 DIY 16m

Take your tool box, but you may not find much use for it. This line up the prow is very attractive and climbs well, but with marginal gear you will want to be solid. No one likes a DIY disaster! *John Allen 1979*

⑪ ✷17 Hotlegs 18m

One of Ross's crowning achievements, and a much loved favourite for many climbers. Strenuous moves through the roof to a left-facing crack with excessive pro possibilities. *Ross Gooder 1970*

⑫ 20 Mirage 18m

Start as for *Hotlegs* and place a high runner to protect the next section. Bridge up the corner and clip the old piton. Commit and pull over on jugs. *Lindsay Main 1982*

⑬ ✷21 Collateral Damage 18m

3 Boulder up to the roof and reach over to clip the 1st bolt. Traverse left on cruxy underclings and slopers to a good stance. The climb continues up the stunning arête with an optional small-medium wire. *Lindsay Main 1996*

'*Moss Guard*, just right of *Nudity*, was climbed by John Allen who spent about an hour going up fiddling with pro, climbing down for a rest and so on. John Howard's belaying, but he hates that sort of mucking around and so he's fully asleep (he'd just done the 1st ascent of Porno without troubling his belayer since he didn't place any pro at all). Finally John yells out 'I'm going to do it this time, look out,' so Howard just pays out metres of slack and goes back to sleep. John lurches up the crux past the crappy wire without noticing the huge loop of rope hanging uselessly to the ground. John H could be pretty slack, but he would've only paid out a bit of rope for anyone else. He knew as well as anyone that once John said he was going to go it was pretty much in the bag, that all the rest was just connoisseuring the route, building up the tension and savoring the moment.'
Dave Fearnley in *Climber* 24, p.31.

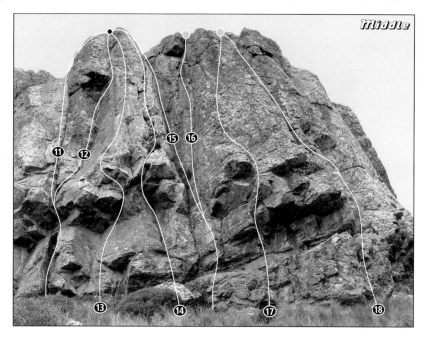

Middle

⑭ ★21 Cat's Cradle 18m

An absorbing climb. First off, bridge up the smooth corner to steep jugs with fiddly gear. After lovely moves through the crux find a rest ledge. The second phase of the climb takes you through fat cracks with bomber gear. *Lindsay Main 1978*

⑮ 16 Gargantua 18m

This climb has got a bit harder in recent years due to some polished holds. It's still good, but the gear placements may need some excavation in the upper section. The crux is accessing the crack at the bottom. This can be tackled from the right (easiest) or straight through the guts. *Ross Gooder 1970*

⑯ ★17 Exposition Crack 18m

A delightful crack. From *Gargantua,* branch right and following the crack onto the face. Good stances, positive holds, great gear, sunshine, views …mmm. *Lindsay Main 1973*

⑰ ★22 Porno 18m

No filth here—just some antics. Crank past the bolt to stimulating climbing on the face above. The abundance of marginal wires and slings will surely amount to something? The original line started up *Exposition Crack* and moved right onto the face. *John Howard 1979. Direct start Tony Ward-Homes 1999*

Right

⑱ ★15 Jambilicus 18m

Start left of *Nudity*. Once 5m up, traverse some airy terrain to reach the crack. Once established here, the line is totally enjoyable, and the nubbins of rock are way cool. *Henry Mares 1977*

⑲ ★★20 Nudity 18m

A leggy route with smooth thighs. The placements tend to be slightly flared and suit small cams (#0.5 and smaller) more than wires. It's a tad easier if you take a breather after the crux on the pedestal. *John Allen 1977*

⑳ ★22 Lickedy Splat 17m

A great looking arête, which climbs well, but contains jeopardy. A steep and unprotected start leads to some gear before the top. *Steve Elder 1989*

㉑ ★22 Moss Guard 17m

Climbs through the middle of the slabby face with nasty gear. After the short bulgy, veer left up the face. *John Allen 1979*

㉒ 17 Gormenghast 15m

A thoroughly enjoyable, leaning corner perched on its own at the right end of the crag. Mostly face climbing with great pro. *Lindsay Main 1977*

'A hex is a man's gift, son. Cams are for poofters and Communists'

Castle Rock

AJ Beaumont on *Gibbet* (18)
CRAIG BUCKLAND/INSPIRED PHOTOGRAPHY

Castle Rock is a striking prow that overlooks the Heathcote Valley. It is the original Christchurch alpine climber's training ground and was the scene of some of the earliest rock ascents in New Zealand. The awesome combination of exposure and great gear on most of the classics still makes this a very popular place on a sunny weekend day.

Geologically speaking, this is one of the best examples of the volcanic dykes that scatter the Port Hills. These dykes point towards the eroded summit of the Lyttelton Volcano and were formed when pressure split the main ridges. Magma was forced into the vertical cracks and if it wasn't fluid, it swelled out to form domes of rock, like Castle Rock.

 Follow the Summit Rd from Dyers Pass past the Sugarloaf TV tower, Rapaki Rock and around a sweeping bend. The Tors is on the right side of the road and Castle Rock is 500m further on the left. The small carpark can get quite congested. Do not leave anything valuable in your car, because there have been some break-ins, especially mid-week when there is not much traffic in the area.

 The walking track goes past The Battlements, around to the front of the outcrop and then to Barbican Wall.

i This guide describes everything left-right.

Two ropes are necessary for rapping from The Keep and may help with some of the leads that wander or have tricky pro.

Take lots of wires (double ups for the long routes) and a good rack of cams.

The gully which leads down to the left side of Barbican Wall is the easiest descent from the top of the crag.

Barbican Wall

This is on the eastern side of Castle Rock and is the furthest wall from the carpark. Most of the routes are marginal leads with poor protection and the rock is flakey in places. However, these adverse elements also make the routes impressive and desirable.

❶ **★18 Alhambra 11m**
Around the left end of the wall, this is an attractive shallow groove. There is no gear down low, apart from a so-so sling, and there are minimal RP placements from there. *Bill Denz 1971*

The climb that changed my life.

What an honour! Being in the Fearnley Castle Rock guidebook, not just my name but a photo of me on one of the test pieces of the crag *Poetry in Motion 25*. I suspect Dave just needed a photo of someone and I was the most willing or perhaps it was a reward for spending hours helping put in the single bolt on *Colossal Youth 24*.

Whatever the reason, my posing on the crux encouraged me to return several days later with Guy Halliburton to attempt my first ever 25 lead.

The first bolt is only 4m off the ground and it hadn't seemed particulary hard to climb up to previously, but it was stick-clipped. This time I also got to it quite easily but as I hadn't warmed up on anything, I was too pumped to clip the bolt. Before downclimbing occured to me my feet skated off and I landed as straight-legged as a tin soldier and promptly cannonaded off the boulder behind me headfirst into the cliff. The three broken metatarsals were extremely painful but the rivers of blood from my forehead ensured prompt service at A&E.

The injury helped me avoid economics lectures which gave me an excuse to quit, build a wall at my parents place and go to Arapiles. Mind you this version is disputed by my girlfriend Jen who thinks I'm a lazy little shit with very indulgent parents.

Roland Foster

Barbican Wall

❷ ★21 Breakfast of Champions 13m
A sexy right-leaning groove. The protection is sparce and fiddly. *Tobin Sorenson 1979 (solo on-sight)*

❸ ★25 Poetry in Motion 13m
Boulder to the bolt and move through to the ledge. Reach high from the ledge for the first nice gear. The crack is adequately protected from here. *Brian Fish 1981*

❹ ★24 Tales of Machismo 13m
One of the hardest and most dangerous routes in the Port Hills. Take the staunch thin crack in the middle of the wall. The gear and rock is diabolical to at least half-height. *John Allen 1979*

❺ ✦★25 Jeni's Gang Direct 13m
A stylin' face climb with intricate and edgy climbing. It's a safe lead if you preclip the 1st bolt. After the 2nd bolt,

keep heading straight up the narrow crack protected with RPs. *Brian Fish 1981/Dave Fearnley 1982 (direct finish)*

❻ ★23 Wall of Shame 13m
Climb the cruxy groove past 2 bolts. From here it's a wee way to the first bomber gear but it's great climbing. Finish up the crack. *John Allen 1980*

❼ 19 Whinging Mick 13m
The crackline just left of the big chimney. Virtually no gear to the ledge. *Dave Fearnley 1979*

❽ 10 Cleft Chimney 12m
Get swallowed into the crack and worm your way to blocky ground.

❾ 15 Orang-utang 12m
Launch up the crack left of the block and trend left to top-out. *Murray Cullen*

John Allen on the first ascent of
Tales of Machismo (24).
IAN WHITEHOUSE

⑩ 15 Baboon 12m
Start right of the ledge and take on
the little crack.

⑪ ★14 Portcullis Chimney 12m
A deep parallel crack. Take big gear
and writhe your way to open space.

Left of the Cave
This is an immaculate section of rock with an
orange hue and lovely views.

⑫ ★19 Corkscrew 7m
A short but spiffy little face climb off
the blocks with a few good wires. *John
Allen 1978*

⑬ ★19 Marc Bollan Memorial Arête 13m
A radiant rounded arête with smeary
slab moves. Place gear in *Escalade*. *John
Allen 1978*

⑭ ★★16 Escalade 13m
One of the classics of the Port Hills.
After the pillar, bridge the corner and
eventually gravitate to the right crack.

⑮ ★18 Rawhide 13m
Slightly contrived, but still a popular
line on good rock. Take the arête right
of *Escalade* and climb placing gear out
left. *Rob Rainsbury 1972*

⑯ ★17 Rampart 13m
Up the face that is criss-crossed with
intermittent cracks. Finish carefully
out left. Spaced gear.

⑰ ★16 Sword in the Stone 13m
A wide crack immediately left of the
cave. A classic jamming bulge.

⑱ 22 Uncompromising Vulture 12m
Do the crux of *Sword in the Stone* and
now go right around the arête and
into the corner. *John Allen 1980*

Castle Rock

27	**10**	Eagle Cleft
28 ★	**15**	Falcon Crack
29 ★	**18**	Gibbett
30 ★	**18**	Gargoyle
31 ★★	**19**	Executioner
32 ★	**17**	Mihrab
33 ★	**19**	Expedition Crack
34 ★★	**17**	Hangman
35 ★	**18**	Buttress Corner
36 ★★	**20**	Judgement
37 ★★	**22**	Peregrinus
38 ★★	**16**	Flying Buttress
39	**24**	Flying Bastard
40 ★	**24**	Ex Cathedra
41 ★	**25**	Ex Cathedra Direct
43	**17**	Inquisition
45	**10**	Hellfire Gully

Carpark 5mins →

Castle Rock

Dungeon Cave

The most outrageous terrain at Castle Rock, this provides steep climbing and shelter from the elements.

⑲ **20 Court Jester 18m**

The classic roof crack at the left end of the cave. Big holds, jams and good gear should please. After the roof, continue up the easy crack. *Colin Dodge 1972*

⑳ **26 Cave Route 18m**

A strange creation with difficult and awkward moves. Climb hard terrain just right of *Court Jester* and join this again for the finish. *Ton Snelder/Dave Fearnley 1984*

㉑ **★29 Ruaumoko 18m**

Difficult bouldery moves from the back of the cave. From a standing start, slap and crank out to join *Passion Play*. Preclip the 1st pro. *Sefton Priestley 2004*

㉒ **★23 Passion Play 18m**

From the right end of the cave, traverse the undercling crack left. Rock onto the face with small holds. Things mellow from now on. *John Allen 1979*

Right of the Cave

The hub of Castle Rock climbing, this is home to most of the classics and has some fantastic crack lines, good gear and more exposure than any other Port Hills crag.

This area has traditionaly been divided into three separate walls; Curtain Wall (above the cave), Gargoyle Wall (ground level and right of the cave) and the Keep (the towering headwall). For convenience, the routes from these three walls have been numbered and listed the way many climbers combine the pitches.

㉓ **★14 Kestrel 11m**

This crack starts right of the cave. Bouldery and balancy for the first few metres to a gear placement, then follow the crack through to 'the aviary' under the roof.

㉔ **★13 Arrow 11m**

Traverse left below the pigeon's self-composting toilet. This can be quite 'out there' but once you join the wonderful wide crack you'll be grinning all the way to the top.

㉕ **★16 Eclipse 11m**

From the base of the *Arrow* crack, traverse right above the roof and don't get the heebie-jeebies. Move straight up the thin cracks in the middle of the face. The pro is okay, with plenty of small wires. *Phil Stuart-Jones 1978.* There is a direct start through the widest part of the roof from the aviary (about 24), added by *Matt Vandenberg 1999*

㉖ **14 Hawk 12m**

The V-shaped corner with a tapered crack. The pro placements are a little hidden but worth a fossick.

㉗ **10 Eagle Cleft 10m**

The body-sized chimney that doesn't require wriggling or massive gear. *Neil Hamilton 1940s*

㉘ **★15 Falcon Crack 10m**

Once you exit the chimney, the crack to your right will beckon. Follow this to the skyline, but take big gear.

> 'Welcome to the employee rock-climbing seminar. You'll learn valuable teamwork skills by doing dangerous things unrelated to your jobs.'
> Dilbert

㉙ ✷✷18 Gibbett 12m

Climb *Hawk* and move into the wide chimney (*Eagle Cleft*), then bridge across to the crack on the right wall. There is an interesting little 5m section of crack climbing to the rest ledge. From here, *Gibbet* continues up a sustained, straight crack line to the top of The Keep. If you love crimps you'll love this. *Rob Rainsbury 1971*

㉚ ✶18 Gargoyle 18m

A V-corner that starts 3m off the deck. Apply some cunning to outwit the crack, then head right as the route steepens. You can rest on the ledge and after the cruxy roof you are well on your way to the gallows.

㉛ ✷✷19 Executioner 15m

A sustained, thin crack that keeps you on edge(s) but a couple of fingerlocks may help you escape the chop. Somewhat of an epic line if combined with *Gargoyle*, in which case a double set of wires is essential. *John Barnett 1974*

㉜ ✶17 Mihrab 18m

Start up *Gargoyle* or boulder up directly (damn desperate and slippery) to the thin crack protected by some pitons, small wires and cams. Once the face peters out, join *Gargoyle* again.

㉝ ✶19 Expedition Crack 14m

A very polished corner which does provide excellent laybacking and gear. Rest in the niche and enjoy neat moves stepping right. *Murray Jones 1971*

㉞ ✷✷17 Hangman 16m

The most iconic of the Port Hills climbs. A sustained, exposed outing up a superb crack. Start at the left end of the ledge where the crack begins.

㉟ ✶18 Buttress Corner 14m

Almost an unpleasant start; bouldery and slippery. After the crux it's a good easy corner.

㊱ ✷✷20 Judgement 16m

Daunting roof moves guard this fine crack. Test yourself and savour pulling over the roof to a pumpy face. *Murray Judge 1973*

㊲ ✷✷22 Peregrinus 16m

The thin crack which bisects the short section of horizontal roof and elegantly points skywards. Once you dangle out over the roof take delight in the crack and the small run-out. *Rick McGregor 1979*

㊳ ✷✷16 Flying Buttress 16m

A wild traverse using underclings (3.5–4 cam or large hex needed to protect this) to the corner/crack. After this the route is quietly enjoyable.

The following four routes are either difficult, dangerous or both. They reside at the right of The Keep and are accessed via Hellfire Gully.

㊴ 24 Flying Bastard 16m

A direct start to the *Flying Buttress* crack through a sketchy roof. *Dave Fearnley 1982*

㊵ ✶24 Ex Cathedra 16m

From the ledge, climb the steep wall to access the crack/arête right of *Flying Buttress*. *Tobin Sorenson 1979*

㊶ ✶25 Ex Cathedra Direct 16m

Same start as *Ex Cathedra* but continue straight into the imposing thin crack (good gear) on the right of The Keep. *John Allen 1980*

42 ★**24 The SS** 16m

1 Around the arête is this snaking crack on a red wall. A bolt protects the start and reasonable gear follows but is hard to place on lead. *Dave Fearnley 1981*

43 **17 Inquisition** 12m

Just right of the *Buttress Corner* arête is a very faint scoop; bridge this and place gear in the *Pegasus* roof before smearing left to the choice arête.

44 **16 Pegasus** 10m

Up the easy crack to the small roof. Haul over this into the laid-back crack with a bush.

The next small wall right provides some good warm-ups and bouldering as well as the entrance of Hellfire Gully.

45 **10 Hellfire Gully** 30m

A fun scramble or descent route from The Keep. *Edgar Williams 1913*

The Fan Cliff

This fan-shaped set of columns is left and a little higher than The Battlements. It doesn't get much traffic, but the climbing is worth the diversion up the hill.

46 ★**19 Lifestyle Asset** 10m

2 The striking left arête. Stay pretty much on the arête to the 1st bolt and follow the line, top-out slightly left. *Joe Arts 1997*

47 **17 Private Popokov** 8m

The small corner which divides the face. The gear appears after the crux. *John Allen 1977*

48 **21 General Malaise** 8m

2 An edgy beginning and then follow the fan left. *Lindsay Main 1999*

49 **20 Marshall Zhukov** 8m

2 Boulder onto the ledge and rock right around the arête and hoon up the corner. *Joe Arts 1998*

The Battlements

This buttress is the first bit of rock you meet after leaving the car park. The climbs are steep but usually well-protected.

50 **20 Camelot** 12m

1 A narrow pillar with a distinctive crack on the right hand side. Follow the vague arête to blocky ground. *Lindsay Main 1998*

The Battlements

51 15 Knight Errant 10m
Mantle onto the ledge and follow the fractured face up the crack. Link back to *Square Table* at the top.

52 14 Square Table 12m
Mantle onto the ledge and move up the corner to good bridging.

53 16 Holy Grail 12m
From the ramp, make a beeline for the blocks up the right-facing corner. Procrastinate before moving through the crux. *Don Hutton*

54 ★21 Dick Barton's Mate 12m
Start next to *Holy Grail* up the thin, daunting crack. From the rest station, the crux involves slapping the arête on the top pillar. This climb is well protected with heaps of small wires/RPs. *Tim Morrison 1982*

55 ★★19 Excalibur 12m
A sustained crack line that lacks good gear for the first few metres, but then yields sound placements. Cruxy through the bulge. *Don Hutton 1967*

56 ★18 Guinevere 12m
A fair maiden, but can play hard to get. Once you've got good pro, don't stall. *Don Hutton 1967*

57 16 Dragon 12m
Start up the short crack that is best protected with cams. Once on the ledge, boulder the big block to the top.

58 12 Knight's Entrance 10m
Follow twin cracks to the gripping chimney. Grovel up this, or climb the face out left.

59 ★★14 Lancelot 10m
A dashing climb that protects in the face of danger. Fine holds up the laid-back crack.

60 ★21 Little Red Rooster 10m
1 Quite nifty. It may be an option to preclip the bolt from the vegetated corner to the left, but the moves aren't too cocky if you go direct. *Dave Fearnley 1981*

153

Mt Pleasant Spur

Mt Pleasant

Upper Mt Pleasant

Lower Mt Pleasant–Left

Lower Mt Pleasant–Right

Cabbage Tree Wall

The Alcove

The Caves

Tiger Wall

Angel Face

The Shelf

The Zoo

Britten Crag

This crag is near the top of Mt Pleasant Spur above the long band of rock that makes up Britten Crag. It has much more compact rock than the lower tier, and with some great crack lines, it is an excellent trad climbing destination. The crag is divided into two main outcrops about 5mins apart. The location is very sunny and the views down on the new subdivision in Heathcote are quite stunning.

Drive towards Sumner via Ferry Rd. Just after Ferrymead, cross a bridge then turn right into St Andrews Hill Rd. This becomes Major Hornbrook Rd, which continues right to the top of the hill past the intersection with Belleview Tce. At the intersection with Madeley Rd, veer right uphill and continue to the road end. Park near the farm gate.

Cross the gate and veer right through the old pine trees until you reach a track cutting along the side of the hill. You should be able to see Mount Pleasant crag ahead, above the track.

This is an easy access crag, with a good grassy ledge to belay from. It is all quite straightforward and the anchors (either blocks or bolts) are sound. Just take your usual rack and a single rope.

Lower Mt Pleasant-Left

The first climbs start 4m right of the 'climbing awareness' sign.

❶ 11 Ray's Climb 15m

A wide crack with nifty bridging. *Ray Begg 1977*

❷ 16 Daryll's Climb 16m

Up the rounded pillar and layback the bulgy crux. *Daryll Thomson 1977*

Just next to the painted 'HB':

❸ 15 Crag Rat 18m

A short bulge followed by easy ground. Start at the painted 'C' and use jugs on either side of the crack to pull up. *Bill Atkinson 1977*

❹ 17 Pincer 18m

An enticing but marginally protected lead. From the 'P' inch up the thin crack to small wire placements in a crack out right. Offsets work well if you have them. *Bill Atkinson 1977*

❺ 16 Left One 18m

A tasty crackline that exits on jugs a little too soon. *Bill Atkinson 1977*

❻ ★18 Right One 18m

Up the left-facing corner to a few awkward moves. Protected well with small cams. *Bill Atkinson 1977*

The next two climbs start from a short, wide crack below the face.

155

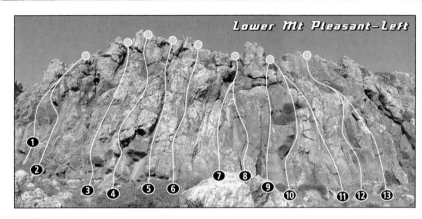

Lower Mt Pleasant-Left

7 16 Henry's Climb 18m
Climb the blocks and follow the short crack to an awkward mantle. Continue to the gully. *Henry Mares 1977*

8 ★18 Lunge 18m
From the block, follow the fractures up the scrummy compact rock. Positive slopers to top-out into the gully. *Lindsay Main 1979*

9 14 Vamit 18m
Ooze up the groove to the kitchen table and waltz up blocky ground. *Bill Atkinson 1977*

10 ★17 Blood 18m
Short, overhanging jam crack. *Bill Atkinson 1977*

11 ★15 Mike's Climb 18m
An groovy crack with orgasmically rounded holds. *Mike Perry 1977*

12 ★16 Mantle Piece 18m
Just like bouldering in your living room. This has a very awkward manoeuvre that usually involves flailing legs and hilarity. *Bill Atkinson 1977*

13 ★21 Orange Energy 18m
A strenuous, bulging crack with good gear. *John Allen 1979*

20m right there is a black wall with two one-move wonders (grades 19 and 15).

Lower Mt Pleasant-Right
A wall with good rock and some charming leads, alongside a couple of more frightening propositions.

14 ★16 Ferret 14m
Champion jamming action up a deep crack. Bridge, wedge or grovel up the groove but watch the flakey rock. For good pro, move right at the top. *Bill Atkinson 1977*

15 ★★19 Crazy Fingers 14m
Climb the block below *Ferret* and step right into the ravishing parallel crack. Savour the twin cruxes on this jamming rarity. *Rick McGregor 1979*

16 ★★★17 Stranger 14m
A wide, left-leaning groove with a bit of everything; bridging, jamming and face holds. Very entertaining. *Bill Atkinson 1977*

(14) (15) (16) (17) (18) (19) (20)

⑰ **✸✸22 In The Night 14m**

A graceful crack with marginal pro at the bottom and adequate but awkward pro in the top section. *John Allen 1979*

⑱ **★18 Little Feet 14m**

A deceptively tricky jam crack. Start up the groove and launch into the crack, keeping the barn door at bay. First climbed solo! *Bill Atkinson 1977*

⑲ **23 The Loom 14m**

Steep and daunting. Start at *Little Feet* and branch off right into the looming crack. Some rock is flakey and the gear is fiddly. *John Allen 1980*

⑳ **★20 Rubber Bullet 16m**

Climb the wide crack just left of the fence. A hidden bonus lies in wait in the offwidth. From the ledge, follow the crack up to the short headwall to an amazing mantle. *John Allen 1979*

Upper Mt Pleasant

The next main section of crag is 5mins walk from Lower Mt Pleasant. The climbs up to grade 20 are all well protected and worth a go. The harder climbs are staunch and serious, but this doesn't detract from the fact that they are fantastic routes on great rock.

㉑ **15 Dead on Arrival 8m**

A chunky, right-facing corner. *Bill Atkinson 1977*

㉒ **14 Moans Coffin 8m**

A right-facing corner right of a small roof (with pocket). Bridging and jamming on good gear. *Bill Atkinson 1977*

The double bolt anchor above Enfant Terrible can service the next 4 routes as long as you watch the swing when abseiling.

㉓ **★18 Neanderthal 12m**

Prominant left-leaning crack line. Use jams and the pocket on the face to get through the crux. *Lindsay Main 1977*

㉔ ✻22 Career Girl 14m
Up the right-leaning intermittent crack to a ledge. The thin crack above is sustained with marginal pro (small cams). *John Allen 1979*

㉕ ★23 Enfant Terrible 14m
Climb 3m up a juggy groove and over a bulge. Protect the start with gear in *Career Girl*. Follow the flake up the face with adequate gear. *John Allen 1979*

㉖ ✻24 Sheltered Childhood 14m
If this climb were a beer it would definitely be a stout. It's a mix of jams and layaways that is full-on to the very end. *John Allen 1979*

㉗ ★25 International Jetsetter 14m
1 🔩 Take off up the crack into a quick stop-over niche. Change course left past the bolt, over the bulge with sparse gear to a single bolt anchor. Happy landings. *Charlie Creese 1982*

㉘ ✻27 Dominion 14m
2 🔩 Boulder up the sinuous arête to the short and steep crux which demands creative moves. *Dave Fearnley 1988*

㉙ ★20 Winters Road 14m
Start on the cracked slab and rest on the juggy ledge. Don't freeze on the offwidth—bridge out and go for it. *John Allen 1979*

The following three climbs finish at the same single bolt anchor.

㉚ ★26 Gruse Power 14m
⚠ Rack up your small wires and boulder up the wall left of *Go*. The top section is an intermittent thin crack. *Dave Fearnley 1983*

㉛ ✻23 Go 12m
Continuous thin crack with a roof at mid-height. Stunning water streaked rock gets you to steep territory with okay gear. *John Allen 1979*

㉜ ★25 Barking up the Wrong Tree 11m
1 🔩 Wide bridging and layaways to the 1st bolt. Tenuous palming right of the overhang gets you over the bulge to a wire placement. *Charlie Creese 1981*

㉝ 28 The Rack 9m
Short but packs a lot of punch. Start up the easy crack and move right to powerful sidepulls. *Derek Thatcher 2002*

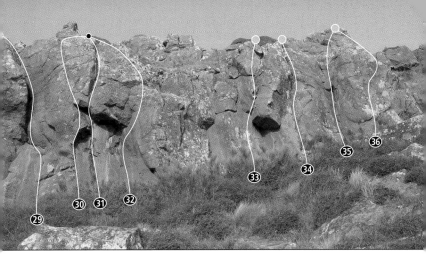

34 **★16 Womble Brothers 9m**
Better than it looks. Lovely edges all the way and good gear from half-height. *Bill Atkinson 1977*

35 **★14 Cobweb 8m**
Follow the crack up fractured wall. Good pro and jugs over the top. *Bill Atkinson 1977*

36 **★16 Wreck on the Highway 8m**
Cruisy, concave slab. Place gear in the slot and reach right to the arête to find the hidden jug. *Dave Fearnley 1979*

Begin Wall
A short wall 20m right.

37 **12 Adolf 6m**
This textured finger crack makes a good outing. *Lindsay Main 1976*

38 **★17 Begin 7m**
A groove with a beautiful short section of finger crack. Blocky exit. *Bill Atkinson 1977*

'In France, a publicly accessible climbing area without bolted lines is viewed like a publicly accessible swimming pool with sharks in it.'
David Kastrup

Face Race **(21).** GUILLAUME CHARTON

Britten Crag is the lower tier of rock on Mt Pleasant Spur. It is up to 16m high and has varied angles from slabs to steep overhangs. Fondly known as 'Brittle Crag,' this is not outstanding rock, but it has become a popular area due to its proximity to the city and the fact that it filled a gap in the Port Hills route climbing library. Before Britten, there were lots of trad crags and stauncher sport routes, but not many well bolted sport climbs. We also suspect that the crag's appeal may have been related to the original rampant overgrading that ruled here. Days here can be productive and social but always be aware of dodgy blocks.

Drive towards Sumner via Ferry Rd. Just after Ferrymead, cross a bridge then turn right into St Andrews Hill Rd. This becomes Major Hornbrook Rd, which continues right to the top of the hill past an intersection with Belleview Tce. At the intersection with Madeley Rd, veer right uphill and continue to the road end. Park near the farm gate.

Cross the gate and head right through the old pine trees until you reach a track cutting along the side of the hill towards the Summit Rd. You should be able to see Mount Pleasant Upper Tier ahead, above the track.

Head downhill gradually until you meet the lower band of rock (5 mins). This is the left end of Britten Crag.

i The gear used at the crag is straight-forward. Most climbs are fully bolted apart from some trad lines at The Zoo and a few other mixed climbs. The routes have double bolt anchors, unless otherwise mentioned in the text.

The Zoo

This is the first wall that you meet after scrambling down a short, steep section of track. It is Britten's only trad climbing destination and has a few good bolted numbers thrown into the mix.

❶ **14 Black Sheep 10m**
Climbed back in the mists of time, when Britten was but a twinkle in sport climbers' eyes. This good old fashioned chimney only takes big cams or hexes—yes, hexes. *Daryll Thomson 1973*

❷ **18 Big Boar 13m**
Long moves through the bulge to a crack with baby buttock jugs. *Joe Arts 2000*

❸ **16 Yellow Splendour 16m**
3 Wouldn't have quite said 'splendour,' but not a bad route. Cruxy moves past the 1st clip, and then it's all over before you know it. *Joe Arts 2000*

❹ **★16 Kingfisher 16m**
⚠ Good-looking corner, truncated by a roof and headwall above. The climb is littered with positive holds but the gear should be treated with apprehension. *Neil Sloan 1993*

❺ **20 Gorilla At Large 16m**
2 A blocky arête right of the roof. With ape moves, swerve right of the 1st bolt then swing back across the arête. A medium cam protects the top-out.

The next two climbs are on the yellow face with a steep headwall. Watch for loose rock in the lower section before the 1st bolt.

Britten Crag

The Zoo

⑥ 18 Ringing the Change 16m

3 🔩 Up the corner past the flake. The traverse across the headwall is most enjoyable. *Tony Burnell 2000*

⑦ 18 Transmogrification 16m

2 🔩 Good climbing up the headwall but sketchy rock up to the 1st bolt. *Neil Sloan 1993*

⑧ 15 Rabid 14m

The right-facing corner with good pro, if you are happy to hang around placing it.

⑨ 15 Rockadile 14m

Delightful wee crack in the middle of the face. Bares no teeth and provides enough pro. *Neil Sloan 1993*

The Shelf

After the trampled fence, follow the track under the roofed section of wall. Continue along the base of the crag for about 100m until you reach an undercut wall, 'The Shelf.' The next routes are at the right end of The Shelf.

⑩ 24 The Big C 16m

6 🔩 Burly moves under the roof lead to the lip. Move up and left to the 4th bolt and then through to a hidden bolt above. *Tony Burnell 2000*

⑪ ★21 Off the Shelf 16m

4 🔩 Start at the right-hand end of The Shelf. Boulder up steep stuff through an excellent crux over the lip. Great finish up the long wall on rounded holds. *Tony Burnell 2000*

⑫ ★18 Legends in the Baking 17m

5 🔩 A route up the middle of the vague wall just right of The Shelf. A bouldery beginning on a short steep section to a long and enjoyable face. *Simon Courtois 1998*

⑬ ★17 Tres Estrellas de Oro 15m

5 🔩 Charming face climbing. Start from a small ledge and follow the crack. *Dave Shotwell 1999*

⑭ ★20 Whispers and Moans 15m

4 🔩 A short arête yielding spicy moves before it chills out in the top section. *Simon Courtois 1999*

⑮ 17 Andele! 14m

4 🔩 Tricky moves at the start lead to pleasurable stemming up the right-facing corner. *Simon Courtois 2000*

> 'If you don't let go, you can't fall off!' Jerry Moffat

The Shelf

⑩ ⑪ ⑫ ⑬ ⑭ ⑮ ⑯ ⑰ ⑱

⑯ 20 Face-Off 14m

4 Up the blank-looking face. Start on the right and traverse leftwards on edges. Continue up the middle of the face to broken ground and over a final headwall. Move left to the anchor. *John Iseli 2001*

⑰ 19 Cereal Killer 20m

5 A neat start with great holds to the faint corner, which steepens and gets difficult. *Lindsay Main 2002*

⑱ ★20 Arriba! 11m

4 Run up the slab to a testy bulge with sneaky laybacks. *Dave Shotwell 2000*

The next two routes are 5m right on a short wall with a white prow above.

4 **17 Get to Jugs 12m**
Cruxy start with delicate edging to a tapering finish. *Lindsay Main 2002*

4 **★21 Get to Grips 12m**
Technical and fingery climbing morphs to surprising slopers and an enjoyable arête. *Richard Kimberley 2000*

Tiger Wall

One of the best walls at Britten, this is a steep, undercut face with some pumpy and juggy lines. It is south-facing, so gets some summer shade.

㉑ 23 Pleasant Point 15m

4 Start at *Where Angels Fear to Tread* and charge past the first 2 bolts over the bulge. Finish at the double bolt anchor out right. *Tony Burnell 2000*

㉒ ★★24 Where Angels Fear to Tread 15m

5 Cranky start left of the black streak, then keep heading rightwards up the face on quality edges. Quite sustained. *Ico de Zwart 2000*

㉓ 24 Sunburst Finish 15m

5 A crusty, steep start on the short roof leads to good holds and a rest. Keep veering right and finish to the right of the last bolt. *Tony Burnell 1999*

㉔ ★★21 Speights Race 16m

5 Follow the overhanging corner/crack, then tackle the face with edges to quench your pump. *Tony Burnell 1999*

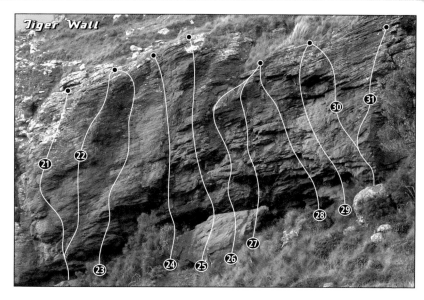

Tiger Wall

㉕ ✳22 American Dream 16m

5 The name implies a shallow illusion, but this is not the case on this thoroughly enjoyable route. In the style of *Getting Rid of Mr Clean* at Lyttelton Rock, it is steep but sports great holds. Climb the yellow boulder and haul up the middle of the steep wall on lovely rounded holds. Continue up the face, veering slightly right. *Tony Burnell 1999*

㉖ 19 Three's Company 13m

3 Start off the boulder and crank robustly up the ledges to the broken crack, where a #1-1.5 cam protects well. *Pere Logan 2000*

㉗ ✳21 Cat's Cradle 12m

4 At the right end of the boulder, reach high and probably cut loose over the roof. Motor up positive jugs to trickiness over the lip. *Tony Burnell 2000*

㉘ 25 Southern Exposure 12m

5 Starts in the middle of the small cave by the nettles. A few hard cranks on steep ground lead to big holds veering left. Finish through a slight notch. *Tony Burnell 2000*

㉙ ✳23 Storm Bringer 12m

4 A steep start up the right side of the cave. Pull over the lip, then keep the pump under control as you move up the wall and over the slight bulge. Finish at a single bolt anchor. *Tony Burnell 2000*

㉚ 19 Big Girls Blouse 11m

4 Start up the arête but head left as soon as possible. Enjoy good holds all the way to the anchor. *Simon Courtois 1998*

㉛ ✳18 The Big Lebowski 10m

4 Up the arête on the far right of *Tiger Wall*. Wicked, juggy moves past the 1st bolt lead to a cruisy finish. *Dave Shotwell 1998*

The next route is 8m right on a mossy wall with a great looking arête above.

7 ★**21 Bathroom Vanity 20m**
Start on the easy wall and veer carefully right to the 2nd bolt. Move up good rock to the beckoning prow above. Nice edges and some balancey moves take you right to exit. *Simon Courtois 1997*

Latin Lover Wall
10m to the right this nice long wall with a few stylish routes.

33 ★**20 It's a Mystery to Me 13m**
4 Up the left side of the wall, where good edges culminate in a crux near the top. Rest and zoom over the small bulge to finish. *Andrew Buist 2000*

34 ★**20 Latin Lover 14m**
4 Leggy climbing to a small roof, where a medium cam protects. Edges continue to the headwall with a gorgeous jug. Single bolt anchor, or move over to the double bolts either side. *Dave Shotwell 1998*

35 **21 Adventure Capitalist 14m**
3 Easy ground to the overlap, which takes a wire. Ramble up from here to a steep wall with a devious exit right. *Andrew Buist 2000*

36 ★**19 What R U Reckon? 14m**
6 On the right side of the wall. Fun, straightforward climbing on dark rock leads to great moves into a groove. *Simon Courtois 1998*

The Alcove
The hardest routes at Britten lurk beneath this long, overhanging wall. It is often the social hub of the crag and a great place to hang out and work some routes. The first climbs included in this guide start at the left end of the large boulder.

37 ★**21 Tropical Storm 14m**
6 Juggy, jolly and steep. Crank past 2 bolts and move left, throwing in a heel hook if you fancy. Continue up the weakness for final steep moves. *Richard Kimberley 2000*

38 **25 It is Pointless to Resist 15m**
6 The direct start. Climb the left-facing notch and wrestle with hard crimping through the horizontal roof. Easy climbing to the anchor. *Andrew Buist 2001*

The Alcove—Left

39 25 Real Slim Shady 15m

6 Directly in front of the large boulder, this is a two crimp wonder through a dark bulge. Easy but crusty up the arête. *Andrew Buist 2000*

The next climb is Deep Impact *27 with a difficult crux and worrying 3rd clip. Next is:*

40 21 Skunk 2 15m

3 Climb the right-leaning weakness past 2 bolts and truck up the broken crack, heading left. *Richard Kimberley 2000*

41 23 A Dog's Life 15m

5 A hard start needs some 'go juice,' then up the bulge to an easy finish. *John Iseli 2000*

42 ✳24 Panda Monium 15m

5 Easy start to a dauntingly steep and pumpy section of wall. *Jeff Shrimpton/ Simon Middlemass 1993*

43 26 Yorkshire Git 15m

5 Start at *Panda Monium* and traverse right and up through a sustained headwall. *Richard Kimberley 2000*

44 ✳26 Hushpuppy Hitched 15m

5 After the lower wall, pull some hard cranks through the horizontal roof to the upper corner. *Pere Logan 2000*

45 ★28 Silence of the Wombats 15m

4 Bouldery up the low face, then a couple of long reaches through the roof and cut loose on the jugs. Once on the upper face veer left to bigger holds. *Sefton Priestley 2000*

46 26 The Great White Wombat Hunt 15m

5 Start right of the scoop/pod of *Silence of the Wombats* and climb to a V-niche. Head left and up to chain anchors. *Richard Kimberley 2000*

47 ★**27 The Zimmerframe Owner Strikes Back 15m.** Steep climbing with big moves on big holds (until they get smaller). Give it some grey power to the chains. *Richard Kimberley 1999*

48 **26 Wall Street Crumble 15m**
A steadily overhanging route leading to a rib, then up the wall above. *Tony Ward-Holmes 2001*

49 ★★**24 Mt Pleasant Butcher 15m**
A favourite, cranky test piece, complete with its very own interesting mantle move. A short corner to a steep roof, gain the ledge, step right and up the wall to finish. *Tony Burnell 1999*

50 ★**23 Weet-Bix Kids 14m**
Tricky slopey start to nice wall climbing. It's steeper than than it looks and bound to cause a pump. Finish as for *Mt Pleasant Butcher. Tony Burnell 1999*

51 ★★**23 Liposuction 12m**
A racey steep wall just left of the cave. Engage crimps and suck it up, before ducking right to the anchor. *Simon Middlemass 1993*

52 ★**24 Thorn Bird 12m**
Boulder the steep stuff and onto the small ledge. Big moves up the face are tough and pumpy. *Tony Burnell 2000*

53 **24 What Mad Pursuit 12m**
Ascend the weakness which gets steadily steeper. Finish over the roof lip to jugs and anchor. *Ico de Zwart 2000*

54 ★**22 Wave of Mutilation 12m**
Start on the left side of the cave up a vague left-trending crack, where fatigue and weakness will surge upon you. *Marcus Thomas 2000*

167

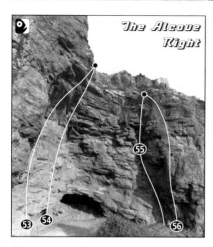

The Alcove Right

55 **★20 U Haul 11m**
3 Funky moves up the steep groove/crack. Starts off tricky, but gives way to big jugs just when the pump gets too much to handle. *Tony Burnell 1999*

Sebastian Loewensteijn on *Silence of the Wombats* (28). TONY BURNELL

56 **22 Disco Logic 11m**
5 Just right of the groove and quite bouldery through the start. After this relax to the top. *Marcus Thomas 2000*

Angel Face
Head back down the track below The Alcove. Just to the right is this yellow wall with several routes before a small cave. There are single anchor bolts with hangers so, to abseil, walk south a few metres to the anchors at the top of *Release The Wombats.*

57 **18 Chocoholic 13m**
4 Climbs the face right of the arête. Pull a few steep moves and then devour the tasty face. The holds are big but it's a little off-balance. *Andrew Buist 2000*

58 **★16 Easter Rising 12m**
2 An appealing route in the middle of the yellow wall. Straight past the bolts to a bit of gear. *Hugh Matthews 1997*

59 **18 God's Teeth 15m**
2 Above the downward pointing tooth. A bouldery start and then casual climbing, but it's tricky to find/place gear near the top. *Hugh Matthews 1997*

60 **18 Angel Wings 15m**
3 Bloody hard start up the corner, but this leads right to a comfy ledge where you can prepare the gear and your psyche for the steep exit through the notch. *Hugh Matthews 1997*

61 **21 10mm Full Metal Jacket 15m**
6 Cranky moves out of the cave on the right-hand side. Once over the lip, engage positive edges to the small overhang, which should be entertaining if you are pumped. *Richard Kimberley 2000*

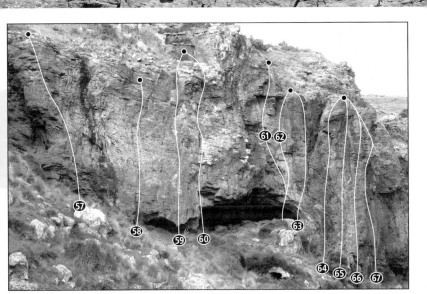

62 ✶✶**21 Release the Wombats 13m**

4 ⚲ Same start as *10mm Full Metal Jacket* but move straight up on nice edges to a fun run-out to the top. *Richard Kimberley 2000*

63 **18 Adios Ingo 13m**

4 ⚲ Boulder up over the roof and veer right, taking the easiest path. Exit out left. *Richard Kimberley 2000*

The next 3 routes are right of the small cave.

64 **21 Happy Ending 16m**

6 ⚲ Up the left side of the face on small and slopey edges. The terrain tapers off until the final roof with good moves. *Patrick Stadie 2000*

65 ✶**20 Out of Africa 16m**

3 ⚲ Up the middle of the face via the Africa-shaped block. A wire can be placed to protect the start and top-out. *Tony Burnell 2000*

66 ✶✶**21 Face Race 16m**

5 ⚲ A fashionable face climb up the right side of the orange wall. Nice technicalities on small but positive edges. Cranky over the lip and an easy finish. *Tony Burnell 2000*

67 **22 No One Expects the Spanish Inquisition 16m.** A bouldery start over a small roof which strikes fear and surprise. Ruthless efficiency and a fanatical devotion will be the chief weapons needed up the arête (a nice red uniform would also help). This exciting route is let down by dubious rock. *Patrick Stadie 2000*

3 ⚲ ✶✶**20 Naughty but Nice 16m**

The thin crack left of the main corner. Hard to reach the face, then move onto the arête. A rest is kindly provided below the last bulge. *Simon Middlemass 1993*

4 **★19 Speak Hers Corner 14m**
The obvious corner which divides the wall. A difficult start to access the pleasant corner and big cams can protect the top section. *Ngaio Colville 1993*

4 **★21 Moss Side 14m**
An edgy face climb. Boulder over the overlap then head up the steepening wall. As your arms start to fade the holds get better. *Tony Burnell 2000*

72 **22 Bit of Rough 15m**
5 Steep start through the overhang via the big block and tricky moves to gain the headwall. *Richard Kimberley 2001*

73 **★23 Pocket Rocket 15m**
5 Start just right of *Bit of Rough* through the blocky notch. Move right and climb the crack to the headwall above. *Tony Burnell 2000*

The Caves
The next routes are about 10m right, perched above two low, incut caves. The rock is good and there are some pumpy routes to play on.

71 **21 Wiggling the Pinky 15m**
6 At the far left end of the twin-caved area. Steepest at the start and then relaxing up through the middle section. *Joe Arts 2000*

74 **24 Bulk Order 15m**
4 Weird, cruxy start below a small roof. Climb left of the first 2 bolts before moving back right to the 3rd. Move over the bulge and up the headwall. *Tony Burnell 2000*

75 **★23 Primitive Man 15m**
2 Start between the caves in a tiny hanging groove and climb through two small roofs. Wire placements in the groove. *Simon Middlemass 1993*

76 ★**23 Total Eclipse 15m**

5 Hard overhanging climbing gets easier once you rock-over onto the face.
Now follow the crack feature. *Richard Kimberley 2000*

77 ★**23 Bulk Delivery 15m**

5 A steep start with long moves on good
holds leads over the roof. Head into
the jug littered corner above. *Tony Burnell 2000*

Cabbage Tree Wall

A nice steep wall with a few strenuous routes.
The right end of the wall is watched over by a
friendly cabbage tree.

78 ★**23 You Beauty 15m**

7 Up the fetching, fused-looking face to
the slopey overlap above. Interesting,
technical moves on this uncharacteris-
tic Britten route. *Dave Shotwell 1999*

79 **24 Bluto 15m**

4 Sloping holds and a few small edges
allow you to climb the steep crux section. Big holds lead to the steep and
airy arête. *Tony Burnell 2000*

80 ★**24 Vertical Plummet**

6 **12m**. Up the steep
s e m i - a r e t e / p r o w.
Long moves with a
crux pulling over the
lip. *Andrew Buist 2002*

81 **25 Popeye 10m**

3 Cranky moves on
good holds at the
start, then small
crimps over the lip.
Enjoyable to the
anchor. *Tony Burnell 2000*

82 ★**23 Cabbage Patch Kids 8m**

3 On the far right side of the wall. Start
on good holds then take on a few
gnarly moves over the bulge. Move
fast and you will be rewarded. *Tony Burnell 2000*

Rachel Musgrave on *Hushpuppy Hitched* (26). TONY BURNELL

Cattlestop

Cattlestop is known mostly for short sport routes, but there are also a few nifty trad lines tucked away. The crag is located at the top of Mt Pleasant Spur. The nature of the climbing and the crag's accessibility from the Summit Road means that you can pack a lot of mileage into one day. Some of the rock is coarse and crumbly, but there is a compact band at the Surgical Strike Wall.

 From eastern Christchurch, drive towards Sumner and head up Mt Pleasant Rd (just before The Causeway over the estuary). At the top, turn right onto the Summit Rd and drive 700m. After 'the cattlestop' and the rock-cutting, pull into a small park on the left.

If you are coming from south or west Christchurch, follow Dyers Pass Rd to the Sign of the Kiwi. Turn left onto the Summit Rd. The Cattlestop car park is 150m past the Gondola.

Cross the road to the stone seat and follow the track past the cave, where there are a few routes. The nitty gritty starts on the Shimmering Jelly Wall.

i Most of the climbs here are reasonably short and they are all set up with double bolt anchors.

The crag faces north-south and is in the lee of the hills in a cold southerly. It also gets reasonable shelter from those nasty north-easterly sea breezes. It tends to get very hot in summer.

Surgical Strike Wall

This is an oasis of bomber rock, the best of Cattlestop. If you want to access this wall direct from the Summit Rd, park at the cattlestop and walk straight downhill.

❶ ✳**21 Satanic Verses 15m**
A frolicsome steep corner littered with flat jugs. The gear below the 1st bolt is negligible but okay thereafter. Enjoy the run-out—it's a ripper of a rock climb. *Paul Tattersall 1990*

❷ ✳✳**21 Surgical Strike 15m**
The classic of the crag, this proud arête is not only aesthetic, it's damn fine climbing. Big edges beckon, but don't be fooled it gets slopey up there. *Lindsay Main 1996*

172

❸ ★19 Midnight's Children 15m

3 🔩 A mystical bridging corner. Clamber high to the 1st bolt then run it out to the 2nd. Move straight up the headwall, then left to the last bolt of *Surgical Strike* to finish. *Peter Sykes 1990*

❹ ★23 Passage to India 13m

2 🔩 A technical climb through a small roof and up the face. After you've clipped the 1st bolt and solved the crimpy crux, the route is out there but not dangerous. There is an optional cam for the finish. *Paul Tattersall 1990*

❺ 25 La Vita e Bella 13m

4 🔩 Traverse right to the 1st bolt and engage in edgy climbing through the crux. Move sprightly up the lovely ledges to finish. *Andrew Buist 2001*

❻ 20 Violet Crumble 12m

1 🔩 A good bouldery start. Place wires above the bolt and watch the top—it's mossy and run-out. The anchor is a single bolt and large block. *Bruce Dowrick 1990*

Sensible Shoes Slab

The next wall is a laid-back slab with a bunch of easy routes. It's great for first ventures on rock or a chilled out afternoon with a picnic.

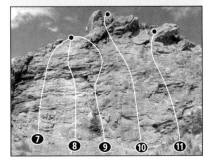

❼ 13 Sensible Shoes 6m

1 🔩 Climb just right of a vague crack. *Stu Allan 1996*

❽ 15 Fast Forward 7m

2 🔩 Zoom up the steepest part of the wall on super good edges. *Stu Allan 1996*

❾ 14 Looking Back 8m

2 🔩 Follows the weakness. Watch the block left of the 2nd bolt and top-out left or place gear and head right. *Stu Allan 1996*

❿ 12 High Heels 8m

2 🔩 Up the middle of the slab to a blocky overhang. Take cams for the top. *Lindsay Main 1996*

⓫ 13 Steel Caps 8m

2 🔩 A slab with great holds and a couple of ledges. Finish up a groove left of the large block. *Phil Stuart-Jones 1996*

Solar Wall

Another pleasant wall with climbs that finish at a double bolt anchor a few metres back.

⑫ **★19 Pssst 13m**

Starts on the seam left of the main face. Really nice moves, but thin gear until cams on the upper headwall get you grinning.

⑬ **★20 Solar Powered 13m**

2 Intriguing face climbing up the middle of the face will amp you up and cams help ease the flow. *Neil Sloan 1992*

⑭ **17 Electricorpse 13m**

1 A thin crack with a gully above. There is decent pro low down but it's run-out to the bolt. *Neil Sloan 1992*

The next route is 12m left of the gully on a small yellow-ish wall.

3 **★17 Nuggets 10m**

A cheeky diagonal line across the face on very nice rock. Traverse right to left past 3 bolts. *Neil Sloan 1992*

Merlin Wall

This wall is left of a wide gully that makes an easy descent and provides good access to this area from the road.

3 **★15 A Slight Thud 8m**

Pleasant face climbing on the wall left of *Merlin the Happy Pig*. *Richard Thomson*

⑰ **19 Merlin the Happy Pig 8m**

1 Hog heaven. Climb left of the arête and grunt your way up through crimpers to the flake. *Marcus Thomas 1990*

⑱ **18 Pigs Can Fly 8m**

3 Interesting climbing with a strenuous start. After the 1st bolt cross the arête onto the face. *Simon Middlemass (solo) 1997*

⑲ **21 Bull in a China Shop 7m**

2 Steep jugs to the 2nd bolt. Pull over, thinking it's in the bag, only to encounter some mean slopers. *Richard Kimberley 1997*

⑳ **16 Flap Flap 6m**

1 This right-trending line is better than you'd think. Lovely holds and top-out. *Peter Sykes*

Shimmering Jelly Wall

This striking wall has a really good selection of trad routes and some enticing sport lines thrown in.

㉑ **19 Nocuous 12m**

1 A blocky start up the arête to gain the jug. Swing right to clip and continue up the face on nice edges. Find good wire placements in the crack (as for *Thin Hedgehog*). *Marcus Thomas 1994*

㉒ 19 Thin Hedgehog 12m

1 🔩
Layback up the crack to the 1st bolt. Veer left to cruxy climbing and find pro in the top crack. The direct start is grade 20. *Richard Thomson*

㉓ ★17 Roadside Attraction 12m

This fetching shallow crack makes for absorbing climbing and the fiddly pro keeps you on your toes. *Lindsay Main 1980*

㉔ 16 Bagatelle 12m

Climb up the twin cracks and veer left. There are some good placements for small cams at half-height, but things get a bit run-out at the top. *Lindsay Main 1981*

㉕ ★12 Gift Horse 12m

Don't bypass this offering, it's one of the nicest, easy trad lines on the Port Hills. There is plenty of gear and creative moves. *Lindsay Main 1974*

㉖ ✷20 Shimmering Jelly 12m

2 🔩
Shimmy up sweet little edges on the face past 2 bolts. A popular climb to test your face climbing prowess. *Pete Sykes*

㉗ 15 Cold Turkey 11m

This follows the rounded crack lines on the right side of the face. Enjoy good holds and gear. *Lindsay Main 1980*

㉘ ★18 70 Cents Worth 11m

3 🔩
Up the slab left of the arête, past the bolts and onwards to a steeper finish. *Stu McConney 1999*

Shimmering Jelly Wall

Richard Kimberley on *Prophet of Doom* (23)

MARK WATSON

Lyttelton Rock is a south-facing band of solid volcanic rock on the crater of the extinct volcano that formed most of Banks Peninsula. The crag has a lofty setting above the Lyttelton Harbour and a great view down onto the busiest port in the South Island and across to the bays of Banks Peninsula. Some staunch natural gear classics, such as *Scratching Julius* and *Citizen Kane* reside here and are a must do for keen trad climbers. There are also a good variety of cranky, bolted routes and edgy face climbs. The crag is well maintained, so expect clean routes and generally good protection.

 Drive towards Sumner and just before McCormacks Bay, turn right onto Mt Pleasant Rd.

Follow this to the top of the hill (7km) and turn right onto the Summit Rd. After 1km you will drive over a cattlestop, through a rock cutting and past the Cattlestop Crag. The road dips downhill and you will see the Gondola terminal ahead. Park on the left at the car park for the Lyttelton Scenic Reserve. You can also access this crag from the Dyers Pass (Sign of the Kiwi) end of the Summit Rd. It is 2.5km past Castle Rock.

From the car park, veer left up the track to meet Susie's Slab.

i One of the best things about Lyttelton Rock is that it is sheltered from the gusty nor'wester. Most of the walls are tucked amongst the native bush, which also makes them relatively sheltered in an easterly and shady in the middle of summer. The crag tends to be a bit grim in winter when the rock is prone to seepage.

The track along the base gets a fair amount of traffic, especially in the weekend. It is a good idea to keep your gear together and off the track. Most climbs are equipped with double bolt anchors.

'Everyone should learn how to weasel out of something. It's what separates us from the animals...except for the weasel of course.' **Homer Simpson**

Susie's Slab

This is the first rock that you meet after leaving the car park. The rest of the crag is further down the track facing the harbour.

❶ ★**19 Susies Slab 6m**

1 Looks very innocent, but is really a bit of a hussy. Superlative rock and a couple of sly, balancy moves make this well worth a go. *Merv English 1983*

❷ ★**22 Pumping Velvet 7m**

2 Layaway to the bolt, then navigate the crimp infested waters. Some cunning is required. *Ton Snelder 1984*

About 15m down the track on the next band of rock:

❸ **16 Sinking Ship 12m**

Awkward but fun (depending on your frame of mind). Follow the wide crack and step left onto the pillar at the top. *Lindsay Main 1978*

Lyttelton Rock

❹ 24 Social Ostracyte Direct 14m

2 ◉ Technical climbing on slopey edges with a devious little crux. The original line bypasses the crux by starting left and moving diagonally right onto the climb at grade 20. *Roger Parkyn (original line) 1984. Pete Smale (direct start)*

❺ 21 Crucifix 14m

Spot the crucifix feature. Great gear to below the crux, then thin/non-existent gear up the top arête. *Lindsay Main 1983*

❻ ★23 Idol Boys 12m

3 ◉ Crank to the 1st clip and curve left through the crux to the slab. Snake back right onto the airy arête.
Paul Jackson/John Chambers 1997

★16 Gooders Line 14m

One of the earliest routes established at this crag. Bridge up the crack to the flared upper section. Get in as much good gear as you fancy; pause to soak up the nostalgia, and pull through some balancy moves. Anchor out left. *Ross Gooder 1971*

❽ ★21 Rubicon 14m

A line of weakness cutting through the steep roof section. Don't be daunted, the gear is surprisingly good. *Lindsay Main 1983*

❾ 20 It's Tough at the Top 14m

Up the thin crack to bigger holds. Step right for slab moves and run it out through easier ground. *Lindsay Main 1983*

Ton Snelder on Pumping Velvet (22)
TON SNELDER COLLECTION

4 ◉ 20 Eight Million Years 14m

Swing onto the arête and move straight up, finding funky moves and a little pumpiness. *Lindsay Main 2000*

⓫ ★19 Dumping Velvet 14m

2 ◉ A testing slab that is bound to get the disco leg going if you're climbing at your grade. A wee way to the 1st bolt and healthy run-outs after this on fun crimps (if a little on the mossy side). *Joe Arts 1983*

Around the corner on a round orange slab:

4 ◉ ★24 Red Wall 15m

Hard climbing on small off-balance holds through the first 2 bolts to a more laid-back slab. *Tony Burnell 1996*

Feeding Time Wall

The next prominant face has some great lines on consistently good, orange rock

⑬ ★23 Prophet of Doom 16m

3 Jolly good edge climbing up this steep wall with holds that resemble fat rolls. Hmmm yum. The holds are positive but the pump may sneak up. *Simon Middlemass 1990*

★21 Feeding Time at the Zoo 16m

1 A popular face climb with a crack start. Boulder up to the bulge where good gear protects the crux moves, then inch your way past the bolt to easier territory. *Joe Arts 1982*

⑮ ★22 Driftnet 16m

2 Climb directly to the 1st bolt, muscle your way through the crux then relax and enjoy the quality rock beneath your fingertips. One piece of mid-size gear protects to the 2nd bolt. *Ton Snelder 1989*

★17 The Promised Land 16m

A saucy route with spaced pro. Ooze up the slab, reach through the overlap to the piton (can be backed up with a #1.5 cam in the horizontal break), then move past the flake with care. Take the steepest line to finish. *Lindsay Main 1983*

⑰ 14 Steppenwolf 15m

A wide crack with a bush in the middle. Big gear. *Paul Drake 1975*

The following 2 routes are short face climbs, accessed via an unprotected but easy traverse ledge that starts at the Steppenwolf *Crack.*

⑱ ★18 Restless 16m

2 An array of good edges and a few burly moves to the 2nd bolt, then head slightly right to top-out. *Joe Arts 1983*

⑲ ★18 Mistery 16m

3 Follow the same traverse ledge as *Restless* (clipping a bolt on the way past), then delicately meander up the face on some good edges. *Simon Middlemass 2000*

179

The three next routes start around the corner in the trees and can be damp in winter.

⑳ ★19 Out on a Limb 18m

3 This bolted classic is in a shady grotto next to a long-suffering tree. It gets a lot of ascents and the small flat edges make fantastic crimps. There is a big run-out to the 2nd bolt (groundfall if you are clipping), but it's all on jugs. Shake out for some steep pumpy ground to the 3rd bolt. *John Birch 1990*

★17 The Environment Centre Bites the Dust 20m. Start at a vague corner right of the tree. The gear is sparse to the obvious flake 4m up, but gets progressively more generous further up the crack. *Joe Arts 1983*

2 ★18 White Lies 18m

Start as for *Environment Centre* and move right along the ledge to the light streak. Interesting moves link up well on the face. Finish on run-out but juggy ground. *John Barnes 1988*

㉓ ★20 Suppressed Personalities 20m

⚠ A long and interesting ex-aid route up the weakness. Steep cranking at the start leads into some technical face climbing with devious gear. *Joe Arts 1983*

Rage Wall

A long wall with excellent rock and an aura of staunchness. It does look intimidating but most routes are quite innocent.

㉔ 24 Cli… Revisited 22m

7 An slightly nasty start on sharp holds and hard moves leads left to pleasant face climbing. *Tony Burnell 1998*

㉕ ★24 Acid Drop 20m

4 Start as for *Rage sur la Plage,* but after the wire placement head left and straight up the right side of the steep prow. *Andrew Milne 1994*

㉖ ★★25 Rage Sur La Plage 20m

4 A hard crimpy start eases off to an easy face where you'll find a big wire placement. When it gets steeper, take a deep breath and hoon up the headwall, drifting left towards the arête. The anchor is around the corner to the left. *Dave Fearnley 1987*

㉗ ★21 The Active Ingredient 23m

4 Embark up the thin crack to the ledge and follow the left-arcing weakness ⚠ until it becomes horizontal. Move

through the roof and, once you've mastered this, the top section is relatively easy but with little pro. *Roger Parkyn 1984*

28 ★22 Bodies 23m

This is not for boys—a fall could turn you into a 'gurgling bloody mess.' Start as for *The Active Ingredient*, go up the crack and onto the ledge. From here be brave and head up the steep wall. Eventually veer left at the top to a cam placement and to join *The Active Ingredient*. *Ton Snelder 1985*

29 ✳23 Victim of Ravishment 23m

An awesome route after some awkward moves to gain the face. Start right of *Rage sur la Plage* and traverse diagonally right to the face. This has beautiful and sustained edging and is a technical and pumpy proposition. Take a #0.5-1 sized cam to finish. *Ton Snelder 1985*

Mr Clean Wall

15m along the track from *Victim of Ravishment*, this is undoubtedly the best wall at the crag. The rock is steep and offers a great selection of trad and bolted routes.

★21 Bombs Away 28m

Quite an explosive little number. It's tucked innocuously around the left edge of the wall, which makes for slabby climbing with interesting falls. Best avoided when wet. *Joe Arts 1983*

181

Lyttelton Rock

㉛ ★26 Drop the Bomb 18m

A steep groove with a high 1st bolt. After this, follow the crack line past the crux and move right at the top. *Dave Fearnley 1987*

㉜ ★24 Clip or Fly 18m

Start as for *Scratching Julius* and head left onto the prow as soon as possible. The climbing is edgy and good value. *Peter Taw 1991*

㉝ ★★21 Scratching Julius 18m

A stellar crack line with great gear, albeit fairly strenuous to place. Exit right to the anchor. Named after John's cat. He originally aided and called it *Rat Fink*. *John Visser 1982*

㉞ ★★25 Fillet of Arnold 19m

Bite into this succulent face climb. It gets steadily more tasty as you ascend and the finale is a slopey exit, which can spit you off if you're tired. *Ton Snelder 1989*

㉟ ★23 Stars and Stripes 19m

An old aid line that follows the natural weakness. It has the same start as *Getting Rid of Mr Clean*, then veers leftwards through crux moves. After this the crack is juggy and receptive to pro. *Steve (Shipoopi) Schneider 1987*

㊱ ★★23 Getting Rid of Mr Clean 18m

Mega-classique (and not as run-out as it looks)! Superlative cranking is to be had on this strenuous test piece. Gymnastic moves on good holds will get you to a decent rest after the 3rd bolt. *Ton Snelder 1984*

Roger Parkyn on the 1st ascent of *The Active Ingredient* (22)
TON SNELDER COLLECTION

㊲ ★★22 Citizen Kane 18m

Just a bit more strenuous than cousin *Julius*. Georgeous climbing and good pro (if you can hang about to place it well). *Joe Arts 1984*

Thunderdrome Area

Before the days of The Cave, climbers spent a lot of time here devising all kinds of pumpy variations. Here are the most classic. They may not look great, but do climb really well.

㊳ ★27 Gone Bimbo 12m

Climb a short face to the horizontal roof, with an undercling crux. Traverse right on crimps along the lip, place a #2-3 cam and move through to the anchor. *Ton Snelder 1989*

39 27 Alternative Traverse 12m

4 Start as for *Gone Bimbo* and traverse right across the roof to join the lip and *Gone Bimbo* again for the last moves. Take a #2-3 cam for the slot. *Andy Cockburn 1993*

40 28 Creatures of Power 15m

5 A very awkward, technical crux low down to a long slabby finish and single bolt anchor. *Peter Taw 1993*

41 ★23 Jug Jockey 15m

4 Climb over several small roofs before the resistance eases on the face. Take a #1 cam. *Tony Burnell 1997*

42 22 Frank's in a Frenzy 15m

3 Go up the left facing corner and rock-over onto the block thing. Continue up the steep wall to a small arête and then slab. *Damian Carroll*

43 ★21 Art for Art's Sake 14m

5 A few metres up the track. Climb a low roof and into the left facing corner. Head straight through another small roof and small arête. *Tony Burnell 1997*

Ataturk Wall

Further along the track, this is a big wall, which is mostly chossy, apart from these two good lines on the right.

44 ★23 Salome Maloney 16m

5 An easy start which soon enough hits challenging terrain on the steep prow. *Tony Burnell 1997*

45 ★22 Colonel Malone 16m

4 An intriguing climb up a vauge corner. Starts off slow but builds up steam to the pumpy and slightly weird crux at the top. *Joe Arts 1989*

Three Sisters

Only two sisters really (the Ugly one is not that flash), this crag is the eastward extension of the Lyttelton Rock volcanic band. The area certainly doesn't get the attention it deserves, which is surprising considering that this is one of Christchurch's major crags with good quality climbs.

Although very close to Lyttelton Rock, the character of the Three Sisters is quite different in places. Some of the best lines follow smooth bulbous arêtes and red, lichenous faces. This is a wonderful place to languish above the harbour. Especially on a sunny evening when the sun lights up the red rock against a backdrop of native bush.

Drive up Mt Pleasant Rd (7km) to the Summit Rd. Turn right and take the next left into Broadleaf Lane. Follow this to the gate and then continue to the end of the gravel road (500m). Park next to the mysterious concrete building.

Walk east from the car park, cutting past the trig station on the Summit Rd side. Cross one fence then continue along the fenceline for about 50m. Cross the fence, then zig-zag your way through long grass and flax straight down towards Lyttelton for 10mins. There is no distinct track but if you stay on the left of the first spur, you will intersect the main walkway.

Turn left onto the main track and after about 30m you will see another track heading down to Lyttelton. It is marked with an orange triangle and will put you between the Sisters, with Middle Sister on your left.

There is also good access to this crag from Lyttelton Rock. After the Colonel Malone Wall, continue along the track for 10mins. After the chossy grey wall, the first track downhill is quite vague and will take you to the left end of the Twisted Sister. The next track (100m along) will take you to the left end of the Middle Sister.

i The climbing here is quite varied. You could happily spend the day doing sport routes, but you would be missing out on some spectacular trad climbing. Some of the cracks do need cleaning and it is a good idea to take a nut key on lead.

It would be great to see more people doing the odd bit of track/crag maintenance. The onga onga is the bain of the crag. It makes sandal and short wearing quite brutal. If you have access to pruning equipment, dealing to the onga onga is a good strategy.

Keeping one track along the base of the crag clear also helps seedling natives grow over the other rambling paths. Be careful not to disturb the climbing rata vines on the crag.

Twisted Sister

The left end of the Twisted Sister has an array of steep, tricky sport routes then some lovely mid-grade lines further right.

1 **26 Ongaphile 16m**

7 Around the corner of the crag and facing west. Clamber onto the ledge and then up the face. *Roland Foster 1996*

2 **28 Big Red 16m**

7 Start as far *Ongaphile* but once you are at the ledge, take the right line of bolts through the red face. *Derek Thatcher 2002*

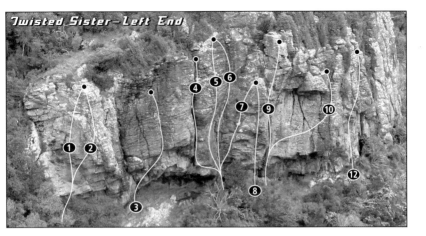

Twisted Sister—Left End

❸ ★26 Deja Jeux 16m

6 Interesting holds past 2 glue-in ring bolts. The roofs lead rightward to a groove with big sidepulls. *Tony Burnell 1999*

❹ 25 Bullworker 17m

6 Start at *Onga Onga via Interflora* but low traverse left to the offwidth which sports nice climbing. *Tony Burnell 1999*

❺ ★★24 Onga Onga via Interflora 16m

5 From the start of *Wages of Fear*, veer left to greet the steep headwall with wonderful climbing. *Phil Higgins 1996*

❻ ★★22 Wages of Fear 16m

3 From the boulder below the crack step up to the corner. Expect enjoyable and safe climbing after the 1st bolt. *Joe Arts 1994*

❼ 25 Soft Centre 13m

5 After the first couple moves of *Wages of Fear* go right to the bolts. Rest on the slab before the last bulge. *Tony Burnell 1998*

❽ 27 Getting Nowhere Fast 13m

4 A hard fingery start to bigger holds through the overhang. The slab provides relief before the last bulge. *Jonathon Wilkinson 1999*

❾ ★27 Swing out Sister 18m

7 The crack which turns into a corner with roofs above. Hoon past 2 bolts into the corner and veer left up the overhanging headwall. *Tony Burnell 1999*

❿ 27 Hatched Matched and Dispatched

5 **18m.** Start as for *Swing out Sister* but move right at the 1st bolt. Traverse accross the whole face to the red groove. The anchor is up and around the corner. *Tony Burnell 1998*

Project 15m

4 A bottomless crack with a nasty hard start.

⓬ ★24 Onga Ongarangutang 15m

5 Diagonaly left up the face and through several small overlaps. *John McCallum 1996*

Three Sisters

Twisted Sister–Right End

⑭ ⑮ ⑯ ⑰ ⑱ ⑲ ⑳ ㉑ ㉒ ㉓ ㉔ ㉕ ㉖

23 The Last Seduction 13m
The short and fairly innocent looking crack which widens considerably at half-height. *Joe Arts 1995*

⑭ ✷18 The Stalker 13m
3 ⚡ Muscle up the bulge left of the chimney past the 1st bolt. Watch the run-out to good mid-size cam placements before the next clip. Great airy moves traversing left and up the arête. The left start is about grade 20. *Joe Arts 1995*

⑮ ✷21 Future Cops 12m
3 ⚡ A beautiful red slab with a few hard moves low down to an easy 1st clip. Classic slab climbing ensues. You can move left to clip the 3rd bolt before tackling the crux out right. The anchor is a wire cable around the tree. *Joe Arts 1994*

⑯ ✷24 Peer Pressure 15m
5 ⚡ A really interesting gem. The consistency and quality of the climbing is rare on the Port Hills. Navigate the slopers and move up a shallow seam on the face. *Tony Burnell 1999*

⑰ ★22 Sloper & Sloper Inc. 18m
3 ⚡ A long commute to work via the right side of the pillar (slinging this isn't such a bad idea). Step into the boardroom at the top of the pillar for an comfy clip, and crux. Technical negotiations and fancy footwork should close the deal. An easy commute home. *Marcus Thomas 1995*

⑱ ★22 The Energy of Dogs 15m
2 ⚡ Follow the slabby, right-leaning ramp to reach the crack. Place gear and continue up the crack finding funky climbing. You'll be greeted with a slopey top-out. *Marcus Thomas 1994*

⑲ ★20 Grunty Falcon 15m
1 ⚡ This apparently refers to the petrol-guzzling beast that Marcus used to drive to the crag. From the scoop at the base of the chimney, grunt past the bolt into a layaway. Follow the crack to the top of the pillar then sling a bush and climb left across the wall to reach the *Energy of Dogs* abseil chain. *Marcus Thomas 1994*

The next grey/green wall is a nice length and the lines are appealing. The rock has a crusty surface, but if you like uncertainty these will be your cup of tea. The routes are all bolted and graded 22, 25, 23.

⑳ ★23 Sister Act 13m

4 A unique climb on the green streaked face, capped with a long narrow roof. Sidepulls and edges on the face lead to the roof. Traverse left and over to the anchor. *Tony Burnell 1999*

㉑ 20 Killing Capitalism with Kindness 13m

2 As much suspense as a good Agatha Cristie on reasonably solid rock. ⚠ Bridge off the large tree below the corner and head right across the face. A big cam higher up the crack can help protect the hard moves to the 2nd bolt, otherwise it is a grounder. Cams also protect the tricky rock-over exit to the anchor out left. *Marcus Thomas 1994*

㉒ 27 More Perverted than Twisted 13m

4 Begin up the steep inverted staircase 4m right of the tree. Hard moves to the roof, then trend right and onto the slab. Continue straight to the anchor on gear. *Tony Burnell 1999*

㉓ 18 Debris Slide 16m

1 The name may hint at the rock quality. Nevertheless, the climb is intriguing. Start in a corner just left of the knarled tree and head straight up for 5m before traversing sharply left. Once on the slab keep trucking left to join *Killing Capitalism. Marcus Thomas 1995*

㉔ 22 Cock in a Frock on a Rock 16m

3 Cross dressing is always a bit of a thrill for the belayer. Starts as for *Debris Slide* and after the pro placement go right to a balancy clip. Keep moving through steep terrain on good holds to a single bolt anchor. *Joe Arts 1995*

㉕ ★17 Making Losers Happy 14m

3 A few moves from the tree to the 1st bolt. After the 2nd, head left across the wall through some large crumbly pockets. The run-out after the 2nd bolt can be protected with a #1 cam. The exit through to the single bolt anchor is steep. *Marcus Thomas 1995*

㉖ 24 Pigs in Zen 12m

2 Power your way right through the small, steep face. Edgy holds culminate in a lunge to the top lip. Mantle over and a small cam will protect the last few moves. *Marcus Thomas 1999*

Middle Sister

Middle Sister is home to trad classics, like *Judge and Jury, Fear of Flying* and plenty of worthwhile sporty lines.

23 Unnamed 7m

2 A good wee climb nestled in native bush at the left end of the crag. This compact angular rock (similar to the good stuff at Lyttelton Rock) is a crimp fest that definitely packs a bit of punch.

㉘ ★24 Gold Soundz 12m

2 A cute rounded arête. Weave your way up slopey holds with balancy moves. *Marcus Thomas 1997*

Three Sisters

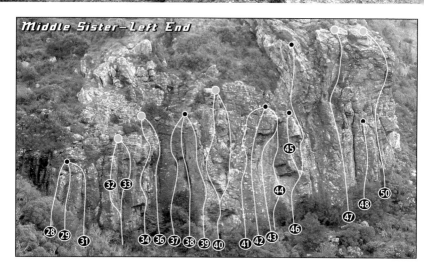

Middle Sister—Left End

㉙ 16 Short Order 12m

An open corner sporting really good gear placements in the crack. Well worth a look. *Lindsay Main 1981*

㉚ 21 Desert Solitaire 12m

Climb the face, veering right to the arête. If you want to protect the moves to the 1st bolt use the crack in *Short Order*. The top half has tenuous smears and good open hand holds. *Brian Fish 1981*

㉛ 23 Caley 12m

Staunch bridging at the base leads to some technicalities. The pro is fiddly on the top section. *Ton Snelder 1990*

㉜ ★22 Penal Rates 14m

A tenuous test piece that starts up *Bridge Too Far*. Delicately traverse to the arête, hug this past the next bolt and look for the 'thank God' edge. A relaxing top-out with small gear placements. *Lindsay Main 1990*

㉝ 17 A Bridge Too Far 14m

A complex corner with surprisingly good gear. Big hexes would drop nicely into the flared constriction. The climbing is sustained and flows well. *Lindsay Main 1977*

The Judge and Jury Wall

An amazing-looking wall in an alcove that has some bomber trad lines. It is one of the highlights of the crag!

㉞ ★20 Joggersaurus Wrecked 16m

Scamper left up the wall following the overlap. Whack a cam in the wide crack, oxygenate, then either find a fingerlock and climb boldly through the groove, or face the face on crimps. Finish up a gentle crack. *Neil Sloan 1996*

★19 Volcanic Café 16m

You wouldn't know it from the ground but there are textbook gear placements 'everywhere' on this climb. Follow the middle crack, step left under the roof and pull a few powerful moves. *Joe Arts 1990*

36 **★17 Corner Dearie 16m**
Enough gear for a supermarket. The corner start is awkward but once this relents everything is fine and dandy. *Neil Sloan 1996*

37 **⚡22 The Monkey Wrench Gang 16m**
An awesome route starting up the overlap with bomber gear. Move left to the 2nd bolt to a classic face with positive edges. *Joe Arts 1990*

38 **⚡17 Judge and Jury 16m**
This crack looks dark and ominous but is a trad treat. Bridge up little ledges and throw yourself into some good old fashioned jamming action through the bulge. A steep finish—oooh yeh. *Lindsay Main 1977*

To the right of the Judge and Jury Wall:

39 **★23 Frog Buttress 18m**
A satisfying excursion on appealing rock. Start behind a tree and gain jugs. It's cruxy through the layaways before you move left to the steepening face. *Richard Kimberley 1999*

40 **19 Jesse Owens 18m**
Pull through the overhang into the corner and climb the crack with pro. There are 2 variation finishes. The left finish moves under the roof, and once you are on the arête drift right to solid rock (the blocks out left are loose). The right variation continues past the tree to a nice crack. *Joe Arts 1990. Tony Burnell (direct finish) 1999*

15 Port Hill Essentials

The Port Hills crags; what they might lack in pure quality of rock they make up for in diversity of climbing style and experience. The development timeline of the Port Hills has been such that they represent a kind of museum (art gallery?) of New Zealand climbing, with all styles and phases of climbing represented in the routes.

Though Port Hills climbing exploration dates back to 1913 it is only since the 1960s that accurate records have been kept and the pace of development steady. What follows is a sampler of classic Port Hills climbing—a selection of routes at a range of grades and crags, from a range of first ascentionists, and chosen from five decades to represent each evolutionary phase. Climbing these routes will test your repertoire of climbing skills, whilst taking you on a historic tour of the best of Port Hills climbing.

Pre-history–sixties
• Kestrel/Arrow combination (14), Castle Rock
• Hangman (17) Castle Rock
• Main Royale (16) Rapaki

Seventies
• Court Jester (20), Castle Rock
• Nudity (20), Tors
• Stranger (17), Mt Pleasant

Eighties
• Victim of Ravishment (22), Lyttelton Rock
• Rage Sur La Plage (25), Lyttelton Rock
• Armitage Shanks (23), Jane Fonda

Nineties
• The Monkey Wrench Gang (22), Middle Sister
• Surgical Strike (21), Cattlestop
• Gorilla Grip (27), The Cave

Noughties
• Mount Pleasant Butcher (24), Britten Crag
• Where Angels Fear to Tread (23), Britten Crag
• Troglodyte (30), The Cave

Mark Watson

Three Sisters

Fear Of Flying Wall

Two red arêtes sandwich this long pale green face. Capped by an impressive roof, this wall certainly has the best aesthetics of the area, along with some staunch lines. The test pieces are bound to instil an appreciation for gravity.

41 ★**23 Suicide Machine 18m**

3 Bulgy overlaps make interesting features on this climb. Devious to the 2nd bolt; stay left of the 3rd and finish up the crack with pro. *Joe Arts 1990*

42 ★**22 Nasty and Unconstructive 18m**

4 Maniacs can charge up to the 1st bolt but those put off by the potential to get yourself mangled, munted and maimed can pre-clip from *Fear of Flying*. After the 1st bolt the moves are great and the top arête exhilarates. *Joe Arts 1991*

43 ★★**17 Fear of Flying 18m**

Touted as the classic of the crag, this is definitely up there with the classics of the Port Hills. While the top section gets the 'thumbs up' for gear and climbing quality, the lower section is very run-out. The first good pro is about 8m off the deck but the holds are all there if your head is. At the top either step left to the *Suicide Machine* anchor or belay from the single bolt. *Henry Mares 1977*

44 **20 Flight Path 18m**

Start to the left of the creeper and skirt over the top. There is no pro until under the roof, then move left around the roof and step right onto the orange wall. Finish at the *Fear of Flying* single bolt anchor. *Tony Burnell 1999*

45 ★**20 Learning to Fly 18m**

4 Start up *Evasive Action* and after the 2nd bolt get some gear in the groove. Move left onto the exposed arête and finish up the horizontal headwall at a single bolt anchor. *Marcus Thomas 1997*

46 ★**18 Evasive Action 25m**

4 An interesting route up the far right of the wall. Keep it together up to the 1st bolt and move onto the red arête. After the 2nd bolt things get a bit run-out, but there is a large cam placement behind the nose at the top of the arête. Trend left and climb the wall past the bolt. A few great moves to the single bolt anchor. Originally established in two pitches. *Lindsay Main 1984. Joe Arts 1994 (2nd pitch)*

47 ★**20 Working Overtime 23m**

1 Another characteristic Three Sisters arête. The bulbous holds give good friction through some technical moves. After the bolt there is an occasional small wire of dubious quality. When the climbing eases off find ample pro through the corner system to the top of the crag. *Lindsay Main 1990*

48 ★**23 No Static at All 11m**

3 Enter this lovely face from the left. Resist the urge to barndoor off the balancy start, then cruise to the single bolt anchor. *Richard Kimberley 1999*

49 **18 Pain in the Arts 11m**

2 Balancy moves on the short arête past 2 bolts. Lower off the single bolt at the top of the arête (as for *No Static at All*), or continue over broken ground (with adequate pro) to the top. *Marcus Thomas 1995*

Middle Sister—Right End

50 **★16 Shark's Nest 20m**

A sinker wire protects the crux start and the remainder of the crack system has nice stances and evenly spaced gear. Once you gain the slab, head slightly right to the final short crack. *Henry Mares 1977*

51 **⚹16 Prometheus Busted 18m**

A mint climb that is one of the best at its grade in the area. Traverse from the right end of the lower face into the wide crack. There's a cam placement in the horizontal notch to protect the slabby moves. Otherwise, climb the left crack which leads to the roof. The roof is quite exciting but no need to have a mongy spaze out, and then veer left over easier ground to the upper crack system. *Lindsay Main 1977*

52 **10 Grand Central Station 12m**

A relaxing adventure up the obvious crack. The vegetation doesn't get in the way of good gear placements. *Lindsay Main 1973*

53 **★23 Kurious Oranji 12m**

Minimalist holds low down lead to better edges through the small bulge. Lovely from here. Pro to finish. *Jonathan Wilkenson 1999*

54 **22 Golden Delicious 7m**

Short but very tricky. RPs may protect to the 1st bolt, then pull through the crux. Single bolt anchor. *Marcus Thomas 1997*

191

The Cave

4

1

3

2

Kaz Pucia on *Dracula* (32). MARK WATSON

The Cave is a massive roof of rock hidden away halfway up the Barnett Park walkway. The terrain is more horizontal than vertical and the routes are quite long. The rock is curvaceous, pleasant to hold and offers varied climbing with lots of heel-hooks. It's a popular place to hang out, flail around and occasionally redpoint. Due to the extreme angle, The Cave houses many powerful endurance test pieces making it 'the' steep sportclimbing crag in New Zealand.

From the centre of the city drive towards Sumner. Just past Redcliffs, turn right into Bay View Rd and park at the end.

Use the walking track up the right side of the valley. The Cave is 100m past a gate and hidden on the right amongst some trees.

i Climbing is possible all year round, but spring through to autumn is the best because it's drier. Winter can be too cold and some routes are prone to seepage. A rope-tarp is essential due to the dusty cave floor.

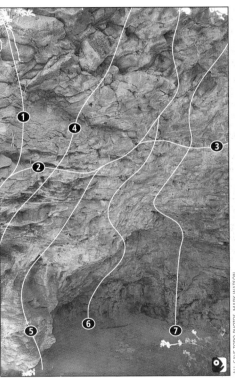

ALL CAVE TOPO PHOTOS, MARK WATSON

❶ 26 Super Glue 11m

7 Short but requires plenty of ooze. Begin at the far left of the cave and traverse right on big holds to the first crux. Now head straight up on small edges until over the lip of the cave. *Tony Ward-Holmes 1998*

❷ ★28 She Devil 16m

10 Unrelenting and solid. Climb past the first 4 bolts of *Super Glue*, but continue traversing right to *Gorilla Grip*. By now you should be quite pumped and there's still most of *Gorilla Grip* to go. *Richard Kimberley 1998*

❸ ★32 Centrifuge 18m

12 The horizontal line which traverses almost half of The Cave. Start as for *She Devil*, pass *Gorilla Grip* and continue across the seam which leads to *Bogus Machismo*. A mediocre rest after the long traverse provides some recovery for the weird and very wide crux. *Ivan Vostinar 2003*

193

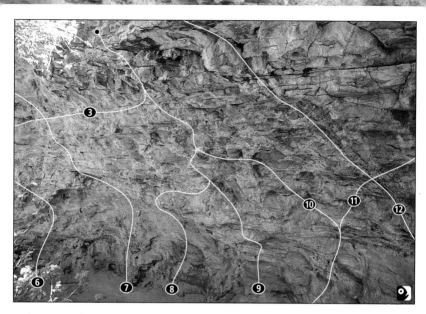

❹ 27 Rubble 14m

7 Starts left of the small slab. Steep climbing crosses the traverse line to holds hopefully better than the name implies. *Tony Ward-Holmes 2004*

❺ ★27 Gorilla Grip 15m

9 One of The Cave classics and always climbed on. Start up the mini slab and climb boldly through three distinct cruxes. It's very steep but good jugs lie in wait after all the hard bits. *Matt Evrard 1993*

❻ ★30 Troglodyte 15m

9 After a cruxy start up the small groove on small crimps, make technical moves left to the big jug. Shake, go left and hang onto the slippery slopers through the main crux. One more tricky section before joining *Gorilla Grip* for the top-out. *Ivan Vostinar 2003*

❼ ★Project 16m

9 Start in the corner and, once up a bit, drift left via a very long section of consistently very hard moves to the lip of the Cave. An impressive straight line on enjoyable holds.

❽ 29 Snake Charmer 18m

13 Up the left-leaning crack thing; set up on small crimps and power up for a big dyno. Traverse right to the pigeon pod and enjoy the rest before joining *Bogus Machismo* via some campusing. Really long but ingenious rests can be found. *Originally climbed to the pigeon pod by John McCallum in 1994 as Hung Like Elvis (26). Ivan Vostinar 2003*

❾ ★32 Ride of the Valkyries 17m

9 The first half of this route is on excellent rock. It involves a dyno and intense fingery moves to the pigeon

pod. After a decadent rest, enjoy some wild moves to link up to the crux of *Bogus Machismo*. *Ivan Vostinar 2003*

⑩ ✹29 Bogus Machismo 18m

11 Great flowing moves make this New Zealand's endurance test piece! Starts in the central, deepest part of the cave. Climb straight up, then veer left at the 4th bolt. The draining start gives way to big holds (relatively speaking) for the middle section. Two cruxes are placed conveniently at the very end for when you are completely pumped. *Peter Taw 1994*

⑪ ✹31 Kaiser Soze 18m

11 Same start as *Bogus Machismo* but head right at the 4th bolt. Generally positive holds with some big stretches, and lightly sprinkled with some rests throughout. *First ascent, Alex Palman in 1998 with manufactured holds (29).* *Ivan Vostinar 2004*

⑫ ✹Project 17m

12 The distinct straight crack that cuts the cave in half. Climb the extremely steep roof on small crimps, gain a rest, cross over *Kaiser Soze* and continue up the feature to the top. Will be a great route.

⑬ ✹32 The Enigma of Kasper Hauser 17m

12 Climbs the crack as for the previous project, but at mid-height turn right and finish as for *Kaiser Soze*. *Derek Thatcher 2004*

⑭ ✹32 Space Boy 16m

10 A milestone in New Zealand's climbing history. Interesting and varied technical moves up the vague arête to the rest hole. Persevere through another bouldery section to a final rest before the last crux. Pumpy finish on good holds. *Originally climbed to just below the last crux by Matt Evrard in 1994. Kaz Puchia 1995*

⑮ Project 14m

7 Same start as *Dracula* but go straight from the 4th bolt. Put the pedal to the metal for two moves and then it's easier.

⑯ ★32 Dracula 14m

7 Start on the right side of the arête-like feature via superb bouldery moves to the 4th bolt. Now go right to join *Nosferatu*. Shake out, get demoralised and hope for the best on the run-out, pumpy finish. *Kaz Pucia 2003*

⑰ Project 17m

9 Climb the steep groove where good holds lead to big moves on nifty slopers. Cross over *Nosferatu* and continue up through the crux and way, way beyond to the top of the cliff.

⑱ 31 Nosferatu 15m

8 A blood sucker. The moves seem alright but putting it together doesn't go easily. After a fingery burst to the only rest, charge left to the cranky crux. Poor footholds require lots of tension and stamina. The route can be extended at grade 32 by traversing from the anchor left onto *Space Boy* and finish up this *(Derek Thatcher 2003)*. *Ivan Vostinar 2002*

⑲ ★26 Urge 13m

7 The big, blocky, bulging beast. An edgy and cruxy start through the mini roof to chunky jugs and an excellent rest at half-height. Another fingery crux leads to jugs, then go right to the anchor. *Brian Alder 1993*

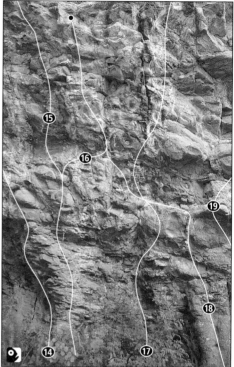

⑳ ✳28 Let There be Bolts 13m

6 Just right of the big blob on *Urge*, you'll find fantastic, funky moves up this sustained and classic route. It's less steep than most of the other Cave routes but really sustained due to poor rests. The interesting moves have kept climbers entertained for years. *Peter Taw 1993*

㉑ 30 Choss Muncher 12m

7 Weird and very strenuous bouldering leads to the crux of *Attack Mode*. Cunning and strong fingers will definitely help, especially since a key hold broke (could be 31). *Derek Thatcher 2002*

㉒ **★28 Attack Mode 13m**

7 Very dastardly for the grade, this sees less ascents than the other 28s here. After the tricky start, head left to a wee rest before committing to serious business on edges through the roof. *Peter Taw 1993*

㉓ **25 Straight No Chaser 13m**

5 Start as for *Attack Mode* and keep going straight up. A draining, bouldery start to a quick rest and steep edge cranking until over the lip. *Tony Ward-Holmes 1998*

㉔ **26 Ice Man 13m**

5 Just left of the waterfall, start as for *Attack Mode*, but at the ledge head right through a difficult roof. *Alex Palman 1998*

Jamie Vinton-Boot on *She Devil* (28). MARK WATSON

Jane Fonda

The Jane Fonda Workout Wall is attractive but also intimidating. It's tucked away in a secluded part of the Port Hills overlooking the Lyttelton Harbour inlet. There is a remote and wild feel to the place and the steep run-off below the wall adds to the exposure. The climbs are long and mostly on excellent rock but what makes this crag require respect is the seriousness of the routes. A few of the climbs are run-out and be cautious of old bolts on a few of the routes. So if you want your adrenal glands to be stimulated by Jane Fonda then come along and get your blood flowing. The wall faces south, so it's grim in winter but great for those hot summer days.

From Sumner drive to Evans Pass, and turn left towards Godley Head. After 3km there is a saddle with a carpark on the right and a stile.

From the stile head west (towards Lyttelton) along the harbour side of the hill. After 7mins the crag should be visible ahead. Keep traversing until above a steep grassy gully which leads down to the right hand end of the wall.

i If you want to rap the routes you'll need either two ropes or one 60m rope, otherwise there is an easy descent on the far left on the crag.

Small wires and RPs will help reduce some of the run-outs.

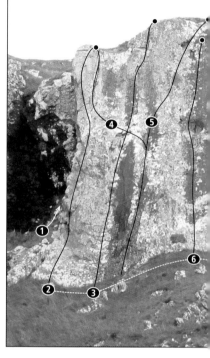

❶ 21 The Penetrator 16m

Around the left side of the wall. Scramble up a short wall to access this west-facing climb. Face climbing on good holds gets tougher to reach the crack with good gear. *Guy Cotter 1989*

❷ ★22 Meat Injection 28m

A long route with varied terrain. Climb the prow directly to *Debauchery,* then step left and continue up the arête. *John McCallum 1986*

❸ ★★19 Polish the Cucumber 28m

A classic climb, somewhat schizophrenic in character. It starts at the left end of the wall just left of the brown

To the crag ➡

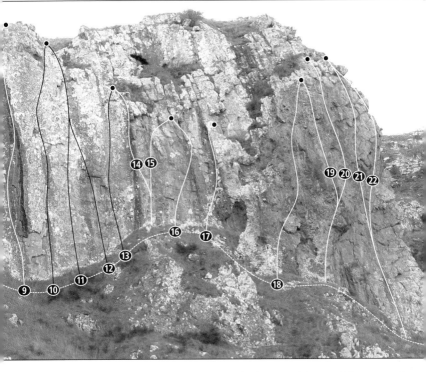

streak up the bolt-protected face. At half-height get your rack ready for a fabulous crack. *Roger Parkyn 1986*

❹ ⚒ 17 Debauchery 29m

A snaking line to access the delicious looking crack. Start up *Purity of Essence* with spaced gear, then traverse left to the crack. As you pass *Polish the Cucumber* the gear becomes good. *Henry Mares 1977*

❺ ⭐ 21 Purity of Essence 30m

Start just right of the brown streak and up to a faint slab/scoop. Continue up the weakness and place a high runner. Traverse right, eventually joining a small roof and exit through this. *Richard Thomson 1986*

❻ ⚒ 22 Whacking Moles 25m

8 Climb the slab directly to the eye and bypass this by veering left. Continue delicately on little edges up the face. *Joe Arts 2004*

❼ ⭐ 22 Spanking Wendy 28m

4 Climb the white slab with mini grooves to a very high 1st bolt. From here it's crusty edging and a bit run-out. Exit left of the cave. *Guy Cotter 1989*

⑧ ⋆21 Half Fact Half Friction 28m

3 ⚠ Start as for *Spanking Wendy* but climb the face a little to the right. Exit on the right side of the cave to join *Cleansing the Stone*. *Gavin Tweedie 1992*

⑨ ⋆⋆22 Cleansing the Stone 28m

4 An exciting climb with big whipper potential. Start just left of the black steak up the brown rock. Once at the 1st bolt, head right and follow the line of good blobby holds. But soon it gets cruxy at the top of the rib. Finish up a short crack. *John McCallum 1986*

⑩ ⋆⋆22 Video Nasty 25m

4 Up a faint right facing corner. There is gear below the 1st bolt and lovely moves up the face to an easier slab. Veer right and save a small cam for the finish. *Roger Parkyn 1986*

⑪ ⋆25 Lard of the Thighs 25m

6 Up the middle of the white lichen face with fingery moves on closely spaced bolts. Once on the slab join *Armitage Shanks*. *Tony Burnell 1997*

⑫ ⋆⋆23 Armitage Shanks 25m

5 A popular and pumpy route up a brown streak. It's quite steep as you veer left and into a small groove. The difficulty relents up the slab, head leftwards. *James Moar 1986*

⑬ ⋆26 Flock to the Rock 16m

2 An awesome looking steep face. Place wires and climb left to the 1st bolt. Now engage the difficult face. *Dave Fearnley 1988*

⑭ ⋆22 Feminine Positions 16m

3 Start as for *Activated Sludge*, but head left at the 1st bolt. Follow the brown and black streak with tricky moves. *Ton Snelder 1986*

⑮ ⋆23 Activated Sludge 13m

2 Face climbing past 2 bolts to a thin short crack. After this step right to the anchor. *Richard Thomson 1986*

⑯ ⋆22 L'Actic Ingredient 13m

3 Up the middle of this small and cute wall. Sustained, technical and veering diagonally right on great rock. *Dave Fearnley 1986*

Kate Finnerty on *Polish the Cucumber* (19). DEAN MACKENZIE

⑰ 14 Spiffhanger 12m

3 🔩 Up the left facing corner, beautiful holds and nice step-ups. *Chris Owens 1995*

⑱ 23 Snotgobblers Revenge 26m

4 🔩 ⚠ Follow a right veering slab onto a block. From here go straight up and at the 3rd bolt step right to run-out territory. *Steve Elder 1990*

⑲ 24 Cinderpath 28m

7 🔩 Start as for the *Artful Dodger* but at the 3rd bolt cut left up the steep and blank wall. Higher up there are lots of blobby bits to pull on. *Tony Burnell 1997*

⑳ ✹20 Artful Dodger 30m

10 🔩 Wild and varied terrain. Traverse right above the overhang to the exposed arête, go around this into a corner. Enjoyable from here only if you have twin ropes or long runners to reduce the rope drag. *Simon Middlemass 1989*

㉑ ✹✹25 Melting Point 35m

10 🔩 Endurance climbing up this long and impressive steep wall. After a short initial slab things get cooking quickly on the weird angles and slopey holds. *Bill McLeod 1989*

㉒ ✹✹26 Tantra 35m

10 🔩 A long and pumpy test piece. From the 3rd bolt of *Melting Point* veer right a little and then tackle the steepest bulge on slopers. *Martyn Clark 1995*

My climbing in the early 80s was witness to…

- Castle Rock being the place rather than Castle Hill.
- Hunting out the tiny arrows where lichen had been scratched away to mark problems at Flock Hill.
- Bouldering with a carpet and no pad.
- *Baby Food* at Cave Stream before instruction groups trashed it.
- Climbing routes at the Homestead but not really bothering to boulder there much.
- No DoC reserve at the Homestead. Sitting at the top of belays and seeing cars stopping on the road for a quick photo opportunity but never seeing tourists wander among the boulders.
- Occassional bus tours driving up to the fence in the Rambandit Valley and parking among the Highland Cattle.
- No village at Castle Hill.
- The jamming pilgrimage trip to Yosemite and bringing back white flares.
- The new haircut trip to Araps on a $30 per week budget.
- The paradise on Earth that was the Bay.
- Purgatory at Long Beach.
- Photocopied and hand-written guides.
- DIY foot long unlined chalkbags. Hell, fleece hadn't been invented yet and then Dave Moss created quilted chalkbags and cornered the market.
- Moulting fibre-pile jackets and salopettes.
- Mountaineers walking up to Castle Rock with heavy packs, wearing plastics and old crampons because rock climbing was but training for the real thing.
- Turning up to Alpine Club slide nights and not really being welcome. Did the club really want to open their doors to these punks?
- Cheap getup, lycra tights for $9 from dance shops, op-shop and market 60's and 70's gear for 50c.
- Being bold, running it out, placing RPs, double ropes and sticht plates with springs.
- Yo-yoing leads with your mates. Having endurance meant you could hang on long enough to place gear.
- Taping the backs of our hands and using 'tinc.'
- Moving out of the cracks and onto the faces using as few bolts as you were game for.
- Hand-drilling with star drills and terriers. Slinging carrots without hangers, using wires or fiddling over an RP keyhole hanger stashed in the chalk bag. Clipping home-made hangers painstakingly hewn from angle stock, every one different and slightly dubious.
- My one moment of retro-bolting shame, which I named *When the Fog Lifts*.

Phil de Joux

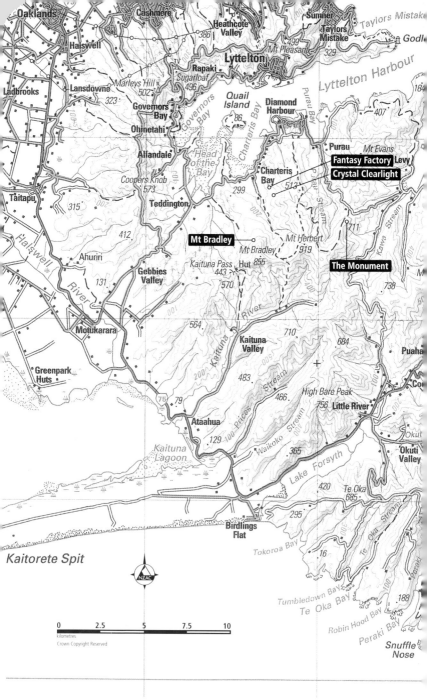

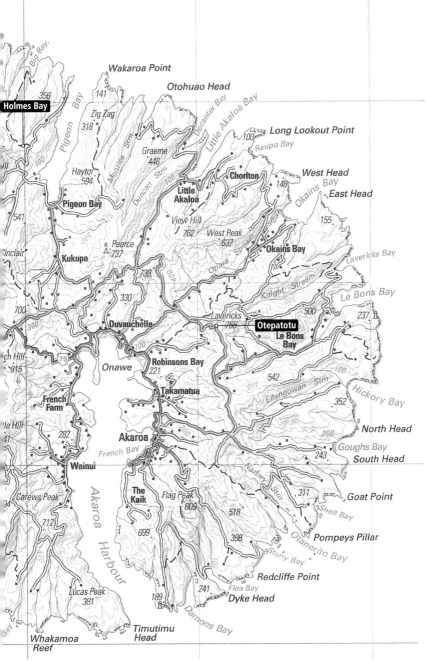

Banks Peninsula

Big Bay

Wakaroa Point

Otohuao Head

356

Holmes Bay

141

Zig Zag

318

Pigeon Bay

Menzies Stm

Duncan Stm

Decanter Bay

Little Akaloa Bay

Long Lookout Point

100

Raupo Bay

West Head

Chorlton

148

Okains Bay

East Head

Graeme
446

Haytor
594

Little
Akaloa

View Hill
762

West Peak
637

Opara Stream

Okains Bay

155

Pigeon Bay

541

Kukupa

Pearce
737

738

Lavericks Bay

Knight Stream

Le Bons Bay

inclair

330

100

500

237

700

300

Laveticks
755

Otepatotu

Le Bons
Bay

ch Hill

815

75

100

Onawe

Robinsons Bay
221

Duvauchelle

542

Ellangowan Stm

Hickory Bay

French
Farm

Takamatua

400

352

le Hill

282

Akaroa

200

North Head

French Bay

Goughs Bay

243

South Head

Wainui

Narbey Stm

Carews Peak

The
Kaik

Flag Peak
809

518

311

Goat Point

712

699

398

Otanerito Bay

Shell Bay

Pompeys Pillar

Akaroa Harbour

Stony Bay

Redcliffe Point

Lucas Peak
381

189

241

Flea Bay

Dyke Head

Whakamoa
Reef

Timutimu
Head

Damons Bay

Mt Bradley

Mt Bradley is the second highest point on Banks Peninsula. The cliffs overlook Lyttelton Harbour and are made of long columns of volcanic rock. The crag is north-facing and catches a good amount of sun, but is very exposed on a windy day. The rock is good quality and the columned features create some mean jam cracks. At the left and right end the lines are short and tend to be easier. The White Wizzard Buttress, is a more daunting proposition, but the climbing is spectacular.

Drive up Dyers Pass Rd to the Sign of the Kiwi and through Governors Bay. Continue to Charteris Bay and turn right into Orton Bradley Park. Check the time that the gate closes. It is on a sign at the entrance to the park.

The cliffs on Mount Bradley are obvious on the right side of the valley. Follow the low track up the valley and head up the hill directly to the cliffs.

At the right end of the Main Cliff there is an easy descent gully. A usual rack is fine, but take lots of slings for the anchors. Some climbers like to use double ropes, and this will be essential if you want to rap off the top of the Main Cliff.

The crag is closed for lambing between September and late October.

Yo-Yo Wall
The first good-looking lines at the left end of the crag.

❶ 18 Pigs On The Wing 17m
Bridge up the short twin cracks to join a wide groove and rounded top out. *Lindsay Main 1983*

❷ ✹21 Yo-Yo 17m
A sumptuous finger crack that just begs to be climbed. The lack of face holds makes it quite unique and quietly strenuous. *John Howard 1979*

❸ 16 Blue Suede Shoes 15m
A wide chimney with a short section of layback. Shake rattle and roll to the last section of crack from the ledge. *Rick McGregor 1976*

Taniwha Wall
15m right, past the next section of vegetated cracks, is a short but adorable wall.

❹ 16 Taniwha 14m
Climb to the ledge for a gripping mantle (gripping the tree that is). Bridge and chimney the rounded, mossy crack to a steep exit. Watch the loose flakes in the crack at the top. *Lindsay Main 1978*

Taniwha Wall

⑤ ★21 Sluds 10m
A thin, lichenous crack. Start straight up the crack and engage edges on the left arête. Join the crack for an easy finish. *John Allen 1980*

⑥ ★20 Prodigal Crack 10m
Twin cracks; one blocky, one smooth. Fingerlock and jam the left crack using the right for good bridging. *John Howard 1979*

⑦ ★22 Worth The Walk 10m
A V-corner. Start on the bulge and head right for delicate manoeuvres to a bomber sequence of jams. *John Allen 1980*

⑧ ✳★23 Science Friction 10m
An incredible climb with twin rounded cracks. These will only provide minor assistance; it is wide bridging, palming and smearing that wins the day. *John Allen 1980*

⑨ 20 Cybernetic Rage 13m
Reach high to a jug and move left into the crack, which eventually curves right. Take your cams. *John Howard 1980*

⑩ 21 Robert Gordon 13m
A corner with a little vegetation, green lichen and devious bridging. Head left near the top. *John Allen 1980*

20m right is a big left facing chimney which separates two narrow walls. These hold the following routes:

⑪ ★22 Unlimited Edition 14m
A weakness up the face with intermittent gear and difficult moves to the bolt. *Ton Snelder 1983*

⑫ 19 Maggie 14m
Just right of the chimney is a wide crack which stops at one-third height. Interesting up to the bolt and challenging thereafter. *Craig Hamilton 1983*

Mt Bradley

13 **★20 Iron Man 14m**

A beautiful crack up the front of this prow to a piton. Hard moves going right to another crack. *John Howard 1980*

The next routes are on the left side of the main buttress.

14 **★17 Crime of the Century 35m**

⚠ Follows a crack, which is steep and difficult at the start, and not good for gear. Drift rightwards and exit up easy terrain. *Lindsay Main 1978*

15 **★22 Prospero 35m**

1 A thin crack which is quite steep at the start and peters out on the face. From the bolt join *Crime of the Century* to finish. *Manfred Oswald 1999*

16 **≉17 Son of Hangman 35m**

A distinct hand crack with a small roof 8m up. The stunning start unfortunately eases off to scrambling amongst the vegetated cracks. *Lindsay Main 1978*

17 **★21 The Grey Ghost 35m**

The thin crack just right of the jam crack. Step right to pass the 1st roof and then step left to avoid the 2nd roof. Move straight up an easier but run-out section. *Richard Kimberley 1999*

18 **≉26 Thorn Mother 35m**

4 Take a thin crack to the roof where bolts protect the moves right and up the awesome arête. *Richard Kimberley 1999*

Main Cliff
Left Side

⑲ ★★22 White Wizard 35m

A mega classic on the front of the buttress. Difficult climbing up a thin crack which just gets better and better up to a delicious upper corner. *John Howard 1979*

⑳ ★★23 Thin White Duke 35m

The other impressive route here and gnarlier due to the roof crux up high. Another hard start to an easier middle section before the daunting, cracked roof. *John Allen 1979*

㉑ ★21 Jubilee 35m

Twin cracks which lead to the left end of the ledge. Finish up the nice deep crack. *Lindsay Main 1979*

㉒ ★19 Cripple Crack 30m

Cracks which reach the right end of the ledge, then continue straight up the crack above. *Lindsay Main 1979*

㉓ ★19 Spring Fever 30m

Really tight bridging between two close columns to a small roof. The crack continues to another roof which is easily navigated. *Marty Beare 1979*

The Castle

Past the next gully is an outcrop with some friendly lines and quality climbing. It is a great place to spend a few hours warming into the Mt Bradley style.

㉔ ★15 The Boston Strangler 16m

The most prominent crack facing up-gully. Nice downward edges all the way. *Lindsay Main 1977*

*Main Cliff
Right Side*

㉕ 14 Satyr 18m

The next crack downslope is a tad mossy but the moves are interesting. The gear is relatively good, even if the placements need excavating. *Bryan Dyson 1977*

㉖ ★16 Guillotine 22m

A striking, straight corner with a sneaky crux below the guillotine feature. Relax on awesome ledges after this. *Murray Judge 1975*

㉗ 18 Henry Crippen 16m

Take the right crack on the narrow face below the nose. Once on the ledge, veer right up the gully. *Henry Mares 1978*

Mt Bradley

㉘ ★16 Genesis 18m
A lovely jam crack on excellent rock. From the ledge, climb the cruxy bulge. *Murray Judge 1975*

㉙ 16 Ecclesiastes 18m
A quality start up a crack on the front of the buttress, but it degrades further up. *Lindsay Main 1977*

㉚ ★21 One Handed Poker 16m
A fine crack up the front of the prow that peters out to a technical slabby face. *Nick Cradock 1989*

㉛ 17 Solomon 16m
A short section of crack to the top of the pillar. Continue up a wide crack. *Henry Mares 1978*

㉜ ★16 Zaccharius 16m
From the short pillar, savour the appetising crack with an easy finish. *Lindsay Main 1977*

The Castle

Right Cliff

Fantasy Factory

Fantasy Factory and its near neighbor, Crystal Clearlight, were borne out of the seventies psychedelic culture when climbers weren't politically correct and didn't need to be. They now sit quietly above Charteris Bay in silent tribute to A class drugs.

Fantasy Factory is the closest crag to the road and has all the makings of a bad trip. It is quite over-grown at the base, and getting around can be frustrating. We've picked the best of the lines but they are variable in quality. Some of the older trad climbs were never cleaned and it is mainly the new sport lines that yield the best climbing.

Drive up Dyers Pass Rd to the Sign of the Kiwi and continue through Governors Bay.

At Charteris Bay, turn right into Bay View Rd (before the yacht club). Turn right into Doris Faigan Lane and continue up the farm road to the gate by the macrocarpas.

 Follow the farm track up to the white tower and continue along the spur. The first dome of rock that you see looks like a crag but is a sandbag.

Instead, stay on the left side of the fence and cross the wooden gate. From here, a forestry road goes sharply right and sidles along the hillside. This is a guaranteed way of finding Fantasy Factory, but it is slightly quicker to continue along the spur and then drop down to the left end of the crag.

i To gain permission call landowner, Peter Nel (03) 3299116.

It is very difficult to get off the crag because of the vegetation at either end.

The only safe way to walk off is by traversing left and descending back to the base.

For the longer climbs, it is definitely easier and faster to take two ropes and set one up as a permanent rap line.

The crag is closed for lambing between September and late October.

❶ **★19 Naming Rights 30m**
Start left of the cabbage tree. Traverse left on so-so gear to join the crack with excellent pro and graceful sidepulls. Keep a lookout for threads. *Alan Hill/Dale Muller 1999*

❷ **20 Mindbender 31m**
Stem up the gully and climb over easy broken ground to the headwall. Be very wary of some of the blocks—they appear to be stuck on with guano! Move right under the roof to some hard-out jamming. An alternative and committing finish is left up the headwall at grade 22 *(John Howard 1979)*. *Tim Wethey 1975*

❸ **★23 Not Crack But Still Ecstasy 31m**
8 ♀ As ethics change, so do the vices it seems. This is a complex wall with many inverted steps capping slick wee faces. After the first section, head towards the right crack and at half-height, traverse left to gain the upper section. *Richard Kimberley 1998*

Fantasy Factory

④ **✷17 Short Cut To Mushrooms 31m**
A deep, jagged crack. Step up to the roof and pull through to the wide groove. Cruise the central section and finish with cruxy moves where the crack narrows. Exit right on a ramp or take the direct finish, which is one grade harder. You will need at least one giant cam. Otherwise big hexes will do the job. *Tim Wethey 1975*

⑤ **★14 Woman's Weekly 28m**
The deep corner/crack. Bridge to the roof and rest. If your horoscope is looking good, forge onwards for more good bridging. *Mike Franklin 1975*

⑥ **★24 Feeling the Paunch 18m**
A smooth brown face capped by a roof and hanging arête. Crimpy moments to master the roof and tasty climbing up the arête. *Tony Burnell 1998*

⑦ **★18 Bruno 30m**
Awkward start to a superb section of crack. The safety degenerates as you climb through a large, loose flake but you will find spaced, solid pro after this. *Tim Wethey 1975*

Traverse along the base of the cliff, and drop down a rocky step to the next climbs.

⑧ **23 Prime Suspect 20m**
Rather ugly and hard all the way. A meandering top-out joins *Older Not Bolder*. *Tony Burnell 1998*

⑨ **✷23 Older Not Bolder 20m**
Very intriguing moves with stunning holds. Start at the right end of the small cave and veer left. *Tony Burnell 1998*

Fantasy Factory
Left Side

20 mins

Fantasy Factory
Right Side

← Descent

---

⑩ ★21 Au Natural 20m

Start at *Older Not Bolder* but continue straight up via thin seams. The gear is spaced and sometimes questionable, but the climbing is brill. *Tony Burnell 1998*

⑪ ✲16 Bitterfingers 30m

This long, weathered groove is sustained and littered with all sorts of good moves. Handle the short pillar at the top with care. *Mike Franklin 1975*

⑫ 16 Rat Race 30m

Bridge up a corner and step right to the first good gear. Sustained climbing follows on nicely contoured holds. *Murray Judge 1975*

The next sporty climbs are just right of the obvious, vegetated corner.

⑬ ★21 Hit the Deck 18m

5 Face climbing kicks back to slabby terrain. *Richard Kimberley 1998*

⑭ ★21 Roll Up 18m

5 Rock onto the face, where a few tricky moves lead to stellar holds. Hard cranks on chickenheads to a slab. *Tony Burnell 1998*

⑮ ★23 Weed Eater 18m

5 Gain the slab then make thin moves up the vague corner. Cranky through the roof and veer right to finish. *Tony Burnell 1998*

⑯ ★24 Weed Killer 16m

5 Beasty moves off the deck to long cranks through the steep bulge. Quite wild really. *Tony Burnell 1998*

⑰ ★24 Magical Mystery Tour 16m

6 Easy up the open corner to bridging and pinching on steep ground. *Richard Kimberley 1998*

211

Crystal Clearlight

Crystal Clearlight is a bolt free zone and has all the hallmarks of a staunch trad crag. It's steeper than it looks and the jam cracks are mainly through overhanging bulges. There are some awesome classics to do and enough climbing for a couple of days.

The rock is remarkably different to Fantasy Factory even though it is only a few hundred metres along the hillside. It is far more solid and the base of the crag is relatively clear and easy access. It's like breathing a sigh of relief.

Access this crag the same as Fantasy Factory, but at the wooden gate (where the forestry road branches off), continue along the spur for about 1km until you can see the left end of the crag. Pick your way down to the base.

i Crystal Clearlight has a number of climbs that require particularly big gear, so it is well worth hauling your mama hexes, cams (up to #5) or carjacks up the hill.

One 50m rope is fine for climbing but another abseil line would help. The anchors are good blocks or shrubs and it is easy to descend off the left end of the crag.

The crag is closed for lambing between September and late October.

❶ 16 T Hex 15m
A pleasant ramble at the left end of the crag. Climb the chimney to the nose and ease rightwards around this feature. Continue straight to the top. *Murray Judge 1975*

❷ ★17 Goodbat Nightman 17m
Practice saying the route name ten times, then climb the direct crackline through to a slopey ledge. Bridge the groove to a blocky top-out. The pro is good but watch where you place it at the top. *Murray Judge 1975*

❸ ★20 Rottcod 17m
Start next to *Goodbat Nightman* and follow the right-leaning crack to an exceptionally devious move over the bulge. Watch the potentially loose block after this. *Rick McGregor 1976*

❹ ★22 Daunt 17m
Start in the dark corner and bridge up the crack. A series of horizontal cracks provide protection and good holds. *John Allen 1980*

❺ ★21 The Four Beasts of the Apocalypse 17m. Climb the right corner of the alcove into a small recess. Exit along the right-slanting crack to join *Tibrogargan*. *John Howard 1980*

❻ ★22 Tibrogargan 17m
A striking crack through the bulging prow. Exit right at the top of the crack and finish up the wall. *Rick McGregor 1976*

❼ ★19 Paranoia Blues 18m
A section of bulging jam crack. Grunt through to the roof and join *Bentley Jam Machine*. *Rick McGregor 1976*

❽ ✷17 Bentley Jam Machine 18m
A deep crack that offers great jamming, but has plenty of other options for the jam-averse. After the bulge continue straight up through the roof (18) or step left into the mellow corner. *Daryll Thomson 1975*

← Descent

9 ★16 **Dreamtree Sequence 18m**
From the painted 'DS,' climb the wall into the notch. With sneaky contortions, climb through the crack and negotiate the trees. *Murray Judge 1975*

10 ✴15 **Gladwrap 18m**
One of the few real chimneys in the South Island. Bridge out through some cruxy moves and chimney to the bulge. Face climbing out right takes you through to the chock stones. *Mike Franklin 1975*

11 ✴✴16 **Black Bitch 17m**
Totally classic—no moss, no loose rock and champion moves. From the fence, move over the bulge and climb with the expectation of finding good holds where you need them. *Mike Franklin 1975*

12 ★15 **Silk Torpedo 17m**
A lovely face split by a shallow crack. Boulder onto the ledge where a #1 cam gets the proceedings going. The weathered ledges make awesome holds. *Tim Wethey 1975*

13 ★18 **Curved Air 17m**
A short, steep section of jamming to a rest ledge, then charge up the splitter crack. The original line finished right at grade 17. *John Barnett 1975*

14 12 **Fancy Woman 15m**
A gaping corner with a roof at half-height. Move up the short pillar and bridge wide to weasel around the roof. *Mike Franklin 1975*

15 13 **Tobias Treetime 15m**
The right-most crack. Start at the painted square and step up on large edges. From the ledge, continue right. Bring your big gear. *Rick McGregor 1976*

The Monument

The Monument is a prominent basalt nipple at the head of the Purau Valley. It is about 40kms from Christchurch and a short walk up the hill, making it one of the most accessible crags on the Peninsula. There is not a huge volume of quality routes, but the selection here will provide a great day out for a mid-grade trad climber. The climbing terrain is challenging with some beasty little finger cracks.

The crag is north-facing and looks over Lyttelton Harbour and across to Pegasus Bay. It is very close to two other areas that we have not covered in the guide. Dawn Wall is directly across the valley from the car park, and Mt Evans is high up on the left side of the road.

From Christchurch, drive up Dyers Pass Rd to the Sign of the Kiwi and follow the road around the bays to Diamond Harbour for about 30–40mins. Continue through Purau and up the road to Port Levy. You will see the crag on the hilltop on the right. Park at the obvious gravel area at the top of the pass.

Travelling on the Akaroa road to Teddington (via Taitapu) is nearly 15kms longer than driving around the bays.

Cross the fence at the stile and walk over farm land to a low saddle. Head straight up through the tussock to the left end of the crag.

The climbs included in this guide are predominantly naturally protected. The gear tends to be small-mid sized cams (double ups are useful) and a range of wires. A single rope will suffice unless you want to rap off the very top of the Andromeda Buttress.

Access around the base of the crag, especially to the Andromeda Buttress, is vegetated and frustrating with a heavy pack.

The crag is closed for lambing between September and late October.

There is no need to call the farmer to ask permission to climb because it's a well known walking area. Just follow the usual courtesies.

The Quicksilver Buttress

This is the high, buttress at the north-east (roadside) end of the cliff. It is easy access and has some glorious lines on totally yummy rock. There is a track on the left to access to top.

❶ ★16 Retrograde Motion 23m

Start off the large blocks (as for *Quicksilver*) and move up the shallow corner using the crack system. At the ledge, traverse left and step-up through a wide crack to a higher ledge. An attractive crack takes you to the top via a 'wake up' crux. *Lindsay Main 1979*

Quicksilver Buttress   Andromeda Buttress

❷ ★17 Quicksilver 23m

An awesome route with gymnastic moves between good holds. Follow the crack system to the ledge as for *Retrograde Motion*. A run-out to the first piton gets the heart rate up, then step wide using positive sidepull action.

❸ ★21 Supernova 23m

The climbing isn't too bad, but placing the gear gets you knackered. Climb the pillar, mostly laybacking off the right arête. From the ledge, step left and climb the crack to the top groove. *Tom Bauman 1978*

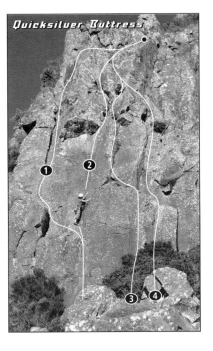

❹ 15 Moonshine 23m

Hoon up three short corner sections, separated by ledges (some big gear needed). Head left through the steep section on good holds. The original finish continues straight up but is sparsely protected.

Andromeda Buttress

This buttress is behind a scrappy gully and has a boulder scree at the base. The foliage has made its way right to the base of the cliff, so it's a bit of a bush-bash, but if you make the effort you'll find some of the best lines at the crag.

❺ 18 Cardiac Arête 37m

A wild start around the overhang takes confidence. After this the incline is more user-friendly, but the gear is sparse. *John Barnett 1979*

❻ 17 Flailing Whales 10m

From the ledge on *Cardiac Arête,* find bouldery moves to the 1st bolt, then it's a free ride on generous edges. The tree to the left is the anchor. *Joe Arts 1994*

❼ 18 Quasar 37m

Start behind the tree and grovel to get established in the wide corner. Plenty of good stances help to place fiddly gear (which is sparse at times). At the roof, move left to meet *Cardiac Arête*. *Lindsay Main 1979*

❽ ★19 Solar Flare 16m

The left-facing corner has a smear, layback crux lying in wait. After initial trickiness, step left onto the arête for casual climbing. There is a single bolt anchor and large block at the top. *Lindsay Main 1979*

The Monument

Andromeda Buttress

← Descent

9 Red Shift–2 Pitches

P1. *18 16m A tempting finger crack with great jams and solid feet where you need them. Plenty of medium cams and wires will see you merrily on your way. Finish at the same anchor as *Solar Flare*. *Marty Beare 1979*

P2. *18 12m Climbs the face on really beautiful edges. Be careful clipping the 2nd bolt. *Joe Arts 1994*

10 *19 Andromeda 16m

An elegant, smooth-sided open corner that lends itself to laybacking. With three #1 cams you will save time phaffing around with wires. At the top, traverse left to the anchor. *Lindsay Main 1979*

11 *20 Giant Space Bunnies From Jupiter 16m. Up the middle of the rounded buttress with virtually no protection. *John Howard (solo) 1979*

12 *17 Steady State 16m

One of the most consistent, pleasant routes on the buttress. Climb the right-facing corner to agreeable laybacks. *Lindsay Main 1979*

'I doubt that the rapid development of many popular climbing areas, particularly in the South Island, would have occurred without the fantastic support from the various overnments of the day which allowed strong cliques of fully sponsored climbers to ply their trade from Takaka to Wanaka. It is a pity that Government support for athletes has been gradually diminishing of late.'
Simon Middlemass

Holmes Bay

This fantastic little crag is set amongst some remnant native bush. The columnar rock offers fine finger and hand cracks with lots of gear placements. At a squat 12m high, it is particularly good if you happen to be a dwarf who loves crack climbing. There is a good range of grades and better still, there is not a bolt in sight.

From Christchurch, take the road towards Akaroa. At the Hilltop, turn left and then left again to Pigeon Bay. An alternative is to take a meandering drive around the bays from Lyttelton. In this case, drive to Port Levy (53km) and continue on a narrow gravel road (10km) to Pigeon Bay. Once you are in Pigeon Bay, turn left at Little Pigeon Bay Rd and follow the gravel farm track up the hill. You will pass one right-veering turn off. Stay left here and keep driving to a farm gate. This is a good place to park.

From the gate, walk over the hill back towards the bay and traverse left to the crag.

You will use cams more than wires at this crag, but a standard rack is fine. The anchors are large blocks, and a long sling is essential. The blocks are sometimes set back from the top of the cliff, and a fixed abseil rope may be the quickest way to descend. Otherwise, walk off either end of the crag.

The crag faces south. It is a great place to get out of the sun and the nor' west wind in mid-summer, but we wouldn't recommend it as a winter destination.

The farm is owned by Mr I.D. Richardson, who is happy for climbers to use the area, but he would appreciate being called in advance if there is a large group going (03) 514 8804.

The crag is closed for lambing between September and late October.

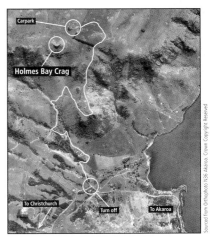

Carpark

Holmes Bay Crag

To Christchurch

Turn off

To Akaroa

❶ ★**15 Magpie 9m**
The four-sided corner with an overhanging block. Start with a tricky mantle onto the pedestal then bridge and use the hand crack. Exit right. *Murray Cullen 1990*

❷ ★**21 Delusions 9m**
This devious layback or jamming crack is a mind bender. The lack of footholds makes it strenuous, but the gear is good. *Joe Arts 1991*

❸ **17 Yellow Matter Custard 11m**
There are nice layback manoeuvres up this line, but watch the loose blocks in the centre section. Scramble right to finish. *Murray Cullen 1990*

❹ ★23 Northwest Passage 12m

Two staunch twin cracks. Bridge up and scuttle right under the roof. *Alan Hill 1994*

❺ ✳19 Cracker Jack Mac 12m

This beautiful hand crack is the classic of the crag. Christchurch face climbers will thrash and scream but eventually enjoy the unavoidable jamming. Finish right through the blocks. *Murray Cullen 1990*

❻ 14 Fallen Idol 12m

An interesting bit of geology makes this an adventurous climb. Start up the 'fallen idol'—a pillar which has sheared off the cliff, and continue up the wide crack. Take some large cams. *Peter Cleary*

4m right past the next pillar:

20 Pinnochio 11m

A curvaceous thin crack with sparse gear. Climb the pedestal (4m) to the crack. At the horizontal break, gain the arête and veer right at the top. *Alan Hill 1999*

Past the shorter blocky columns (8m):

❽ 21 Escalade du Jour 10m

Left-facing open corner behind the matagouri grove. A bouldery start leads to good holds/ledges high on the left. The gear is good but it needs traffic to clean up. *Murray Cullen 1990*

❾ ✳19 Crack of Delight 10m

Indeed it is! Step off the block and bridge wide up the parallel-sided finger crack. *Joe Arts 1991*

7m right past the small roof:

⑩ **21 Fox on the Rocks 9m**
Three thin cracks provide fine, fingery climbing. *Alan Hill/Nigel Thompson 1994*

⑪ **15 Broadleaf Lane 9m**
This crack has been colonised by small ferns, but with some judicious gardening it's a lot of fun. The top (crux) is bulgy and bouldery. *Peter Cleary 1990*

⑫ ★**20 The Spies Are Out 8m**
A mellow finger crack that opens up to a vicious wide thing. The heat continues until over the bulge to the groovy pocket. *Joe Arts 1991*

⑬ **14 Hump the Lump 8m**
A mantle/hand jam combo. Better than it looks and excellent pro. *Peter Cleary 1990*

6m to the right (after small roof):

⑭ **24 Abandon All Preconceptions 11m**
Place gear from the left pedestal (under the roof) then descend and climb from the ground. Awkward bridging leads to the thin finger crack. *Joe Arts 1994*

⑮ ⚞**22 Death by Blocklets 12m**
From the pedestal, climb the thin crack and four-sided corner. Hard bridging takes you to good holds under a small roof. Finish through the wide exit. *Joe Arts 1991*

⑯ ★**23 The Pigeons Have Flown 12m**
A distinct, right-trending finger crack. Bridge and haul up on good jams and top-out over the steep bulge. *Joe Arts 1991*

⑰ **17 Space Aged Medasin 12m**
A meandering route that starts off a pillar. Climb right to another pillar and follow the crack. *Murray Cullen 1990*

Nobble

A method of putting a climber off their stride by making disparaging remarks about their ability, style or the difficulties and dangers of a climb. Nobbling is usually done by groups of friends climbing in a competitive spirit on outcrops or problem climbs. It is sometimes used by local climbers to upset a well known visiting climber, who may be trying to ascend some notorious local climb or problem. Nobbling, of course is nearly always carried out in a friendly and joking manner. **Peter Crew** the *Dictionary of Mountaineering* (1950s).

Otepatotu

This is a small crag offering a few good routes that are likely to appeal to keen trad climbers. The rock is excellent quality but some of the cracks are a little vegetated. Only the cleanest routes have been included but there are plenty more good lines that need renovating (fortunately it's mostly gorse and therefore a viable target). The crag has nice views of the Akaroa harbour and is surrounded by native bush making this an enjoyable place to visit for a day. Many of the climbs have less pro at the bottom as the rock is blobby and the cracks only begin higher up. The crag faces south and can be vicious in a southerly.

From Christchurch drive towards Akaroa. Once at the Hilltop, turn left into the Summit Rd. 3km after the turn-off to Okains Bay, on the left hand side is the Otepatotu Scenic Reserve (with a carpark).

After a nice 10min walk through the bush, turn left and take the lookout track to reach the top of the cliff.

i As the vegetation is rather thick at the bottom of the crag, abseiling in is the only sensible option. Leaving a permanent rap line speeds up the climbing.

❶ ✴12 Diploma 15m
The beautiful crack line up the rib at the left end of the wall. Once up a little leave the main crack and head left, which leads to a wonderful finish. Plentiful holds and gear. *Warwick Anderson 1973*

❷ ✴18 Eliminator 17m
A hairline crack up the middle of an attractive face. Tenuous smears and finger locks to the horizontal break, followed by edgy climbing on the arête. *Hugh Logan 1978*

❸ 19 Falaise Malaise 18m
The arête right of the overgrown crack. It's a wee way to the 1st bolt and higher up the pro is a bit fiddly. Take RPs and cams to #3. *Hamish Dunn 1992*

❹ 16 Oblivion 18m
A run-out face start leads to a well protected corner. Fun climbing with a couple of mantles. *Mike Franklin 1973*

❺ ✴17 Voie Classique 18m
Awesome, edgy face holds up the twin cracks. Start in the right crack, move-up the left one and back again. After the face, heave over the mini roof/arête to gain the easy top. *Hamish Dunn 1992*

❻ ✴22 Falter 18m
⚠ Climb the face which is basically gearless. Once under the imposing headwall, arrange the gear as best as possible for the fantastic looking face with more holds than it appears. *John Howard 1980*

❼ ✴21 Altar 18m
⚠ The most imposing line of the crag, this ascends the bold arête. The gear lacks substance low down but does improve in the top crack and horizontal breaks. *John Allen 1979*

❽ 14 Claymore 16m
The deep corner with some vegetation and a little clay. The climbing however, does stay on good clean rock with plenty of bridging. *Hugh Logan 1973*

⑨ ★20 Cheniv de Pierre 16m

Start up *Little Vibrator* and move left to join the face. Lovely edgy step-ups past the bolts and exit up the finger crack. Climbing the face directly to the bolts is fabulous but unprotected (a good top-rope). *Rob Battersby 1992*

⑩ ★16 Little Vibrator 16m

A pleasurable route which follows left leaning cracks. Start up the crack in the middle of the face and soon go right to join another crack. *Tim Wethey 1973*

⑪ 22 Cabbage Milkshake 16m

A route which should receive more interest than a fiberous milkshake but it needs a rebolt. A steep groove with a powerful crux gains an easy crack. *Roddy McKenzie 1983*

A cragging legacy left by a giant

The Port Hills and Banks Peninsula are what remains of a volcano that was once both an island and home to a two-headed, magma-spewing beast. This inferno was the volcanic centre of the South Island and began to erupt about 12 million years ago. At its peak, the volcano may have been as high as Mt Ruapehu, which would mean that the level of the Summit Road is less than half way up the old volcano.

The lava flows of this volcano initially built crags like The Tors and, in a later phase of eruption, produced a trachyte band which runs up Mount Pleasant Spur (Britten Crag and Cattlestop) and over to the Three Sisters. The volcano also produced dykes of rock that radiate from the centre of the old volcano. These include Rapaki Rock and Castle Rock.

9.7 million years ago, the second crater began to erupt and the volcanic centre moved towards Akaroa, building Mt Bradley and The Monument. The Akaroa volcano grew until it overtopped the Lyttelton cone and formed crags like Otepatotu. In one final burst of activity, the basalts of Diamond Harbour were formed on the south side of the Lyttelton caldera. Fantasy Factory and Crystal Clearlight are both from this era.

Mt Somers

Meat Grinder

Christian Principals

Fog Buttress

The Pinnacles

This sub-alpine area has some of the best cracks and volcanic columns in the South Island. The rhyolite domes were forced up about 136 million years ago and fractured during the cooling process to form long parallel crack lines. On the Upper Cliffs the climbs are steep and sustained, while some of the smaller outcrops are tilted back to make friendly, short lines. As a whole, the cracks are not regularly climbed and may be vegetated. If you are willing to do some cleaning en route and don't mind a good old fashioned hike in, you will love this place.

If trad is not your preferred medium but you want to check this area out, The Pinnacles are fully bolted. The rock is geologically totally different from the columnar cracks higher up the hill. It was produced from a fissure eruption of concrete-like slurry and tends to be quite crumbly, but is still fun to climb.

Mt Somers

3 hours

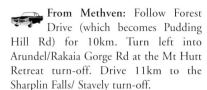

From Methven: Follow Forest Drive (which becomes Pudding Hill Rd) for 10km. Turn left into Arundel/Rakaia Gorge Rd at the Mt Hutt Retreat turn-off. Drive 11km to the Sharplin Falls/ Stavely turn-off.

From Christchurch: Travel to the Mt Hutt turn-off and follow the road south for 20km to the Sharplin Falls/Stavely turn-off.

From Geraldine: Take the road to the Mt Somers township. Drive 10km to Staveley on the road north until you reach the Sharplin Falls/Stavely turn-off.

From the Sharplin/Stavely Falls turn-off, turn right into Symes Rd. After the bridge, turn right into Flynns Rd and travel 4km to the Sharplin Falls car park. Leave your car here, but make sure you take valuables with you.

Take the track to the Pinnacles Hut. Do not go to the Mt Somers Hut as this is the wrong end of the loop track! Follow the high level track (sub-alpine walkway) over Dukes Knob. The first section is steep but the track soon flattens off along the river. The average walking time with a heavy pack is 2.5 hours, but some groups move a little faster.

The Pinnacles Hut is DOC owned and costs $5 per night, which is good value for this well-maintained abode. It has 19 bunks and tends to get busy with trampers, climbers and hunters in the weekends. There is a mountain radio for emergencies and daily weather forecasts. The hut is stacked with many things that may help lighten your pack including pots, cups, plates and cutlery. There is no cooker or fuel, but there is a log burner.

The crags are 10–20mins from the hut and are north-facing. The valley is quite sheltered and it may be too hot to climb in mid-summer. Autumn and spring (after the snow melt) are the best seasons.

Double ropes are useful for rapping and leading the twin cracks. Take double-ups of wires and plenty of draws, as some of the Main Cliff classics take a lot of gear. It is also good to have two nut keys per pair (one for cleaning on lead and one for removing gear).

Most climbs have double bolt anchors, but some bolts on the routes are older-style (8mm).

The environment is very fragile and the sub-alpine vegetation is vulnerable to human impact. Please try to stay on the main tracks and build/follow the cairns around the cliffs.

There is some amazing insect life living in the rock. Be especially careful not to disturb the wetas. This species is unique to the Mt Somers region and is under threat from introduced pests.

'Murray certainly came up with a good find at Mt Somers. Still it isn't as popular as it deserves to be…I think the problem here is a matter of perception. While we're well used to walking in to climb some alpine choss heap the thought of carrying a pack for a couple of hours for a spot of cragging makes most of us cringe. If it's not roadside, it's not a crag. If it's not alpine, it's not worth walking to.' **Andrew MacFarlane** *(The Climber issue 19 1996 p.24).*

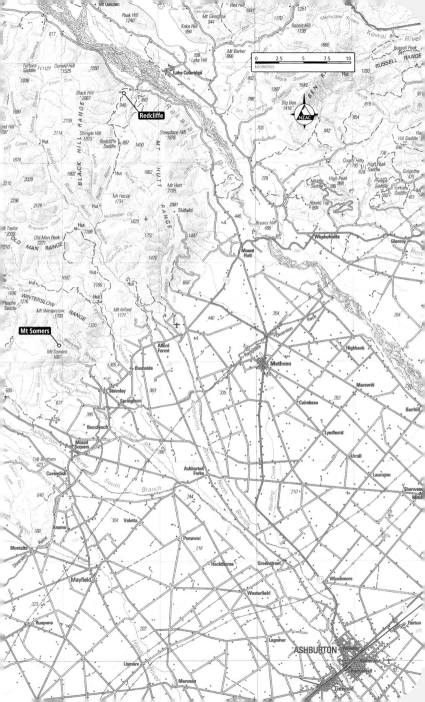

Mt Somers

Christian Principals Wall

This enticing columnar wall is on the ridge above the East Pinnacle. It sits just left of the groovy, warped scarp and looks more commanding from a distance than it is up close. Be careful of the stacked blocks on the arêtes and rubble at the anchors. Otherwise, the rock is sound and the gear is generally good.

❶ ⁎⁎15 Bring Back the Cane 22m
The most uniform crack line on the wall. Superlative gear and an all-round good time for naughty children. *Murray Judge 1998*

❷ 16 Sunday School Felching 22m
A deep V-corner with good gear. Not as unsavoury as the name. *Chris Burtenshaw 1995*

❸ 19 Buns of Steel 22m
Gain the arête as soon as possible and smear up cruxy terrain. Doing this purely takes discipline. *Murray Judge 1998*

❹ 16 Screams in the Night 22m
Start left of the scrubby gully. Follow the arête and sidle right. Excavation may be required to get good gear and watch the loose stuff. *Sean Waters 1995*

❺ ⁎15 Sleeping with the Nasty Boys 22m
The wide crack between two prominent arêtes. A quality start, but degrades a little up the top. Jolly good gear though. *Sean Waters 1995*

❻ ⁎16 Corporal Punishment 24m
Follows the arcing crack right of the arête. Pass left of the roof and climb diagonally right to the highest anchor. *Tom Riley 1998*

❼ ⁎16 The Staircase 31m
Long, twin cracks lead to antics through the roof at half-height. Delicate moves up the slab to a rightward exit. *Chris Burtenshaw 1995*

226

Meat Grinder Wall

This wall is seldom visited but deserves more attention. It is a great beginners wall and sits about 100m above the Christian Principals Crag in a panoramic location. The climbs are on laid back columns with bomber gear.

To reach the crag, walk right from the Christian Principals Wall and scramble up a steep gully, veering left. Continue straight up the ridge for 5mins.

⑧ 17 A Springtime Festival in Autumn 19m
Scamper up the rounded slab. This is split by a thin crack. The top section is a wide, jagged crack with primo gear. *Sean Waters 1995*

⑨ 13 Spare Rib 17m
A line up the left of two central arêtes. Bridging moves lead to a thin crack on the arête. *Chris Burtenshaw 1995*

⑩ 15 Weta Waltz 16m
Very wide bridging up the twin cracks is augmented with edges.

⑪ ★17 Misty Mountain Hop 16m
The groove up the wide arête. Move up the slab to the horizontal breaks (good cams) and skip lightly up the crack to finish. *Sean Waters 1995*

6m to the right is a featured wall with small, sharp arêtes.

⑫ ★14 Frankfurter Duet 15m
Climb the twin cracks with mesmorising amounts of gear. *Ivan Vostinar 2004*

⑬ 14 Saveloy Heaven 15m
Up the middle groove using bridging manoeuvers.

⑭ ★13 Beef-Flavoured Sausages 15m
The right-most groove on this section of wall.

Around the corner on the vegetated wall:

★15 Porno Star 15m
A wide groove, split by three cracks. Find gear in both the left and right cracks. *Chris Burtenshaw 1995*

Meatgrinder Wall

Mt Somers

Fog Buttress

This is a small crag between the Meat Grinder Wall and the Upper Cliffs. Most of the wall is quite chossy but at the left end there is one section of solid rock with some classy crack lines.

To reach the crag from the Main Cliffs, traverse directly across from the Far Side through the main gully. This takes about 10mins. From the Meat Grinder Wall, the crag is right and slightly downhill. It is an easy, undulating traverse.

⑯ 19 Terrible Tales of Teenage Angst 13m
A left-slanting finger crack. Climb with the help of the arête and take lots of small wires. *Sean Waters 1995*

⑰ ✻16 Parthenope 14m
A very yummy hand crack on the right side of the arête. Awesome foot jams. *Chris Burtenshaw 1995*

⑱ ★17 Bucket of Fino 14m
Use the arête and finger crack. Low down, this can be protected by gear in *Foggy Notion*. *Grant Piper 1995*

⑲ 15 Foggy Notion 14m
A comfortable crack with several cruxy sequences. *Sean Waters 1995*

The Upper Cliffs

This is the most dominant group of columns that you see when you emerge sweaty and triumphant from the tramping track. It is where most climbers concentrate their energies because the rock and lines are fantastic. Access to the Orange Wall is straightforward from the track. The walls further left, near the waterfall, are best approached from the top track (abseil from the top of the cliff).

The Far Side

Next only to the Orange Wall in terms of quality, this is clean, steep and demands good bridging technique. The easiest access is to follow the track from the Orange Wall rightwards and up. You can then rap from the top of the Main Cliff.

⑳ ★18 No Weasels 30m
A wide, bridging chimney on the left end of the wall. Step wide and palm your way through the crux to a couple of good rests. There is a good anchor (big cams) just before you top-out. *Kate Sinclair 2004*

㉑ ✻19 The Far Side Buttress 32m
The enticing splitter crack up the buttress. *Jay Kinsman 1994*

㉒ ★21 New Age Deceit 33m
Wide bridging up the prominent right-facing corner. Clip 3 bolts out right on *Dubious Means*. *Andrew Macfarlane 1994*

㉓ ✻24 Dubious Means 33m
Climbs the next main crack with delicate bridging and fingerlocks. *Andrew Macfarlane/Murray Judge 1994*

228

Track to the hut →

㉔ ✹22 The Contortionist 38m

6 Start below the large truncated pillar and bridge up the groove to the next roof. Move left again onto the face to find protection between the bolts. *Murray Judge 1995*

㉕ ✹24 Pain and Pleasure 38m

11 A blank face and shallow crack make for a staunch lead. Start right of the truncated pillar and cling to the crimps up the unceasing face. Some gear is needed for the start and finish. *Al Mark 2001*

㉖ ★21 Gecko 38m

5 A journey on interesting terrain. First, bridge the corner below the angled roof and slither right into the crack.

At the horizontal break, hand traverse left to the top-out crack. *Murray Judge 1994*

㉗ ★21 The Longest Hardest Climb I've Ever Done 42m. Climb right of the roof and up the crack to reach the groove on the left. *Murray Judge 1994*

5

㉘ Once a Jolly Swagman–3 Pitches

This is a good adventurous climb close to the waterfall. You can get to the base of the route in two abseils from the top, but it is probably safer to do three to avoid the swing under the waterfall. *Murray Judge/Andrew Macfarlane 1995*

Mt Somers

P1. 16 20m Start at the pool and scramble up left to a single bolt belay. Climb the easy groove to the break and traverse left to the upper groove (original line) or continue up the groove and traverse at the top.

P2. 16 20m Traverse across the bushy ledge and layback the start. Trend right up the cleanest rock and step left at the top.

P3. ★20 32m Follows a superb groove to the ledge, then heads left up broken blocks.

㉙ **★19 Where's My Jolly Jumbuck? 32m** From the last belay of *Swagman*, traverse right and up the next groove to rejoin the route at the ledge. *Murray Judge 1995*

P2. 15 20m The route steepens here. Head left and up a short slab and then move back right to a short buttress.

★P3. 24 32m Climb the steep wall to the top.

㉜ **★★24 Hang Ten 32m** Abseil to the *Tsunami* belay and climb directly up to the triple roof for wild moves through the overhangs. *Wayo Carson 1997*

㉝ **★23 Pipeline 32m** Abseil to the belay. Layback up the crack as high as possible then clip the bolt and reach for the holds. Step to the left to start the top section. *Murray Judge 1997*

Waterfall Wall

This is a spectacularly aerial place to climb. There is a beach at the base of the waterfall that is easily accessed by abseiling in from the top. It is quite tricky to get to this area by traversing from the base of the other walls and if the waterfall is pumping, there may be spray and wet patches of rock.

㉚ **★22 Wailing Wall 32m** Best approached by abseiling in, this route follows the right-facing corner to the roof. *Murray Judge/Andrew Macfarlane 1994*

㉛ **Tsunami–3 Pitches** Starts off 'the beach' at the foot of the waterfall. *Wayo Carson/Dave Brash/Murray Judge 1995*

P1. 16 18m From the beach climb the low-angled slabs to a belay on the bushy ledge.

230

The Fortress

This is a wide buttress between the Waterfall Wall and the Orange Wall. The left-end climbs can be approached carefully from the base of the Orange Wall. This is quite an exposed traverse and some parties prefer to abseil from the top. The first abseil is 30m, or a safe 5m downclimb to the lower anchor which is nicer to rap off.

To the Orange Wall

㉞ Scimitar–3 Pitches
Murray Judge 1994

P1. 14 20m A fun access pitch up the low-angled column that slowly and steadily steepens.

P2. ⚹21 20m A stunning open book corner with mint gear. Bound to make you smile.

P3. 15 30m A short crack that leads to an easy, vegetated scramble.

㉟ Banana Split–2 Pitches
Murray Judge/Wayo Carson 1995

P1. ⚹20 40m A wonderful excursion on an arcing column. The climb slowly builds momentum, making the last mouthful quite hard to chew.

P2. 15 30m As for Pitch 3 of *Scimitar*.

㊱ Mississippi Mud Cake–2 Pitches
Murray Judge 1995

P1. ★17 40m A nice meander up the slab on edges to join the crack. Lovely edgy step-ups, a great view and cruxy finish.

P2. 15 30m As for Pitch 3 of *Scimitar*.

㊲ ⚹18 Hotline to Jim 40m
A long, rounded arête that climbs well, but spartan bolting makes it an interesting undertaking. Take some mid-sized cams for the horizontal breaks. *Andrew Macfarlane 1994*

㊳ ⚹23 0800 Butch 40m
Wonderful climbing up the groove. Start at the double bolt anchor and venture up the crack using face holds. *Tony Pine/Murray Judge 1998*

㊴ 24 Psychological Trauma 40m
A wide corner with some shrubbery. Follow the weathered crack and be careful of chossy rock on the arête. *Chris Burtenshaw/Sean Waters/Grant Piper 1995*

Jon Sedon on *Skate* (22). MARK SEDON/OFF PISTE PHOTOGRAPHY

Orange Wall

This lustrous wall looks down on the hut. The crack lines are the Mt Somers draw card and there are some totally stellar routes. Take lashings of wires, a range of small-mid sized cams, a fistful of draws and go hither.

⓵ 19 What's Up Doc? 38m

8 A long line with two distinct sections. Start up the crack with minimal pro. At the bushes, follow the bolts up the face and arête. *Murray Judge 1994*

㊶ ★19 Have you been Stung? 38m

4 Climb past the bolts under the protruding block and feel your way up the crack. The gear is good but it is too tempting to escape to nearby bolts. *Murray Judge 1994*

㊷ ☀23 Steady Eddie 38m

10 A searing, challenging line that climbs just left of the crack. Some gear is needed after the 1st bolt and at the top. *Murray Judge 1994*

㊸ ☀☀25 A La Weta 38m

10 Climbs just right of the rounded arête. An unrelenting face and arête classic that puts your footwork to the test. *Bolted by Murray Judge, FFA Unknown*

㊹ ☀☀21 Uno 38m

The superlative Mt Somers classic that follows the chimney left of the roof. It is a sustained, bridging corner with awesome gear at every stance. Take plenty of draws and gear. *Andrew Macfarlane 1994*

Orange Wall

Descent →

45 ✳✳ **22 Skate 38m**

2 ⊘ An extraordinarily good crack line through the wide, bridging corner right of the roof. Fingery climbing with uncertain feet will lead to bomber jams. *Murray Judge 1994*

46 ✳✳ **24 Snapper 38m**

6 ⊘ Parallel twin cracks. Follow the bolts and climb the steepening wall with gear. *Wayo Carson 1997*

47 ✳✳ **23 Kentucky Fried Kea 38m**

A pumpy and aesthetic left-facing corner. Fairly generous jams and lay-aways, but it's thin for the tootsies. *Jay Kinsman 1994*

48 ✳ **16 Orange Roughy 32m**

4 ⊘ Start up *Kentucky Fried Kea* and tra-verse right at the horizontal break. The rest of the climb follows the arête with bolts. *Murray Judge 1994*

49 ✳ **16 Red Herring 32m**

Sparse but easy through the lower slab. Above the break find lovely moves with improving gear. *Murray Judge 1994*

50 **15 Dogfish 31m**

2 ⊘ Not bad if you are well within your grade. Climb past 2 bolts and place ⚠ gear out right before a long run-out. Move into the groove to good wires before the crux. *Wayo Carson 1994*

51 **15 Sardine 31m**

1 ⊘ A long, quite consistent crack that takes good wires and small cams. Most people clip the 1st bolt on *Dogfish* before moving right into the crack. *Murray Judge 1994*

The Pinnacles

The Pinnacles are made of conglomerate, con-crete-like rock. The good holds are chunks of solid rock that have been set into a slurry and climbing here is all about having blind faith that the holds will stay on. Weird as it may seem at first, the moves are good fun and the climbs are quite long.

East Pinnacle

This leftmost pinnacle has lengthy climbs with positive holds. It is about 15mins from the hut.

1 **16 Crunchie Nuggets 29m**

7 ⊘ Move up the lower wall, hoping the nuggets don't crunch. Mosey up the arête to finish. *Wayo Carson 1994*

2 **19 Hokey Pokey 32m**

8 ⊘ Head up the ramp then straight up the short cruxy wall. Easy run-out to the anchor. *Murray Judge 1994*

3 **19 Pixie Caramel 32m**

8 ⊘ Start as for *Hokey Pokey* then move right and ride the grooves. *Murray Judge 1994*

4 ✳ **20 Hound Dog 37m**

17 ⊘ In places this climb has the worst rock on the pinnacle, but there's a perverse sense of enjoyment to be found on the crazy terrain and weird moves. It will test your quickdraw rack to the limit. *Murray Judge 1994*

5 ✳ **16 Perky Nana 36m**

8 ⊘ One of the more interesting lines here. Bridge up the groove and move left onto the arête. Watch the run-out up to the 5th bolt and move method-ically up to the slab. *Toby Judge 1994*

The Pinnacles

Central Pinnacle

This pinnacle has a large, very high face with some crumbly rock, but the following climb is the totally worthwhile.

❻ Rocky Road–3 Pitches
Murray Judge 1994

1 **P1. 17 12m** Start on the detached boulder. A few balancy moves will take you to a belay ledge.

11 **P2. ✳20 36m** This is an airy pitch with lots of excitement. Good incut holds provide relief from the crimps.

5 **P3. ★18 23m** Steep, cruxy moves to a slab that rounds off the climb nicely. Abseil off the back side (25m).

❼ ★21 Send the Bill 36m

8 An alternative second pitch to *Rocky Road*. Edgy climbing on pretty good rock, relatively speaking. *Murray Judge 1996*

West Pinnacle

Overall this pinnacle has the best lower grade climbs on excellent rock.

❽ 16 Nameless Girl 12m

3 A bouldery arête that requires lateral force. The top is run-out. To retrieve the anchor, there is a grade 12 scramble on the back side of the block. *Sash Nukada 1995*

❾ ★18 Same, Same but Different 20m

4 Steep, edgy climbing kicks back to a ramble up the slab. *Sash Nukada 1995*

❿ ★22 Fresh Start, Dude 20m

4 Just left of the water streak. Steep and hard before a slabby run-out. *Jason Crichton 1995*

⓫ Zephyr–2 Pitches
A nice adventure and a good introduction to this type of rock.

6 **P1. ★15 22m** An entertaining climb that rolls up the end of the pinnacle to a ledge. *Wayo Carson 1995*

Mike Brown on *Rocky Road* (20)
KESTER BROWN

Hut Pinnacle

5 P2. **14 23m** The rock deteriorates somewhat on this pitch, but it makes a good lofty outing. Follow the groove and move onto the rounded top-out.

Around the right side of the pinnacle, 10m up the track is:

4 **14 Cloak and Dagger 21m**
This climb follows a groove on slightly mossy rock. Good, blobby holds. *Murray Judge 1994*

Hut Pinnacle

This pinnacle has easy access and some of the more compact rock on these monoliths.

13 **18 Strong 22m**
6 Pull through the problematic bulge and amble the easy slab to the top. *Murray Judge 1994*

14 **★19 Silent 22m**
5 ⚠ A stealthy start past the 2nd bolt and ground fall potential to the 3rd. Cruxy moves through the bulge onto the slab. *Murray Judge 1994*

15 **★18 Type 23m**
5 A tricky rock-over to get you started, through to a fun traverse and thin crux. An easy but stoic run-out to the top. *Murray Judge 1994*

16 **★22 Eh? 23m**
8 After a steep start, traverse right to a climactic bulge before the terrain tapers off. Head slightly left to the anchor. *Murray Judge 1994*

The next climbs are 35m right. The route that you pass in the middle of the wall is a strange and very sketchy grade 19.

17 **★23 Zesty 25m**
7 Intricate moves straight up the scalloped face to a slabby top out. The line that diverges left is a grade 22 on lower quality rock. *Murray Judge 1995*

18 **24 Feisty 25m**
8 At the right end of this wall, move up thin ground to a laid back top section. *Wayo Carson 1995*

> 'Consider what you want to do in relation to what you are capable of doing. Climbing is, above all, a matter of integrity.' **Gaston Rébuffat**

Redcliffe

Redcliffe is a cluster of small limestone walls on a sheep station up the Rakaia River. From a distance it looks very scrappy, but amongst the flakey rubbish, there are a few pockets of awesome rock. At its best, it is hard, grey limestone with subtle holds and tufa features. There is not a huge volume of climbs at the crag, but the classics make it worth an outing, particularly if you want to wile away a few hours doing a bunch of unique routes.

From Christchurch: Take the main road west for 45km to Darfield and turn-off to Mt Hutt. Follow this winding road for 45km through Glentunnel to the Rakaia Bridge.

Take the next right to Double Hill (before the Mt Hutt turn-off). Continue along the banks of the river over the Little River Bridge and continue on the gravel road through a couple of fords.

Just after Redcliffe Bridge (22km from the main road) and past Redcliffe Station turn left into Glenn Rock Station. Take the farm track which winds up to the quarry.

This access road was put in recently and there may be a small fee to help pay for it.

Walk up the fenceline to a track with a rope handrail. This takes you up to the Top Cliff.

i It is very important to call the landowners, Fiona and Duncan Ensor, before climbing at the crag. They can be contacted after 7.30pm on (03)318-5055.

The crag is closed for lambing during September and October.

The 'extreme' abseiling platform at the top of the main wall is used by commercial groups.

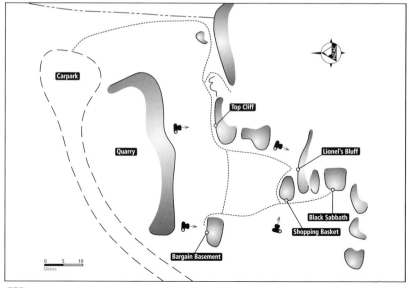

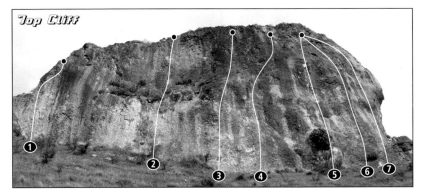

Top Cliff

One of the access conditions is that climbers do not use or stand on the platform.

The crag is very sunny but has no shelter from the nor' wester which rages through the gorge some days.

There is a camping spot 5km before the crag, after the 2nd ford, at Kowhai Flat.

Top Cliff
This is right of the large wall above the quarry. Follow the handrail and veer right.

❶ 25 Last Bus to Hale Bob 12m

5 ● At the left end of the cliff, this route starts on blocky layaway holds. The wall gets consistently steeper before a dynamic move right to finish. *Pat Deavoll 1997*

3m right is a project which needs hangers. 10m right of this is:

❷ 20 Split Personality 20m

6 ● Move up the centre of the low wall to the garden ledge past 3 bolts. The route continues on the vague arête past tricky laybacks. Single bolt anchor. *Tony Burnell 1997*

❸ ★22 Monkey See 18m

6 ● Follow the streaky wall on thin holds over a rounded top-out. Easier terrain to the anchor. *Sean James 1990*

❹ 25 Bottle Shop 18m

5 ● A blank-looking face that is edgy to start and very sparse over the bulge. Veer right to another bolt and head straight up to a single bolt anchor. *Tony Burnell 1997*

❺ 21 Hard Rock Café 17m

6 ● Start by a crack and large bush. Layaway up awesome holds and pad up the easy slab to the anchor. *David Newstead 1990*

❻ ★21 Shell Shop 17m

4 ● Follow a vague arête to a more sparsely protected slab with a couple of balancy moves. *Bill McLeod 1990*

❼ ★23 First Among Sequels 17m

5 ● A direct line up the attractive gray streak. After the 4th bolt, head left up the slab to join the *Shell Shocked* anchor. *Tony Burnell 1997*

239

Redcliffe

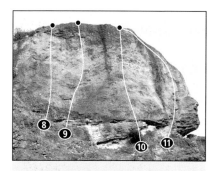

Bargain Basement

This is a short wall, with some great rock. Walk downhill from the Main Wall about 20m. Along the top there are several single bolt anchors which can be backed up to each other.

⑧ ✹22 Smiths City 13m

3 ⚡ An elegant face climb on immaculate rock. From a single bolt belay, move past a grunty start onto the wall. *Bill McLeod 1990*

⑨ ★23 Super Value 13m

3 ⚡ Inch up carefully to the 1st bolt through the scooped out face. This will get you pumped before you know it. *Bill McLeod 1990*

⑩ ✹26 Armourguard 15m

4 ⚡ A superb, rounded face that is intricate and sustained. Start at the cracked rock, where a medium cam protects to the 1st bolt. *Bill McLeod 1990*

⑪ ★21 Price Chopper 15m

3 ⚡ On the far right of the wall, up the slight groove. A medium cam can protect to the 1st bolt. After the 3rd bolt, head left up the arête. *Bill McLeod 1990*

Shopping Basket

Another excellent wall. From the Main Cliff or Bargain Basement, traverse south-west around the hillside. The next climb is on the north-facing side of the buttress.

② ⚡ 18 Stretch's Seventeen 8m

Compact rock and neat, edgy moves. *David Newstead 1990*

The next climbs are on the main wall with a high, horizontal break.

⑬ ★20 Dollar Wise 14m

4 ⚡ Technical, open hand moves relent at the break. Head right to the anchor. *Bill McLeod 1991*

⑭ ✹23 Mobil Mart 14m

3 ⚡ Boulder to the tufa blob and mobilise all resources for the crux. Coast to the anchor. *Bill McLeod 1990*

⑮ ★16 The Wide Crack 14m

A gaping fissure that takes big gear (#4–5 cams). If you didn't bring a rack, it makes a good top-rope.

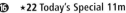

⑯ ★22 Today's Special 11m

3 Up the middle of the narrow, calcified wall, which features hard-to-read crimps. *Bill McLeod 1990*

Lionel's Bluff

This unique wall should be visited. It has some long, technical routes and is reached by traversing across from the Top Cliff or take the narrow gully above Shopping Basket.

⑰ ✹✹23 Verdid 20m

6 A smooth ride past the break onto a stellar gray wall. A long, cruxy section takes you to the anchor. *Lionel Clay 1989*

⑱ ✹✹22 Verdone 23m

6 An inspiring line up the centre of the face past a large tufa nose. Start through the jagged crack and ooze up a cruxy section of wall. Crank up good edges to a rest on the tufa and muster some energy for the last link up to join *Verdid*. *Lionel Clay 1989*

⑲ ✹✹23 Vernicious Kid 25m

10 Worm up the hard face to a tufa section and a break at the wee grassy ledge. Tackle the crux to reach the next large ledge and follow this up with more fine moves. *Pat Deavoll 1997*

⑳ ★24 Versed 25m

9 Bridge the broken corner and embark up the difficult face to a rest ledge. Sublime rock above this leads to the arête. Watch for loose rock. *Tony Burnell 1997*

From the Shopping Basket, traverse right and uphill to a compact black wall with this route:

㉓ ★23 Black Sabbath 14m

4 Takes the central line of solid rock past 3 bolts to a clipping ledge and some final sneaky moves. *Tony Burnell 1997*

'The first in a series of challenging, thrilling and dangerous outdoor adventure games that lets kids experience the realism, excitement and achievement of going Beyond the Limit. Ultimate Climb lets kids experience the thrill and challenge of a real climbing adventure.' *Excerpt from the cover of the Microsoft game 'Beyond the Limit: Ultimate Climb.'*

Hanging Rock

Mayan Smith-Gobat on *Dreamweaver* (28). DERÉK THATCHER

Hanging Rock is a tranquil limestone crag on farmland overlooking the Opihi River. The rock is pocketed and more featured than Castle Hill and if you've honed your skills at the boulder fields, this is a great place to apply similar moves to sporty routes.

The main walls at Hanging Rock are covered in full in this guide, apart from the routes at the Jungleland area. This is down by the river and is not visited very often. It does have some good routes around grade 20–22, but may need a big cleaning effort.

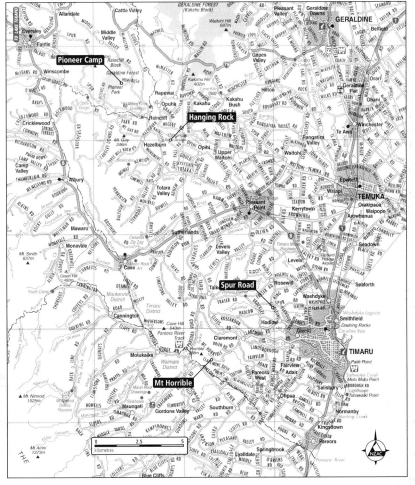

The Slabs • Antman Area • White Wall • Black Wall • Under Pressure Wall • Conquistador

From Pleasant Point, turn right into Tengawai Rd (also signposted as the turn-off to Hanging Rock Bridge). After a few kilometres, turn right into Omihi Rd. After about 5mins, turn left into Gays Pass Rd and right into Goulds Rd. Park off the road at the gate before the farmhouse.

Follow the grassy lane to a wooden stand by the barn. This houses the logbook, which should be filled out before you climb. Walk past the barn and through a heavy gate. Continue along the fenceline to a track on the left and follow this downhill. You will end up at the base of the crag with the White Wall on your right and the Black Wall on your left.

The farmers, Mr and Mrs Gould, are happy for climbers to use the area but please make sure that you close the gates and respect their property.

The crag is closed for lambing between the end of August and mid-October.

The bolting varies. The best are the 12mm stainless carrot bolts with hangers, or 12mm glue-in bolts. These are more trustworthy than the 10mm galvanised (usually hangerless) carrot bolts.

A single sport rope is fine, and take a handful of wires for threading naked bolts.

Take a couple of plastic brushes; one big one for dusting off the slabs, and a tooth brush for fine-tuning the small, feisty holds.

There is excellent camping 10mins away at Pioneer Park (water and toilet). From Raincliff drive down Middle Valley Rd and the park is on the left.

The Slabs

Hanging Rock

Mad Gesture Wall | Dreamweaver Area | Knights of the Reich | Momentry Lapse Wall | Pretty in Pink Wall | Speed King Wall

The Slabs

As you drop down the hill to the base of the crag, the slabs are about 150m right. You will pass the White Wall and the Antman Area first.

❶ ✹17 Broken Head 16m
3 🔩 From the groove, follow smears left to the 1st bolt and enjoy toe-sized pockets all the way up the slab. *Russell Shanks*

❷ ★16 Sweet Dream 16m
3 🔩 Climb the corner, and bridge the water groove up to the top slab. *Ian Binnie*

❸ 25 Hairy Tails 16m
3 🔩 A bristly direct start to *Nursery Crimes* using small slopers on the bulge. *Ivan Vostinar 2000*

❹ ✹10 Nursery Crimes 16m
2 🔩 An easy slab that is nevertheless technical and demands a good head for run-outs. *John Fraser*

Antman Area

This outcrop is uphill, about halfway between the toilet and The Slabs. It sports some devious slab and face climbing.

★V5 Neutron 12m
A line of great pockets to a slopey mantle.

V3 Proton 12m
Reach high to a good hold, then step up to small edges.

❼ 14 Electron 13m
3 🔩 A leftward traverse that starts below the matagouri bush. A step-up takes you to an easy slab. *Ivan Vostinar 2000*

❽ ✹22 Generating Hassles 16m
5 🔩 A grunty start up jugs to a slab. The crux moves take you left of the scoop to a hard top-out. *Terry Murray 1996*

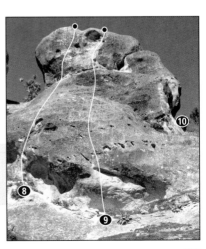

⑩ 17 Desertion 12m

3 🔩 Tricky rock-over into the groove, then waltz up, heading right. *D. Clarke*

White Wall

Below the power lines, 50m right of the Antman Area, is a white pocketed wall. It houses a few short but popular climbs.

⑪ ★20 Pond of Ripples 16m

4 🔩 Big holds on the face lead right. Finish up a small groove.

⑫ ★20 Nothing Too Serious 10m

3 🔩 Long moves on sharp incuts link up well to make this sustained. *Ian Binnie*

⑬ ★19 Sunset Strip 9m

3 🔩 An amazing array of moves for such a short climb. Layback past 2 bolts and crank to a sequence of pockets. *Ian McLaren*

⑨ ★17 Antman Black 16m

6 🔩 Big, prickly jugs through the steep start to glorious slab moves. Exit right of the yellow scoop. *Mike Robertson/Grant Piper 1989*

Black Wall

Black Wall

Next to the access track, this is perhaps the finest wall at Hanging Rock. It is littered with a sea of pockets and dimples; the routes are a decent height and all of the climbs on the main face are excellent value.

3 **21 What's in a Groove? 12m**
Not much! After a strenuous rock-up to the slab, the moves are very thin.

15 **22 Monteiths at Point 13m**
3 A trivial start leads to a very slopey bulge. This must be well-cleaned to ensure victory. The top section is an easy slab, but has with ground fall potential. *Grant Piper 1992*

16 **★★21 Indentity Crisis 16m**
5 Reach high to the first holds (use cheat stones if you need to) and boulder through the crux. Surf on through to the anchor. *Ian McLaren*

17 **★21 Black as Your Hat 16m**
4 A reachy first move and low crux eases back to a run-out but enjoyable top section. *Ian McLaren*

18 **★18 Desire 15m**
4 The first route established at the crag, and a good one at that. Some crank needed for the moves from the 1st bolt. *Ian Binnie*

19 **19 Lichen Bandit 15m**
3 ⚠ Nice climbing but, although the stances are good, there is ground fall potential at every bolt if you slip while clipping. *Grant Piper 1991*

Under Pressure Wall

The next wall to the right. The routes are quite varied and reasonably long.

20 **★21 Under Pressure 15m**
7 From a teetering pile of rocks, hop to the sinker pocket. Groovy moves up the long water streak. *Ian McLaren*

21 **★20 Toolong Left 14m**
5 Up the scoops to crux moves heading left at the 2nd bolt. Cruisy ground past the belly-buttonesque super jug. Rocking onto the stomach requires stealth. *Milo Gilmore 1996*

Conquistador Wall

5m right is a lovely little wall with two subtle water grooves.

㉒ **★25 Unnamed 17m**

4 The impressive arête. Start just right of the bush and after a grunty start head right onto the face. Cut back left at the arête to a mantle. Slabby climbing to the top.

㉓ **★21 Conquistador 17m**

3 The striking water groove in the middle of the face. Climb the steep weakness and rock into the groove. The slab mellows out after the crux. *Pete Hunt*

㉔ **★21 Rhythm Roulette 17m**

3 Good jugs get slopey soon enough. Push through the pump up the pocketed groove and top-out face-to-face with a steel monster. *Russell Shanks*

Mad Gesture Wall

A few minutes further right are some quite splendid climbs set amongst the foliage.

Tom Hoyle on *Pretty in Pink* (25). DEREK THATCHER

㉕ ✹18 Mad Gesture 14m

3 🔩 Follow an awesome sequence of pockets, veering left. There is a bonus bird's nest in every one. Cross right again to finish with a few sneaky slab moves. *Milo Gilmore 1996*

㉖ ★16 Rhythm Divine 14m

2 🔩 Wander left along the ledge to sinker jugs up to the 1st bolt. A few tricky moves to the exit. *Ian Binnie*

5m right by a gnarled tree:

㉗ 16 Terminal Frost 13m

3 🔩 Follow the tree up the gully and swing off a branch to clip. The slab moves are tenuous but fun if the foot smears are clean. *John Fraser*

Dreamweaver Area

Two minutes along the base of the crag is this impressive, blank and bulbous wall.

㉘ ★22 Ya'ma Points the Finger 18m

5 🔩 You don't want to cross Ya'ma. A powerful start through the first bulge is followed by intriguing slab moves. *Ian Binnie*

㉙ ✹✹28 Dreamweaver 16m

3 🔩 An immaculate face serving up consistently technical climbing. Unrelenting until the anchor. *Tony Rooney 1989*

㉚ ★23 Mystique 12m

3 🔩 Lovely pockets morph into evil slopers past the 2nd bolt. Finish through the big scoop. *Tony Rooney*

Through some bushes and on the next decent sized wall is the following route:

㉛ 22 Ole Memory Lane 15m

2 🔩 Casual pockets lull you to a desperate undercling and hideous top. *Ian Binnie*

Picnic Wall

Just to the right of *Ole Memory Lane* is this buttress with two perplexing routes.

㉜ ★21 Knights of the Reich 14m

3 🔩 Incredibly devious moves up the blank groove. A technical test piece. *John Fraser 1989*

㉝ ★20 Picnic at Hanging Rock 15m

4 🔩 Big cranks on positive pockets, then muster some psychological stamina for the slab. *John Fraser 1990*

249

Hanging Rock

Momentary Lapse Wall

This massive buttress is undercut at the base and has some awesome lines. All of the routes start either at the far left or right to access the climbable rock.

34 ★**22 Unnamed 24m**

6 🔩 Start out left and at the 3rd bolt veer right. Continue straight up a thin technical face.

35 ★★**23 Momentary Lapse of Reason 25m**

8 🔩 Start uphill of the undercut and traverse across jagged jugs. Once in the centre of the face, grapple with thin moves near the top. *Ian Binnie 1989*

From the right side of the buttress are these routes which all require a couple of threads for protection low down.

36 Margins of the Mind–2 Pitches
Simon Middlemass 1990

2 🔩 **P1. 15 15m** Start at the far right of the wall and traverse sharply left on massive pockets to the exposed arête.

2 🔩 **P2. ★★21 12m** Freaky climbing up the arête on pockets.

37 ★★**24 We Got Bananas 24m**

5 🔩 Traverse to the left-most water groove, where delicate pocket climbing takes you to a rounded top-out. *Brian Alder 1990*

Speed King Wall

38 **★26 Murder on the American Express 20m**
3 Traverse left and strain through the crux above the small cave. Subtle moves to finish. *Dave Fearnley 1990*

39 **★26 Doctor Doolittle 17m**
3 Traverse past the sharks tooth and out of the cave. Follow the shallow scoop to the garden. *Jeremy Strang 1991*

Speed King Wall

An enticing piece of rock, in fact, the pilgrimage to sample the delights of *Speed King* is an essential part of climbing at Hanging Rock.

40 **★23 Poison to Poison 15m**
6 A couple of nasty pulls on sharp pockets leads to a brilliantly cunning crux. *Ian Binnie*

41 **⚡21 The Antidote 17m**
6 The amazing groove moves up high provide the remedy for sharp pocket action at the start. *Ian McLaren*

42 **⚡★15 Speed King 22m**
6 A wandering line of pockets that kicks off with big moves under the arête. Meander up the slab and eventually move left at the last bolt to a rounded top-out. *John Fraser*

43 **★19 Brittlemania 22m**
6 Houdini antics to stand up in the scoop, then escape out left to an excellent line of pockets. Another wily move to master the slab. *Geoff Ellis*

On the next buttress:

44 **★29 Protoplasm 25m**
6 The white streak on a supremely overhanging face. A slightly crusty start leads to improving rock and increasing difficulty. Move right to the arête to finish. *Nick Sutter 1991*

Pretty in Pink Wall

㊺ Open project 25m

8 ⚑ An impressive line up the bulbous arête.

㊻ ★27 I Might Like You Better If We Slept

5 ⚑ **Together 23m**. Likely story! Start up the corner and traverse left to a powerful crux. Finish through big scoops. *Brian Alder 1990*

㊼ 23 Hanging Around Like a Dog on Heat

3 ⚑ **13m**. Follow the white, overhanging corner to the cave anchor. *Al Mark 1990*

㊽ ⚡25 Grippton Factor 21m

7 ⚑ A burly start to beautiful climbing on great pockets. A classic bouldery top-out. *Ian McLaren*

㊾ ★25 Pretty in Pink 18m

4 ⚑ Climb past the white flake to desperately thin crimps. Save some juice for the slab. *Ian Binnie 1989*

㊿ ★19 Lycra Bandit 16m

3 ⚑ Smear up to good pockets and pull a Wolfgang Gullich manoeuvre to rock up through the crux.

Spur Road

10 mins

Spur Road is a south-facing basalt crag. Like Mt Horrible, it has many good natural gear lines between 10 and 15m high with plenty of options for protection. The rock has rounded edges, which make great holds and there are plenty of cracks.

Volcanic rock is quite unusual in this area. Most of South Canterbury is underlaid with limestone and soft sandstone. These cliffs are a remnant of the last lava flows in the South Island, which drained out to the sea near Timaru.

North of Timaru, turn inland onto Washdyke Flat Rd (just south of the SH8 turn-off to Mt Cook). This road leads to an intersection with Spur Rd. Follow Spur Rd for 4km to a sweeping corner (100m before the turnoff to Kings Rd). Park by the deer fence.

Over the fence is a track which leads through trees to another deer fence. Turn left and follow the fence to the pine trees. Turn downhill and cross the stile, then veer right to the base of the cliff. The right-most routes are about 30m from the track exit at the base of the crag.

i Sometimes the top of the crag can be a little dirty after rain and some of the blocky rock should handled carefully.

The routes often have painted letters to identify them. The abbreviations are included with the route name in the guide.

★21 Gnome's Nightmare (GN) 13m
Left of a tree, climb the concave face to a bolt. Mantle and finish up the crack. *Russell Shanks 1985*

★18 Living After (LA) 13m
Up the smooth face and finger crack, then move right into the hand crack.
Murray Judge 1985

Just right of the tree:

18 Top or Drop (ToD) 13m
A zig-zagging finger crack which culminates in a mantle crux top-out.
Lindsay Main

The next 3 climbs start in a shallow, orange recess:

18 Ghostbuster (GB) 13m
Juggy start to the lip, then head left into the wide upper corner. *Russell Shanks 1985*

★16 Lion of Judah (LJ) 13m
Up a broken start below the roof, then head into the left-facing corner. *Pete Axford 1984*

15 (T) 13m
The short right-leaning crack, which joins the vertical crack out right.

Around the prow, 21m right of 'T':

17 Fame Not Fortune 13m
A nice line through flake features to a wide crack. *Andrew Macfarlane 1986*

Spur Road

⚒ ✹17 Cavalry Road (CR) 13m
Awesome rock up the face with vague cracks to a distinct left facing corner. *Andrew McFarlane 1984*

⚒ ★18 Two Drops (TD) 13m
Up the steepening corner to a mini roof, then continue up the fat crack to top. *Pete Axford 1984*

6m right past the banded face:

⚒ 13 Confidence Crisis (CC) 13m
Easy oozing on big holds and jams. *Andrew McFarlane 1984*

⑪ ⚒ ✹17 Shanks Sandbag (SS) 14m
A classic finger crack with exceedingly good bridging. *Russell Shanks 1984*

4m right:

⑫ ⚒ ★15 Stone Age Romeo (SR) 14m
Good holds up the long corner with some loose-looking blocks up top. *Russell Shanks 1984*

⑬ ⚒ ★15 The Two of Us (T2OU) 14m
After a cruisy start, boulder past the big broken blocks and up the easy slab. *Charlie Hobbs 1984*

⑭ ⚒ 13 Victory (V) 14m
Up the Y-shaped cracks into a slabby corner. *A. Crosbie 1984*

⑮ ⚒ ★18 Number of the Beast (NB) 14m
Superb climbing which gets better and better. Be careful on the lower blocks then there are bomber holds and gear on the upper twin finger cracks. *Russell Shanks 1985*

⑯ ⚒ ★18 Room to Move (RTM) 14m
Climb up the fractured crack and worm up the squeeze chimney. *Andrew McFarlane 1985*

⑰ ⚒ ✹17 Eliminator (E) 14m
Jugs for thugs through two bulges. Rest well, then commit to arm jamming on the upper wall. *Russell Shanks 1984*

⑱ ★22 Staying Power 14m

A bouldery start on the bulge before a thin crack. Climb left of the nose and head right around the arête to finish up a blank face. *Murray Judge 1985*

⑲ 13 Pin Ball 13m

The prominent crack with a green hue. Move around the block to the wide corner.

⑳ 15 Andy's Arête (AA) 12m

Up the short face, then tackle the arête. Veer right on the final section where you'll find a small cam helps the proceedings along. *Andrew Macfarlane 1985*

㉑ 12 Bush (B) 11m

Beware the big blocks at the start, then enjoy the offwidth. *Andrew Macfarlane 1985*

㉒ 11 What Goes Up 10m

Doesn't always come down. Climb the blocks to twin cracks in the corner.

㉓ 17 Eternal Legs 10m

Scramble past the blocks and climb the face using the crack. All over before you can say 'on belay.'

㉔ 13 Metamorphosis 10m

A pure jug haul up the broken crack. *M. Mason 1986*

Ben Yates bouldering at Spur Road.

255

㉕ 17 Hot Tin Roof (HTR) 10m

Up the broken crack and over the roof to a blocky finish. *Andrew Macfarlane 1984*

㉖ 14 Magician's Birthday 10m

Up the slab to an overlap. Take the short crack to the top. *Lindsay Main 1985*

㉗ 10 Honbun (H) 10m

The short corner sporting lovely holds. *Charlie Hobbs 1984*

㉘ ★17 Zorro 13m

Scramble up the ledgy groove to access the twin cracks. *Murray Judge 1985*

㉙ 14 Wee Wettle 13m

Climb the jagged crack to mid-height and gallivant up the wider crack to finish. *Charlie Hobbs 1983*

㉚ ★15 House on Fire (HOF) 13m

Immaculate holds and pro on a gentile slab. One of those must-do things. *Russell Shanks 1984*

㉛ ★19 Pleasure Victim 13m

Start up the finger crack to the bulge, and succumb to lovely rounded holds. Finish up the crack. *Luke Newnham 1985*

㉜ 15 One Sunday Afternoon 13m

A broken crack, then climb through the groove. Good holds line the way. *Pete Axford 1983*

㉝ 14 Rabbit Hole (RH) 12m

Up over blocks, then ferret your way into the crack. *Charlie Hobbs 1983*

Mt Horrible

Mt Horrible is a plug of quality basalt very close to Timaru. If you enjoy trad climbing on bomber pro and unpolished rock then you should check this area out. The routes are quite short but have an abundance of well-rounded holds and cracks that vary from finger width to offwidth. All of the prominent lines are covered in this guide. The other routes are shorter, blocky lines on both sides of the main wall. Some of these can be treated as boulder problems.

From Timaru: Just north of the Timaru city centre is an intersection with Wai-iti Rd. Turn right here and drive 4km to Gleniti. Veer left into Claremont Rd and follow this for 7km past Claremont School to Whalebone Corner (intersection with Fairview Rd). Turn left on to Fairview Rd and take the next right, which is Mt Horrible Rd. After 5km, there is a farm gate on the left (see photo). Park here but please do not obscure the gate access.

From Dunedin: Turn off just before the Pareora Bridge into Pareora River Rd. After 12km, turn right into Holm Station Bridge Rd. Turn left into Fairview Rd and travel for 3km before turning left into Mt Horrible Rd.

Cross through the gate and walk along the hedge on your left. Go through another gate and head slightly right for the next 300m, through the gate and to the big pine trees on the other side of the paddock (see photo). Either use the single pine as an abseil anchor or scramble down one of the gullies to the crag.

Abseil tree *Gully track* *Gate*

There is no need to contact the landowner before climbing. Just observe the usual courtesies.

Expect clean, solid rock with ample gear possibilities. Bring a standard rack with a couple of large cams for the wider cracks.

A single rope is fine for leading but an extra rope is handy as a rap line.

The top of the crag is totally flat and provides a convenient tree anchor.

The first routes are on the far left of the main wall before it gets vegetated or blocky:

Gate *Foot access*

❶ 17 Potato Head 12m
Start as for *Jelly Roll* and head left to the deep stemming corner.

❷ ★16 Jelly Roll 12m
Tricky start to fantastic holds. Raspberry jam your way up the right hand crack.

❸ ★23 Turn to Gold 12m
Tackle a cranky move on the steep face then mantle over (tenuous with nasty fall potential). Place gear in the left crack and shimmy up the face/arête to finish. *Tony Rooney*

❹ ⚹22 Hyperformance 12m
A finger fissure up the steep face gives way to a flared crack. In true Fearnley style, this is an awe-inspiring line. *Dave Fearnley 1982*

❺ ⚹18 Pareora Corner 13m
A continuous fat corner that serves up excellent climbing from start to finish. *Andy Cambell*

❻ ⚹19 The Bird 13m
Follow the finger cracks to the bulge then put in a high-step. Rock-over and cruise the wide crack. *Andy Cambell*

❼ ★22 The Arête 14m
Boulder up the left side of the arête and veer left into the crack. This continues straight up the bulging arête. *John Howard*

★16 Slim Jim's Jam 14m
The delightful, arcing corner. A challenging start gives way to easier climbing.

❾ 17 Groove in High 14m
Technical climbing on the narrow face capped by blocks. The finger cracks lead to a big rest and easy ground through the corner.

★17 Twin Cracks 14m
Funky moves up the steep start, then rock-over and engage both luscious cracks. The route eases off to low angle, blocky climbing.

⑪ ★14 China Boy 13m

Start just right of the tree. Bridge up twin cracks to the ledge and continue up broken terrain through the right facing corner.

⑫ 18 Blue Monday 13m

Up the offwidth (next to the nose) to divine layback moves. Finish up the left crack.

⑬ ★17 Arch Dig 12m

Magic climbing through the pea pod and up the wide right-hand crack.

⑭ ★★19 Wildman 12m

Bridge up the small arch and hand jam the crack. Gain the rest ledge and head up the crack to the right side of the roof. *Andy Cambell*

⑮ 15 Young Coronary 11m

Tricky start to the easy broken corner.

Integrations

This is a story about the last few years. It finishes today. Obsessive focus and single mindedness are great, these things have allowed me to do some wonderful things. Things that helpful folks said I could never do. Things like living in a van and having a decent income. I've had an ongoing obsessive streak since before I can remember; my first recollections of life are about obsessive things, comfort things. Rock climbing has been a lasting obsession for me for quite a few years. My obsessions have all been about being afraid that I can't have everything and about escapism. The great thing about obsessions is that if you do them long enough, you start to wonder why you do them and you start to get amazing insights into your mind. I can recommend them as a great personal growth tool. Rock climbing as an obsession has the added benefit of keeping you fit. People like obsessions, when folks talk about me to their friends it's often been about my obsessions: Chris the rock climber, Chris the van-dweller, Lizzard, the...whatever he is, whatever you do don't give him your phone number. We love to compartmentalise anything, people included, it keeps life simple and gives us a false sense of safety. Climbing lead me to a whole bunch of other things in my life: learning about the natural environment, New Zealand history, geology, developing businesses, love of nature, teaching and friends, really good friends. Now I'm getting the same hit that I got chasing numbers through my early climbing years from all these things. Less obsessive and more integrated. Yum.

Chris Burtenshaw

Sebastapol Bluffs

The Aoraki/Mount Cook National Park is more well known for mountaineering than rock climbing. The greywacke is damningly referred to as 'weetbix' by frustrated alpine rock enthusiasts, because it is notoriously loose and fractured. Fortunately, Sebastapol Bluffs has some of the most solid rock in the area and is but a stones throw from the comforts of the village. The weathered greywacke has a wonderful texture with lots of incut edges and often a red tinge.

There are a number of other routes not included in this guide, but these are on dubious quality rock and rarely get climbed. If you would like more information about the area, a pamphlet guide is available at the Alpine Guides shop in the village.

Alpine Rock

Aside from Sebastapol Bluffs, the most accessible rock climbing is at Twin Stream. Although this is a 'crag,' the 4 hour approach is committing and the area definitely falls in the alpine rock genre. It is seasonal and is only really 'on' for rock climbing in high summer.

The best guide to this area is the NZAC *Barron Saddle–Mt Brewster* mountaineering guide by Ross Cullen or visit www.geocities.com/~nzclimbing/guides

The road to Aoraki
NICK FLYVBJERG

10 mins

From the village, walk or drive back along the main road for about 1km. Park in front of the bluffs and follow the tracks across the river bed.

Most of the climbs are bolted, but take a rack for the mixed and trad lines. Make sure that you treat the rock with usual alpine caution. There is a fair amount of rubble on the ledges so helmets are essential and as many of the routes are over 25m long, two ropes are necessary for descents.

There is cheap camping at the DOC site on the way to the Hooker Valley and two mountaineering club huts near the village. Wyn Irwin is near the camp ground and is owned by the Canterbury Mountaineering Club.

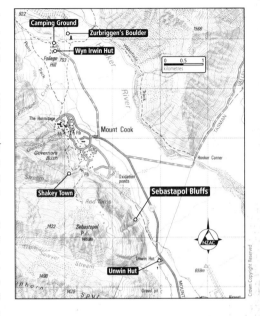

Unwin Hut is owned by the NZAC and is about 3km back down the main road from the village. Both huts have great facilities, but club members will get preference if it is busy. Wyn Irwin is locked in winter and Unwin has a full-time warden.

Sebastapol Bluffs

Sebastapol Bluffs

Twin Cracks Wall

This is a small wall at the left end of the crag. Follow the main track and then take the fork which leads left.

❶ 19 Balls 17m

3 A nice start via a fat wire placement to the slab. Bravery through the crux is rewarded with great holds and bomber gear. *Murray Ball*

❷ ★21 Ethical Debate 18m

4 Absorbing and sustained climbing up the centre of the face. It is wise to place the start wire as for *Balls* or *Twin Cracks*. *Kiersten Price*

❸ 16 Twin Cracks 20m

A distinct, jagged crack. Watch the loose blocks down low and take a wide range of cams.

Crucifix Wall

This is the first wall that you meet while ascending the scree slope at the left end of the crag. It is about 100m right of the Twin Cracks Wall. The cracks are rarely climbed but do have some good sections of rock. The wall above and left has three climbs in the 18–19 grade range.

❹ 18 Crucifix 23m

1 A thin crack that cuts through the most solid rock on this wall. At the top, clip the bolt and scramble up to the anchor.

❺ 17 Doubtful Thomas 23m

1 Thin moves to a piton and solid climbing up the crack. The top third is on broken ground.

❻ 14 Crucifax 20m

1 A flared crack on the right hand side of the wall. It takes good gear and has some nice layback moves.

The Gully

There are quite a few routes in this area, but they do not get much traffic. The rock is quite patchy but where it is good, it is really good. The following climb is uphill from the Crucifix Wall at the apex of the scree fan.

❼ **★21 Tremor 30m**

Gain the ledge via 3 bolts and continue past a single bolt anchor to the smooth, inset face. There are amazing moves over the bulge and an optional #1–1.5 cam protects to the roof. *Brent Shears 1999*

Climb 5m up to the belay ledge on the right.

❽ **★21 Revenge of the Podge 37m**

If winter decadence has been weighing you down, this one will be a challenge. It's a sweet 'n' sour creation with stunning sections of rock mixed in with looser stuff.

❾ **★★19 Magic Messiah 37m**

Crimps and technical face moves past the bolts to a lovely crack. This links the first 2 pitches of the original line; a 7 pitch adventure that deteriorates further up. *Peter Dickson/Alex Palman/Jo Kippax 1991*

20m around the base of the cliff is a narrow brushed wall between two bands of vegetation.

★20 Poison Dwarf 12m

A groovy sequence of crimps that is short but nuggety. *Kylie Wakelin 1999*

Lunar Wall

This expanse of rock sports two airy routes. These don't match up to the Red Arête Area in terms of rock quality, but have a certain alpine vivaciousness.

Sebastapol Bluffs

⑪ ★17 Lunar Landing 55m

10 Not immaculate rock, but still a pitch of intergalactic proportions and stellar exposure. *Brent Shears 1999*

⑫ ★19 Lunar Tick 46m

10 An adventure up the right side of the wall. Start up the vegetated rock and veer left to a light, streaked section. A lot of fun, but treat the holds with caution. *Brent Shears 1999*

Red Arête Area

An outing up this bluff on a sunny day is magnificent. It is a great place to get some height, practice multi-pitch climbing or just enjoy linking up primo slab pitches. The rock is an alluring shade of red and is incut with juggy edges. The anchors have been well set up by local guides for instruction and you will find abseil points in all the right places. Be aware of other parties, especially when pulling ropes, as this may dislodge loose rock.

⑬ ★14 Let's Go Bushwalking 35m

8 This is a multi-pitch climb, but things get a little vegetated after the 1st pitch. Start at the left end of the slab and hike straight through to the anchor. If you feel like completing the climb, head out left among the shrubbery (grade 16).

⑭ Shark Attack–3 Pitches

Put up with minimal gear by Nick back in the day, this big fish was retro-bolted with recycled hangers made out of snowstakes. From the ground these resembled shark fins. *Nick Cradock 1980s*

4 **P1. ★12 23m** A laid-back start to a big old slab. Follow a ladder of solid ledges.

6 **P2. ★15 27m** Yet more beautiful slab climbing. The rock-over move through the little roof adds to the excitement.

8 **P3. ★★16 37m** A sublime face climb on the best greywacke you are likely to get your digits on.

⑮ Red Arête–2 Pitches

This pilgrimage to lofty heights above the village is a place to ponder the mountains and all that is good. Legend has it that Tom Fyfe climbed this in 1894 as training for the 1st ascent of Mt Cook, sans rope of course.

7 **P1. ★13 37m** The second line of bolts from the right end of the slab, this is a great warm up and beginner lead. Although the holds are plentiful, don't expect a monotonous scramble.

9 **P2. ★★13 36m** The best grade 13 we've found in the South Island. For total immersion don't stop at the midway anchor.

⑯ 12 Unnamed 37m

8 An alternative start to the 1st pitch of *Red Arête* that starts 3m right and continues to the same anchor.

⑰ Mako–2 Pitches
Chris Burtenshaw & AATC 2000

8 **P1. ★16 30m** To reach the start of this pitch, climb 5m left from the top of the 2nd pitch of *Shark Attack*. The face is technically interesting after a slightly crusty start.

8 **P2. ★15 33m** From the anchor, head left though the small roof and then right to the slab.

Red Arete Area

15m abseil to track

P2

To the scree slope

17

P3

P2

P2

13 14 15 16

Descend by abseiling the route (twin ropes) or bring shoes and rap 12m off the back/right side of the bluffs into a gully. Walk 10m down and traverse right all the way to the scree. Scramble down to your gear.

Kingfisher Slabs

From the main track head right and follow cairns up to the smooth, red slabs. Don't miss a sharp left turn before the matagouri. If you end up battling through vegetation, you are definitely not on the right track. The next two climbs are on the left slab and are accessed from the scree. The middle and right slabs are reached via the track which takes you to the base of *Sustalyte*.

⑱ ⚡20 Clean Hands 20m

4 Excellent edges on a fine piece of wall. A #4 wire can protect the cruxy moves to the jugs before the bolt. *Paul Aubrey*

⑲ ★16 Conservation Crack 20m

Some voluntary park management succeeded in pulling this fissure back from extinction. Dust off your hexes and put in as much stonking gear as you want. *Alan Adams*

The next climbs are on the middle slab.

Sebastapol Bluffs

Kingfisher Slabs

⑳ ✶19 Dirty Digits 40m

An awesomely long excursion with alpine charisma. Start up the face and move left of the crack. After the small tree, the route follows the pillar on stunning rock. *Ray Button 1999*

㉑ 16 Kingfisher 40m

A neglected old thing that needs some lovin'. Apparently it was popular in the '70s? *Alan Adams*

㉒ ✶✶19 Seriass 35m

Immaculate slab climbing. Cling to the edge of adhesion on a testing and run-out finish. *Tony Dignan 1982*

The next climbs are on the right slab.

㉓ ✶✶17 Keep Left Arête 35m

This jagged arête makes a sustained and lengthy climb. Use the arête and face.

㉔ ✶18 Sustalyte 32m

Delicate dancing on the slab, then a few casual run-outs to the anchor. Take wires for the middle third.

Johnny Davison on the *Keep Left Arête* (17)
KATE SINCLAIR

Aoraki Bouldering

There are several bouldering spots around Aoraki/Mt Cook Village that are frequented by locals on their days off and alpine climbers waiting out the weather. The most popular spot is the Pukaki Boulders. Close to the village, the best place to check out is Zurbriggen's Boulders. These are north of the campground, just off the Hooker Valley track. Both the Pukaki and Zurbriggen's boulders have good top-rope anchors.

There is also a okay traverse called Shakey Town near the village. This is about 5mins up Black Birch Stream from the Red Tarn footbridge. It is on the right as you walk up the stream bed. 'The Pebble' is on the same stream bed (lower down) and has several top-rope routes.

Pukaki Boulders

The Pukaki Boulders are a great place to go for a spot of low key climbing. They are clustered on the right (lake) side of the road a few kilometres from the Mt Cook turn-off on the way to the village. There

Brigid Allan on *Pukaki Arête* **(V1)**
KATE SINCLAIR

Memorial Boulder

Carpark

Pukaki

① ② ③ ④ ⑤ ⑥

Pukaki Boulder

is no car park, but the area is signposted and managed by DOC. There are several top-rope anchors on the Pukaki Boulder. We have included all of the lines on the front faces, but there are other good problems to scope out around the back. The Memorial Boulder is next to the Pukaki Boulder.

Memorial Boulder

- ❶ **VE** Low angled slab.
- ❷ **VM** Short wall.
- ❸ ★ **V5** Sit-start the short, rounded arête. Dyno from slopers to the jug.
- ❹ **VM** Reach high to good holds.
- ❺ **VM** Sidepull to good holds.
- ❻ **V0** Mantle.

Pukaki Boulder

- ❼ **VE** The left arête. The usual descent.
- ❽ **V0** A few positive edges.
- ❾ **V1** Reachey moves off crimps.
- ❿ **V0** Through the massive jug with a comfy top-out.
- ⓫ ★★ **V1** **Pukaki Arête**. Sustained moves up the striking arête.
- ⓬ ★ **V3** Traverse right–left.
- ⓭ ★ **V0** Diagonal line up the face.
- ⓮ **V1** Up the face with a thin finish.
- ⓯ **V1** Up the centre of the face.
- ⓰ ★ **V0** Follow the biggest holds and ledges.
- ⓱ **V6** The ledgy arête with a sit-start. The standing start is much easier and worthwhile for the high arête.

Duntroon

Duntroon limestone is well known for its bouldering. Elephant Rocks has an array of technical, smeary problems and pocketed top-rope routes. The powerful and pumpy, Hulk Hogan is a roadside attraction near Elephant Rocks. It's a totally unique overhanging scarp with huge limestone jugs that create crazy dynos and dynamic moves.

This area was also the site of New Zealand's first international sport climbing competition in the late '80s. In the valley behind Hulk Hogan and at the Y intersection to Danseys Pass, the chipped routes and painted competition lines still linger.

The limestone was formed in a basin produced by the fault that pushed up Fiordland and the Takitimu Mountains in Southland. This wide, shallow area stretched from the Waiau Valley north to the Eglinton Valley.

Sam Mangai on *Livewire* **(V5).** DAVE WOODMAN

The first people to explore this area were late Neolithic people who drew animals, humans and mythical forms on the rock. About 2km west of Duntroon is one of the most well-known rock art sites in New Zealand, *Takiroa*. The other interesting site near Duntroon is *Maerewhenua*. This is north of Hulk Hogan, about 500m after the turn-off. The art portrays birds, human and reptilian forms and abstract designs. Some of the later images are of European sailing ships and copperplate script.

Duntroon

From the south: Turn towards Weston just before Oamaru. At Weston, turn left towards Enfield and continue to Ngapara. Just after Ngapara is a Y-intersection (signposted to Danseys Pass). Drive straight through the intersection and continue for 1km until you see Hulk Hogan on the right side of the road. Elephant Rocks is 3km further down the road on the left.

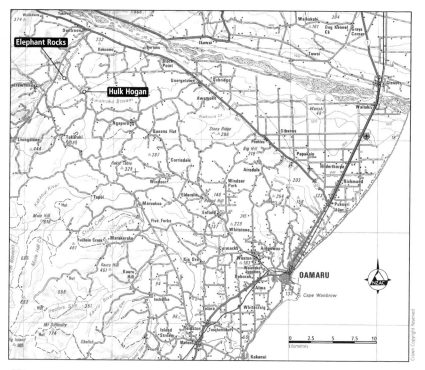

From the north: 5km north of Oamaru, turn off SH1 at Pukeuri onto SH83. This road runs west up the Waitaki Valley. Drive for approximately 35mins, then turn left onto the Island Cliff–Duntroon Rd.

From Duntroon: Cross the bridge and take the first right to Ngapara. Follow the signs to Elephant Rocks (6km). Hulk Hogan is 3km further down the road on the left.

i There is awesome camping at the Duntroon Domain. It costs $5 a night and has sublime showers, cooking facilities and a common room. Book/pay at the Duntroon pub.

Andre Dahlman on *No. 22*, Map 3 (V6). ANDRE DAHLMAN COLLECTION

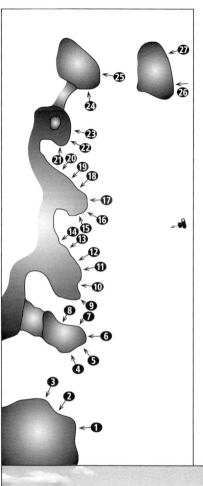

❶	**V4**	Slopey left hand hold.
❷ ★	**V6**	**The Butt Mantle.** The overhanging scoop.
❸	**V7**	**Fat Roll.** Climb over the bulge.
❹	**VE**	Slab.
❺ ★	**V0**	Short but cool slab.
❻	**V5**	Frustrating small bulge.
❼ ★	**V3**	Bridge the shallow scoop.
❽ ✷	**V5**	The pocketed face, veer right.
❾	**V4**	Small bulge.
❿ ★	**V1**	The groove with mini headwall.
⓫ ★	**V0**	Nice steady step-ups.
⓬	**V4**	The hideous-looking scoop.
⓭	**V3**	More hideousness.
⓮	**V1**	A scoop—more conceivable.
⓯ ★	**V0**	Pocket and smearing.
⓰	**V4**	Tenuous smear.
⓱ ✷	**V2**	Pockets on the steep arête. Drift left to the slab.
⓲	**V5**	**Extension.** Pockets straight up.
⓳	**V5**	**Ninja.** Over the bulge using a mono.
⓴ ★	**V2**	Smear up the shallow groove.
	V2	Smear up the blunt arête.
㉒ ★	**V0**	Tricky step-up to the pocket.
㉓	**V3**	Little pockets on the bulge.
㉔	**V0**	Long, flat slab.
㉕	**VE**	Low-angled slab.
㉖	**VM**	Stand up using the hole.
㉗	**V0**	Reach high and smear up.

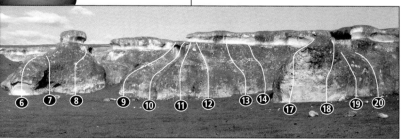

Elephant Rocks Map 2

(1) **V4** Small pockets, over the lip.
(2) ★ **V3** Pockets, finish over lip.
(3) ★ **V1** Nice climbing heading left.
(4) **V1** Dishy smears.
(5) **VM** Big holds up the weakness.
(6) **V0** Nice undercling.
(7) **V1** Smear up the mini arête.
(8) **VM** Small arête.
(9) **VE** Short arête.
(10) ★ **VM** Up the split rock.
(11) ★ **VM** The corner.
(12) **VM** Short arête.
(13) **VM** Nice step-up.
(14) **VM** Stand in the big pocket.
(15) **P** Very small, crimpy holds.
(16) **V1** Mono and crimp.
(17) **VM** Smear up the little scoop.
(18) **VM** Pad up the slab.
(19) **V3** Mono pockets.
(20) **V2** A gentle rock-over.
(21) ★ **V0** Pockets head left.
(22) **VE** Long, easy arête.
(23) ★ **V1** Up the long groove.
(24) **V4** Crank to the big pocket.
(25) **V3** Devious top-out.
(26) ★ **V3** Delicate moves on the slab.
(27) ★ **VM** Up to large pockets.
(28) **V3** Cunning moves up the groove.
(29) **V0** Reach high to the break.
(30) ★ **V5** Straight up over bulges.
(31) ★ **V5** Weird moves up the groove.
(32) ★ **V0** Drift right on pockets.
(33) ★★ **V0** Steep start, slabby finish.
(34) **V3** Small holds, smeary scoop.
(35) **V4** Crank on the two-finger pocket.
(36) ★ **V0** Reach lip and mantle.
(37) **V0** Reach to slopers.
(38) **V3** A short and smeary grovel.
(39) **VM** Low-angled groove.
(40) **VM** Nice pockets.
(41) ★ **V1** Layback and smear.
(42) ★ **V1** Smear up.
(43) ★★ **VM** Up through pockets.
(44) **V3** Small pockets.
(45) **V6** Tiny crimps.
(46) ★ **VM** Wide bridging up the scoop.
(47) **V4** Awkward, small holds.
(48) ★ **V3** Nice palming.
(49) **V5** High, with a daunting top-out.
(50) ★★ **V1** Steep pockets, exit left.
(51) ★ **V3** Footholds in the scoop.
(52) ★★ **V0** Slab.
(53) ★ **V0** Slab.
(54) ★ **V1** Blunt arête.
(55) **V2** Mantle to the large sloper.
(56) **V1** Rock up on pockets.
(57) **P** Blank face.
(58) **V2** The large, shallow pocket.
(59) **V0** Mantle.
(60) **V4** Slopey mantle.
(61) ★ **V1** Pockets.
(62) ★ **V2** Pockets.
(63) **V5** Up the arête.
(64) **V5** Mantle using the two-finger mono.
(65) **V0** Slopey slopers.
(66) **V2** Slopers.
(67) ★ **V5** Dyno to the top.
(68) **V3** Small holds, slopey top.
(69) ★ **V1** Pockets and edges.
(70) **V1** Pockets.
(71) ★ **VM** Great pockets.
(72) ★ **VM** The eye-shaped pocket.
(73) **V2** Reach high to the mantle.

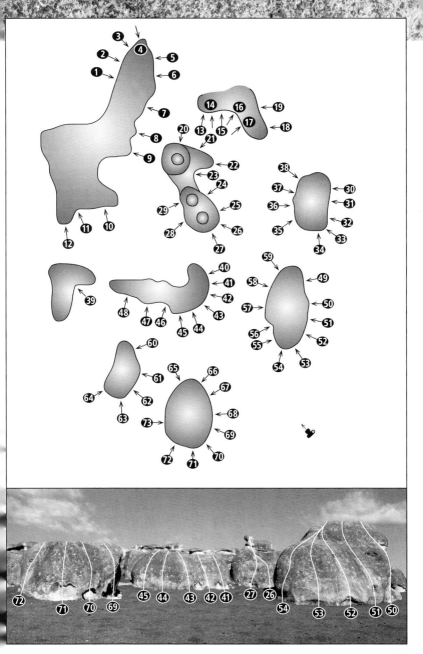

1 ★ **V2** Small holds on the blob.

2 ★ **VE** Long, blobby walk up.

3 **V6** **Erosion.** Blank face with nasty crimps.

4 ⚹⚹ **V2** Desperate to the big pocket.

5 ⚹⚹ **V0** Big pockets and funky moves.

6 ⚹⚹ **V0** Straight up the slab.

7 ★ **VM** Head left up the weakness.

8 ★ **VE** Nice long slab.

9 **V3** Pockets.

10 ★ **V0** Slab.

11 **V1** Reach to the pocket.

12 **V4** Two-finger pocket.

13 ★ **V4** Smear and crimp.

14 **V0** Slippery slab.

15 ★ **V2** Up to break, then slopers.

16 ★ **V2** Over bulge.

17 ⚹⚹ **V3** Up the groove with a technical start.

18 ⚹⚹ **V0** Slab with pockets.

19 **V2** Small pockets.

20 ⚹⚹ **V0** Lots of pockets, head right.

21 **V3** Pockets, some loose.

22 ★ **V6** Big moves between pockets.

23 ★ **V5** Hop to the slopey pocket.

24 ★ **V8** **French Kiss.** Small, crimpy pocket.

25 **P** Very tiny holds.

26 ★ **V3** Lovely pockets then slopers.

27 **V2** Rock out left.

28 ⚹⚹ **V3** Tricky arête.

29 ⚹⚹ **V2** Pockets with a tenuous top-out.

30 ⚹⚹ **V0** Jam crack; wow!

31 **V7** Exciting over the hard bulge.

32 ★ **V0** Pockets with tricky top-out.

33 ★ **V1** To the break and up.

34 **V1** Tricky before and after the break.

35 ★ **V0** Use the break.

36 ★ **V0** Layback crack.

37 ★ **V6** Ferocious small pockets.

38 ⚹⚹ **V5** Delicate test piece up small pockets.

39 ★ **V7** **Inside a Quiet Mind.** Small holds.

40 **V3** Edges.

41 **V1** Underclings on yellow rock.

42 ★ **V1** Charming pockets and edges.

43 ★ **VM** Short slab.

44 **V1** One pocket at waist height.

Donald Duck

45 **V1** Smear up.

46 ⚹⚹ **V2** **Donald Duck.** A mantle test piece.

47 **V1** Edges.

48 ★ **V1** Smear up with scoop.

49 **V3** Crank to the mono pocket.

50 **V1** Step-up and smear.

51 ★ **VM** Smear up using the mono.

52 ★ **VE** Easy slab with a hole.

53 ★ **V0** Sit-start, follow the jugs.

54 **V1** Generous holds eventually lead right.

55 ★ **V1** Pockets, veer left.

56 ★ **V1** Pockets then mantle.

57 ★ **V6** A hard problem with miniscule holds.

58 ⚹⚹ **V2** A tenuous and classic smearing problem.

59 ★ **V1** Smear up.

The Elephant

60 ⚹⚹ **V0** Nice and long, brilliant holds.

61 ⚹⚹ **V0** Big moves at the start to a slab.

62 ⚹⚹ **V0** Into the scoop and over the bulge.

63 ⚹⚹ **14** Lead using two bolts. Big holds.

64 **V2** Mantle with a mono.

65 **V2** Mono crank.

66 **V0** Short and smeary arête.

67 **V3** Slopers and smearing.

68 **V2** Bridge up.

69 ★ **V5** Long face climb on pockets.

70 ★ **V6** Same, same but different.

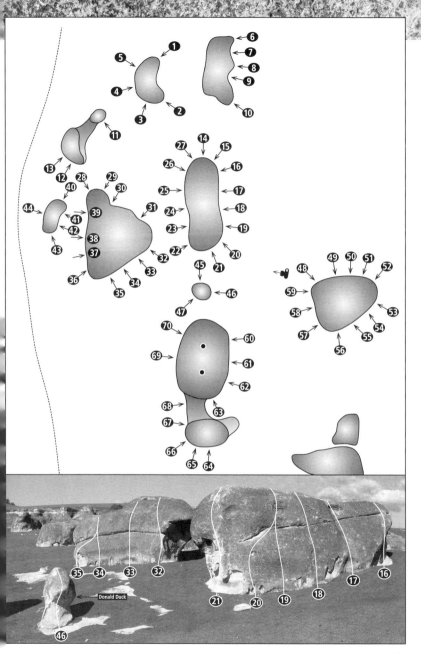

Donald Duck

❶ **V0** Short smear-up.
❷ **V2** Offwidth groove.
❸ ★ **V2** Face with small pockets.
❹ ✹ **V1** Pockets to underclings.
❺ **V4** Up the middle of the face.
❻ ✹ **V0** Groove.
❼ **V5** Up the face.
❽ **V1** Up the arête.
❾ **V0** Smear up all the way.
❿ **VM** Pockets.

The White Slabs

⓫ ✹✹ **V3** The lovely, pocketed groove.
⓬ ✹✹ **V0** The distinct groove.
⓭ ✹✹ **V1** Face with hundreds of pockets.
⓮ ✹ **V0** Up the dark face.
⓯ ✹✹ **VM** The beautiful slab.
⓰ ✹✹ **VM** The prominent chipped slab (one from the dodgy days).
⓱ ✹✹ **V4** Zesty problem with small holds.
⓲ ★ **V3** Tricky start.
⓳ ★ **V3** Small pockets.
⓴ ★ **V0** The usual descent.
㉑ ✹ **V6** Face climbing test piece.
㉒ ★ **V6** Crimp and high rock-over.
㉓ ★ **V2** Step-up into the pocket.
㉔ ★ **V2** Tricky step-up.
㉕ ✹ **VM** Head right along the break.

㉖ ★ **V2** Through the scoop.
㉗ **V2** Undercling the pocket.
㉘ ★ **V2** Crusty, pocketed face.
㉙ **V5** Crusty, pocketed face.
㉚ ★ **VM** Groove to large pockets.
㉛ **VM** Beautiful arête.
㉜ ✹ **V1** Up shot-gunned pockets.
㉝ **V0** Climb through to a large pocket.
㉞ ★ **V1** Two big pockets. Does not top-out.
㉟ **V1** Reach high to the edge.
㊱ **VM** Reach to the horizontal break.
㊲ ✹ **V2** Pockets. Smear up the face.
㊳ ★ **V1** Long slab with cruxy top.
㊴ ✹✹ **V0** Lovely, long face.
㊵ ✹✹ **VM** Up the smeary corner. The usual descent.
㊶ ★ **V2** Long, blank slab.
㊷ ★ **V1** High but lots of holds.
㊸ **V7** Up the arête/face on glued edges.
㊹ **V2** On sharp holds to big jug. Does not top-out.
㊺ ✹ **V0** Positive climbing through the small scoop.
㊻ ★ **V0** Past the bush and sidepull.
㊼ ✹ **V1** Lovely pockets.
㊽ ★ **V2** The groove.
㊾ ★ **V1** Step high into the pocket.

Jodi Apiata on *No. 8* Map1 (V5)

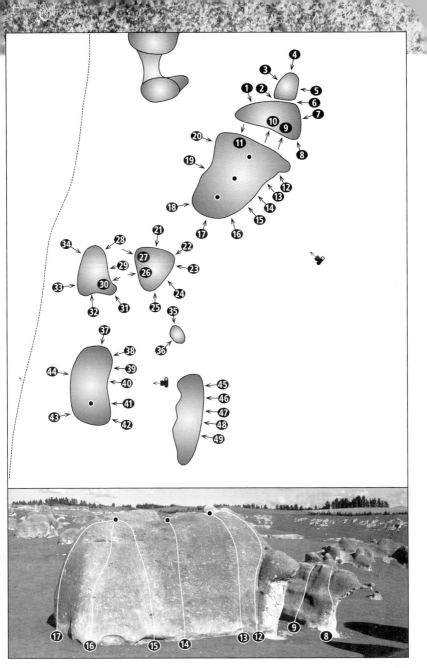

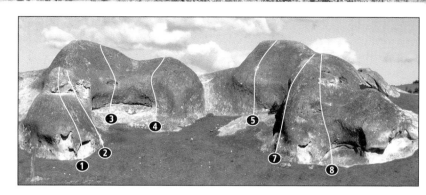

1 ★ **VM** Interesting move onto the slab.
2 **VM** Crumbly, yellow pockets.
3 ★ **V1** A strange, high step-up.
4 ★ **VM** Reach to the pocket.
5 ★ **V3** Cranky rock-over.
6 ★ **V0** Groove.

7 **V3** Big pocket then crank.
8 **V0** Pockets in the scoop.
9 ✹ **VM** Nice big pockets.
10 ★ **VM** Low-angled slab.
11 **VM** Best jug at Elephant Rocks.
12 **V1** The nose.

Daniel Ussher on *Donald Duck* (V2). ANDRE DAHLMAN

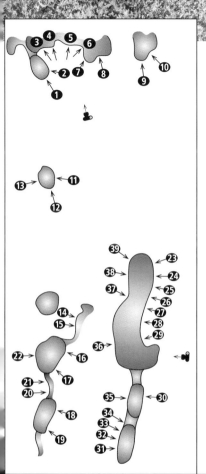

⑬ ★ **VM** Magnificent holds.

⑭ ⚹ **V1** The twin monos.

⑮ ★ **V0** Mantle the sloper.

⑯ **V2** Pockets and bulge.

⑰ ★ **V0** Two step-ups.

⑱ ★ **VE** Smear up and around.

⑲ **V1** Layback the arête.

⑳ ★ **V0** Reach to good holds.

㉑ ★ **V0** Smear up the runnels.

㉒ ★ **V5** Mantle to the good pocket.

㉓ ⚹ **V0** Layback the high crack.

㉔ ★ **V0** Through the yellow scoop.

㉕ ⚹ **V0** The multi-pocketed face.

㉖ ★ **V0** Shallow groove.

㉗ ★ **V2** Pockets and smearing.

㉘ ★ **V1** Wonderful slab.

㉙ **P** Over the high bulge.

㉚ **V0** Reach high to chunky, yellow holds.

㉛ **V2** The high, crusty lip.

㉜ ★ **V1** Smear up and over the lip.

㉝ ★ **VE** Up the shallow groove.

㉞ ★ **VM** Find the top jug.

㉟ ★ **V1** Long reach to jugs.

㊱ ⚹ **V3** Up the faint scoop.

㊲ ★ **V4** Delicate smearing.

㊳ **P** Pockets over the bulge.

㊴ ⚹ **V4** Access the ledge and head up left.

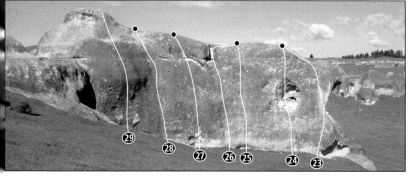

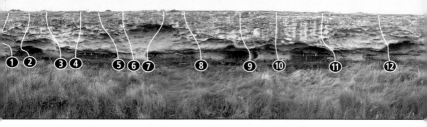

The boulders are not usually topped-out. It is considered good style just to match both hands on the top hold or lip.

Some of the high problems near the fence have a fall zone onto the road. Make sure you have a traffic spotter and good boulder mat manoeuvrerer.

❶   **V8**   **Dag Muncher.** Tiny holds with a tricky toe lock.

❷ ★ **V7**   **Momentum.** A few desperate slopers.

❸ ★ **V0**   Left on jugs.

❹   **V1**   Left end of grille, straight up.

❺   **V2**   Right end of grille.

❻   **V0**   From pillar, big holds through roof.

❼   **V3**   Veer right to crux.

❽   **V3**   Angle left on a couple of smears.

❾ ★ **V1**   Pillar start; up and over.

❿ ★ **V5**   Left of grille; jug to a hard pinch.

⓫   **V0**   Right of grille; cruise the jugs.

⓬ ★ **V2**   From scooped cave; sloper to big jug.

⓭   **V4**   Knee bar to a dyno.

⓮   **VM**   From undercut ledge. Good holds.

⓯   **VM**   From the small scoop on good jugs.

⓰   **VM**   More luscious cranking.

⓱   **V0**   Left of the *Matrix* cave, veer right.

⓲ ✷ **V6**   **Matrix.** Traverse the lower lip of the cave with long, powerful moves.

⓳   **V5**   **Inversions.** Sit-start at the back.

⓴ ★ **V4**   Straight through the roof between the dish and blob.

㉑   **V5**   Veer right to finish.

㉒   **V7**   **Tobin's Traverse.** Climb past the blob and move left under the roof.

㉓   **V4**   Straight through the high roof.

㉔   **V5**   On the far right of the cave.

㉕ ★ **V6**   Move up on slopers and dyno.

㉖ ★ **V3**   From protrusion, haul on jugs.

㉗ ★ **V2**   Big moves and holds.

㉘ ★ **V4**   Tricky moves up faint groove.

㉙   **V2**   Start at the lip of the small cave.

㉚   **V3**   Right of the cave, a couple of sloper moves.

㉛   **V3**   From the grey ledge, snake up.

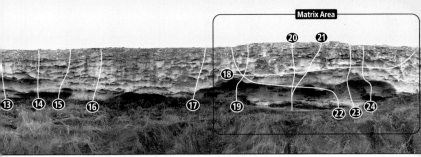

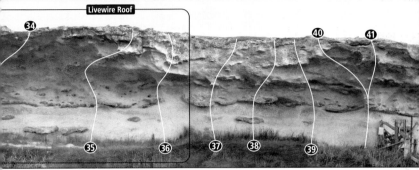

32 ✳ **V4** Massive cranks on good holds.

33 ★ **V5** **8mm.** Spaced climbing. Beware of landing on hidden rocks.

34 ★ **V8** **Road Kill.** Move right to a wild dyno which can land you on the road.

35 ✳ **V5** **Livewire.** Straight up and then traverse right.

36 ★ **V5** Climb through the wicked pinch.

37 **V2** Up and veer right.

38 **V3** Over dark ledges, straight up.

39 **V5** Slopey holds to a dyno.

40 **V7** Veer left on small holds.

41 **V2** Next to the fence.

Andy Milne on *Night Nurse* (V7). ANDY MILNE COLLECTION

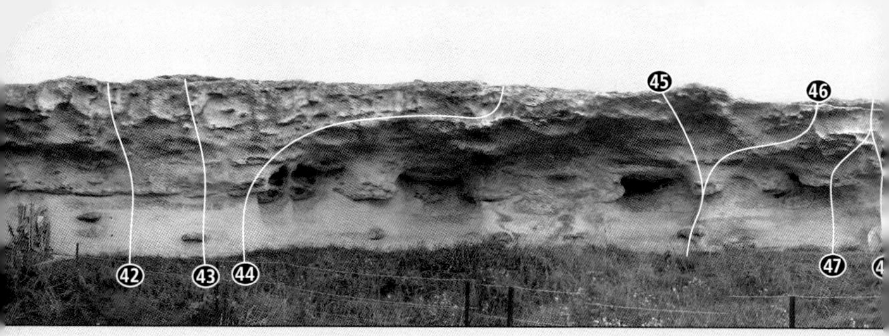

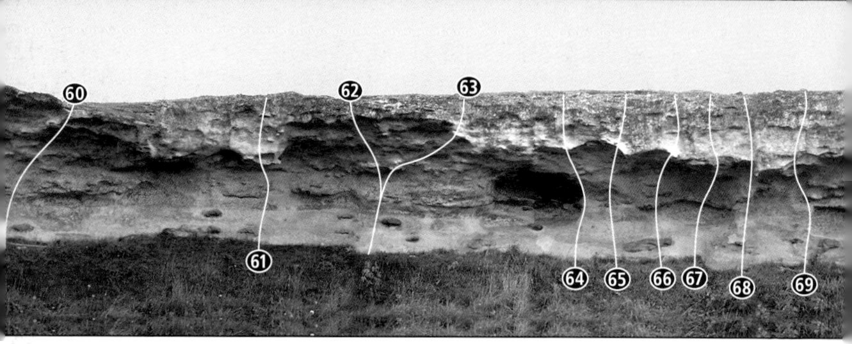

㊷ **V5** **Barbed Wire.** Big moves, small holds.

㊸ **V7** **Derek's Dyno.** Very long and crazy.

㊹ ★ **V6** **Springfield Monorail.** Start left of the scoop and go right about 6m.

㊺ ★ **V7** **Night Nurse.** Straight up from the pillar.

㊻ ★ **V5** **What Becomes of the Broken Hold.** Traverse right on jugs.

㊼ **V5** Left of the boulder through to the lip.

㊽ ★ **V2** From the boulder, veer left to the lip.

㊾ **V0** Cruisy jugs.

㊿ **VM** Through to the 'mother jug.'

(51) **VE** Short face.

(52) **VE** Left of the flake.

(53) **V1** Through the roof, heel hooking.

(54) **V3** Dyno left to a crimp.

(55) ★★ **V4** Ooze past two good holds.

(56) ★ **V7** **The Breaks Co-op.** An old test piece. Dyno from fingery holds.

(57) ★ **V2** From the scoop, lovely-jubbly holds.

(58) **V3** Lunge to small hold.

(59) **V5** Veer right.

(60) **V5** Up and right from a small ledge; hoon up right.

(61) **V2** Heel hook through the small roof.

(62) **V5** **Special K.** Big move off blob to average holds.

(63) **V5** Move right with body tension.

(64) **V8** **The Incredible Hulk.** Gain the undercling and slap the sharp lip.

(65) **V7** **Silence of the Lambs.** Static problem through roof.

(66) **V6** Crank out right.

(67) **V1** Heel hook through the roof.

(68) **V0** Nice jugs, use heel hooking.

(69) **V1** From the chiselled scoop to a sloper. Exit left.

(70) **V6** 2m right of scoop, to the crimp and throw left to good holds.

(71) ★★ **V4** **Riverworld.** 2m right of scoop/blue paint. Long and exciting.

(72) ★ **V5** Variant, veering left.

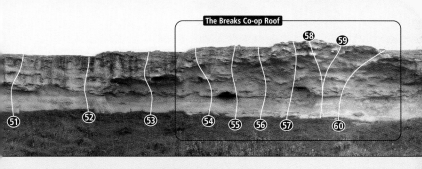

The Breaks Co-op Roof

51 52 53 54 55 56 57 58 59 60

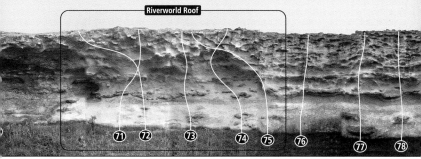

Riverworld Roof

71 72 73 74 75 76 77 78

73 ✹ **V5**	Direct to lip.	**76** **VM**	Face.
74 **V5**	Up through right side of roof.	**77** ★ **VM**	Face.
75 ★ **V4**	Long, high left traverse along the lip.	**78** **V0**	Face.

Nathan Campbell on *Matrix* (V6). ANDY MILNE

Bill Bradshaw on *Horace Has a Bricky Hiccup* (22). DAVE WOODMAN

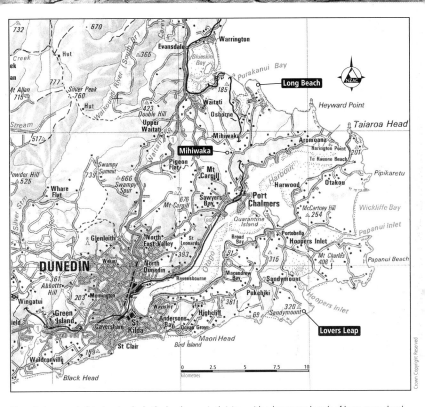

Dunedin is a wonderful place to climb. The local scene is thriving, with a long term bunch of keen route developers and transient student-types. The oldest and most popular locale is Long Beach and the new hot spot is Lovers Leap. Perched out on the Peninsula, this cliff is columnar basalt with closely-spaced, searing crack lines. The other crag included in this guide is Mihiwaka. The grades here are easier than Long Beach and Lovers Leap and it is one of the few bolt-free crags in the South Island.

We highly recommend Dave Brash's *Dunedin Rock*. It has full coverage of the major crags we've included along with the less-visited areas; fascinating historical anecdotes and a CD-Rom (designed by Andre Dahlman) packed with awesome images.

Local wildlife above Port Chalmers.

Long Beach

Good sea cliffs are rare in New Zealand and Long Beach has to be one of the best and definitely the most frequented. Many of the old climbs are steeped in history and the first ascents were often completed using minimal protection. Like most early rock climbs in New Zealand, they were seen as training for the mountains and at the time, routes like *Kindling Crack* (19), on The Pinnacle, were cutting edge in terms of technical difficulty.

In the 1980s route development boomed with the availability of bolting technology and some of the most classic sport and mixed lines were put up. Long Beach now remains a unique melange of adventure climbs (on sometimes less than perfect rock), naturally protected classics and sporty test pieces, but it has retained its trad crag atmosphere.

From Dunedin, follow the road around the northern side of the harbour to Port Chalmers (12km). Just after the 50km speed limit sign follow the signs to Purakanui/Long Beach. Turn left into Borlasses Rd and after 200m, turn right into Blueskin Rd.

Weave along the hills for about 10km before turning right towards Long Beach. Once you are at beach level turn left and park at the northern end of the domain.

Follow the sandy track under the macrocarpas for a couple of minutes. You will see Dragon's Lair from a small rise on the track. The cove ahead is Bolt City.

The trad lines at Long Beach require a good rack that includes a range of cams (down to the small sizes) and some RPs. Offsets are also useful.

Unless you stick to the bolted lines, adventure climbing will be the order of the day. Be careful of friable rock and make sure that your gear placements are in a solid medium. Helmets are a good idea for most routes—especially for the belayer.

The base of the crag is either hard packed dirt, sand or both. A rope tarp will minimise the amount of sand that gets into your rope. Cams can also get gummed and gear will corrode due to the saline environment if it's not cleaned occasionally.

The view from Mihiwaka

Dragons Lair | Bolt City | Main Cliff | Perfect Skin Wall | Drury Lane Wall | Pinnacle Sunnyside

Dragon's Lair

This is a small but gutsy wall set amongst a nettle grove just off the main track. The rock is of a high calibre and generally the climbs require finger strength.

❶ ✵26 Instrument of Torture 14m

5 A dauntingly steep start gives way to spartan face moves up the top section. *Dave Fearnley 1988*

❷ ★29 Satan's Sidepull 14m

2 Climb a short, devilish crux then lay-back the seam. *Ivan Vostinar 2000*

❸ ★24 Now That the Love Has Gone 14m

3 Bouldery up to the obvious ledge, then make thin moves up the face. Place a cam in the horizontal break and top-out gymnastically right of the V-groove. *Dave Fearnley 1986*

Dragon's Lair

① ② ③ ④

---

④ **✳18 When the Fog Lifts 13m**

3 An engaging and bouldery climb. After big moves past the 1st bolt, indulge in classic face moves. Place pro and mantle. *Phil de Joux 1984*

Bolt City

This small alcove is a great place to play. There are a bunch of well-bolted lines that are classic and technique intensive and two that will require a healthy head space.

⑤ **✳24 Philanderer 12m**

1 A route with personality. Weave up the chequered face on big holds and protect it with a #00 cam. Hard but totally awesome moves up the crack with good gear. *Richard Thomson 1986*

⑥ **✳30 Nautilus 12m**

5 Hard crimping and an intricate start leads to some delightful cranks and dynos on nice holds. It's not long, but it's sustained. *Ivan Vostinar 2004*

---

⑦ **✳24 Jeremy's Route 12m**

3 Big ledges to the mother of all rock-over moves. Once you've mastered this, head left on pleasing holds. *Jeremy Strang 1988*

⑧ **✳✳24 Labours of Love 13m**

6 A technical test piece on supreme rock. The climb follows a vague groove which produces delicate sequences and the odd bridging rest. *Phil de Joux 1985*

⑨ **✳✳26 Twenty Twenty 20m**

7 Cruxy face climbing leads to a rest at half-height. Very tricky, off-balance moves up the arête. *Andy Milne (to the Labours of Love anchor) 1988. Mike Simpson 2002*

⑩ **Day of the Vijaks–2 Pitches**

John Allen/Dave Fearnley 1980

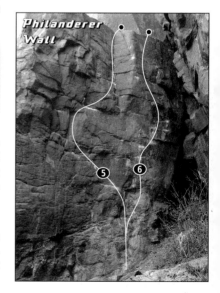

Philanderer Wall

⑤ ⑥

Andre Dahlman on *Twenty Twenty* (26)
DANIEL USSHER

Long Beach

P1. 20 12m A bold undertaking that follows a fractured crack. Quite serious to the piton but lush gear after this.

P2. ✳21 18m Head right from the anchor, following underclings to the groove. This has a reputation for spitting out gear because of the fall angle and has been the site of some mega-wingers.

⓫ ✳**23 Acid Queen 12m**
After a sketchy start, barely protectable with RPs, this shapes up to be a fantastically technical route with good gear. Take some cunning with you. *Graham Love 1984*

Main Cliff

This is the most public face of Long Beach. The wall is next to the main walking track and is a mosaic of lichen covered faces bisected by vertical crack lines. The landmark is the red fishing buoy quite curiously hanging about 20m above sea level at the *Fleet Street* anchor. The rock quality is patchy and it pays to have a healthy respect for the high band of choss that looms above the climbs.

Bolt City

⓬ ★**21 Swiss Version 25m**
The central face line that sports slopey, lichenous holds. A tenuous excursion. *Al Mark 1985*

⓭ ★**16 Keeping on the Straight and Narrow 25m**
A comfortable lead with a great mid-section. Look forward to a wee crux before the top-out. *Brian Alder 1985*

⓮ ★**20 Call Me Wanker 25m**
Climb delicately up to the bolt and breathe deep before mantling the roof. A compelling section of crack tops it all off nicely. *Dave Vass 1984*

⓯ ★**18 Noxious Vapus 25m**
Way cool. Climb boldly up the V-corner to get gear in the horizontal break. Commit and step across the void and up the good crack. *Graham Love 1984*

Main Cliff Left Side

⑯ 20 Freddy Fudpucker 21m

4 A less than tantalising blocky section takes you past the bolts and into a crumbly corner. All this aside, it is not bad if you like things adventurous. *Graham Love 1984*

⑰ ★20 Fleet Street 25m

3 Stroll up to the bizarre crux using an array of underclings, sidepulls and eventually a smeary step-up. Stride left to the buoy.

Crime and Punishment Wall

Just around the corner from the Main Cliff you'll find the exhilarating *Crime and Punishment,* along with some other very classy lines.

⑱ ★19 Burning Sky 24m

1 A graceful crack. Climb to the bolt and bridge artistically up the corner to the crux. *Dave Fearnley 1980*

⑲ ★22 Strenophobia/Xenophobia 25m

6 An invigorating line up a imposing strip of rock. Strenuous up the lower face then relax through the middle to a final, gutsy crux. *Al Mark 1985*

⑳ ★20 Love Al Root 28m

If adventure climbing is what you're into, look no further. Climb the wide groove and take the left branch that leads into a spectacular layaway crack. Finish left at the *Burning Sky* anchor. *Graham Love 1984*

㉑ ★★22 Crime and Punishment 33m

4 Synonymous with Long Beach, this classic is exhilarating and just run-out enough to encourage beads of sweat on your brow as you hone your powers of concentration at the crux. From the ramp, move up the pockets to a small corner and run it out to the ledge. Majestic climbing up the arête to the top. *Graham Love 1984*

㉒ 21 Whine and Botherment 7m

2 🛠 A cute one up the freestanding pillar 4m right of *Crime and Punishment. Jo Kippax 1994*

To access the next route, either climb up Whine and Botherment *or scramble up the dirty slab to the marcrocarpa tree.*

㉓ 20 Fringe Benefit variant 18m

5 🛠 Start behind the tree and climb the face for tricky moves on the arête, finishing right. *Graham Love 1984 (original route going left). Jo Kippax 1994*

From the right end of the Crime and Punishment Wall, scramble up the steep dirt slab to a short, rounded arête:

㉔ 20 Rick's Arête 16m

3 🛠 Climb the crack and tackle balancy moves to a mantle top-out. Good moves, just a little dirty at the top. *Rick Kershaw*

Perfect Skin Wall

This wall is tucked behind a macrocarpa grove and doesn't get many visitors. The clay above the cliffs seems to get washed down onto the rock, which makes some climbs a bit dirty, but there are a few very worthy lines that stay clean.

15m right at an old tree stump:

㉕ 18 Fluid Ethics 18m

3 🛠 Scramble up the choss band to the 1st bolt and cruise on great rock until you encounter a manky crack. Take #1.5–2 cams to protect this. *Steve Carr 1998*

Crime and Punishment Wall

㉖ ★25 Never Enough 16m

4 🛠 Face climbing just right of the arête. Massive moves link good edges. *Andy Milne 1991*

㉗ ⁂25 Perfect Skin 12m

3 🛠 A superbly devious route with an intellectual element bound to perplex most young punks. *Andy Milne 1991*

㉘ ★13 Meals on Wheels 14m

🛠 A good lead up the corner crack. The bomber placements are interspersed with flared sections.

㉙ ★18 Fraggle Rock 14m

2 🛠 Starts just right of the corner crack and gains independence higher on the face. Go right over the bulge. *Al Mark 1984*

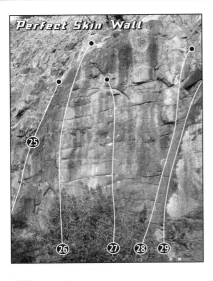

Perfect Skin Wall

❷ ✳19 Jumping Jellyfish 22m

Start up *Drury Lane* and traverse right from the hand jam. Follow the arcing corner and step left for the last few moves. *Murray Judge 1976*

❸ ★22 Love Don't Live Here Anymore 22m

3 Classy start up the pocketed wall. Reach through the vacancy from under the roof to wonderful, airy moves on the arête. *Al Mark 1986*

❹ ★21 Cuttlefish 22m

3 Up the faint crack to leviathan jugs. A cruxy rock-over takes you to join *Jumping Jellyfish*. *Al Mark 1985*

Pinnacle

The Pinnacle juts out onto the beach and is the most popular venue in Dunedin. Sunnyside is north-facing and has a mixture of easy-access top-roping and a healthy sprinkling of very challenging leads. The base of the crag is on the beach and a generous rope tarp to accomodate all of your gear will keep the sand at bay.

Pinnacle Backside

This immaculate section of rock is the pick of the pinnacle. It is on the east side and although often chilly, it is well worth your energy. The rock is very solid and the climbs are sustained and charismatic.

❶ ✳✳20 Drury Lane 22m

This striking line usually provides an entertaining performance for onlookers. Follow the crack and cower in the cave for as long as you like. Teeter out, place a medium cam and schaa-wing out on the hand traverse. Finish up the right hand crack. *Graham Love 1985*

Pinnacle-Sunnyside

The balmy microclimate, easier lead grades and top-rope access makes this wall eternally popular. If you are planning to top-rope here, be careful moving around between the anchors.

⑤ 11 Bandura 13m

Low-angled slab and crack climbing with plenty of good stances to sort out some gear.

⑥ 14 Bumpkin 18m

Quite a nifty line up the face into a groove that sucks up medium cams. Go for the easy top-out left, or give yourself a thrill by exiting right over the blocks.

⑦ ★19 Leap of Faith 18m

Start up *Bumpkin* to bomber pro below the roof. Pull up to the alluring face protected by small wires. A sneaky move takes you to an easy top-out. *Steve Carr 1984*

⑧ ★★14 Alesia 18m

A sustained climb up the blocky corner. It has most likely seen more ascents than any other route on this wall.

⑨ ★17 Not 18m

Start right of *Alesia* up blocky ground and make a beeline up the arête. Some balancy moves and high steps lead to an exhilarating finish. *Jo Kippax 1990*

⑬ ★22 Horace has a Bricky Hiccup 22m

Reachy climbing follows the undercut prow. Stay left of the 4th bolt. *Jeremy Strang 1988*

⑭ ✦20 Surreptitious 22m

Boulder up on good sidepulls and aim for the permachalked jugs. Grit your teeth and bridge high for mega moves. *Graham Love 1984*

⑮ 21 Naked Doom 22m

The arête right of the obvious gully. Start up the jam crack to the right, and move up to the arête. Fun climbing on RPs degrades to increasingly sketchy blocks. *Graham Love 1984. Rick McGregor (direct start) 1984*

⑯ ★26 Crimpsentration 22m

Moderate climbing to a hard move from thin crimpers. Use a small cam between the 1st and 2nd bolts. *Mike Simpson 2003*

Kim Cousins filming Jonathon Clearwater on *Kindling Crack* (20) for *Southern Faces*.
DAVE WOODMAN

⑩ ★17 Kennedy's Crack 22m

An epic battle. Employ your full arsenal of knee bars, hand jams and body wedges. Climb the angular blocks to get to the gully, summon up some courage and launch yourself at the offwidth. Take plenty of big cams. *Calum Hudson 1971*

⑪ ★23 Watching the Defectives 22m

Up the easy, broken face of *Alesia* to the slab. Fossick around for the crimps and exit through the right-leaning top crack. *Al Mark 1986*

⑫ ✦20 Kindling Crack 22m

A beautiful old crack. After styling the offwidth crux, move up the thin fissure to the cave and clip. Step left and dyno to the jug. The original line finished right after the crux (grade 19) and was first attempted using wooden wedges for protection. *Bob Cunninghame 1966. Jeremy Strang (direct finish) 1987*

⑰ ★**20 Oui 22m**
A great line following the lightning bolt crack. Climb past 2 bolts and kink right to more classic climbing.
Greg Aimer 1985

⑱ **16 Go 19m**
Start at *Oui* and follow the fat crack in the left-facing corner. Trek up the ledge until you meet the next vertical crack. Save a couple of big cams.

⑲ ★**13 Hominid 15m**
Take one of two starts to reach the right-facing corner. Finish up the *Go* crack.

⑳ **12 Overkill 15m**
A well-protected lead with an adventurous flavour. Veer left towards the obvious gully and pull up on good edges to the crack.

Bouldering

A few minutes down the beach north of The Pinnacle is a long undercut basalt outcrop, split into three roof sections and arches. It has some easy problems on the outside faces and some very strenuous problems and projects on the roofs and cave lips. It is loads of fun for a warm up or to let off steam on a drizzly day. The landings are nice and soft.

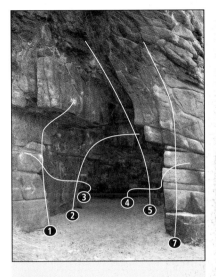

Cave 1

This high cave faces back towards The Pinnacle and has some long traverse problems which start deep in the cave.

❶ **VM** The short arête to a single pocket.

❷ **V5** Inside the cave on the roof arch, traverse left from underclings to a crucifix dyno.

❸ ★ **V6** Traverse out from deep in the bowels of the cave—yes, under that dark claustrophobic roof. Don't ever let any one tell you climbing is weird (head torch optional).

❹ ★ **V3** Traverse out rightwards from a sit-start at the back of the main cave.

❺ ★ **V5** The terrifying bridging exit in the roof of the cave.

❻ ★ **V5** Full traverse of the inner cave (left-right is best).

❼ **V0** The right arête.

Mike Simpson on *Watching the Defectives* (23). DAVE WOODMAN

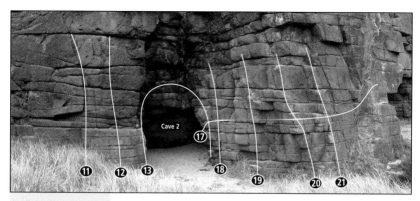

Cave 2

Seaward Face

This is the long, blocky wall that starts at the right hand edge of Cave 1 and finishes at the edge of Cave 3. It has numerous easy problems, only limited by your imagination.

⑧   **VE** Up the staircase to a wonderful pocket.

⑨ ★ **VE** Up the lay-back to stand on the slab.

Sam Mangai bouldering _Jodi's Traverse_ (V8). ANDRE DAHLMAN

⑩ ★ **VM** The round arête onto slopers.

⑪   **VE** The blocky, layback crack.

⑫   **VM** Up the horizontal breaks on crumbly holds

⑬   **V1** Traverse the lip of the cave up the left side of the arch, swing through the middle section and down-climb the right edge.

⑭   **V5** Low traverse inside Cave 2.

⑮   **V5** High traverse inside Cave 2.

⑯   **P** Roof traverse of Cave 2 from back to front (sea-side).

⑰ ★ **VM** Traverse from the arch out right to the obvious ledge before Cave 3.

⑱   **VM** Big, bulbous jugs.

⑲   **VM** The weakness.

⑳ ★ **V0** Lovely arête with curvaceous holds.

㉑   **VE** Easy blocks.

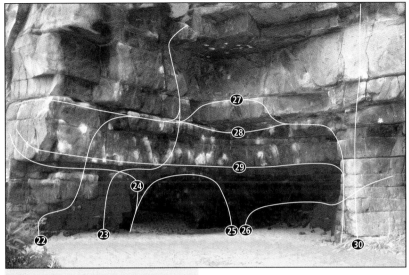

Cave 3

At the north end of the caves is a large arch with some magnificent rounded holds. These are the pure lines but there are lots of great variations.

The next problems start at the left end of the archway.

22 ★ **V3** Sit-start and heel hook to jugs. Traverse right along the break and past the hole to touch the block, which you may not want to yard off!

23 ✷ **V4** Sit-start out to the small horn to the same finish.

24 **V0** From the left-inside arch, stay low and traverse the wall to the edge of the outside arch.

25 ★ **V8 Jodi's Traverse** Traverse the inside edge of the cave.

26 **V0** A low traverse from the back of the cave, along the right hand wall to the edge of the arch.

27 ✷ **V4** A high traverse above the archway. Start at either side and gain the top seam.

28 ★ **V5** Low traverse of the arch.

29 **V8 Seam Eliminate**. Use the slopey hand holds along the lip of the arch below the bottom seam.

30 **V1** 2m right of the arch. Move straight up to the jug.

Jonathon Clearwater bouldering on the Town Hall wall.
DAVE WOODMAN

Mihiwaka

Mihiwaka is a small crag overlooking Carey's Bay on the way to Long Beach. It has been used by locals as a training ground for the big hills since the 1950s. This was mainly top-roping and soloing until Calum Hudson and friends developed it over six years from 1972. Not one bolt has been placed, although we are sure many have been severely tempted. So don your old jersey, leather boots (at least for the approach) and dust off your hexes. In keeping with the theme, these work amazingly well in the wide cracks – if you young tykes don't have any, don't fret you can protect with cams and wires, but it won't be quite the same.

In total, about 20 routes and variations have been established and these either fall into the classic and well-protected, or the run-out and serious category. We have selected those that climb well and are adequately protected. This should be a good start, but it is the kind of crag that you can explore and find interesting variations.

From Dunedin, follow the road around the northern edge of the harbour to Port Chalmers (12km). Just after the 50km speed limit sign, follow the signs to Purakanui/Long Beach. Turn left into Borlasses Rd and after 200m turn right into Blueskin Rd.

200m before the turn-off to Waitati, pull into a car park on the coastal side of the road. The track starts at the #25 orange marker.

Follow the track through the bush for 15mins. You will emerge beneath *Deep, Wide and Frequent*.

Take a standard rack and hexes. The ground is muddy after rain and you will need sturdy footwear for the track.

The best place to fill up your water bottle is at a spring just before Mihiwaka. There is a concreted outlet two corners before the carpark on the left.

Access to the top of the crag is from the right end of the cliff. Anchors usually consist of several small trees. Take long slings to extend these.

'John Wayne never wore Lycra.' **Ron Kauk** (about why he climbs in blue-jeans).

❶ ★19 Uneasy Rider 35m

You'll be uneasy too, especially if the climb is wet at the top. Start up the striking diagonal crack and use the slab and jugs to get to the base of the wide corner. This crux section has minimal gear. Exit up the groove. *Rick McGregor 1975*

Melanie Bell on *Aqualung* (17). DAVE WOODMAN

Carpark 15 mins

❷ 14 Top Cat 35m
Start as for *Living in the Past*. Once you are over the bulge, head into the left corner via the flake. Exit left on easier, vegetated terrain. *Murray Jones 1973*

❸ ✷13 Living in the Past 35m
The line follows a water runnel that has formed the most incredible jugs, chickenheads and slotter wire placements. Climb over the bulge and launch yourself at the corner. A runout but easy top-out. *Calum Hudson 1972*

❹ ✷✷17 Aqualung 35m
A much-loved oldie that takes the long, jagged crack through the bulges. *Calum Hudson 1973*

❺ ✷14 Mandrake 35m
A left-arcing, fat crack that crosses below the upper roofs. There are two options to finish; either head up the

vertical crack (*Bombay*, grade 16) or finish left around the block. Watch rope drag and take lots of large gear. *Calum Hudson 1972*

❻ ✷13 Deep, Wide and Frequent 35m
An ideal warm up for *Aqualung*, with good stances to place gear and plenty of options. Start at the seam, 4m right of the big boulder, hang out on jugs and enjoy the view. *Bruce Clarke 1972*

❼ Transmagnificantupantransiality 2 Pitches. This can easily be linked together as one pitch, but the scenic belay ledge is hard to resist. *Calum Hudson 1972*

P1. ★ 16 18m A right-leaning, dominant crack. This leads through a roof to the ledge.

P2. 13 12m From the belay, follow an easy crack heading left.

Lovers Leap

Simon Kennedy on *Pink Cadillac* (22). STEVE CARR

Out on the fringes of the Otago Peninsula, Lovers Leap is a much talked about addition to the Dunedin climbing scene. The main wall is one of the best in the South Island. It forms the steepest side of a narrow cove and the climbs follow long basalt columns. Because some cracks are very narrow, bolting is a necessity. This does not dilute the intensity of the climbing and most people find that their technique is tested to the limit.

It is quite remarkable that the first route was only established here in 1998. Perhaps this could be put down to the daunting environment and air of mystique that surrounds the crag. When you are high on the Orange Wall, looking across a misty ocean into southern nothingness, the atmosphere borders on spooky. The waves crash into the gaping zawn below the wall and the echoed yelps of seals drift across the crag. This is a wild place.

From central Dunedin drive south towards the Peninsula. Link up with Andersons Bay Rd and instead of following the road around the inner harbour, veer right towards Musselburgh on Shore Rd. Turn left into Musselburgh Rise and follow it around a bend to Silverton St. Turn left onto Highcliff Rd and meander along the top of the Peninsula for 10km. Turn right into Sandymount Rd and continue for 4km, past the Hoopers Inlet intersection, to the reserve car park.

Walk through the avenue of macrocarpas and veer right past the sign to 'The Chasm.' About 100m before the Lovers Leap viewing platform, head downhill towards the spur. You can either walk down the ridge track, which is a bit daunting, or scramble down the gully to the left. The access track links to the right hand end of the crag.

The only downside of Lovers Leap is the south-facing aspect. This limits the climbing windows to long fine spells of weather. Solar radiation totally bypasses the crag in winter and if there has been heavy rain, water seeps through the rock from the farmland above. It would be a good idea to ask locals about the conditions before you head out.

The crag is on farmland and is closed for lambing from August to October.

A good rack of cams is essential and you will probably need double ups in small sizes. Offset wires are particularly handy for these cracks.

Double ropes are the only way to descend off many routes. We have not included the fixed lines in the route heights.

Be very wary of the choss band at the base of the cliff and bear in mind that the rock above the columns is loose and friable. A helmet is needed for the belayer and climber.

'Man, I thought you always carry your grigri and a backup grigri on those trad climbs? You can rap down double ropes if you bring two... then if you bring another two, you can use them for backups instead of prusiks. I usually bring 8 grigris, in case my partner forgets his set.' **Jason Liebgott**

Ridge track

Valley track

7 ★ 20 Don't Cry For Me Argentina
8 21 Slap Stick
9 ★ 20 Al's Jam Crack
10 ★ 18 The Affliction
11 ★ 20 The Cure
12 ★ 19 Walk Of Shame
13 ★ 19 Stereo Cameo
14 ★ 20 Brave Dash
15 ✸✸ 28 Maximum Pseudo Likelihood
16 ✸ 27 Orange Peel
17 ✸ 23 Seawitch
18 ✸✸ 27 Demilitarised Zone
19 ✸ 25 Balls of String
20 ✸ 24 Welcome To Failure
21 ✸ 22 Pink Cadillac

Fixed line A
Fixed line B
Fixe
Fixed line C

1 15 Access Gully
2 23 Cardboard Chaos
3 ★ 22 Just the Tick-it
4 ★ 18 Crying Time Again
5 ★ 19 Triple Treat
6 ✸ 22 Side Effect

Lovers Leap

Fixed line E

Fixed line F

Fixed line G

Lovers Leap

Left End

This end of the crag is a good introduction to Lovers Leap. The gear is exceptionally good on most climbs and odds are on that it is just going to get better with age!

❶ 15 Access Gully 16m
A clean, left-facing corner and a good lead for tentative first steps at the crag. There is good gear after the first blocky section. *Dave Brash 2002*

❷ 23 Cardboard Chaos 16m
A distinct, thin finger crack with a pumpy start. Good placements if you hang in there, but make sure you take small cams. *Keith Riley 2002*

❸ ★22 Just the Tick-it 16m
Up the faint corner to a jamming crux midway. Take small wires and cams down to #0.5. *Steve Carr 2002*

❹ ★18 Crying Time Again 19m
Head right from the belay bolt and bridge/jam the twin cracks. Exhilarating moves out left make for an airy top-out. *Dave Brash 2001*

❺ ★19 Triple Treat 25m
Aptly named, this is three sections of climbing split by truncated pillars. Step left after each rest ledge into a new section of crack. You will appreciate the occasional big cam. *Al Ritchie 1998*

❻ ★22 Side Effect 24m
5 A luscious line up a dark, brooding corner. Start up *Triple Treat* and move right to engage the 1st bolt. The corner steepens through a bulge to become slab on the top section. *Dave Brash 2002*

❼ ★20 Don't Cry For Me Argentina 24m
From the belay bolt, traverse right and pick your way up the face using mainly the right hand crack. Towards the end, move left into the groove. The rock will clean up well. *Keith Riley 2002*

❽ 21 Slap Stick 17m
2 The bolted traverse gives access to a splitter crack up the buttress. Small cams are the ticket. *Steve Carr 2004*

From Fixed Line A:

❾ ★20 Al's Jam Crack 24m
You can't avoid the jamming on this one. Start from the belay at the top of the fixed line and traverse left. Plunge your digits into the hand crack and at the middle anchor move into the left-facing corner. An alternative start is to traverse in from the start of *Slap Stick*. *Al Ritchie 1999*

❿ ★18 The Affliction 20m
A good old fashioned crack line to put your jamming prowess to the test. From the fixed line, climb up and left along ledges to the base of the crack and go for it. *Steve Carr 2001*

⓫ ★20 The Cure 20m
4 This mind excursion can be accessed via any of the previous four routes. Cruxy bolt-protected climbing on knobs before bridging up the easier groove. Step left to an atmospheric anchor. *Steve Carr 2001*

⓬ ★19 Walk Of Shame 14m
Directly above the fixed line, this is a crack the way they used to make them; sinuous and sustained. Nice bridging and yes, jamming. *Dave Brash 2001*

⑬ ★19 Stereo Cameo 14m

Twin cracks between the buttresses. Cruise the first section on pleasant edges to a steepening crux through the left crack. *Dave Brash 2001*

From Fixed Line B:

⑭ ★20 Brave Dash 16m

Quite lovely. Traverse left into the crack. This widens in the upper section and produces awesome layback moves all the way. Take plenty of big cams (the finish takes #4-5's). *Milo Gilmour 2002*

Orange Wall

This is an impressive section of wall with steep, stunning columns and very challenging climbing.

⑮ ⚹⚹28 Maximum Pseudo Likelihood 20m
10⚑

A classic addition to Dunedin rock climbing. The orange rock is bullet hard and the climbing is technical, powerful and sustained. It's all that you could want in a route of this style, no real rests and it is not over until the very end. *Bill Bradshaw 2004*

From Fixed Line C:

⑯ ⚹⚹27 Orange Peel 25m
6⚑

The orange rock left of *Seawitch*. Fairly sustained with one crux that climbers regularly peel off. Mainly bolts and a few medium wire placements. *Mike Simpson 2003*

Dave Brash on the crux bulge of *Killer Wall* (23). STEVE CARR

⑰ ⚹23 Seawitch 25m
8⚑

An impressive quasi-chimney. Stem the well-protected crack line. At the top, mosey out right for an optional rest (watch for the dodgy pillar above), before cutting back left to the anchor. Nicest if you continue straight past the rest. *Steve Carr 2001*

From Fixed Line D:

⑱ ⚹⚹27 Demilitarised Zone 23m
10⚑

From the 4th fixed line, clamp your way up the faint pillar until devious moves enable you to access the upper crack on yellow rock. *Steve Carr 2002*

Lovers Leap

The next four routes start from the anchor at ground level. Either use double ropes or back-clean your draws to avoid excessive drag.

⓳ ✳**25 Balls of String 40m**

13 Traverse way left to the edge of the Orange Wall. Layback on good-sized holds and tip-toe up some very balancy moves. *Steve Carr 2001*

The Right End

The columns continue along the right side of the crag. There is some awesome climbing here, but be very wary of the choss band at the start, especially when it is damp because lumps do break off.

⓴ ✳**24 Welcome To Failure 30m**

9 Twin cracks on the right-most section of orange rock. Traverse out left to the line of bolts, where classic, sustained bridging takes you to an excellent crux. Take some small offsets and small cams to #1. *Steve Carr 2001*

㉑ ✳**22 Pink Cadillac 28m**

8 Veer left to the multi-cracked brown face. Sustained moves lead to some awkward sequences and just when you are hoping for a change of pace, get ready for an exciting finish out left. There is a 2nd pitch (grade 19) that links to *Balls of String*. *Steve Carr 2001*

㉒ ✳✳**22 It Always Ends In Tears 26m**

3 The scene of the Leap's longest whipper to date. After not clipping the 1st bolt and breaking a hold, Steve Carr tumbled 20m; from 5m up the climb,

The Zawn

to the ground and past his belayer. He was unscathed and assures us that this is a classic and safe line. Sideways undulations provide tentative finger-locks and lots of trickyness. Start at the belay chains and scramble via 3 bolts to the crack (unclip the first 2) and take a good sized rack. *Dave Brash 2001*

㉓ ✳✳**25 Parallel Universe 30m**

10 A cosmic phenomenon that is stiff for the grade. Start at a small pillar on the track and tackle outrageously technical climbing up to the triangular roof. A supergalactic move to the upper crack enables you to seize a rest, but there's a way to go yet! *Steve Carr 2002*

From Fixed Line E:

'Following the first ascent of *Killer Wail*, Derek Chinn, Simon Kennedy and I began the trudge back up the ridgeline when we noticed two huge black and white shapes streaking through the sea below. Two orca were making their way down the coastline to the chasm below. The chasm is home to several adult fur seals and their offspring. High tide had driven them out to sea and the orca were now circling them and making short work of terminating their existence. The sea was slowly turning red, so much so that Simon's partner, Jess, could make out the change in colour from the platform several-hundred metres away.' **Steve Carr**

㉔ ✶ 20 Long and Winding Road 42m

4

This meandering line links good sections of crack. From the fixed line, follow bolts up the *Unrequited* groove and weave left across the top of three truncated pillars. Aim for the crack under the left end of the roof and exit around the bulge. Double ropes are essential. *Steve Carr 2001*

㉕ ✶ 21 Wicked Corner 32m

Starts as for *Long and Winding Road*. After the ledge go up the deep corner. A testing route with bridging to the anchor directly under the roof. It is advisable to belay from the ledge under the corner to cut down rope drag. *Dave Brash 2001*

㉖ ✶ 24 Unrequited 41m

7

Directly above the fixed line, stem up the rounded groove. Move right towards the lichenous face into the corner. The peapod is a great lark. *Dave Brash 2001*

From Fixed Line F:

㉗ ✶ 23 Via Magma 40m

9

During the development of Lovers Leap, one of the original pillars on this route ejected itself from the cliff one night and wiped out the track below. Once it cleaned up, the climb was even better! Start up the left-slanting twin cracks with tenuous smears. Veer left to sustained moves into the left-facing crack. *Steve Carr 2000*

Fixed Line G:

㉘ ✶ 23 Killer Wail 26m

7

A graceful, arcing corner that follows the line of bolts to the roof. There are good intermediate gear placements (wires and cams to #2). *Steve Carr 2001*

㉙ ✶ 22 Date With Destiny 31m

Once you've grovelled over the lower choss, this route is awesome. In usual Lovers Leap style, the gear placements can sap your energy. If you can, save some go-juice for the cruxy finale. *Steve Carr 2001*

Windswept macrocarpa. ANDRE DAHLMAN

Wanaka

Wanaka's climbing is concentrated up the West Matukituki Valley. The walls have been developed to be user-friendly and, along with easy access from the road, this has made Wanaka one of the most popular places to go for a casual climbing trip.

The crags are on the glacial-worn schist hills that characterise this landscape. The flat cut faces can be anywhere from slabby to overhanging and the horizontal quartz seams make many of the moves quite crimpy.

This select guide covers some of the best, most accessible climbs in the area, but there are other crags to explore in the valley. These are comprehensively covered in the local climbing guide, *Wanaka Rock*. This is updated anually and is available from outdoor stores in Wanaka or by joining the Wanaka Rock Climbing Club. Send $30 to: the Secretary, PO Box 427, Wanaka. Proceeds are used for bolting and crag development.

Riverside

The Alcove

Roadside Attraction

Trackside

The West Matukituki Valley

Wanaka

From Wanaka, follow the road out of town towards Treble Cone ski field. It is 10km to Glendhu Bay and another 5km to the West Matukituki Valley.

The crags are described as you meet them up the valley. The climbs are characteristically short sport routes but there are also some very nice trad lines dispersed around the valley.

Most climbs have chain anchors. Please don't wear these out by top-roping directly through the anchor (use your own locking biner).

Most of the climbing is on pastoral lease farmland. The Wanaka Rock Club has negotiated access with farmers and it is very important to respect their climbing guidelines. This includes no fires, no dogs and no rubbish. Please cross the fences at the stiles and leave all gates as you find them. There are lambing restrictions from the end of August through to October.

There are no camp sites in the valley. The closest camp ground is at the Glendhu Bay Motor Camp. There is one toilet on the way to The Diamond, one in the shrubbery opposite the Main Cliff car park and one opposite Roadside Attraction.

Hospital Flat

This is an open, flat area with the landmark Tombstone on the left side of the road. The car park is at the end of the straight stretch of road across the flat. This is the access point to Main Cliff (along with The Tombstone, The Engine Block and Sunnyside). Please do not walk across the paddock; there is a track by the fence. The climbs are described from the far left (Tombstone) through to the right (Sunnyside).

The Tombstone

To reach this striking monolith cross the fence, continue back towards Wanaka past Main Cliff, and wander up the hill.

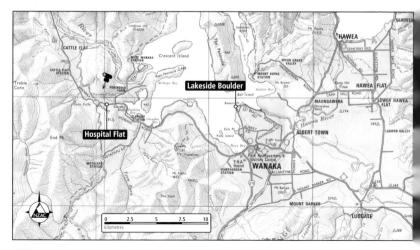

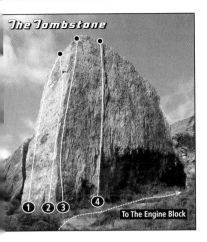

The Tombstone

To The Engine Block

① ⚡16 Lincoln Blondes Have More Fun
4 ⚡ **15m.** This top notch face climb starts
at the left arête. *Kevin Nicholas/Guy Cotter*

② ★17 Fingers Columbia 15m
5 ⚡ Scenic climbing that starts on the
right arête, and veers left to solid
quartz holds and a funky under-
cling/overcling thing. *Russell Braddock*

③ ★18 Rusty Pins 14m
6 ⚡ On the left side of the face, lay off the
arête to ecstasy. *Guy Cotter*

④ ⚡17 The Crack 14m
This is one of the oldest and most aptly
named routes in Wanaka. It's a much
loved trad route that splits The Tombstone and needs big cams at the top.
Dave Fearnley

3 ⚡ **★21 Disco Inferno 13m**
Etched on the back of The
Tombstone, this route follows the
scooped out arête. Balance up the
groove and rock onto the thin fin of
rock. Very photogenic. *Guy Cotter*

4 ⚡ **★24 Lung Starter 13m**
Wicked climbing on juggy scoops.
Huff and puff up the top wall and
wheeze your way over the top. *Lionel Clay*

The Engine Block

A very big boulder 20m uphill from The
Tombstone. There are two easy top-rope lines
left of *The Radiator*.

⑦ ★12 The Radiator 12m
4 ⚡ Some vroom to get started, but there's
no need to overheat. *Glenn Einam*

⑧ 29 Engage 13m
3 ⚡ On the underbelly of the Engine
Block, vertical layers of schist make
for a short but beasty route. Wind up
to the crux and put pedal to the metal
for the undercling move. *Max Farr 2000*

317

Main Cliff

This Wanaka hot spot is only a few minutes from the Hospital Flat car park. The easier grade sport lines are often used for instruction, but the trad climbs are equally good and usually free of top-ropes.

❾ ★19 The Nutty Professor 13m

A wicked finger crack that gets better 'n' better. Pull on a jug and reach high to finish. Take a large cam for the horizontal break after the overlap. *Ed Nepia*

❿ ★20 Senstra Dextra 15m

A mighty fine trad route. Start up *The Nutty Professor* and traverse right to the finger crack that runs all the way to the roof. Exit right to the anchor.

The line through the roof goes at the same grade, but take a wire for the hanger less bolt. *Callum Hudson*

⓫ ✯14 The Big Corner 15m

An outstanding route and one of the best trad lines in these parts. Head up the corner before moving out left onto the flake.

⓬ ✯✯17 Headbanger's Arête 17m

A sharp, aesthetic arête. Thrash up the free standing block and layaway. *Murray Ball*

The next routes start off a grassy ledge right of Headbanger's Arête.

⑬ ★22 Thin and Germanic 15m

3 Very cruxy and thin until after the 1st bolt. Finish up the face where both your frame of mind and the holds get a positivity boost. *Jochen Lenfert*

⑭ ★14 Wasted on the Wing 13m

1 This wide, diagonal crack takes big gear and finishes on the short headwall past the bolt. A very good first trad lead.

⑮ 13 Do I Have To? 14m

5 This is a well-bolted beginners lead. Give it a whirl (Shirl).

Sunnyside

This crag is above the the Hospital Flat car park. Walk up the road 50m before heading up the track. The routes described here are on the right hand end of the wall. There are easier routes out left, but the rock quality is not as good.

⑯ 26 Life in the Fat Lane 14m

5 Gain the ledge and engage the crimps. Veer left up the wall. *Ian Binnie*

⑰ ★25 Who Stole My Doris? 14m

5 Boulder onto the ledge and move through trickyness on slopey crimps. A satisfying finish. *Kevin Nicholas*

⑱ 27 No Sweat 14m

6 A sustained number that gets harder and harder, reaching a crescendo at the end. Take a fridge-full of chalk. *Jochen Lenfert*

⑲ ✳24 All That Remains 13m

6 This climb is split by two gigantic rest ledges but cruxy sequences will keep you entertained in the interim moments. *Allan Uren, Ed Nepia & Clinton Beavan*

⑳ ✳25 Mental as Anything 12m

5 A super-sustained crimp fest. One of the classics. *Glenn Einam*

㉑ ★26 Ode to Powergel 11m

2 After a rather hard start on crimps, charge past 2 bolts to good natural protection. *Ed Nepia*

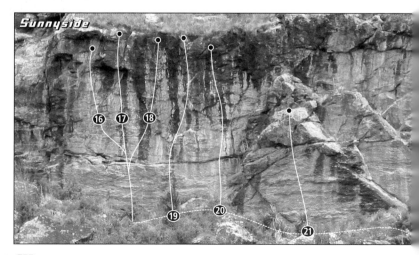

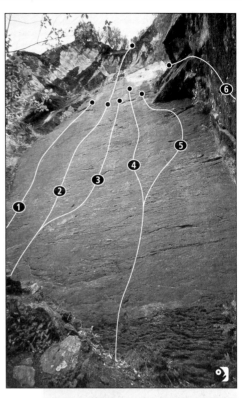

The Cutting

Directly across the road from the Hospital Flat car park, The Cutting has a few shady walls with mid-grade slab climbs. *Falcon Steep* is on the prominent face visible from the car park. Walk across the road towards the toilet and look for a discreet track on the left.

㉒ **✹✹22 Falcon Steep 24m**

9 🔩 This mega-classic is absorbing right to the anchor. *Guy Cotter*

Trackside

This is a small wall has the same access as The Diamond, but turn left at the lake.

✹30 Humble 14m

5 🔩 The steep wall just left of the crack has hard crimping on excellent quality rock. Exit rightwards onto a tenuous slab. *Chris Plant*

The Diamond

This beautiful slab is just off the Diamond Lake walkway. The climbs are lengthy undertakings and as it is south facing, the wall gets very good shade in summer.

Around the corner from Hospital Flat, turn right into the car park and follow the track up the hill. Take the path on the right side of the lake up to the obvious diamond-shaped slab.

❶ **✹18 Get a Job 24m**

6 🔩 Simply a long, pleasant line with a couple of cruxy sequences. *Glenn Einam*

❷ Naked on the Néve–2 Pitches

This climb can be run together to make one mega pitch. Use double ropes to descend or abseil twice. *Clinton Beavan/Allan Uren*

4 **P1.** ⭐**20 18m** Up thin edges to the ledge and anchor.

6 **P2.** ⭐**19 20m** An exposed continuation. Move up the wall and straight through the roof. The next section is run-out on an easy slab. Be careful of rope drag around the roof.

❸ ⭐17 Got a Job 16m

4 A good face climb to a ramp staircase. *Glenn Einam*

❹ ⭐19 Ex-squeeze Me 28m

9 Four technical sections of slab with rest ledges to recuperate at the end of each quarter. *Mark Sedon/Johnne Sedon*

❺ 15 Sand Gropers 20m

6 Slither up the edgy slab and reach the ledge via the crack. *Glenn Einam*

Naked on the Néve (20). DANIEL JENKINS

Venus Wall

❻ ⭐18 Feeling Rampant 21m

3 A thin crack with fantastic gear and bolts after the crack tapers out. Groovy terrain with hidden holds over the bulge. *Clinton Beavan*

❼ 19 Dried and Bagged 20m

4 Gradually wean yourself away from the crack and onto the face. Slopey edges make this feisty. *Freewheelin Franklin*

❽ ⭐23 10 Dollars is Cool 13m

3 Spicy and sequency. After bold moves off the ground, treat the 2nd clip as you'd handle a scorpion. *Dave Vass/Geoff Ellis*

❾ ⭐22 Venus in Furs 13m

4 It's certainly got spunk. Slappy start up the corner to foxy moves on the slab. *Clinton Beavan*

Hotline Wall

The next wall houses some robust routes and an exquisite crack. Walk around the corner to the right to find these hidden gems.

❿ ⭐17 Big and Chossy Bedroom Sossy 20m

A voluptuous crack that takes large gear and lots of it. *Anna Keeling*

⓫ 21 Penance 17m

4 Start as for *Hotline*. Place a wire and head out left to the bolts. *Nick Cradock*

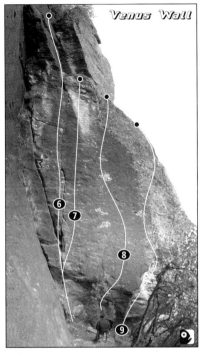

Venus Wall

⑫ ★★22 Hotline 17m

Could this be a trans-Tasman immigrant hiding in the dark recesses of Wanaka? This fine splitter crack is totally unique in the schist lands of Central Otago. Take double-ups in small pro. The angle is vertical but be warned, the indecisive will wilt. *Nick Cradock*

⑬ ★20 Hey George 40m

10 A wide corner crack sporting a bizarre mixture of face and crack moves. It tops out onto the slab. *Trevor Streat*

⑭ ★19 Fuckity Fuck Fuck 18m

6 Not to put too fine a point on it… This is a nice line up the black wall. Really balancy moves may unleash expletives. Just think of it as an ode to Nick's powers of expression. *Nick Cradock*

Hotline Wall

John McCallum on *Hotline* (22).
MARK SEDON/OFF PISTE PHOTOGRAPHY

Riverside

This is an idyllic, east-facing area overlooking the river. It is split into a few different walls with a wide grade range.

Turn left off the road after the bridge and drive through the shingle pit to the car park. The first wall you pass is about 20m from the car park has and has 6 easy climbs (grades 13–16). The numbering in this guide starts at the far left of the scarp at the Garden Bar.

The Garden Bar

This is a shady grotto down at river level with some pleasant climbing and swimming. Abseil off the bolts at the left end of the Riverside Wall. Climb out once you're finished.

5 ✸ **24 Just Add Sausages 16m**
Some sizzle is called for on this technical and sustained arête. *Dave Vass*

6 ★**22 The Oatmeal Savage 18m**
Start as for *Who the Fuck...* and branch left up the face, finishing up the arête. *Davie Robinson*

8 ★**23 Who the Fuck is Nick Cradock? 23m**
Totter up the ramp and negotiate reachy moves on the face. *Davie Robinson*

Riverside Wall

The rock on this wall is some of the best in the area. The wall has some really stunning, long face climbs with short roof sections and bulges.

From Te Whanau Wall, there is a fixed rope up a slab to the right end of the cliff.

❹ ✸**24 The Engorger 18m**
8 Start as for *Zoot Alors*, but move left into the overhanging corner to finish at the same chains. *Ed Nepia*

❺ ✸**24 Zoot Alors 18m**
7 Start through the bulge and head straight up to the overlap. *Ed Nepia*

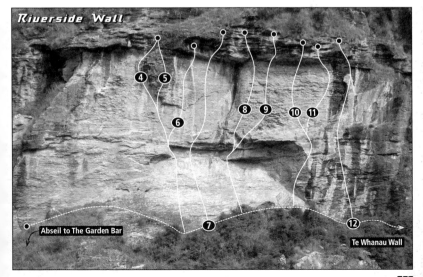

Riverside Wall

Abseil to The Garden Bar

Te Whanau Wall

❻ **★30 Te Timatanga 18m**

8 Do-able to the overlap, then it's all on up the face through two intensely crimpy sections. *Brendan Perkins 2002*

❼ **★★25 Lollapalooza 19m**

9 Something special. Classy roof moves onto a refined face, then one more small roof to finish. *Clinton Beavan*

❽ **★25 Changes in Time 19m**

10 Cruxy rooflets to a relaxing face and final exertion through the roof. *David Hiddleston*

❾ **★27 Moana Magic 19m**

7 Start as for *Changes in Time.* Head past the nose, into the sickle and negotiate the roof. *David Hiddleston*

❿ **★25 Inshallah 19m**

9 Start as for *Anti Walk Device* to the ledge then embark on the slab and pull through the roof. *David Hiddleston*

⓫ **★★23 Anti Walk Device 18m**

9 Left of the black streak, move up the arête on colourful rock. Track right-wards up the face and through the roof. There is an alternative 2 bolt start to the right, at about grade 24. *Ed Nepia*

⓬ **★★22 Jack Be Nimble 20m**

6 Very cruxy past the 1st bolt, then ease up to the candlestick. Dance carefully up this to a short roof section. *David Hiddleston*

Te Whanau Wall

⓭ **16 Get Kerfuffled 16m**

5 Hoon up the crack then gently-does-it onto the arête. Enjoy an airy finish. *Sarah Adcock*

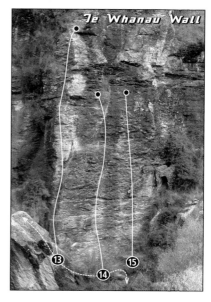

⓮ **★18 Te Whanau 16m**

5 A challenging start through to glorious laybacks. *Davie Robinson*

⓯ **★17 Terrain Spotting 14m**

5 Reachy to the flake then it's all good thereafter. *Sarah Adcock*

The Alcove

The Alcove is above and left of Roadside Attraction, about 5mins up the track.

❶ **★23 Where's Dr Holdfinder 17m**

7 Up the wall using the crack. Reachy moves keep coming as the pump creeps up. *David Hiddleston*

❷ **★★22 The Colonel's Secret 16m**

6 Steep cranking to the best handjams in Wanaka. *Clinton Beavan*

The Alcove

❸ ★19 Chinese Hospitality 15m

6 🔩 A welcoming warm up (damn it's pumpy clipping all those bolts). *Guy Cotter*

❹ ★22 The Ferocious Weasel 19m

8 🔩 A little beast that plays innocent and then goes for the jugular. *Clinton Beavan*

❺ 24 The Fearsome Flounder 19m

8 🔩 Utterly relaxing until devious moves take you left to join the *Ferocious Weasel*. *Ed Nepia*

❻ ★25 Misguyded 17m

7 🔩 Face climbing up the black streak to a staunch horizontal roof. *Ed Nepia*

❼ ★23 Roche Moutonnée 16m

9 🔩 Flow up the face and ooze over the roof. Heel and toe hooks on jugs help the cause. *Allan Uren*

❽ ★24 Bob The Builder 10m

4 🔩 Sustained and crimpy cranking on the white face. Knuckle down and work those digits. *Bruce Dowrick*

❾ ★25 Huha 11m

6 🔩 An Alcove test piece with moves that will drill you to the very end. All that and a bolt to height ratio that will blow your chalk bag off. *Ed Nepia*

❿ ★20 Cunning Linguistics 15m

5 🔩 Quite a tongue twister. Bridge up the corner and move left through the roof. *Whitney Thurlow*

She had told him expressly NOT to bolt the crack!

Roadside Attraction

Roadside is a couple of hundred metres down the road from Riverside. There is a car park on the right, directly opposite the crag. The toilet is towards the river in the willows.

❶   14 Elvis Trashes His Car 14m
6 🛢 Diagonal climbing on holds as big as The King. *Steve Henry/Maree Horlor*

❷   15 Strawberry 15m
6 🛢 Start at the right leaning corner/crack and pick your way up the face. *Paul Aubrey*

❸   ★16 Aratuatahi 14m
5 🛢 Waltz up the face to the mother of all underclings. According to John Entwistle 'you could bring a family up under there.' Easy to the top. *Clinton Beavan*

⓫   21 Reefer Madness 16m
7 🛢 From ground level, rollick up the white face via a small conundrum. *Ed Nepia*

⓬   ★19 The Army Route 14m
5 🛢 Start as for *Reefer Madness* and lay-back the seam. *Guy Cotter*

⓭   ★24 Screamin' Norwester 12m
5 🛢 An unusual but captivating outing with a bouldery sequence off the deck. *Ed Nepia*

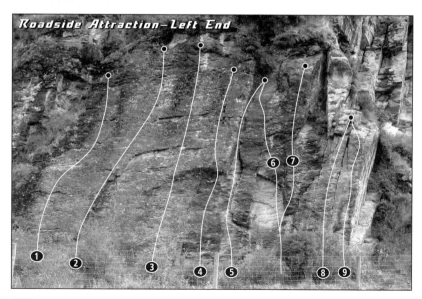

Roadside Attraction—Left End

❹ ★20 Practicing Arms 14m

2 Warm up your limbs on the start and feel the pump over the bulge. The top section takes good wires. *Lydia Bradey*

❺ ★15 Aspiring Arseholes 14m

Layback the buttocks and take some large gear for the sphincter. *Brian Dyson*

❻ ★17 Slightly English 14m

3 Follow the diagonal crack to a flake that sucks up wires. Rock up the bolted face on great pockets. *Nick Cradock*

❼ ★18 Nasal Excavations 14m

4 Start as for *Slightly English* up the crack, but veer right onto the pocketed face after clipping the 1st bolt. Fantastic moves up the arête. *Dave Packman*

❽ 18 Papals Nasal 13m

And so the nostril fixation continues…The cruxy start needs a good spot until the first piece of gear. Shake out and go for it. *Nick Cradock*

Roadside Attraction–Right End

⑨ ✹21 Arêtenaphobia 13m

3 The kind of off-balance fiasco that causes tantrums and retrospective enjoyment. *Paul Aubrey*

Around the corner on the next face:

⑩ 21 I Need A Pie 16m

4 Right of the small pillar, bridge up the corner and pull through to a rest ledge. Ease up through the next roof. *Allan Uren*

⑪ ✹23 Up Your Scud 13m

6 From the arête, engage in crimp warfare. Victory will require subterfuge and no quarter will be given 'til the chains. *Guy Cotter*

⑫ ★23 Free Barry 14m

6 Move right from the chains. Big holds and big moves may cut you loose through the roof. This can be nicely teamed up with *Up Your Scud* for a mega-pitch. *Ed Nepia*

⑬ ★29 Onion 12m

4 Loose a few layers of skin on the bottom crux, but save a bit for the top (you may well need it). *Ivan Vostinar 2000*

⑭ Short Cut to Exposure–2 Pitches
Paul Aubrey/Allan Uren

6 **P1. ✹✹17 20m** Chimney, layaway, bridge (or any combination of the above) up the cleft left of the ramp. Step right onto the arête and continue straight up. To protect the second from a potential swing, clip the 1st bolt of the next pitch before moving right to the anchor.

4 **P2. 17 18m** Move left from the anchor, tackle the reachy bulge and scuttle up easier terrain.

⑮ ★24 Nasal Discharge 16m

6 A beautiful combination of wild thuggery and delicate moves up the arête. *Hugh Barnard*

⑯ ★27 Crumble 16m

5 Start as for *Nasal Discharge* but head right on tiny crimps. Eases off past the last bolt. *Chris Plant*

⑰ ★21 Nasal Ecstasy 17m

7 Either boulder from the ground onto the ramp or wander up to the belay station. Layaway into the corner and take an airy traverse left. Banana back to the anchor. *Allan Uren*

⑱ ★25 What's My Mission Now? 17m

5 Climb *Nasal Ecstasy* and take the right crack to the steep bulge. Clip on crimps then charge on through. *Colin Pohl*

⑲ ✹22 Everything but the Formalities 16m

5 From the top of the steep ramp, veer right for elegant climbing up the black corner. *Allan Uren*

> 'The rules of the game must be constantly updated to keep up with the expanding technology. Otherwise we overkill the classic climbs and delude ourselves into thinking we are better climbers than the pioneers.' **Yvon Chouinard**

Lakeside Boulder

This is a lone boulder on the lake front with short, steep problems. This guide is a start but there are plenty of possibilities and variations.

From the lake front follow Beacon Point Rd past the yacht club until it turns to gravel. The boulder is on the beach where the road meets the lake.

❶ **V3** One move wonder from small crimps to good holds.

❷ ★ **V4** From the good start hold, veer left.

❸ ★ **V4** From the good start hold, veer right.

❹ ✹ **V5** Up the arête from the start pockets.

❺ **V7** From the start pockets, head straight up the small face on crimps.

They all agreed, it was a truly amazing sit start.

❻ **V5** From the start pockets, head left.

❼ ★ **V3** From the start pockets, head right.

❽ ★ **V2** Slopey dishes to start and a couple of cranks.

❾ **V5** Weird slopey moves. Quite awkward.

Queenstown

Beyond the hustle and bustle of the busiest resort town in New Zealand, there are a few excellent schist crags. Wye Creek is the most extensive and has a variety of good walls in a beautiful setting. The Queenstown Hill crag is also superb quality schist and Arawata Terrace is small but sports a few standout lines.

Chinaman's Bluff is 70 kilometres west of Queenstown, up the Dart Valley. This is an excellent multi-pitch venue with the best trad climbing in the region. The Remarkables Range, which fills the eastern skyline of Queenstown, is an alpine rock and ice climbing area. The best source of information about the rock routes on The Remarkables is *Rock the Wakitipu Way*.

Anna Dwyer on *Deam Thing* (21). KATE SINCLAIR

Gorge Road

Gorge Road is a new addition to the Queenstown climbing scene. It has a mixture of trad and sport routes and its proximity to central Queenstown makes it an easy place to go for a spot of cragging. All of the crags face north-west and enjoy an abundance of sunshine. The whole crag has potential for new routes including easy multi-pitch lines. Take note that this is a new crag and therefore the rock may be loose.

The Gorge Road crag is 5mins from the centre of Queenstown. Take the road out of Queenstown heading north towards Arthur's Point and Coronet Ski Field. Gorge Road Commercial Centre is on the right just before the 70km/h speed sign. Turn into the commercial complex and park.

The track to the crag starts on the other side of the small stream, directly south of the complex. Follow the track up for about 5mins and you will see Leonardo's Wall on the left.

ALL GORGE ROAD TOPO PHOTOS, DAVE BOLGER

View from Gorge Road crag. DAVE BOLGER

ℹ The crags are located on a recreational reserve and there is no need to obtain permission to climb. However, the land beyond the Black Wall and the Main Wall is private and climbing is strictly prohibited.

Leonardo's Wall

After about 5mins up the main track, turn left and follow this track to a rope and handrail. You will pass an arête *(Tel Aviv Express)*. To reach the next route, follow the handrail all the way to the left end of the wall.

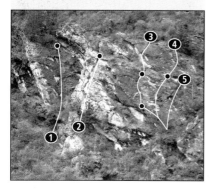

❶ ★18 Heart of Darkness 25m

10 Nice moves on sound rock. *Scott Kennedy 2004*

❷ 19 Tel Aviv Express 30m

9 A couple of bridging moves get you out of the trees. Clip a bolt out left before the crux and be careful; if you fall off at the crux you may swing under the overhang. Above the crux, the climbing is a lot easier (grade 15) and well protected. *Ofi Fischler 2004*

❸ Assessor or Assassin–3 Pitches
Dave MacLeod 2004

4 **P1. 12 8m** Traverse left on a ledge system from a belay chain shared with *Cliptomania* to an anchor.

9 **P2. 14 15m** Follow the snaking line of bolts. Nice easy climbing to a large ledge which can be gained using a knotted rope.

5 **P3. 19 8m** From the belay on the ledge, follow a short steep bulge of bolts.

Rap 40m to the ledge, then another 15m to ground.

❹ Cliptomania–2 Pitches
Dave MacLeod 2004

7 **P1. 15 12m** From the chain, climb the left hand line of bolts. The large ledge is gained by using a knotted rope. Belay at the ledge.

5 **P2. 17 15m** From the ledge, commit to a steep start then follow nice holds to a crux move at the top. Well protected.

❺ 14 The Man That Was Not Here 12m

5 Nice warm-up route with plenty of bolts. *Ofi Fischler 2004*

Bolt Wall

Walk for about 15mins up the access track to at a large sycamore tree. Turn right and follow a small track for about 5mins to reach Bolt Wall.

9 **17 Carey's Arête 25m**
After a vegetated start, the climb follows a winding arête at a mellow angle. Watch the loose block at the start. *Carey Vivian 2004*

6 **Open Project 10m**

6 **Open Project 10m**

5 **23 Punked in the Gorge 10m**
Steep climbing with a couple of big moves. The last bolt is mid-crux and some people prefer to bypass it. *Dan Martin 2004*

Main Wall

Main Wall

Access to the climbs involves a 20min walk up the steep track. Once this levels out you will pass an currently undeveloped crag on your right. Keep walking until you meet a large recession topped with a roof.

⑩ ☀23 Andy's Arête 25m

8 ☕ The obvious arête at the left end of the wall has some fantastic climbing with interesting moves in a great location. Start at the right side of the arête or do the variation on the left (both are the same grade). *Andy Thompson 2003*

⑪ 25 Beaten into Submission 20m

2 ☕ Clip 2 bolts on the face, then lunge up the wee overhanging block to the crack. Great pro in the crack, however its super, sustained and keeps firing at you. Very testing for a natural pro route. *Aaron Ford 2004*

⑫ ★17 Hapu Crack 15m

2 ☕ Clip 2 bolts then surmount the block (crux), then follow crack with excellent protection. *Dave Bolger & Chris Prudden 2002*

⑬ 18 Suicide Possum 20m

6 ☕ 5m to the right of *Hapu Crack*. A chossy start leads to varied climbing over the flake and up to the chain. *Carey Vivian 2002*

⑭ ☀18 Dog in Town 18m

5 ☕ A classic with holds in all the right places. Place gear at the start and climb to a small overhang with 1 bolt. Follow slab to the chain and avoid moving out right past the 2nd bolt. *Dave Bolger 2002*

⑮ ★20 Bungfinger 25m

8 ☕ Thin moves at the start lead to a small overhang. Charge through on good holds and follow the slab past a nice hand crack. Move right to a small ledge. A fantastic move creates a nice climax to the route. *Dave Bolger 2002*

⑯ 23 Mr Green Finale 25m

7 ☕ Sustained thin climbing leads you to a overhanging V-block. Surmount the block and follow slab for 2 bolts then traverse out left to finish up *Bung Finger*. *Dave Bolger 2004*

Coronet Crag

This is a small roadside crag in the Coronet Valley. The flavour of the crag is slightly dirty but it does provide some titillation for climbers and passing drivers. It is not known for its ambience, as you'll be sucking in car fumes on busy days, but there are some good rock features that require more technique than your average schist climb. Its quite smeary and slopey in places. This alone makes it a good place to wile away an afternoon or evening.

 Drive out of Queenstown on Gorge Rd towards Coronet Ski Field. Continue through Arthurs Point, cross the Shotover River and head up Arthurs Point Rd for approximately 3km. The crag is clearly visible on the right hand side just before the turn off to the ski area. Please do not park beneath the crag.

i The crag is north-west facing. It gets the sun later in the day but it is a very cold place to be in winter. The Queenstown Lakes District Council has asked that climbers do not use the crag during the ski season because distracted drivers on this narrow road cause chaos.

The crag is an instruction venue and occasionally gets quite busy,

Left Side
The left end of the crag has some long, good quality lines.

❶   16 The Moist Nun 16m
6 🌂 Apparently habits aren't waterproof? Start up the crusty corner and then negotiate the face on slopers and small edges. This is often used for abseil practice.

❷   18 Bryan's Route 16m
8 🌂 Move up to the bulge then follow the ledges up the face.

❸   ★17 Blond Bimbo 13m
6 🌂 Negotiate the small roof with a balancy move onto the face. Bridge up the corner to the hawthorn tree.

Left Side

❹   ★21 Retroman 13m
6 🌂 Balancey over the roof, then technical moves take you up the face to a crimpy crux. Top-out at the hawthorn tree. *Dan Ross*

❺   18 Young Women Are Passionate and Must Have Their Way 13m
5 🌂 A sustained and crimpy face before moving up to fondle the arête feature.

Right Side
This is the next section of wall, 20m right of *Young Women...*

❻   15 The Chutney Chute 12m
8 🌂 Start up *Ladder in My Stocking* and move left under the roof. Reach to the ledge and crank up to the face.

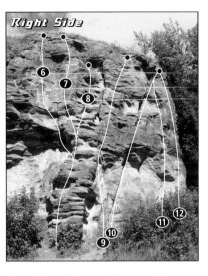

❼ 15 Hung, Yawn and Quartered 15m

7 Start up *Ladder in My Stocking* and move to the left scoop. Reach over the blunt arête and continue onwards.

❽ ★12 Ladder in My Stocking 15m

6 Scoops and hollows make this a great looking line and it is just as good to climb.

❾ ★15 Make the Clip or Take the Plunge

6 **15m**. Devious to the 1st bolt but once you are there, it's a cruise up the long slab on jugs.

❿ ★17 Flaps 14m

A nice trad climb with bomber cam placements. Climb up the deep, right-leaning crack and rock-over to join *The Pain Centre* at the top.

⓫ 19 The Pain Centre 13m

1 Tenuous moves past the bolt to casual crack climbing.

⓬ ★18 Pecker Breath 13m

4 Fortunately more charming than the name. This is fascinating, sustained climbing. *Mark Whetu 1992*

Rock Star Area

7m right through the bushes is a small wall with two climbs that are well worth a look.

⓭ 14 Liquid Smoke 12m

5 A slabby arête on the left side of the buttress. Interesting moves but quite odd rebolting.

⓮ 18 I Want to Be a Rock Star 12m

3 Tricky moves up the arête take you a step closer to the dream. *Gordy Watson 1997*

7m to the right is a small, hollow pillar:

⓮ ★12 Mall Rats 12m

4 Weave up the arête past the column of rock to a crux on the aesthetic face. The anchor is 5m back on the wall.

This is the most central rock climbing area in Queenstown. There are two crags, both at the top of the Queenstown Hill walkway. It is a hike, but the rock quality is well worth it. The pick of the Queenstown Hill area is the 'Hospo' Wall. The rock is arguably the best schist climbing to be found in Queenstown, if not Otago.

From central Queenstown, drive up Ballarat St, left onto Kent St, then turn right into Kerry Tce. The car park is immediately on the left.

Head up the walking track through the pines. When you meet the loop walkway, take the left branch of the track and continue to the saddle (total 40mins). There is a sculptured iron seat to the right.

To reach Hospitality Wall, turn left at the saddle (opposite the iron seat) and continue on the summit track. After 5mins, once you get a clear view of the summit, turn left at towards the Coronet Valley and walk for another 5mins past a pond to the crag.

To reach the Queenstown Hill crag continue on the loop track and just before the treeline, take the first small track left. After 1min you will meet the Lower Tier. The Upper Tier is a little further along the track on the left.

These crags have been well equipped with good bolts and anchors. The climbs are short, but have up to 10 bolts. The only additional gear that we placed was a #3 cam at the Upper Tier.

The land is a farm reserve and should not be treated as public land. Dogs are absolutely banned (one unfortunate fox terrier has already been shot on-site).

Hospitality Wall

This main wall has some long and interesting climbs on super good rock.

❶ ★19 Sun Machine 15m
4 Scramble up the gully around the left end of the wall and move carefully to the 1st clip. Gymnastic moves on ledges through to a steep finish. *Gordy Watson 1999*

❷ ★★22 Squirm Baby Squirm 20m
7 A wild journey through impressive orange rock. The holds keep coming if you keep moving. *Mark Woodward 1996*

❸ ★24 Boschie Britches 21m
10 The slab below the roof is a short warm up before big cranks through the roof. A stimuating face to top-out. *Rupert Gardiner*

❹ ★19 Corporate World 20m
7 A big investment required for the 1st quarter and enjoy positive growth on the upper face. *Russ McRae/Dave MacLeod 1994*

❺ ★17 Ascent of a Cat 18m
6 After a cruxy start, it's feline frolics in a jug ridden crack. *Dave MacLeod/ Katrina Benecke 1994*

❻ 17 Sleazy Politics 18m
5 Watch the slippery start (it can be protected with a #4 cam) then you can afford to be ruthless on the face. *Dave MacLeod 1994*

Hospitality Wall

Carpark 40 mins

Little Hospitality Wall

❼ ★19 Spouting Junk 13m

4 Intricate face climbing on little crimpers. *Ian Binnie 1994*

to a long, meandering slab. Don't fall off the top, it's easy but run-out. *Dave MacLeod 1995*

Little Hospitality Wall

This is about 40m right of the Main Wall and has some excellent routes. Below the Little Hospitality Wall is the Patriach Wall, which has two bolted routes on the left (18 and 21). There has been little development here, but the rock definitely has potential!

❽ ★20 Pump Fiction 12m

3 Climb to the 1st bolt of *Natural Born Drillers* and traverse up angled schist

9 ✶**21 Natural Born Drillers 12m**

3 Beautiful climbing on amazing schist edges. *Pete O'Connor 1995*

10 ✶**16 King Sperm 11m**

3 Climb through the featured middle section of the crag and move up the tilted layers of quartz past another hole. *Dave MacLeod 1995*

11 **15 Wanaka Wanabeez 8m**

2 Smeary moves up to the 1st bolt then climb through sculpted scoops.

12 **16 Captain to the Engine Room 7m**

2 Short and groovy. Jam the crack to the 1st bolt and move past the small cave.

Lower Tier

This outcrop has short climbs on good rock. It is a popular place to top-rope and take beginners to learn leading techniques.

342

1 **15 High Voltage Simulator 11m**

4 Climb up to the ledge and negotiate some tricky smears through to the anchor. *Dave MacLeod 1992*

2 **13 Electric Eel Down My Pants 10m**

4 Cruisy moves on good holds. *Dave MacLeod/Alex/Mark Foley 1992*

3 ★**13 You Should Have Been a Blonde 10m**

4 Lovely sustained climbing on knobs and ledges. *Dave MacLeod/Alex/Mark Foley 1992*

4 **12 Alex and His Epic Machine 9m**

4 Easy to the diagonal break and a few slopey moves to jugs. *Dave MacLeod/Alex/Mark Foley 1992*

5 **10 Spannakourn a Kova 10m**

2 Mantle onto the ledge and tackle the casual slab above. *Dave MacLeod 2001*

Upper Tier

Another east-facing wall, this is just up the hill from the Lower Tier. The rock has a spectacular array of gold and black streaks and the climbs are very crimpy and quite feisty.

6 **19 Tank Engine 12m**

4 Start at the crack and move up the arête to the break. *Dave MacLeod*

7 ★**21 Little Toot 12m**

3 Fine, fingery climbing that doesn't ease off until the break. A #3 cam protects moves to the anchor. *Bill McLeod 1993*

8 **22 Hickory Dickory Dock 11m**

3 Fairly edgy to the break and then really crimpy to the next bolt. *Bill McLeod 1993*

9 ★**20 Rumping Sax Joop 15m**

6 Crimpy climbing to good sidepulls then mantle onto the ledge. *Dave MacLeod 1993*

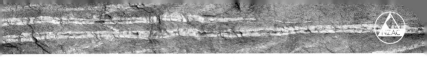

Upper Tier

⑥ ⑦ ⑧ ⑨ ⑩ ⑪ ⑫ ⑬ ⑭ ⑮ ⑯

⑩ ★**21 Lotions, Potions and Creams 15m**

5 Follow the slanting cracks to the bulge with a two finger pocket. Mantle to easy stuff. *Dave MacLeod 1993*

⑪ **21 Body Hate 14m**

4 Left of the golden block, climb through a small roof to a sustained face. *Ian Binnie 1993*

⑫ ★**18 A Jerk on a Rope 14m**

6 Move up the black face to the right of the broken crack and propel yourself on great edges. *Dave MacLeod 1994*

⑬ ★**19 Frog's Demise 8m**

4 Cruxy past the 1st bolt, then move through a small roof to good sidepulls.

⑭ **19 A Walk in the Clouds 9m**

3 A few longish moves to start then easy ground to a top crux. *Mark Whetu 1994*

On the next yellow-streaked buttress:

⑮ ★**18 You're Not a Good Human 13m**

6 Big holds via the crack to a sustained face. *Dave MacLeod 1993*

⑯ ★**15 Unlawful Entry 13m**

5 Start at the bottom of the crack. Follow positive edges all the way up the vague arête. *Dave MacLeod 1993*

Spaniard (not to be trifled with)

343

Arawata Terrace

Set amongst the Cabbage Trees overlooking Lake Wakitipu, this is a very scenic place to hang out. There are a couple of small walls that match some of the best Wye Creek faces in terms of quality but are much easier to access if you are only keen to do a few climbs. It is a really good place to do some easy leads.

Drive from Queenstown towards Glenorchy. At the Fern Hill roundabout turn right up Sunshine Bay Rd, then left into Arawata Tce. Pass Evergreen Place and then Moss Place on the left. Park just past Moss Place.

Walk up the unnamed lane (street #45) and continue to the 4WD track. After about 5mins turn right onto a narrow track leading to a radio aerial. Follow your nose uphill past another aerial and by now you should be able to see the Upper Tier. Turn off the main track and pick your way up to the base of the crag.

The anchors are all double bolts and you will only need to take a single rope and a handful of quickdraws.

Upper Tier

This wall has a roof protruding from the left end and some fantastic routes.

❶ ★24 Haggis Burger 21m
6 ⚑ The prominent line of the crag, with a roof that presents some bizarre moves. Climb the slab and swing out over the roof (use long quickdraws to cut down the rope drag). Cruise the fat arête to the anchor. *Ian Binnie 1990*

❷ ★20 Happy Hooker 20m
9 ⚑ A wild ride over the roof to an easy face. *Ian Binnie 1990*

Upper Tier

❸ ★17 Biggles Wiggles 21m
6 ⚑ Start with a few solid moves right of the roof, then waltz up the juggy upper face. *Craig Biggs/Pete O'Connor 1995*

❹ ✳15 Job for the Jobless 21m
6 ⚑ Carefree fun on a lengthy, sustained slab. *Ian Binnie 1990*

❺ ★16 Priapism 18m
5 ⚑ Roam over two ledges, where face climbing leads to a rock-over through the overlap. Pretty nifty really. *Pete O'Connor 1995*

'The absolute simplicity, that's what I love. When you are climbing, your mind is clearer, free of all confusions. You have focus and suddenly, the light becomes sharper, sounds become richer and you are filled with the deep, powerful presence of life.' **Heinrich Harrer**

Lower Tier

This is slightly right and below the Upper Tier. Either traverse from the Upper Tier across the hill, or continue along the main track for another few minutes before turning uphill.

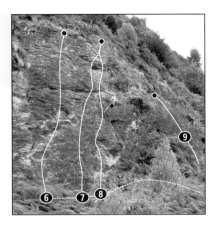

6 **17 Wobbly Bits 16m**

5 A crimpy start eases off to relaxed, quality climbing. *Donna Matheson 1995*

7 **18 Pillow Moments 18m**

4 Head up the diagonal crack (optional wire placements) to the 1st bolt. After the 3rd bolt veer left to join *Prodigy*. *Tarn Pilkington 1995*

8 **17 Prodigy 17m**

6 After a crimpy start, there are funky moves through the overlap. *Tarn Pilkington 1995*

9 **14 BLB 12m**

3 Positive edges and smears make for a good warm up or first lead. *Tarn Pilkington 1995*

Lake Wakitipu, looking towards Glenorchy. PETER ALLISON

Wye Creek

Tucked away in a steep snow-fed valley above the eastern shores of Lake Wakatipu, Wye Creek has some of the best schist climbing in Otago. The walls are compact and heavily featured with quartz veins and protrusions that make awesome holds. The setting is splendid, with fantastic views over the lake and across to the jagged ranges that frame Queenstown.

The valley is bisected by a creek and both sides have different character traits. On the South Side there are some long, fluid lines that are some of the most exposed undertakings around. The North Side has a number of smaller walls with hard, crimpy lines on beautiful rock. There are some natural pro and mixed lines on both sides of the valley, but the cracks tend to be too brittle and crumbly for bomber gear placements. It is on bolted faces where Wye Creek really comes in to its own, and whether it is endurance testpieces or intense overhanging lines, you will find some outstanding sport climbs to do here.

From Queenstown, drive to Frankton and turn right towards Te Anau. Follow the road out of town and cross the Kawarau River. From here, it is 14km to Wye Creek on the open road. There is a cluster of houses on the lake front opposite the Wye Creek valley (Drift Bay Rd). Drive through the farm gate on the left side of the road and follow a 4WD track to a wide clearing. Most climbers leave their cars here.

The walk up the 4WD road from the lower car park takes about 10mins. From where the narrow walking track starts, Black Wall is 100m up the hill on the left. The other North Side walls take anywhere from 5 to 15mins to access, and the South Side is a 20min walk up through the bush and across the dam.

Take at least 12 quickdraws and one 60m rope or two 50m ropes for long climbs. A brush is a convenient accessory for the dusty or flakey holds.

i It seems to be okay to camp in the field before the 4WD track. It is sunny in the morning and hidden from the road.

It is best to get water from higher up the creek where there is no livestock.

North Side
The North Side of the valley is sprinkled with small walls. These stay in the shade for most of the day in summer, but may be prone to seepage in winter. They are generally steep with hard, bouldery lines on very solid rock.

Black Wall
This wall is right next to the walking track, about 100m after the 4WD track ends. The first 2m is crumbly but the upper section is solid and well-featured.

20 mins

NZAC

North Side

Rainbow Wall

Wow City

Project Wall Eweniverse Wall

Bush Wall

Homage Wall

Dam

South Side 3 mins

Carpark

---

❶ 20 Black Widow 15m

5 ⚡ Start off the grassy ledge at the left end of the crag. Interesting moves through the flakey roof lead to the upper face. *Aaron Ford/Sally Carter 2002*

❷ ★20 Matt's Joke 18m

8 ⚡ Generous jugs lead smoothly onto the slab. After this the climbing is steep with wonderful holds. *Swenja Stellfeld/ Rupert Gardiner 1999*

❸ ★20 He Who Laughs Last 18m

8 ⚡ A steep crank onto the face, then it's plain sailing apart from some thin moves halfway up. *Gordy Watson 2000*

❹ ★21 Cheers Papa 18m

6 ⚡ Fairly chossy up to the 1st bolt then a cruxy rock-over onto the face. Delectable climbing ensues on quartz knobs. *Swenja Stellfeld 2000*

❺ 19 Full Empty 16m

7 ⚡ Up the lower face to funky moves around the hebe. The crux lurks past the 6th bolt. *Mark Woodward/Jos Firth 1998*

Project Wall

After the Black Wall, head up the track for 5mins until you approach the pipeline. For *Blood on the Tracks* and *Xenalasia*, turn uphill and cross under the pipeline to the bottom of the cliff. For the other climbs, continue up the track and traverse left along the base of the next cliff. Scramble up the boulders at the end of the track to find *Rogan Josh* and the other routes to the right.

❻ ★★23 Blood on the Tracks 25m

12 ⚡ A tricky, blank start leads to a good rest and looming headwall. This keeps coming at you with lots of good holds. *Russ McRae 1997*

347

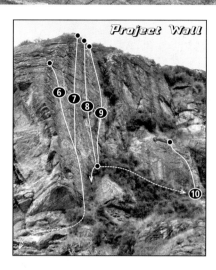

Project Wall

❼ **✦✦25 Xenelasia 30m**

13 🔩 A very striking line. Climb as for *Blood on the Tracks* and keep charging straight up the face. *Ian Binnie 1997*

❽ **✦25 Roganjosh 23m**

8 🔩 A challenging, technical masterpiece with an array of crazy moves. Not your average schist climb. *Pat Deavoll 1997*

❾ **26 Tikka to Ride 23m**

9 🔩 Mild to begin, but there's no way to tone down the spicy crux. After working up a sweat, cruise through to the anchor. *Ivan Vostinar 2004*

10m right along the track is a slab route:

❿ **★24 Equilibrium 22m**

9 🔩 Delicate foot placements, undercling action and sideways vision should get you up—all things being equal. *Sally Carter/Aaron Ford 2003*

Back on the main walking track, the next black wall (by the pipeline) has this lone route:

5 🔩 **22 The Small English Bogan 12m**
An interesting diversion on good rock. *Doug Smellie 1999*

Homage Wall

Before the pipeline ducks into the bush there is a short track that leads sharply left to the Homage Wall. The climbs are very diverse for such a small wall and there are a couple of awesome projects waiting to go.

⓬ **16 Henry's Slab 10m**

4 🔩 The slab around the left corner of the wall. Definitely a few challenging moves. *Henry Weir 2000*

⓭ **20 Silly Arête 10m**

4 🔩 Some steep moves before a rock-over onto the face, then it's all over before you can say 'vertically challenged.' It may be a good idea to stick clip the 1st bolt. *Ian Bull 1999*

⓮ **★18 Reflective Times 10m**

5 🔩 A crag curiosity. Frolic up the crack to the cave. A freakish left traverse takes you way, way, way around the corner to join *Silly Arête*. *Doug Smellie 1999*

⓯ **25 Peter 10m**

4 🔩 Solid sidepulls but floundering feet. Teeter to the cave jugs and meet more resistance to the anchor. *Laurent Simoni 2000*

⓰ **Homage Project (open) 10m**

6 🔩 Visionary bolting from Ian Binnie has produced what will be a classic testpiece. It's the angle not the size of the holds that is the problem.

⑰ **★Open Project 11m**

7 ⚷ Visiting Frenchman, Laurent Simoni, was doing his part to make up for the Rainbow Warrior. Sustained climbing on fiendish slopers. Ooh la la…

⑱ **★23 Wackybacky 12m**

5 ⚷ Access the ledge and make taxing moves through the crack. Pull around the corner on amazing quartz jugs. Good stuff! *Gordy Watson/Andy Mills 2000*

Bush Wall

Before the dam turn left (uphill) on the marked walking track. 30m up the track you will stumble across the Bush Wall. This is not visible from lower down, but is an excellent hideaway if you like your face climbing technical.

3 ⚷ **23 Gift of Grace 12m**

The first brushed streak on the far left of the wall. Start left of the tree for some very fingery climbing. *Ian Binnie 1997*

4 ⚷ **★24 Shared Vision 12m**

A pale, streaked line that is crimpy and sustained. Pumpy for the grade. *Ian Binnie/Ben Yates 1997*

5 ⚷ **★25 Wombat 13m**

Left of the green, mossy streak. Move up past big slopers to a crimp fest. *Laurent Simoni 2000*

5 ⚷ **★26 Weeping Emerald 14m**

More technicalities up this fine face. Start between two thin trees, right of the moss. *Ian Binnie 1997*

4 **25 Tasmanian Devil 12m**
A vicious little monster. Crimp to the break and hurl yourself up the face. *Laurent Simoni 2000*

Continue past the Black Wall for 2mins to the next small wall with one route:

4 **22 Year of the Splat 12m**
Crimpy to the ledge, then sustained up the yellow and black streaked face. *Ian Binnie 1997*

Wow City Wall

The climbing at this wall is steep and powerful. A stick clip is essential for many of the starts because the drop off is nasty, to say the least. 15m past *Year of the Splat,* turn right at the orange triangle then descend right through the bush for 20m.

㉕ ★**26 Torn Soul 12m**
4 Thin, steep climbing past glue-in ring bolts. *Ian Binnie 1997*

㉖ ★**23 Little Bo Steep 18m**
6 Luscious cranking on clean, curvy jugs. Not too cruxy and great to do as one of your first roof climbs. Take a #2 cam to finish. *Ian Binnie 1997*

㉗ ★**25 D,D For Girls 18m**
5 Hard start, but there is more than a handful of voluptuous jugs to see you on your way. Finish as for *Little Bo Steep* with a #2 cam. *Ian Binnie 1997*

㉘ ★**24 Mixed Devotions 18m**
7 Motor up to the layback crack and take a sunday drive to the next crux. Face moves to finish. *Neal Withers 1997*

㉙ **25 Today 11m**
3 Continuous hard cranking on steep ground. *Rupert Gardiner 2001*

㉚ **22 Let's Get Electrified 12m**
5 The second pitch of *Today.* Move up the face to the top section and take some gymnastic crank in your bag of tricks. *Gordy Watson/Andy Mills 2000*

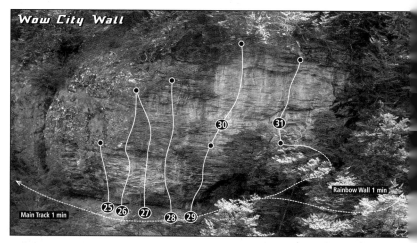

Wow City Wall

Rainbow Wall 1 min

Main Track 1 min

㉕ ㉖ ㉗ ㉘ ㉙

Use the traverse line to access the next route:

31 20 Between Tribes 13m

5 From the belay, climb the face to meet the corner crack. A primitive but positive finish. *Ian Binnie 1998*

Rainbow Wall

This is a spectacular chunk of rock. Its multi coloured streaks are hidden away in the beech forest, but once you find it, you'll be hooked on these steep little numbers. After the Wow City Wall, traverse right through the forest for about 20m, then head up hill another 20m.

3 ★24 Rhythm Annihilator 7m

At the far left of the crag, this is a short but crimpy one. *Dan Martin 2002*

3 25 Magic Karma Ride 8m

After a cruxy start off sidepulls, move through the bulge to generous holds. *Rupert Gardiner 2002*

3 ★27 Leaping Leprechaun 9m

Massive moves to crazy slopers with an edgy finish. *Mike Simpson 2003*

3 23 Aurora 10m

A wild-looking line let down by poor quality rock through the middle section. *Gordy Watson 2001*

36 ★23 Pot of Gold 15m

4 From below the arête, take the angled traverse crack past a dark section of rock to the exit anchor. *Aaron Ford 2002*

37 23 Wildfire 10m

3 Follow 2 bolts to the bulge. After steep ground through the crux, see if your forearms will hold out through the juggy section. *Gordy Watson 2001*

Rainbow Wall

㊳ ★24 Rainbow Connection 10m

3 ● Starts below the mid-point of the sideways crack. Either make a wild lunge left or move straight up on micro crimps. Unrelenting from the break. *Dave Bolger 2003*

㊴ 24 Shoe Route 9m

3 ● Boulder directly up to the small ledge to a well-heeled middle section. *Jodi Apiata 2003*

㊵ ★26 Rainbow Warrior 7m

2 ● Technicolour climbing up psychedelic streaks. *Aaron Ford 2002*

㊶ ★26 ROYGBIV 7m

2 ● A beige streak of devious climbing up snaky quartz seams. *Mike Simpson 2003*

㊷ 23 Rainbow Child 8m

3 ● Starts up the black streak through slanting holds. From the 3rd bolt reach right until you can catch the break, then move left to the anchor. *Gordy Watson 2001*

㊸ ★24 Punch it! 8m

3 ● Starts just left of the brown streak. Goey, awkward moves ease off as the holds get better. *Mike Simpson 2001*

South Side

This side of the valley houses most of the mid-grade lines at Wye Creek but there are also some steep, hard challenges to be found. The prominent faces catch sun for the whole day from spring to autumn.

It takes about 20-30mins to reach this side of the valley from the car park. Head up the walking track on the north side and cross the creek at the hydro dam. At the next dam, a short track takes you up to the base of Harold's Wall. The cliffs are described from far left to right.

Zippity Zappity Wall

From Harold's Wall, follow the base of the crag left and up towards the waterfall. This is a great place to hang out, but be aware that you may not be able to hear your partner's calls over the waterfall.

South Side

Zippity Zappity Wall
Harold's Wall Upper
Proud Monkey Roof
Harolds Wall Left
Harold's Wall Lower
The Mission Wall
Main Wall
North Side 3 mins
Dam
Liver Abuse Buttress

The Mission (16). DANIEL USSHER

Wye Creek

❶ ★**19 Punching Out a Redneck 15m**

4 🔩 Muscle through the roof and rock-over. The face is cruisy but a little fight is needed through the top crux with a healthy run-out. *Gordy Watson 1999*

❷ ★**17 Ballisticfibrosis 18m**

5 🔩 A most enjoyable face climb. You'll find good holds all the way. *Gordy Watson 1999*

❸ ⚡**18 Unlawful Discharge 20m**

6 🔩 A brilliant route with very sustained climbing. Good holds with the odd sloper and pinch thrown in. *Gordy Watson 1999*

❹ ★**19 How's that Zap? 25m**

8 🔩 Careful up to the 1st bolt then continue on classic schist jugs. The slopers get tricky past the 7th bolt. *Gordy Watson 1998*

Harold's Wall

This large and imposing wall consists of three distinct faces. A ledge system cuts the wall across the middle and it is also split by a vertical crack that marks the division between the left and right side of the wall.

Left Side

This area has the best quality rock on Harold's Wall. The classic *Fata Morgana* starts on the far left, slightly around the corner. The other routes start directly off the track.

❺ Fata Morgana–2 Pitches

The longest and highest route at the crag and an achievable adventure at the grade. Two ropes are recommended for the descent and be careful route finding—it can be confusing. *Ian Binnie/Swenja Stellfeld 1998*

8 **P1. 13 30m** Accesses the upper face. Start on the slab that faces up-valley, just right of the Zippity Zappity Wall and traverse sharply right. After the tussock ledge, cross the niche and move past an anchor (for *Little Rivers of Anticipation*). Continue right and up to meet the anchor for the next pitch. It may be hard to hear your partner's calls from here.

6 **P2. ✷✷15 26m** A superb pitch with solid rock and wild exposure. Head up the slab, veering slightly right to the arête. Finish at the boulder perched above the crag.

Abseil on two ropes to the ground.

❻ ★24 Babaganoosh and the Fabulous

6 **Freak 15m.** A dainty start up the wee arête, then figure out the short, weird crux. Over the bulge to the anchor. *Ian Binnie 1998*

❼ ✷24 Little Rivers of Anticipation 22m

8 Climbs just right of the crack. Sidepulls through the roof may make you quiver. An alluring face to finish. *Ian Binnie 1998*

❽ ✷✷22 B27 Positive 25m

8 A sustained and airy test piece. Slightly tricky to clip the 1st bolt, then take a breather before the roof. Incredible pockets line the way to the upper face. *Ian Binnie/Russ McRae 1997*

Right Side (Lower)

The right side of Howard's Wall is separated in to an upper and lower face by a ledge and handline.

❾ 15 Rejection 10m

5 A sweet thing on solid rock. Good bridging in the groove, but take a feather duster.

❿ ✷✷24 Nu Energy 18m

8 A supercharged face climb that doesn't relent. Slopers keep the pump going but the edges are just where you need them. It is rare to find a route that is this sustained all the way. *Ian Binnie 1997*

⓫ ★24 The Vision 18m

9 Fun climbing through three horizontal breaks. Enjoy calm before the storm then weather the bulge before easy ground. *Ian Binnie 1996*

⓬ Launch Pad to Hype Her Space 3 Pitches

Mark Woodward/Dave McKinley 1997

7 **P1. ★18 24m** From the right end of the lower wall, climb the featured face.

4 **P2. 15 15m** Straightforward climbing up the juggy but crusty face. At the 4th bolt, head right to the anchor.

Harold's Wall—Right Side

P3. ★★24 18m Full value exposure with good gear placements. Climb two small bulges to access the stunning face above.

Right Side (Upper)

The climbs on this wall start off the mid-way ledge and are hard. Not only are they steep and airy, they are also psychologically intense.

⑬ ★25 Barophobia 25m

Great climbing, especially the upper two-thirds. The line shares the start with *Projection*, but heads straight up the rounded crack. Use a medium wire in the crack to protect the slopey moves before the overhanging section. *Mike Simpson 2004.*

⑭ ★★26 Projection 25m

Mentally project yourself onto this at night and dream about the sustained climbing on immaculate rock. A medium wire is optional to protect the right-angling traverse section after the 1st bulge. *Mike Simpson 2004*

⑮ ★25 Perry's Other Crack 20m

10 Follow the left-slanting crack over the roof to the easy face above. *Perry Beckham 1999*

⑯ ★25 Massive Attack 20m

10 Steep climbing that demands finesse through the longest section of roof. *Bruce Dowrick 1999*

⑰ ★24 Move It or Lose It 20m

10 Good holds all the way, and a pumpy rock-over to the easy face above. *Ian Binnie 1999*

⑱ ★23 Perry's Crack 12m

1 Climb the crack using fixed pro. It may be a good idea to back this up with your own. *Perry Beckham 1999*

Main Wall

This wall looks very slabby from down the valley, but is actually quite sustained. It has the longest climbs in Queenstown and is the most-visited area at Wye Creek. All of the routes are long, so be careful not to rap off your rope.

⑲ ★18 Almi 30m

13 A leggy face climb up quartz jugs to a mini roof. Pull through by the seat of your pants and meander to the anchor. *Swenja Stellfeld 1999*

⑳ ★★18 88 Chocolate Treats 25m

11 An appetising start up the slab, then veer left through a cruxy bulge. The upper face is strewn with protruding quartz seams. Fantastique! *Swenja Stellfeld 1997*

㉑ 15 Beyond the Pale 27m

5 Clip the first 4 bolts of *88 Chocolate Treats* and step right into the corner. Move onto the face past a run-out section of crack and clip the last bolt of *Bigger than Big*. *Simon Middlemass 1998*

㉒ ★17 Bigger than Big 27m

8 Crank over the bulge on jugs, rock over at the 3rd bolt then weave up a spectacular ladder of quartz knobbles. *Ian Binnie 1996*

㉓ ★★16 The Mission 27m

9 This long, cruisy arête is a rare treat. Follow the weakness past the 2nd bolt and go left to the arête. Find a good perch on the way to enjoy prime-time views. *Mark Whetu/Russ McRae 1996*

㉔ ★18 Lucalucki 32m

14 Wend your way up the centre of the face on consistently positive holds. The ochre rock is on the loose side, but there are bolts aplenty.

㉕ ★17 Don't be Decieved 32m

8 A sportingly bolted climb that is exhilarating if it's at your grade. It shares the first 3 bolts with *Lucalucki*, then trends right. A fingery section past the 7th bolt. *Mark Woodward 1996*

㉖ ★19 Smellie Crack 24m

10 A combo of bridging and face climbing makes this intriguing. Follow the bolts on the left side of the off-width crack, then bust through the lip where the crack narrows. *Doug Smellie 1999*

㉗ ★★22 Aratika 28m

10 This lofty arête dominates the Main Wall and just asks to be climbed. Hook, clamp and weave up the sustained pillar. *Russ McRae 1996*

㉘ 16 Aramuru 28m

4 Follow the bolts up the face into a wide and quite crusty crack. If you have lots of massive cams, you can protect this well, but otherwise it would be better tackled as a top-rope excursion. *Doug Smellie 1999*

357

Main Wall–Proud Monkey Roof

㉙ ⚡**18 About Time 28m**

13🪝 A classic, well-featured face, 4m right of the corner. Expect the odd jug and heaps of 'thoughtful' holds. *Mark Whetu/Russ McRae 1996*

Proud Monkey Roof

An iconic overhang at the far right of the Main Wall, the Proud Monkey Roof is the most photographed spot in Queenstown (after the bungy platform). Horizontal antics on quartz jugs will satisfy your primal urges and the upper face takes you gliding over the lake. For most climbs it pays to stick clip the 1st bolt to save your noggin if you do happen to peel off.

㉚ ⚡**24 Drunken Monkey 18m**

9🪝 A few long moves under the roof, then exercise your fingers on a thought-provoking upper face. *Gordy Watson, Andy Mills 2001*

㉛ ★**23 Proud Monkey 20m**

7🪝 A couple of strenuous pulls, then steep moves on chunky jugs. Reach over the lip and tackle the steadily more demanding upper face. Beautiful moves on the top section will make you a happy primate. *Ian Binnie 1996*

as you heel hook over the lip. Cruise up the slab. *Ian Bull 1999*

③④ 21 Drop Kick to the Head 12m

4 A leftwards traverse under the roof to the arête. A potentially vicious second clip if the climber or belayer are complacent. *Doug Smellie 1999*

③⑤ ★22 More Monkey Business 18m

7 Scramble up jugs, and after cranking over the bulge, you'll have earned a banana. Find the sneaky jug for the 3rd clip and run up the delightful slab. *Doug Smellie 1999*

③⑥ 21 Raining Body Parts 18m

7 Sidepull through a steep section and wander up the slab. *Ian Bull 1999*

Liver Abuse Buttress

A small buttress directly below The Proud Monkey Roof that is a great warm up for some of the longer routes on the Main Cliff. Either scramble down from the ledge to a safety rope and belay bolts, or rap in from the double bolt anchor on the top of the buttress.

③⑦ ★14 Liver Abuse 10m

4 A nifty wee line up the left side of the face. Good for detox days. *Elanor Slater 1997*

③⑧ 15 Te Koha 12m

6 The first bulge is easy going, but the second half gets you cranking on smaller holds. *Sally Carter 2002*

③⑨ ★14 Windy September 16m

6 Good relaxed climbing that starts at the bottom of the access rope. *Steve & Judy Logan 2002*

④⓪ 14 Wet Sunday 15m

5 The slab on the right side of the cliff. Better wet than gloomy. *Sally Carter 2002*

③② ★23 Red Curry Pot Climb 10m

4 The spiciest roof moves on this wall are helped along by good use of toes and heels. All over once you reach the lip. *Doug Smellie 1999*

③③ ✹21 Dream Thing 20m

8 Hang horizontal over Lake Wakitipu and make sure your mates have cameras in hand to catch your silhouette

Chinaman's Bluff

This crag is well set up for pseudo-alpine adventures. It is perched above the Dart River in an awesome location with spectacular scenery and guaranteed good times—don't let the walk put you off! The classic climbs, such as Ravages of Time, are mainly long multi-pitch outings that take most of the day, but there are some new bolted routes that are less time consuming.

From Glenorchy, take the sealed road to the Rees River Bridge and the gravel road up the Dart Valley to Chinaman's Bluff. The road is well graded but watch the fords during heavy rain.

Follow the DOC track up the river for approximately 40mins. At a downhill hairpin bend there is a large cairn on the right hand side by a stream (see photo). Turn off towards the cliffs and follow the orange ticker tape along a vague path for about 10mins. When you reach the cliff, veer left along the track. This doubles back on itself to the base of *Ravages of Time*.

This is a multipitch area and double ropes are essential. Take a standard rack, 15 quickdraws and a few slings. The

descents can be time consuming, but the anchors are well set up for abseiling.

Some parties on *Ravages of Time* end up descending in the dark so it is a good idea to bring a headtorch, warm clothing, lots of water and a small pack per pair for the climb.

There are plenty of great camping spots up the valley and there is a shelter with toilets by the start of the walking track. The sandflies are the only downside. Campers have been known to wake up to what they thought was the pitter patter of rain on their tent, only to be attacked by swarms of little biters when they emerged. The only solution is to either to grab your pack and try to out-run them or camp away from the river.

A short walk down the track towards Chinaman's Bluff is a new crag called 'China Wall.' The climbs here are well equipped sport lines in the 17–23 grade range. The rock is quite flakey and dusty in places. This is not to say that it won't clean up in the future and if you are interested there is a pamphlet guide for sale at the Glenorchy Café.

The first two routes are best found by locating the start of Ravages of Time; *a clean, bolted slab. From here, follow the track left for 50m, and cut back right up a rocky gully for 30m. The starts are up on a ledge, right of the gully. These routes may be easier to access if you climb* Chink in Shining Armour *first and rap directly to the base.*

Chinaman's Bluff 15 mins

1 ★ 22 Browsing Time
2 ★ 23 Time Machine–3 Pitches
3 ✦ 21 Chink in Shining Armour–4 Pitches
4 ✦ 20 Ravages of Time–8 Pitches
5 ✦ 21 Tick Tock
6 ✦ 21 Blue Lagoon–3 pitches
7 ✦ 20 Third World Assassin–4 Pitches
8 19 Mystery Route

P8

P7

P6

P5

P4

P3

P2

P4

P3

P2

3

1 2

P2

8

6

5

7

4

ginal first pitch of Ravages

❶ ★22 Browsing Time 38m

16 Start a few metres left of *Time Machine* in an overhanging corner. Pull up to a feisty rock-over, past a ring bolt and roam casually to join the 2nd pitch of *Time Machine*. *Gordy Watson/Steve 'the Aussie'*

❷ Time Machine–3 Pitches

This is a long, fully bolted number that starts off the track. *Gordy Watson/Andrew Mills*

10 **P1. ★21 20m** Teleport yourself through a cruxy start and rove up easier terrain to the anchor.

11 **P2. 19 22m** A weird pitch that boomerangs. Head left on crusty rock and kink right in a roundabout kind of way. Nuzzle through the foliage to the belay ledge.

Andrew Macfarlane on the first ascent of *Ravages of Time* (20). MURRAY JUDGE

10 **P3. ★23 24m** A nice finale on a slab with technical interest and perplexing moves.

❸ Chink in Shining Armour–4 Pitches

After the 2nd pitch of *Ravages of Time,* this climb diverges left and cuts up the centre of the monolithic slab. As you can see on the topo, a lot of elbow grease went into cleaning this route! *Nick Cradock/Murray Ball 2003*

6 **P1. 17** As for *Ravages of Time.*

5 **P2. 18 26m** Climb as for *Ravages of Time* and after 16m head left past the bolts to the anchor.

10 **P3. ★20 30m** A splendid, steep line that works the forearms on good edges.

11 **P4. ✳21 30m** An elegant continuation up the wall that throws out some mischievous moves near the top.

It's easiest to abseil straight down from the top of pitch 3 (40m) and scramble down the gully to the left. Cut back 50m through the bush to the base of *Ravages of Time.*

❹ Ravages of Time–8 Pitches

This climb has seen many ascents and for good reason. Hanging from a belay a few hundred metres off the deck, watching the Dart River snake its way towards Glenorchy, is a charming way to see one of the most beautiful parts of the region.

The climb is a mixture of bolt protected face climbing and good cracks with a bit of scrambling between belays. It was originally done with a lower pitch, which is seldom climbed because a new track leads directly to the base of the original Pitch 2.

A good rack of cams is essential and double ups in the larger sizes comes in handy. An average ascent time is about 7 hours. It may then take up to 2 hours to rap the route. *Murray Judge/Andrew Macfarlane/Steve Carr 1999*

6 **P1. 17 20m** Follow the line of bolts up the clean slab. Exit right to an anchor.

1 **P2. ★18 36m** Climb past the bolt and up ledgy, suspect rock. Where the crack thins, (at the start of *Chink in Shining Armour*), move right to undercling the roof. Pull tricky moves over the arête to a jam crack. The anchor is above the gnarled tree.

P3. ★18 30m Climb a right-leaning crack to join the corner system (*Tick Tock*) and move right over the arête into a wide crack. Keep climbing to a comfy belay ledge at the big tree.

8 **P4. ★20 30m** From the ledge, charge up the crack on the left. Veer right for sustained face climbing on good edges.

From the anchor scramble up past a tree with abseil slings. Walk 30m right along the base of the cliff, past a bolt anchor to a steep arête.

8 **P5. 17 21m** Climb the sharp arête and take an airy traverse out right to the main arête where you will find the most scenic belay stance on the route.

6 **P6. ★18 34m** Step around the arête onto the striking face. Pass 3 bolts and continue straight up a weakness, with oodles of gear, to a tree belay.

6 **P7. ★16 30m** Cruise up the slab, over a wee ledge veering right to a tree belay.

Scramble right over boulders and head straight up into the bush for 25m. Follow the base of the crag right for 10m to a jagged crack.

4 **P8. ★20 34m** A superb, juggy crack on sublime rock that eventually leads to a slab. A pumpy finish makes a satisfying finale to this grand adventure.

It may take 2 hours to rap the route on double ropes. An alternative descent of pitches 1–4, is to rap Chink in Shining Armour. *This is more direct line on clean, steep rock. From the top of pitch 4 (the forested ledge system), walk 50m left and look for the sling around a tree. Two long abseils will get you to the base of* Time Machine. *Walk off.*

5m right of the start of Ravages of Time, *scramble up a bank to reach the next route.*

❺ **★★21 Tick Tock 55m**
A long and classic crack line up a left-facing corner that joins the 3rd pitch of *Ravages of Time*. It is gear intensive, needs a 60m rope and is arguably a more consistent start to *Ravages*. *Nick Flyvbjerg/Allan Uren 2003*

The next route starts just right of Ravages of Time. *Scramble up a goat track at the right end of the wall.*

❻ **Blue Lagoon–3 pitches**
An awesome trad route, which links up with the top half of *Ravages of Time*. *Murray Judge/Matt Squires 2000*

'Andy and I spent seven days working on *Ravages* at New Year through a hot dry spell. We would get back to our tent at dusk dehydrated and burnt after a day of scrubbing and climbing and sit by the stream drinking water and unable to eat. The climb gradually emerged from the wall as we linked bare rock and vertical jungle. The final crack and wall was done on lead with the overhanging top-out completed the following summer with Steve Carr. *Ravages* opened up a large expanse of rock which will produce quality routes for many years to come.'
Murray Judge

Paul Coggan on the 2nd
pitch of *Ravages of Time* (20)
KATE SINCLAIR

P1. ✳**19 35m** A beautiful, naturally protected crack with wonderful lay-backing.

P2. ✳**21 35m** Move past 3 bolts up a steep wall to a great finger crack. Belay under vegetation.

P3. 17 18m A short pitch to the top climbing past vegetation.

From the start of Ravages of Time, *follow a ledge system right for 60m (tread carefully) to a broken corner with bolts.*

➐ Third World Assassin–4 Pitches
An elegant trad route that follows an impressive crack line. *Wayo Carson/Kate Wolfe/Jamie Foxley/Murray Judge 2003*

P1. 17 17m Follow the square corner past the bolts, but treat the flakes with suspicion. Exit left to a belay ledge.

P2. ✳**20 24m** A blank wall, bisected by a foxy finger crack. Tantalising but unabating.

P3. ✳**19 24m** The playful continuation of the crack line with joyous gear. From the belay, scamper over a small roof and upwards to the face.

P4. ★**15 22m** A darling, right-slanting crack with generously proportioned holds. A cruisy finish to a prime route.

➑ 19 Mystery Route 32m
From the spacious ledge after the 1st pitch of *Third World Assassin,* head right and up the face. Comfy set-ups eventually lead to a testing roof and groove. *Murray Judge/Jamie Foxley 2003*

There is another pitch above Mystery Route, *but this is needs further brushing.*

> 'The best way to push yourself the hardest and do the most amazing things is by having fun. Not going up something because someone said it would be impressive, but because you can't imagine any other place on the planet you'd rather be.' **Peter Croft**

Wayo Carson stepping out the 2nd pitch of *Third World Assassin* (20). MURRAY JUDGE

The Chasm

Andy Cockburn on *Contact Neurosis* (29). PAUL ROGERS

5 mins

The Chasm is an atmospheric crag hidden behind a wall of rainforest above the Milford Sound road. The angular granite is split into distinct sections with varied terrain and the wall is capped by an over-hanging roof. Rain water tumbles off the lip of the crag and the rock stays dry unless it is very windy.

The first route was established at the Chasm in 1993 when Paul Rogers decided to take a closer look at the wall. He was inspired to continue establishing lines up most of the classic features.

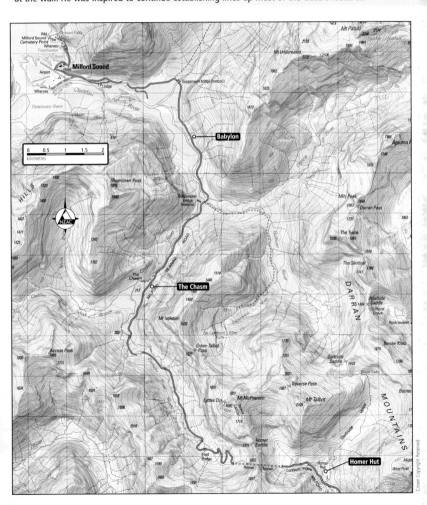

The Chasm

Cleddau Valley. PAUL ROGERS

From Homer Hut, drive towards Milford Sound through the tunnel and down to the Cleddau Valley. 9km from Homer Hut, you will see signage reading 'The Chasm 400m' on the left side of the road. This does not refer to the crag (the 'real' Chasm is a water-worn gorge and tourist attraction down the road). About 50m before the sign is bridge #132, which is marked by a small cairn. Park at the bridge.

There are two access tracks 30m apart:

Track One: From the Milford Sound side of the bridge, follow the wide creek bed for 5mins then duck through the bush to the left end of the crag.

368

Track Two: At the bridge, follow a steep creek bed marked by orange tape for 5mins. This takes you directly to the base of the wall. *High Ideals and Crazy Dreams* is opposite the track exit.

i The crag is well set up. There are double bolt anchors on all climbs and where the gear is sparse you will find well-placed bolts.

A fat 60m single rope is fine for most routes, but two medium diameter ropes help reduce rope drag on traversing pitches. Be very wary of thin ropes because the granite edges are very abrasive. There has been one accident caused by a climber's rope being severed mid-abseil.

Climbers tend to pick their way around the crag by climbing access pitches and then traversing or rapping to other anchors. A happy day can be spent linking up climbs without having to descend to the soggy forest floor. When lowering someone off the steep upper pitches, you may need to throw them a line to pull the climber in and it may be better to down-climb steep routes to retrieve gear.

Please do not pee off the crag!

After much deliberation Geoffrey and Roger decided there was no way they could pee into the forest from the Chillout Ledge.

The Left End
The left end of the crag is accessed from Track One. Otherwise, follow the crag around from the right end for about 60m.

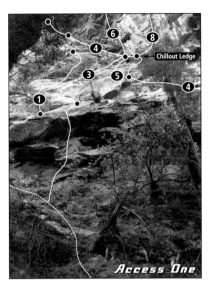

Access One

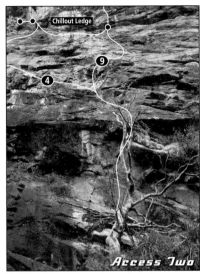

Access Two

From Access One:

❶ Dread Zone–3 Pitches

Paul Rogers/Polly Stupples 1994

P1. 18 15m From the forest floor, reach up through the blocks and rock-over onto the slab. Veer left to a single bolt belay below 'the guillotine,' a V-shaped wedge of rock.

P2. ✷ 21 30m Follow underclings out left and move left up the slab. A grunty rock-over takes you to another section of slab and after the next reachy crux, climb the left-trending crack.

P3. ✷24 15m Move left into the diagonal corner and climb with conviction through a difficult bulge. Keep charging and things will taper off quite nicely. From the 4th bolt, head straight up to join *Jack the Biscuit.*

❷ ★19 Pro Rata 16m

A lovely trad route. Start from the pitch 3 anchor of *Dread Zone* and traverse left via lush holds and bomber gear. Double ropes and long runners will smooth out the ride. *Steve Henry/Dave Roberts 1994*

❸ Mr Wolf–2 Pitches

Murray Ball/Paul Rogers 2003

P1. 18 15m Start as for the first pitch of *Dread Zone.* After the rock-over, continue straight up the slab to a single bolt anchor, which can be backed up with a fat wire. With long slings you can belay from a small ledge below the anchor.

P2. ✷22 26m Sublime climbing on a diagonal undercling. Rock onto the slab and start drifting right through some gnarly slopers. Plain sailing to the Chillout Ledge.

The Chasm

- 4
- 1
- 2
- 4
- 7
- 8
- 6
- P2
- Chillout Ledge
- P2
- P2
- 5
- 4
- 9
- 4
- 1
- 3
- Access One
- Access Two
- Track One

Hidden Wall Ledge

Access Three

Track Two

The Chasm

The next climbs start at Access Two.

❹ Jack the Biscuit–4 Pitches
Hugh Barnard/Paul Rogers 1993

P1. 17 22m From the tree, climb to the slab via bolts. Cruise up another few metres before following the vague ramp sharply left. The belay is hidden behind the right-facing corner. Double ropes or lots of long quick-draws are recommended.

P2. ★19 15m Bridge up the short open corner with gear and rock out right to a very funky slab. Wander right to a wide crack with bulbous quartz holds. Exit to the Chillout Ledge.

P3. ★18 25m From the left end of the ledge, this route traverses hard left. The climbing is comfy but the setting is way out there.

P4. ★24 12m Start left of the belay and head up steep ground. Splendid holds beckon the unwary to surprisingly slopey territory. Anchor out left. *Rob Wigley 1999*

❺ ★22 Granite Gringo 15m
After the first pitch of *Jack the Biscuit*, climb the ladder of ledges towards a sickle crack. Some sneaky slab moves take you through to a juggy top-out, protected with medium wires. *Kate Sinclair 2004*

The next few climbs start from the Chillout Ledge. They are accessed via Mr Wolf, Jack the Biscuit *or* Granite Gringo.

❻ ★26 Buster Gonad 24m
Possibly the wildest line at The Chasm, yielding surprisingly good holds in an outrageous setting. It's

The Chillout Ledge. PAUL ROGERS

certainly quite pumpy but good rests make this well worth trying. From the middle of the Chillout Ledge, climb the corner and continue up the featured weakness. Just before the roof there is a sitting rest. *Paul Rogers/Steve Walker 1993. Chris Plant extended it in 1993*

❼ Project 23m
From the ledge, traverse right 2m then climb the corner and arête. This line joins *Buster Gonad* for 1 bolt then climbs straight up through the cruxy dyke feature.

❽ ★★27 Bus t'Milford 18m
An awesome test piece. Traverse right via tricky moves around the arête to be greeted with a juggy section of radical pockets. Big cranks on friendly edges to finish. *Chris Plant 1994*

❾ Contact Neurosis–2 Pitches
P1. ★17 30m From the tree, climb onto the slab via bolts. Ramble up a faint corner and head right over the slab. Once it starts to steepen, move left up a fetching wall. *Paul Rogers/Toni Bryant 1994*

Scott Kerr on *High Ideals and Crazy Dreams* (22)
KATE SINCLAIR

The Chasm

10 **P2.** ✳**29 18m** Moves from the ledge lead to a fingery section then generous jugs. Either bust out long moves ape style, or sort out a technical solution on intermediates. Funky top-out over the lip. *Andy Cockburn 2003*

3 **12 Contact Neorosis to Chillout Ledge 12m.** Traverse left and down 1m, then up a short crack to the ledge.

Long live New Zealand granite!

The pure thrill of weaving my way up the featured pockets and edges on *Laybrinth* have had a lasting impact on me. The uncrowded journey to Black Lake, Gertrude Saddle and beyond, with new and old friends have helped to cement my lasting commitment to Fiordland Granite.

Recently the exploration and development of new walls in the Cleddau Valley (Babylon), by the likes of Brooze Dolwrick, Derek Scratcher and Myan Gobsmack Smith will light a fire of adventures that will last for many a year in this range best described as 'the Warehouse of crags!'

I hope we can take on the challenge of establishing high multi-pitch free routes on the big walls above the bush. Sinbad Gully is just the start!

Paul Rogers

The Right End
This is accessed via Track Two, or by following the base of the crag for 60m from the left end.

The Hidden Wall
From the Track Two exit, move 20m left, hugging the base of the cliff. Scramble up a short track to a rata tree. The following climbs access the Hidden Wall Ledge.

10 ✳**21 Proximity Infatuation 21m**
7 From the tree, head up the slab using opposing side pulls. Rock straight through the bulge to easier ground.

374

Tackle the small flake and move through to the anchor. *Paul Rogers 2002*

11 ★**22 Safety in Numbers 19m**
8 From the tree, climb the steep slab past 3 bolts. Devious moves go slightly right to a hard sequence over the bulge. Climb straight through to the last bolt. *Mark Sedon 2002*

These next climbs start off the Hidden Wall Ledge, which is accessed from either Proximity Infatuation *or* Safety in Numbers.

The 2nd pitch of Retrosexual *starts 2m below, and just right of, the ledge.*

12 ✳✳**23 Groove Armada 23m**
10 Sensational moves from the belay take you to technical ground with the odd rest. *Paul Rogers/Will McQueen 2002*

13 **26 Tardomania 20m**
5 From the belay in the centre of the ledge, follow the bolts to a rooflet. Pull through and move left up the ramp to find a couple of gear placements before the anchor. Be careful cleaning the route as the anchor is off to the side. Down climbing is the easiest. *Derek Thatcher 2003*

14 ✳**24 On the Prow 16m**
6 A pumpy and balancy climb that follows a vague arête on the upper wall. From the right end of the ledge, move straight up. A medium cam protects to the first bolt, then trend right to good holds and sort your feet out to keep the barn door action under control. A few pulls and you'll be on the slab. *Paul Rogers/Jon Sedon 2002*

Back at ground level:

To the Hidden Wall

Access Three

⓯ Retrosexual–2 Pitches
Originally climbed on natural gear, this climb has been retro-bolted and makes an engaging, sporty outing. According to Paul these are 'the biggest holds you'll ever fall off.' Avoid swinging when back cleaning or rapping the route to ensure that you don't sever your rope on the abrasive edges.

7 P1. ★22 18m Starts as for *Safety in Numbers*. At the 3rd bolt, traverse right through edges and ledges. Mantle over to the anchor. *Paul Rogers 2004*

6 P2. ⚡23 15m Bridge into the corner and charge through balancy moves onto the arête. At the top of the arête, move right onto the slab and suck it up to finish. *Paul Rogers/Hugh Barnard 1993*

The next climbs start at Access Three.

To reach the next two routes, head 7m up High Ideals and Crazy Dreams, *then traverse sharply left to two separate belay anchors. The* Vertically Challenged *anchor is higher and further left.*

⓰ ⚡25 Vertically Challenged 20m
7 Follow the darker line of weakness to the roof. Pull through into the fantastic scoop where powerful moves on slopers lead to the lip. Mantle over and tackle the short headwall to finish (as for *Retrosexual*). *Kevin Nicholas/Paul Rogers 1993*

375

⑰ ⚡24 One Way Ticket 24m

8 Elegant face moves to the roof, where positive holds lead to a tricky exit. The rest of the route is superb face climbing up a vertical line of weakness. A #1 cam protects the initial steep moves below the roof and medium wires can reduce the run-out between bolts. *Steve Walker/Paul Rogers 1993*

⑱ High Ideals and Crazy Dreams
Paul Rogers/Steve Walker 1993

P1. 19 15m Climb the lower slab and rock-over on good holds to the right. Stack some good gear in the horizontal break before steep moves up and left lead to a layaway. Follow this and trend right to a small belay ledge at the bottom of an obvious flake.

2 **P2. ⚡22 19m** Move left and crank the flake. Laybacks left lead to a dyke, which is climbed past 2 bolts to a belay bay. A 30m rappel will put you on the ground.

The far right end of the crag is accessed from a short track at the left end of the hedge under the waterfall.

⑲ ⚡24 Day Tripper 25m

5 Negotiate the finger of rock where easy climbing leads to a nifty slab. Now the fun begins up the steep corner. Good jugs give you just enough respite from the two crux sections. Exit right. *Paul Rogers/Steve Walker 1993*

Brigid Allan on *On the Prow* (24). PAUL ROGERS

⑳ ★27 Doobious Tendencies 25m

7 Weave through the scoop and over onto the ladder-like slab which will escalate you to the challenging top bit. Weasel your way through the edges to a climactic finish. *Ivan Vostinar 2004*

㉑ ⚡23 Stoned Immaculate 25m

9 This stunning line follows an intermittent overlap to the slab below the roof. Layback open hand holds to the ledge and push through a mantle move to the face. Follow the overlap to a powerful top section. *Paul Rogers/ Hugh Barnard 1993*

Derek Thatcher on *Requiem* (30)
TOM HOYLE

Babylon

This awe inspiring cliff is near Milford Sound. The right wall is slightly overhanging orange rock with lots of tiny edges, sidepulls and underclings. This makes the climbing style very fingery and technical. Development only started a few years ago with Bruce Dowrick bolting the first route *'Fuel.'* This area is bound to get a lot more attention, both from the addition of new lines and repeat ascents of the test pieces. If you like hard, intricate climbing then it's too good to ignore.

The wall is next to the big slip halfway between the Donne and Tutoko bridges. 1.7km past the Donne Bridge, park on the left.

The best approach is to walk up the stream bed for 15mins, which leads to the middle of the wall. Then it's a short traverse right to reach the right wall.

i You can climb here in most weather apart from heavy rain, as water will seep down the wall. In wet weather belay at the top of the slab.

Some of the routes that have been established here have spaced bolts and stick clipping may be the only way to start working them.

The left side of the crag has some easier lines that are not recorded in this guide. It will get more traffic in the future and there is plenty of scope for new lines. Homer Hut has all the new route information.

'Only two things matter, energy and action.'
Zen Master **Taisen Deshimaru**

❶ ✷26 The Whore of Babylon 16m

5 The warm up route! Start at the base of the big orange streak and head diagonally left. The moves are committing to the 5th bolt and there's a burly crux sequence before the chains. *Jonathon Clearwater 2004*

❷ Project 25m

8 Starts just right of the *Whore of Babylon*. Climb to the 6th bolt (grade 27) for an awkward set up into some underclings. This leads to an insane five-move crux. Joins the next project at the end.

❸ Project 25m

8 At the rata tree, this route has amazingly hard climbing the whole way. It starts slopey then gets unbelievably fingery!

❹ ✷✷29 Rage 18m

6 Access this route by climbing to the last bolt of *Fuel,* then traverse left to the project belay. Clip the bolt to the left and lower onto jugs for the start. It's hard moves all the way to the break, including an obscene high step. After sitting down for a breather in the break, head out right to a bolt then move left along the slopey diagonal feature. *Derek Thatcher 2004*

❺ ✷✷27 Sinanthropus 18m

4 Straight up from the project belay. An intricate sequence makes this a thinking person's climb. *Derek Thatcher 2004*

❻ Fuel–2 Pitches

9 P1. ✷✷29 24m. Just right of the rata tree, this is a continuously fingery climb with lots of subtle body positions and a baffling crux. *Derek Thatcher 2003*

P2. ✸26 18m. Straight up from the belay, a #3 cam protects easy moves left to the 1st bolt. A cool crux to the next bolt, then an entertaining run-out on easy ground to the break (a #0.75–2 cam will tone this down). *Derek Thatcher 2003*

❼ ✸32 Katalepsis 25m

The hardest face climb in NZ! This is a direct start to *Requiem*, and heads straight up from the belay. Super hard moves after the 3rd bolt lead to seven underclings in a row. Join *Requiem* at the 5th bolt and try to keep your composure. *Derek Thatcher 2004*

❽ ✸✸30 Requiem 26m

Belay next to a small tree halfway up the slab. Start right then head diagonally left to the *Fuel* belay. A hard move at the 2nd bolt, then you'll need power endurance to finish. *Derek Thatcher 2004*

❾ Project 19m

Go right from the *Fuel* belay and weave your way up the wall to a desperate finish—don't grab the chains!

Castledowns

North End Slabs

North End Buttress

Sycophrantic Ar

Castledowns

This quality limestone area in the heart of Southland is a favourite cragging destination for Invercargill locals. The rock is definitely on par with the best South Canterbury limestone crags and has way better route climbing than Duntroon. There is great potential for new routes at various grades and the bouldering is largely untouched. Hopefully will also see more action in the future. If you are heading to the Darrans, Wanaka or Queenstown, this charming crag will be well worth a look. It also makes a good weekend trip from Dunedin.

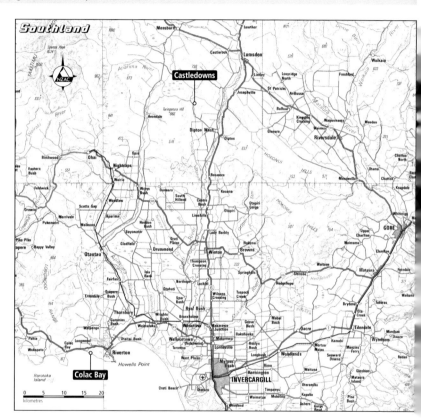

Drive to Dipton. By the garage, turn into the Dipton–Castle Rock Rd and cross the Oreti River. Take the 2nd turn left (2km after the garage) onto the Dipton–Mossburn Rd. Drive for 14km past the first large outcrop (with a limeworks). The crag is the next series of limestone ribs near the road. Please use the farm gate and close it after you.

i Not all of the climbs see regular ascents and the rock tends to grow fine lichen that feels like ball bearings under your toes. It helps to top-rope clean the climbs before leading them (it can make several grades difference). Take an arsenal of plastic brushes from toothbrush size to large scrubber.

The galvanised bolts have chain hangers and most double bolt anchors have lower-off shackles. There are single bolt anchors on some routes. These can often be backed up with a matagouri bush, so it helps to have at least one long sling.

The farmer, Stephen Clearwater, is happy for climbers to use this area but he would like to know when people are on his land. Please call before cragging (03 248 5057 or 025 301 360) and do not camp here or bring your dog.

The crag is closed for lambing in September. If you are going to the crag a couple of weeks either side of lambing it is a good idea to check that it is open.

If it has been wet, take sturdy shoes that you don't mind getting slathered in a glorious mixture of mud and cow poo.

There is no fresh water near the crag, but there is a toilet at the south end courtesy of the Southland Section of the NZAC.

Basic groceries can be found at the Dipton Store but the nearest accommodation is 3km south of Dipton at the Benmore pub ($20 per night). It is difficult to find a place to camp near the crag, but there is a reserve near the Oreti River Bridge (David Milligan Park) in Dipton. It seems okay with locals to pitch a tent here, but there are no facilities.

Andy Mills on one of the boulders. KRISTEN FOLEY

North End Slabs

This is a bulky, rounded outcrop with four single bolt anchors for top-roping. These can be backed up with matagouri bushes.

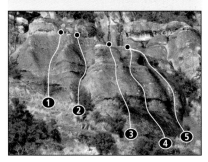

❶ **★14 On Your Marks 10m**
A slab with a rounded and cruxy step-up. This becomes more featured on the upper section. Makes a good boulder problem.

❷ **18 Gordon's Groove 10m**
The groove by the tree. Bridge and daintily mantle to the upper groove, where things ease off.

❸ **16 Opportunity Rocks 10m**
A hard, cruxy rock-over, then it's easy up the slab. Reach high to good holds near the top bulge.

2 mins

NZAC

❹ 22 Centre Plot 10m
Reach high to a sloper, then palm down through the crux.

❺ ★21 Powder Ates 10m
Lots of edges lead to the bulge. Clamp your way through using slopers.

North End Buttress

This north-facing wall is 50m right of the North End Slabs.

❻ 19 Climbing By Numbers 16m
3 ⚡ A slabby start with some awkward
⚠ climbing past the 2nd bolt. Sidepull through another crux on the water-grooved bulge, then there is ground fall potential on easy ground to the anchor. *Andrew Macfarlane 1995*

❼ ✴21 Don't Miss the Dish 18m
3 ⚡ Up the deep groove with exciting moves on textured slopers to the 1st

clip. Rock left via two mono sidepulls and smear past the break. Bridging to the top is pure loveliness. *Andrew Macfarlane 1995*

❽ ★22 Black Doris 20m
5 ⚡ The diagonal water streak makes a staunch line with some feisty side-pulling past the 2nd bolt. At the ledge, traverse right to an enjoyable arête. *John McCartney 1995*

❾ ★23 Toeing the Line 23m
7 ⚡ A well-protected and testing face climb on the front side of the wall. Positive holds soon become dishy. Finish up the arête. *Andrew Macfarlane 1995*

Hidden Gully

The Hidden Gully is a complex series of ribs, blocked at the entrance by some large boulders. There are a few routes in the gully (not included here) that are accessed by abseiling in from the top.

Sycophrantic Arête

The next wide gully has two proud arêtes on the left side and some good face climbing on the opposite wall.

5 ⚡ **★21 Sycophrantic 20m**
A high, weather-beaten pillar cut with horizontal breaks. Traverse left to the 1st bolt and use opposing pressure to shimmy past the mid-way break. The last section is pleasantly exposed. *Jo Kippax 1996*

5 ⚡ **Open Project 16m**
Sustained pocket climbing that gets slopey at the top. Will be a good one.

There is a grade 14 slab at the head of the gully. The next climbs are back down at the gully entrance.

Politics Wall

This wall has excellent rock and moves that demand everything from crimp power to mono manoeuvres.

⑫ 16 Slip-Slop-Splat 9m

3 Looks cute, but could spit you off at any of the three cruxes, as it did the 1st ascentionist who had a grounder from the 2nd bolt (apparently due to excessive cow poo on his boots). *Jo Kippax 1995*

⑬ ★20 Writer's Blank 15m

6 A sneaky traverse along the groove. After some dainty footwork, the last reachy move will be easy or a total calf stretcher, depending on your height. *Jo Kippax 1995*

⑭ 20 Reiter's Bonk 12m

3 A sequencey climb that joins *Writer's Blank* mid-way along the traverse. From behind the bush, good holds lead to the bolt. A crimpy crux to blank slopers. *Jo Kippax 1995*

⑮ ★★23 Sad State of the Socialist State 12m

4 A beaut climb. Find good jugs off the ledge and head left where subtle moves take you to the diagonal seam. Go right on shifty slopers to a 'sigh of relief' top-out. *Jo Kippax 1995*

Gravitron Gully

This is the next wide, cirque-shaped gully. It has amazing rock formations and a spectacular overhanging prow at the head of the gully.

⑯ 27 Stalker 12m

4 Start at the right side of the bulge and grunt through to the horizontal groove. The single bolt anchor can be backed up with a bush. *Ivan Vostinar 2004*

⑰ ★16 Feminist Wiles 15m

6 Climb the leaning arête, aiming for the smooth face. Head left past a generous undercling to top-out. *Jo Kippax 1995*

At the head of the gully, left of the roof:

⑱ 20 Ethics is a Place in England 12m

2 Intimidating and bouldery moves to the 1st bolt, then it's nice and steep over the bulge. *Jo Kippax 1996*

⑲ ★23 The Gravitron 10m

4 Wild terrain takes you in a rightward arc under the roof. *Al Ritchie 1996*

Castledowns

Gravitron Roof

Classic Wall

This wall extends from the right side of the Gravitron Roof down to the base of the gully. The first climbs are on a slender pillar of rock.

⑳ 19 Competitive Networking 15m

6 Start at the scoop and pull through the steep section using mighty big pockets. Delicately smear up the rounded and cruxy bulge. *Jo Kippax 1995*

㉑ ★16 The Dead Go Direct 18m

8 On the front face of the pillar, inch up to consistent slab climbing. Once named the *Dead Goat Arête,* Chinese whispers must have worked their magic on the route name. *Jen Purdie*

From the base of the last climb, follow a track around to a rock groove and scramble up to a high ledge. This short wall has some great climbing and the cabbage tree makes a handy belay.

㉒ ★17 Vociferous Resistance 9m

4 Pad up rounded holds and follow the rib right of the groove. A Castle Hillesque top-out. *Jo Kippax 1996*

㉓ ★17 Vertiginous Existence 8m

2 Head for the small, yellow roof and palm down to rock into the groove. Pleasant bridging from here. *Jo Kippax 1996*

㉔ 16 Flatulent Persistence 7m

2 The dimpled section of rock behind the cabbage tree. Fancy footwork gets you over the lip. *Jo Kippax 1996*

㉕ 18 Grunt 'n' Go 6m

2 Steep moves on good holds lead to a two-crank crux. Single bolt anchor.

㉖ ★24 Solaris 24m

7 A bulbous wall with two weird cruxes over the blobs. Start at the bright orange rock and pull over the bulge using great pockets. Rest well for the top moves. *Ivan Vostinar 2004*

㉗ **⚷15 The Castledowns Classic 30m**

9 ⚷ A consistently intriguing adventure with many little cruxes and curious moves. It's easiest to collect the draws by bringing the second up and abseiling off the front face. You can just reach the ground on a 50m rope but two abseils are possible. *Al Ritchie 1996*

The Shelf
This is the front wall of the turret. There are two pitches of climbing, radical pocketed moves and overhanging jamming in pockets!

The lower pitches are:

㉘ **★23 Omelette 13m**

4 ⚷ Steep climbing up the pocketed crack. Well worth a go and not too daunting once you find the holds. Short and cranky. *Jo Kippax 1995*

㉙ **★20 Chicken-Shit 12m**

4 ⚷ Fantastic jugs up the pocketed wall to a slopey top-out. Sidepull the slight arête to a welcome chickenhead. *Richard Kersel 1995*

㉚ **Anti-anhedonia–2 Pitches**
Jo Kippax 1995

3 ⚷ P1. **21 12m** Casual moves up the central face to a mantle that takes gusto.

4 ⚷ P2. **⚷24 15m** Way-out climbing up the amazing headwall. From the ledge, work through the first wee crux and slab, then jam and undercling your way up the steepness.

The top pitch is:

㉛ **21 Wombling Woozle 18m**

4 ⚷ Charge up the slab and grasp slopers on the arête, throwing in a heel hook for good measure. *Jo Kippax 1995*

The Picnic Spot
The most social and sunny locale at the crag, this is where most beginners top-rope or take tentative leads. It is also a great spot for more challenging lines.

㉜ **★15 Womb with a View 8m**

3 ⚷ Classic smearing and palm-down manoeuvres make this challenging. Start on the short slab and use the crack right of the bolts. Finishes left up the spine. *Jo Kippax 1995*

㉝ **Shellfish Desires–2 pitches**

3 ⚷ P1. **★12 12m** This could feel harder if you are not used to this style of climbing. Head straight up the middle of the face and top-out on the bushy ledge. The last hold is a fossilised shell! *Janine Wiles 1996*

Castledowns

The Picnic Spot

Top Hat

Bunny Gully

32 — 33 34 — 35 — 36

3 **P2. 16 10m**   A harder, but satisfying finale to this line. *Jo Kippax 1996*

34 **★18 Girl on a Swing 11m**

3 A tactical enterprise that curves rightwards over quality rock. Good body tension through the crux will fight the swing.

35 **★21 Gumboot Revival 19m**

5 This wide scoop has apparently been responsible for a few reverse skin grafts. Start on the rocky ledge and feel your way to steep ground. A heel hook and rock-over makes the crux look stylish. *Andrew Macfarlane*

Bunny Gully

This is a long, narrow gully with quite a lot of vegetation. There is some good climbing at the entrance but it is also worth checking out the climbs at the top.

36 **★★19 Kingston Flyer 24m**

7 This is an outstanding line at the entrance to the gully. Boulder across the scoop and smear up the slab, finding the occasional pocket. Finish straight up the small prow. An alternative finish is to move left up the exposed arête. *Andrew Macfarlane 1996*

37 **★16 Never Say Nevis Again 22m**

8 A long route with stealthy moves between rests. Holding your breath helps? *Jo Kippax 1996*

Scramble to the head of the gully to find the streaked, south-facing wall.

3 **★21 Suicide Bunny 13m**
A radically dimpled wall. Climb the yellow rock to a jug band, then ease up a steep section. Traverse left along the top section of pockets to a dastardly mantle. The single belay bolt is 3m back and can be backed up with a long sling. *Al Ritchie*

The Hauler Area

The Hauler Boulder

Top Hat

At the very top of the Bunny Gully is a fascinating collection of featured walls. The most distinctive is an archway called Top Hat. The first route is on the uphill side of the arch.

20 Jiggy With It 8m 3
A north-facing slab on the left boulder. An easy start through aerated rock thins out considerably up the face. Single bolt anchor.

On the right side of the arch:

19 Ornithology 8m 3
A powerful start through to some mega pockets, topped off by a reachy move.

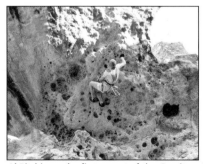

Al Ritchie on the first ascent of the *Gravitron* (24)
JO KIPPAX

On the front side of the Top Hat:

★14 Top Hat 14m 4
Start smartly up the arête and put on the ritz on the headwall.

The Hauler Area

Right of the boulders, at the entrance to Bunny Gully, are some quality face climbs.

④② ★16 The Hauler 15m 3
Named after the gouges left by a winch during a Search and Rescue training exercise. Boulder onto the slab and creep past difficult moves to reach the top groove.

15m right is a soaring water groove:

④③ ✦20 Parsimonious Bastard 15m 3
Outrageous fun and games. Bridge and wedge various body parts in the groove. *Andrew Macfarlane 1995*

④④ ★23 Tunnel Vision 15m 3
Think laterally for this. A juggy start leads to the base of the groove where some sidewinding should help the cause. *Andrew Macfarlane 1999*

Colac Bay

Colac Bay is on the South Coast near Invercargill. Countless storms have pounded this shoreline and the crashing waves have sculptured the fine grained granite into smooth dishes and scalloped patterns. It is exceedingly hard and sometimes streaked with marbled rock that looks and feels like greenstone. Ambling and beachcombing along the deserted beaches and rocky headlands is a great way of seeing this area. This guide covers the best bouldering and top-roping that we found in our travels.

Andrew Macfarlane did do some development in this area, but little was recorded. We have named the top-rope routes for convenience, but some would make good trad leads in the future and there is plenty of scope for more bouldering.

The Colac Bay Tavern

Happy local at the Tavern

Drive west along the coastal highway from Riverton towards Tuatapere. Just before the Colac Bay township, turn left into Tihaka Beach Rd. Follow the gravel road to the eastern end of the beach.

Walk east along the beach past the first rock outcrop. About 100m past this area, cross the first rocky headland by either traversing on the coastal side over a chasm, or walking around the back over stock tracks. The Octopus Wall is straight ahead.

The area is sandy, but it is handy to have a boulder mat

for the high stuff and occasional rocky landings. A carpet for keeping shoes clean and dry will be useful.

For top-roping, take a sling to set up block anchors. These are up to 10m back from the edge of the cliff and need extending with a short rope or long sling. Some anchors can be backed up with cams.

The nearest accommodation is the Colac Bay Tavern, a lively pub with a camping ground attached. Tent sites are $9 per night and cabins are $22 per person.

Octopus Wall

This wall has several good top-rope lines up sea-weathered weaknesses. There are anchor possibilities about 10m back from the edge.

❶ ★16 Mullet Arête 12m
A juggy arête with sinker pockets and rounded edges.

❷ 17 Honki Dory 12m
Up the face on good holds, then traverse along the horizontal break. Cruxy moves to the groove left of the octopus head.

❸ ★18 Suction Cup 12m
Traverse into the crack from the right and move up to the notch. Hand traverse right under the head to a slopey top-out.

❹ 18 Fishy Fishy Oooh 12m
Start at *Suction Cup* and follow the fractures on angled holds. Exit right around the block.

❺ 23 Flounder 12m
Over the roof onto small crimps, then wrap your tentacles around the arête and grunt up.

Crayfish Wall

From the Octopus Wall, head up the beach a short way to the next long headland. The Crayfish Wall faces east and has two sections; one short and featured and the other smooth with inverted steps.

On the first short buttress there are two boulder problems:

❻ ★V0 Up the big slots and mantle over.

❼ ★VM The arête.

❽ 14 The Black Corner 9m
Up the lichenous corner.

❾ 17 Sea Snake 9m
Take the line of least resistance up the face.

❿ 15 Zig Zag 6m
Follow the zig-zag overlap.

⓫ ★16 Sand Jam 6m
This face has more friction than the Darrans along with a couple of stellar handjam moves. Three stars if it was three times longer.

Colac Bay

Crayfish Wall

On the next face:

⑫ ★17 New Romantics 12m
Wind your way up the slab and move into the corner on slopers and smears.

⑬ 20 Indie 12m
Up the slab to the short corner with lots of tricky sidepulls.

⑭ ★18 Jellysquish 12m
Wicked underclings. Veer right.

⑮ 24 Blistering Barnacles 12m
Bouldery moves up the face.

⑯ ★15 P40
Bridge up the corner and layback the sandpapery arête.

Neptune Area

There is some brilliant bouldering on the other side of the headland. The two incut gullies have fantastic traverse lines over streaked, green rock.

❶ ★ V2 From the green ledge move up the face on edges.

❷ ⚑ VM Slanting crack

❸ V5 From the slanting crack, traverse right along the big ledge.

Neptune Area

4 **V2** One hard move to the big jug.

5 **P** Short, cracked face.

6 ✷ **V1** Traverse line on big jugs. Terrible feet.

On the opposite wall is a band of scalloped rock:

7 ★ **VM** Directly opposite *No.5*, up smooth, slopey scoops.

8 **VM** Slopers into the notch.

9 **VE** Opposite *No.4*, step up and mantle.

In the next narrow gully:

10 **V0** Sit-start and mantle.

11 **VM** Up the corner to the notch.

12 **P** Low traverse on slopers.

13 **VM** A short arête.

14 **V1** Dyno to jug.

15 ✷ **V1 Submarine Traverse** Traverse high along slopers; right to left.

Kate Sinclair on *Foveaux Arête* (V1)

Pounamu Cove

This is the seaward face of the next buttress.

16 ★ **V3** Slopey holds lead left and up.

17 ★ **V2** Georgeous holds lead right across the face to a jug on the arête.

18 ✷ **V4** Sit-start the slopey arête.

19 **P** Slopers lead to sidepulls up the weakness. Finish at the break.

20 **P** Traverse at mid-height along slopers.

21 **V0** Up a short, left-facing corner.

Pounamu Cove—left

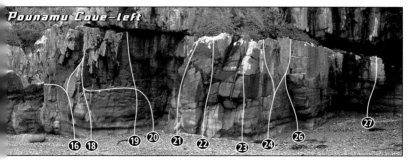

Pounamu Cove-right

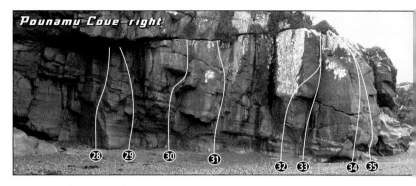

㉒ **VM** Up the face with a small chimney.

㉓ **V1** Arête.

㉔ ✹ **V2** Up the smooth face on edges, then head left.

㉕ ✹ **V1** Amazing edges up the face to the staircase.

㉖ ★ **V2** Sit-start under the staircase and lay back the crack.

㉗ ★ **V4** Right of the slime patch, slap and clamp your way up bulbous holds.

On the right wall of the cove:

㉘ **V0** Jugs up to the roof.

㉙ **V0** Jugs up to the roof.

㉚ ★ **V6** Technical stemming and sidepulling.

㉛ **V0** Awesome sidepulls up the weakness.

'Do or do not, there is no try.' **Yoda**

㉜ **V1** Edges on the arête lead right into the corner.

㉝ ★ **VM** Up the corner.

On the next buttress:

㉞ ✹ **V1 Foveaux Arête** Up the seaward face, laybacking the arête.

㉟ ★ **V5** Sit-start and up the face.

㊱ ✹ **V3** Up the undercut arête on slopers.

㊲ **V4** From slopers, reach to undercling the roof.

In the next cove on the left wall:

㊳ **V0** Off the ramp, up the middle of the face.

㊴ **V0** Up the slabby ramp and headwall.

㊵ **P** Staunch-looking arête with an undercut start.

On the face, right of the next rock cove:

㊶ **V3** Hard bouldering to the break and top-out right. High!

The Teapot

30m along the beach is a freestanding block about 3m high with a few good problems. On the face east of The Teapot there are some good top-rope lines.

Foveaux Arête

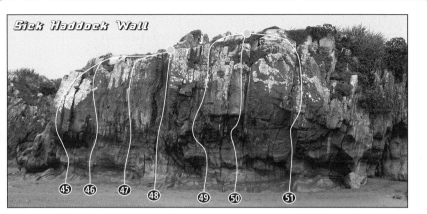

Sick Haddock Wall

㊺ ㊻ ㊼ ㊽ ㊾ ㊿ ㊾

㊷ ★ **VE** On the seaside.

㊸ **VE** On the east side.

㊹ **VM** On the back side. Use the spout.

Sick Haddock Wall

This is the third big outcrop after the Neptune Area. The following climbs are on the serene front face. There is potential for these to be short but outstanding bolted lines.

㊺ **Project 12m**
Climb the bulging overhang.

㊻ **Project 12m**
Slopey, cruxy climbing through smooth pockets.

㊼ **Project 12m**
Up vertical lines via slopey holds on the technicolour face.

㊽ ★**14 Sea Shanty Corner 12m**
Bridge up the corner following the wide crack.

㊾ ★**20 Sonic Oscillations 12m**
Gain the ledge, reach high to slopers and rock-over.

㊿ ⁂**15 Sick Haddock 12m**
Bridge the wide groove.

㊾ **18 Drunken Sailor 12m**
Start up the corner, rock onto the arête and hoon up the face.

Ivan Vostinar on *No. 36* (V3)

395

Glossary of Terms

Abseil: To descend by sliding down a rope. Also known in as 'rappel' or 'rap.'

Adventure climbing: A style that involves heading into unknown territory and having to make ongoing assessments of the rock and gear quality, which may not always be optimal.

Aid climbing: Moving up a route using fixed or placed protection as a means of progression by pulling on equipment.

Alpine butterfly knot: Used in the middle of a rope to create a loop that can be loaded from any direction.

Anchor: A point where the rope is fixed to the rock. Anchors can be natural features, such as trees or blocks or artificial placements, such as bolts and natural protection.

Arête: A narrow, vertical ridge which can be sharp, blunt or rounded.

Barn door: Off-balance climbing, which causes the climber to swing out from the rock.

Belay: To provide safety for the lead climber by controlling the rope through a friction device.

Belay station: A place where a belayer is anchored between pitches. This usually involves at least two independent connections to the rock that can withstand the load if the lead climber falls.

Beta: Information about a climb that can range from moves, sequences, to tips about the gear needed. If a climber gets beta before a climb, it ruins the on-sight. The term is derived from 'Betamax' (early videotape format).

Beta reflex: The uncontrollable urge of male climbers to issue unwanted Beta to female climbers.

Bolt: Permanent bolts which have been placed for protection. They have hangers most of the time.

Bomber: Used to indicate that something is exceptionally solid, e.g. an anchor, the gear or a hold.

Booty: Gear left behind on a climb by a previous party usually because they abseiled off it or it got stuck. Finders commonly spend hours dislodging stuck bootie.

Bouldering: Climbing unroped on boulders to a height where it is still safe (more or less) to jump off.

Bouldering mat: A mattress-sized foam block used to minimise falls while bouldering.

Bowline: A popular knot used to attach the rope to a harness. Its main advantage is easy untying after it has been loaded.

Bridge swinging: Doing a giant swing under a bridge with a climbing rope. Construction cranes can be used for swinging as well. Often it's illegal.

Buildering: To climb buildings. This usually occurs surreptitiously under the cover of darkness.

Buttress: Part of a rock wall that juts out from the main face.

Cam: Generic reference to the family of spring loaded camming devices (SLCD's) such as Friends, Camalots and Aliens. These are all removable pieces of protection that 'cam' when loaded to lock into a crack in the rock.

Campus: A dyno using the arms only with the legs dangling helplessly below.

Chalk: Magnesium carbonate; a white, powdery substance helps dry sweaty hands.

Cheese grater: To scrape skin off various body parts while sliding down a slab.

Chickenheads: Protruding lumps of rock, which make excellent hand or footholds. Can also be used for protection by slinging.

Chimney: A wide crack that is usually big enough for a climber to slide into, at least part way. Techniques for climbing chimneys include wriggling and groveling or elegantly bridging, if it's wide enough. 'Chimneying' means using the back and feet to brace against the walls of the crack.

Chockstone: A stone wedged in a crack or chimney. These can be tied off with a sling for protection.

Choss: Poor quality or loose rock.

Clean climbing: Using only removable protection which does not damage the rock. This movement developed in the 1960's and was against the use of permanent protection (such as pitons and bolts).

Clove hitch: A useful, easily adjustable climbing knot most commonly used to connect the rope to anchor points.

Corner: The junction of two planes of rock. A corner may also be referred to as an 'open book corner' or dihedral.

Crank: To pull on a hold as hard as you can.

Crimp: An edge held only by the fingertips.

Crux: The most difficult section of a climb. The crux could be a single move, a sequence of moves, or an entire pitch on a multi-pitch climb.

Deadpoint: A dynamic move made by lunging upwards and grabbing the next hold just before you start falling again. By catching a hold 'in its 'deadpoint,' you place the smallest possible load on the holds and your fingers.

Deep water soloing: Climbing a cliff above water (sea or lake) without ropes.

Dogging: Climbing, resting, aiding and lowering to 'work out' sections of a route until a sequence is mastered. Short for 'hangdogging.'

Double fisherman's knot: Used to tie two ropes together.

Double rope: The use of two half (smaller diameter) ropes for long, wandering pitches or dangerous trad routes. It reduces rope drag and minimises the shock load on individual pieces of protection in a fall.

Dynamic belay: A belay method in which some rope is allowed to slip during severe falls. This can reduce the impact force during a serious fall.

Dyno: A dynamic climbing movement usually involving a jump or lunge to a distant hold.

Edge: A tiny ledge of rock. 'Edging' is using the inside or outside edge of the foot to stand and make moves.

Elvis: A suprisingly common, paranormal event which can occur during a challenging climb. In a moment of weakness or fatigue, the spirit of Elvis is channelled through the body causing it to vibrate, particularly in the legs.

Epic: A prolonged, grueling experience on a climb.

Exposure: The feeling that occurs when there is a great distance between the climber and the ground. Multi-pitch or steep routes provide lots of exposure.

Fall factor: The length of the fall divided by the amount of rope paid out. This is a way of calculating how much force will be exerted on the equipment.

Figure of Eight: A popular tie-in knot. It's easy to learn and clear to see if incorrectly tied.

Glossary of Terms

Figure Four: A peculiar climbing move which you won't believe until you see or try it. Useful when you have a brilliant handhold but absolutely no footholds. With one hand on the hold, wrap the opposite leg over the holding wrist. From here it is possible to get enough leverage to reach up to higher holds.

Fingerlock: A masochistic technique of twisting and wedging fingers into a crack.

Fixed pro: Unremovable pro that may include bolts, pitons, stuck wires and cams.

Flagging: Extending a foot or entire leg out to provide the counter-balance to reach for a hold in the opposite direction.

Flake: A thin wafer-like fin of rock that is usually detached from the main face.

Flapper: A piece of skin torn off a hand or left barely attached. Caused when a callus peels off during a move.

Flash: Leading a climb with no falls or rests on the first attempt, with beta or information about the climb beforehand.

Free climbing: A style of climbing where ropes and gear are only used for protection and not pulled on for assitance. This is the most common rock climbing style.

Free solo: Free climbing while using no protection. Although dangerous, many consider it to be the most pure and exhilarating expression of the sport.

Friend: Trade name for the first spring loaded camming devices made by Ray Jardine.

Gaston: This manoeuvre is the opposite to a layback and involves pulling sideways on a hold (as you would if you were trying to open a lift). Named for French climber Gaston Rébuffat.

Gripped: To feel as if some icy, white claw has emerged from the great beyond to ruthlessly clasp your throat and freeze you in your tracks. It may be related to exposure.

Grounder: To fall and hit the ground.

Gym rat: A term for those that climb predominantly indoors.

Handjam: A technique where a climber wedges their hand in a crack, locks it in place and makes the next move.

Headpoint: An English term for a traditional route led after top-rope practice and sometimes with pre-placed protection due to the dangerous nature of the route. The traditional equivalent of a redpoint.

Headwall: The top section of a wall or climb that is steeper than the face below.

Heel Hook: The act of bringing one foot to chest height and hooking it on a hold.

Hex: Short for Hexentric, this is a type of nut with an hexagonal shape. They work for wedging (as a wire) but also for camming when they are placed long ways in nearly parallel cracks.

Highball: Term used to describe high bouldering problems.

Horn: Spike of rock that may be used for protection or as a hold.

Italian hitch: Also known as a münter hitch, this loose free moving knot can be used with a karabiner for belaying or abseiling.

Jug: A very large, positive hold.

kN: An abbreviation for kilo Newton, imprinted on karabiners and other climbing gear to indicate their load rating. One kilo Newton is about 100kg.

Layback: A climbing technique used in cracks or on a vertical edge, where feet push against one surface while the hands and arms pull in the opposite direction.

Lead: To climb ground up either placing protection or using bolts.

Lock-off: To hold the rock with one arm bent while using the other arm to reach up for the next hold or to place/clip protection.

Manky: This can describe anything dirty, oozing, repulsive, seeping, rotten or shabby in regards to the rock, climbing gear or a placement.

Mantle: A technique to get established on a ledge, especially when topping out. Various techniques are possible and amusing; the last desperate measure being the bellyflop. If you've never seen a mantle, try visualising the stylish way of getting out of a swimming pool.

Nut key: A long and slender piece of metal that can be used to remove stuck wires or cams.

Offwidth: A crack that is too wide for good jams, yet too narrow to fit a climber's whole body. Exotic techniques for climbing offwidths include hand stacks, heel-toe locks, knee bars, 'chicken wings', levitation and a lot of grunting, swearing and thrashing around.

On-sight: Leading a climb with no falls or rests on the first attempt, without any information about the climb beforehand.

Pitch: A section of climb between two belays that is no longer than the length of one rope (usually up to 50m).

Piton: A metal spike that is hammered into a crack for use as protection or an anchor.

Pocket: A hold formed by a small depression in the rock.

Protection (pro): Removable pieces of gear which wedge in cracks to protect the leader.

Prusik: A sliding knot used to ascend a rope (named after its inventor Dr. Karl Prusik).

Pumped: The feeling of swollen, limp and sometimes painful forearms. This happens due to lactic acid build up the muscles.

Quickdraw: Short sling with karabiners on either end. To be hip, just call it a 'draw.'

Rack: Refers to hardware carried during an ascent and often doubles as a status symbol.

Redpoint: Derived from German word 'rötpunkt,' the term came in to common usage in the Frankenjura in the 1970s. It originated from the practice of painting a an empty red circle at the bottom of a climb that was unclimbed. When completed with no-falls, the circle was filled in.

Originally, if the quickdraws were pre-placed, this would be called a 'pinkpoint,' but because pre-placed quickdraws have become the norm, this term is obsolete.

Resin: A sticky alternative to chalk which permanently damages the rock because it does not wash off. It has been banned by consensus in New Zealand. The French call it 'pof.'

Rock-over: A complex but enormously satisfying move that requires stepping a foot-up high and pushing the bodyweight over and onto the raised knee.

Rope: Modern kern-mantel climbing rope consists of bundles of continuous nylon filaments (kern) surrounded by a braided protective sheath (mantel).

dynamic ropes are used for leading and have about 10 percent stretch. Static ropes are used for top-roping and abseiling and have about 2 percent stretch.

RP: A tiny brass nut on wire designed to fit well in small cracks.

Runnel: A groove caused by water erosion.

Runner: A loop of tape or webbing, either sewn or tied that is attached to protection.

Run-out: Distance between two pieces of protection. A route is run-out when the distance between the climber and the last piece of pro becomes uncomfortably long.

Sandbag: To underrate the difficulty of a climb in an effort to either appear cool and confident or to tempt others into trying the route.

Second: The person who belays the leader and takes out the protection on the way up.

Sidepull: A hand hold that needs to be held with a horizontal (sideways) pull.

Sit-start: A bouldering craze sweeping the world and coming to an obscure wall near you. It means to start a bouldering problem from a sitting position.

Slab: Flat and seemingly featureless, off-vertical piece of rock that is usually climbed using smearing.

Sling: Flat nylon webbing that is usually hollow (tubular). It is used for anything from setting up anchors to making runners.

Sloper: A rounded hold that is grasped with an open hand and often gorgeous to touch.

Smearing: When the balls of the feet are used to generate as much friction as possible between the shoe and the rock.

Sport climbing: Routes completely protected with bolts.

Spot: To catch, or reduce the momentum of a falling boulderer. The ideal spotter is fat, soft, slightly inflatable and can move very quickly into position. Standing around nonchalantly and failing to catch someone is called a 'Kiwi spot.' Grasping the climbers buttocks is referred to as a 'French spot.'

Stopper Knot: A knot in the tail of a rope that prevents the possibility of the tie-in knot loosening.

Tape knot: A knot that joins sling/tape.

Top-roping: Climbing when the rope has already been set up through the anchor (the rope extends from the climber up through the anchor and then down to the belayer).

Trad: Short for traditional climbing. 'Trad' is characterised by placing removable protection in cracks etc. It is more than just a climbing style; it is a school of thought with its own set of ethics and perspectives.

Undercling: A type of hold that only offers a positive grip when pulled on in an upward direction.

Whipper: A very long fall.

Wires: Removable metal pieces of protection that climbers wedge in cracks. They are also called nuts and get their name from the fact that they were originally large machine nuts with webbing tied through the centre hole.

Wired: Knowing the rock and a sequence of moves completely and intimately, i.e. having the route 'wired.'

Zipper: A fall where the protection pulls out one after the other as the leader falls.

Other Rockguides

This is a list of the local rock guides availiable at the time of printing. These are on sale in local areas as well as through the NZAC, which stocks most New Zealand rock climbing and mountaineering guides.

If you are interested in alpine rock, the NZAC mountaineering guides also contain long multi-pitch rock routes.

Barron Saddle–Mt Brewster.
By Ross Cullen.
This covers Twin Stream comprehensivly, as well the region's alpine routes.

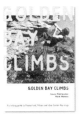

Golden Bay Climbs
By Simon Middlemass and Mark Watson.
A comprehensive guide to Paynes Ford, Pohara and Sandhills Creek.

Dunedin Rock.
By Dave Brash.
A complete guide to all of Dunedin's climbing areas, complete with a CD-Rom.

Paynes and Beyond
The Handog Camp Guide.
A guide to all Golden Bay climbs up to grade 22.

Wanaka Rock
The Wanaka Rock Club Guide.
A comprehensive guide to climbing crags and boulding areas around Wanaka.

Port Hills Climbing
By Lindsay Main.
A comprehensive guide to Christchurch's Port Hills.

Rock The Wakatipu Way.
By Kerri Dann and Andy Mills.
A comprehensive guide to most of Queenstowns crags.

The Definitive Spittle Hill Climbing Guide
By Alan Davison and Matt Pierson.
A guide to all boulder-ing and route climbing in Spittle Hill.

The Darrans Guide
By Murray Judge and Hugh Widdowson.
A guide to the alpine-rock routes in the Darran Mountains.

Climbing Walls

Nelson

Vertical Limits
34 Vanguard St, Ph 0508 VERTICAL
www.verticallimits.co.nz
info@verticallimits.co.nz
Hours: Mon–Fri 10am–9pm Sat–Sun
10am–6pm.
Admission: $10, + gear $15; Student $8/$13,
Under 16 $6/$10. Memberships and concession cards are also available.

Christchurch

Canterbury University
Ilam Rd. Ph (03) 364-2433
Hours: Mon–Fri 7am–10.30pm, Sat
9.30am–6pm, Sun 10am–10pm.
Admission: $5 public, $2.50 student. Gear
hire: $5 for two.

Twizel

Twizel Events Centre
Admission: Child $6 (school children, any
age), Student $8 (tertiary student, ID
required). Adult $10 (no age limit).
3 month pass $150, 6 month pass $240, 1 year
pass $399.

Franz Josef

Franz Josef Community Centre
The Guiding Company
Ph (03) 752-0047 or 0800 800102
Hours: Thurs and Sun 7-10pm. Tues 7-10pm
(summer only).
Admission: $5 members, $10 non members.
Membership $50 for 6 months and $80 for 1
year. Half day courses and gear hire available.

Queenstown

Queenstown National Bank Rec. Centre
Joe O'Connell Drive, Frankton
Ph (03) 442 3664
Hours: Mon–Thurs 9am–9pm, Fri–Sat
9am–5pm, Sunday (winter only) 11am –7pm.

Admission: Adult $10, U16 $4. Gear Hire:
Boots $5, Harness $5 - Both for $7. Unlimited
climbing options also available. Open Nights
for adults Tuesday and Thursday 7-9pm NB:
Always call before coming out as special events
sometimes disrupt climbing availability.

Element
Remarkables Park, Frankton
The wall is free of charge to climbers with their
own equipment upon completion of a belay
license. Without their own gear we charge
$10.00 for hire of shoes and harness.
Hours: Monday–Thursday 9:00am–6:00pm.
Friday 9:00am–7:00pm. Saturday/Sunday
10:00am–6:00pm.

Oamaru

Waitaki Recreation Centre
Orwell St. Ph (03) 434-6932
Hours: Mon–Fri 9am–8.30pm, Sat
10am–12pm.
Admission: $5; Annual membership: Family
$80, Adult $60, Student $30. NB: the wall is
not open to inexperienced or unsupervised
climbers.

Invercargill

YMCA
77 Tay St, Invercargill. Ph (03) 218-2989
Hours: Mon–Thurs 6am–9pm, Fri 6am-8pm,
Sat 8am–12pm.
Admission: $4; NZAC members discount;
Students $3.50 YMCA rockclimbing instructors available to take groups. Gear available for
hire to groups with instructor.

Stadium Southland Climbing Centre
Surrey Park, Isabella St, Invercargill
Ph (03) 217-1200
Hours: Open 7 days, 7am–10pm, bookings
recommended.
Admission: Adults $6 (off peak $4). Students
$5 (off peak $3). School Children $4 (off peak
$2.50). Peak period is 5–8.30pm. Discounts
apply for group bookings. Gear hire also available: harness $5, shoes $3, chalkbag $2.

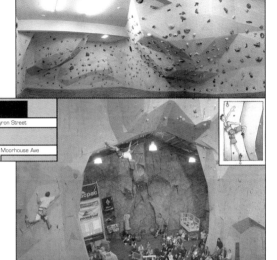

the roxx climbing centre

- Top-ropers & leaders
- Boulderers & coffee drinkers
- Socials & hard-outs
- Hirers and buyers

Hours:
Monday–Friday
4:00pm–10:00pm.
Saturday/Sunday
10:00am–10:00pm.

Cnr Waltham & Byron,
Christchurch.
Ph (03) 377–3000
climb@theroxx.co.nz
www.theroxx.co.nz

YMCA CHRISTCHURCH EST 1862

Hours: Training room - Everyday 9am–10pm. Main wall - Top-rope times: Mon, Tues, Wed, Thur, Fri, Sun 4–9:30 pm. Sat 1–7pm. Leading: All week 9am–10pm.

Christchurch's largest indoor climbing wall offering 32 lead climbs and 21 fixed top ropes

12 Hereford St. Ph (03) 366-0689.
buzz@ymcachch.org.nz
www.ymcachch.org.nz

Admission: Adult $8, student $6.50, children under 13 yrs $5. Gear Hire: Harnesses $5, Shoes $5. Instruction & courses available.

Related Services

Alpine Guides Ltd

Guided ascents,
instruction courses,
ski touring, heli and
glacier skiing.

address:	Bowen Drive, Aoraki/Mount Cook 8770
post:	PO Box 20, Aoraki/Mount Cook 8770
ph:	(03) 4351-834
fax:	(03) 4351-898
email:	mtcook@alpineguides.co.nz
web:	www.alpineguides.co.nz
	www.heliskiing.co.nz
	www.skithetasman.co.nz

Alpine Recreation

Guided climbing, trekking, ski
touring and instruction courses in
the Aoraki Mount Cook region.
Ball Pass and Fitzgerald Pass cross-
ings. Operator-owned huts.

Anne & Gottlieb Braun-Elwert

address:	PO Box 75,
	Lake Tekapo
ph:	(03) 680-6736
fax:	(03) 680-6765
email:	climb@alpinerecreation.com
web:	www.alpinerecreation.com

Aspiring Guides Ltd

Specialist guided ascents of
NZ's classic peaks, moun-
taineering, rock, ice climbing,
alpine rock courses, trekking,
ski touring, private charter
helicopter skiing, international expeditions.

address:	Level One, 99 Ardmore Street, Wanaka
post:	PO Box 345, Wanaka
ph:	(03) 443-9422
fax:	(03) 443-9540
mobile:	025-301-677
email:	climb@aspiringguides.com
web:	www.aspiringguides.com

Good Sports

For all your outdoor equipment and clothing needs,
plus a wide range of rental
equipment. Bookings for
Alpine Coachlines.

address:	17–23 Dunmore
	St, Wanaka
ph:	(03) 443 7966
fax:	(03) 443-7033
email:	info@good-sports.co.nz
web:	www.good-sports.co.nz

NZOIA

Provides qualifications for
outdoor instructors in
alpine, rock, bush, kayak,
cave and sea kayaking.

address:	PO Box 11090,
	Manners Street, Wellington 6034
ph:	(04) 385-6048
fax:	(04) 385-9680
email:	ao@nzoia.org.nz
web:	www.nzoia.org.nz

Physiosouth

For your all your physiotherapy
needs by experienced staff who
understand rock climbing.

address:	9 clinics in Christchurch
ph:	(03) 332-6487
free ph:	0508 4 PHYSIO 7 days
	(for appointments at
	any clinic)
email:	physiosouth@physiosouth.co.nz
web:	www.physiosouth.co.nz

Wanaka Rock Climbing

Professional instruction from qualified guides. All skill
levels catered for by Wanaka's only rock climbing specialists. Introduction to rock climbing, technical
courses, alpine sport climbing and private guiding.

post:	PO Box 383 Wanaka
ph:	(03) 443-6411
fax:	(03) 443-6811
email:	info@wanakarock.co.nz
web:	www.wanakarock.co.nz

Dave Brash

Dunedin Climbing – Instruction and Guiding Service. Novice to advanced, all ages, all abilities. Local crags, alpine rock guiding. Traditional and adventure climbing courses a specialty. Publisher of *Dunedin Rock* – there's more to Dunedin rock than South Island selected!

address: 44 Grey St, Dunedin
ph: (03) 473-9970, 027 222-1195
email: davebrash.climbing@xtra.co.nz,
web: www.dunedinclimbing.co.nz

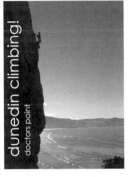

dunedin climbing!
doctors point

NEW ZEALAND ALPINE CLUB

KRISTEN FOLEY ON THE SOUTH WEST RIDGE OF MT ASPIRING. PHOTO: MARK WATSON

- Access to alpine and rock climbing trips and instruction courses via local sections

- Half rates at Club huts, discounts at some DoC alpine huts

- Free annual subscription to *The Climber* and the *NZ Alpine Journal*, discounts on a wide range of NZAC guidebooks and other climbing publications

- Discounts to many indoor walls

- The NZAC supports your climbing overseas with cash grants, endorsements, and reciprocal agreements for use of club huts overseas

- DoC Annual Hut Pass discount

- Eligibility for travel insurance which covers climbing

- Affiliation to FMC who supply discounts on maps, guidebooks and travel within NZ

www.alpineclub.org.nz

Phone or email the NZAC National Office
to find out your closest section:
03 377-7595, office@alpineclub.org.nz

Castle Hill Route Index

Castle Hill Boulder Index

V6

Castle Hill Boulder Index

Grade Comparison Chart

NZ	USA	France
10	5.5	3
11	5.5	4
12	5.6	4
13	5.6	4+
14	5.7	4+
15	5.7	5
16	5.8	5
17	5.8	5+
18	5.9	5+
19	5.10a	6a
20	5.10b	6a+
20	5.10c	6b
21	5.10d	6b+
22	5.11a	6c
23	5.11b	6c+
23	5.11c	7a
24	5.11d	7a+
25	5.12a	7b
26	5.12b	7b+
26	5.12c	7b+
27	5.12d	7c
28	5.13a	7c+
29	5.13b	8a
30	5.13c	8a+
31	5.13d	8b
32	5.14a	8b+
33	5.14b	8c
34	5.14c	8c+

Sebastian Loewensteijn on *Futurism* (28) Paynes Ford

MAYAN SMITH-GOBAT

Index of Routes by Grade

Index of Routes by Grade

23

Index of Routes by Grade

Index of Routes by Grade

Index of Routes by Grade

Index of Routes by Grade

15

Index of Routes by Grade

13

12

11

10

'I am a Christchurch based artist and climber who preferes oils and slopers as tools of the trade. I love stimulating discussion (particularly about politics), listening to music, (primarily King Crimson) and really slow foreign films (Akira Kurosawa). I'm also partial to a bit of bouldering, Monty Python and 80s fashion.' Ivan

'I am an environmental scientist from Christchurch, now based in Canada studying snow and climate change in the Rockies. I like blue cheese and experimenting with ways of looking at the world—dabbling in writing, photography and film. My favourite rock climbing medium is trad but I am partial to sunny days at 'the Hill' and a spot of sport climbing.' Kate